CIVIL PROCEDURE AND PRACTICE

GREENS CONCISE SCOTS LAW

CIVIL PROCEDURE AND PRACTICE

THIRD EDITION

By

Charles Hennessy, LL.B
Solicitor Advocate

W. GREEN

 THOMSON REUTERS

Published in 2008 by W. Green, 21 Alva Street, Edinburgh, EH2 4PS
Part of Thomson Reuters (Professional) UK Limited
(Registered in England & Wales, Company No 1679046. Registered
Office and address for service: Aldgate House, 33 Aldgate High Street,
London, EC3N 1DL)

Typeset by LBJ Typesetting Ltd of Kingsclere

Printed and bound by CPI Group (UK) Ltd, Croydon, CR0 4YY

Reprinted 2012

For further information on our products and services, visit
www.wgreen.co.uk

ISBN 978-0-414-01751-1

No natural forests were destroyed to make this product;
only farmed timber was used and replanted

A CIP catalogue record for this book is available from the British Library.

CONTENTS

ACKNOWLEDGEMENTS TO THE THIRD EDITION

The commencement of the Civil Justice Review in 2007 lulled me into a false sense of security that the previous edition would be my last but then, after ten years of deliberation and prevarication (although not necessarily in that order) a sudden change was made in the financial jurisdiction limits for Summary Causes and Small Claims in January 2008. I would like to thank the Scottish Government for providing the principal reason whereby, in the summer of this year, I was dragged back kicking and screaming to a re-examination of the text of the second edition. I have now tried to reflect procedure and practice at April 1 (a mere coincidence) 2008.

Whilst revisiting chapters I had hoped never to see again, I felt obliged to update other parts of the 2005 edition primarily by incorporating obvious rule changes and adding more recent case illustrations and examples from the last three years. I resisted the temptations to rewrite the whole text and to anticipate some of the possible changes to come under the Review in much the same way as I have so far resisted the temptation to take up skiing. Premonitions of serious accidents on slippery slopes came to mind and frankly I am not that brave nor that foolish.

I should thank the insidious flatterers at Greens who assured me that this could be done at breakneck speed without explaining how. From that acclaim I should exclude Rosemary Johnston who actually helped me out as my editor. My friends and colleagues provided the usual constructive support by gleefully pointing out all of the shortcomings once again.

Finally, by popular request and as obliged in my contract, I have to "finish with my family". Pausing only to discard the most attractive interpretation of that clause, I should recognise them briefly for their massive contributions, or massively for their brief contributions, depending on your point of view. My wife was kind enough to go to the South of France for a long holiday to enable me to work on this edition, blatantly misinterpreting my suggestion of which one of us was supposed to do what and where. I would imagine she will be returning fairly soon. My daughter agreed to stop phoning me daily to check on my well being or "her inheritance" as she put it. Number one son got married which seemed a rather extravagant reaction to my frequent requests for IT support. Number two son moved out *permanently* (his emphasis). I miss them all terribly but the room rentals have come in handy.

ACKNOWLEDGEMENTS TO THE SECOND EDITION

To a certain extent I was duped into writing this second edition. Without thinking too deeply about the topic (a recurrent theme since childhood) I agreed to write it when asked to do so by Greens. I assumed that a bit of updating and fiddling with the syntax of the first edition would suffice and this could easily be achieved in between routine callings in the ordinary court. Even though, to the best of my recollection, I had actually been doing civil litigation for the last four years, I was taken completely by surprise when it dawned on me that there had been umpteen procedural changes during that period.

Once I had started, however, I swiftly noted the more obvious changes which necessitated re-writing about a quarter of the book. It became prudent to rely upon the support and assistance of many people who appreciated the psychological damage this exercise could have caused to a vulnerable personality. My thanks go to Sheriff Lindsay Foulis, Geoff Clarke, Gordon Keyden, Donald Bruton, Sheriff James Taylor and Terry Fafferty who read over some draft chapters for me. Thanks also to Clare Crawford and the other students who were my sample audience and ensured that the "Jackanory" quality of the book was not lost. Finally, thanks to Valerie Malloch who was responsible for the original con, and Philippa Blackham who was responsible for dragging me over the finishing line in time for publication.

For those readers whose appreciation of the first edition began and (apparently) ended with the original acknowledgment, and who have expressed concern for my domestic wellbeing, may I give some small reassurance. My family continues to suffer for my art in the creation of this book. My short suffering wife has defied medical science and proved that she could, in fact, care even less about this edition than the first one. Two of my children have left home although they may not have gone far enough away to make this arrangement mutually satisfactory. The remaining child (their names will come back to me soon I am sure) has become a lawyer "just to spite me". They really deserve all of the credit and, according to the latest bank statements, have indeed received it.

ACKNOWLEDGEMENTS TO THE FIRST EDITION

I can still remember there were times when I thought it was a good idea to write this book—I think it lasted for 10 minutes about two years ago. I have a number of people to name, and perhaps shame, for keeping my nose close to the grindstone with one arm up my back—learning to type under these circumstances was possibly my greatest achievement.

Karen Taylor of Greens must shoulder most of the responsibility for persuading me that it could be done and encouraging me throughout. Neil McKinlay of Greens ("The enforcer" as he was introduced to me) made me finish it. Luisa Deas of Greens, my editor, was wonderfully reassuring. My friend Ronnie Conway led by example and kept me going in the dark hours, a time with which, as a resident of Airdrie, he was very familiar. The ritual abuse and ridicule from my professional colleagues in Glasgow was, as ever, a powerful incentive.

Many individuals were kind enough to read over drafts of some of the chapters. In no order of importance or priority I would like to thank David Shand, Tom Cruikshank, Stewart Walker, Geoff Clarke, Sheriff John Fitzsimmons, James Kelly and all my office co-workers who kept me on track. Thanks also to my group of 1999 at the GGSL (aka "Charlie's Angels") who gave some of the chapters a test run and said nothing grossly offensive. I accept full responsibility for any negligent acts or omissions—even if it was their fault.

Finally I would like to pay tribute to my wife Annette and my family. Their unstinting apathy and general disinterest was a constant source of strength. I can only speculate on why they tolerated so many weeks and months without my companionship. Maybe some day they will tell me—or perhaps start speaking to me again.

PREFACE

Aims

The principal aim of this book is to make the rules and practice of the major forms of civil procedure in Scotland understandable and accessible to those who have limited knowledge and experience. There are so many different procedures in Scotland and so many detailed rules that it would be impossible to explain and analyse them all fully without writing many volumes of impenetrable prose. It has been necessary on many occasions to sacrifice precise detail and strict accuracy in favour of an approach which gives the reader a broad appreciation of the more important features of civil procedure.

The book does not deal with family actions. The practice and procedure in family actions has become highly specialised in recent years. The rules of procedure have proliferated recently and whilst the general principles of procedure in family actions are the same as in other forms of procedure, they have to be regarded as distinct.

The book is intended as an introductory guide to law students who will understandably have difficulty in grasping what civil litigation procedures are about until they have been closely involved in civil cases in practice. It is also intended as a starting point for readers who are coming upon the civil procedure rules in practice for the first time or are dealing with a case for the first time under a form of procedure with which they are unfamiliar. There are explanations for why rules are framed to deal with particular situations and illustrations of the way in which they actually operate.

No matter how intelligent or diligent he might be, no student, trainee lawyer, or newly qualified assistant has any prospect of fully understanding procedural rules until he has actually experienced them in practice. This book attempts to put a little more emphasis on the reasoning behind the rules and upon the practical application of the rules. I hope that this will assist readers to understand them better and encourage readers to see all court rules and procedures as a means to an end, and not as an end in themselves.

The book only scratches the surface of certain aspects of procedure. That may be no bad thing. I make no apologies for it, but it is important to emphasise that when I am discussing some of the rules and practices I have had to make generalisations which may not be entirely accurate. The book is inevitably concise, and reference should always be made to the rules themselves for the full picture. There are a number of excellent text books which deal with one or more of these topics in much greater detail and readers are encouraged to look to them for a far more author-itative explanation and exposition of the rules of procedure and practice in these particular areas. I have provided suggestions in each chapter for other text books and further reading which would provide a more thor-ough treatment of the specific procedures concerned.

There are certain matters I have chosen to ignore. I have omitted any reference to title and interest to sue in civil proceedings. I have made only passing reference to jurisdiction rules. It is of course vital to deter-mine that a court has jurisdiction over a defender before one can even begin to consider the procedural rules of the particular litigation. In prac-tice, in non-family litigation, jurisdiction is rarely a major issue and the detailed rules are so complex that I confess I have never fully under-stood them. I certainly do not understand them sufficiently to try and explain them concisely. My principal daily experience of litigation is in the sheriff court so there is inevitably an emphasis on those procedures with which I am particularly familiar. These rules have proliferated in recent times, and I think that any attempt to explain them would compli-cate the overall aim of the book. However, I do provide details of the most helpful sources and textbooks which cover this area.

Practical Context

It would be a mistake for any person coming new to civil procedure to make an effort to memorise the rules. It is much more helpful to grasp why they are there and to see the logic underlying them and the way in which they are applied in practice. With this in mind, I have attempted to include in each chapter comment on, and an illustration of, some of the practical issues which procedure in litigations will raise. It should be remembered that clients rarely come into a lawyer's office for the first time and immediately demand that a court action be raised. Litigation is often a final resort, and I am going to use three realistic examples of sit-uations in which court actions may be raised after efforts have been made to resolve the disputes without going to court. In the book I have in mind these typical scenarios from a civil practitioner's filing cabinet:

1. Your client, Mr X, was driving a car with three friends as passengers, when he had an accident. You act for all of them in relation to their claims for damages for personal injuries following the accident. They were all injured to varying degrees, ranging from a grazed elbow to a severe neck injury which has disabled one of them. They have all decided that they should raise court proceedings.
2. Mr X happens to be a self-employed joiner and builder. He operates in partnership with two friends. The firm ordered a large quantity of tim-ber from a supplier. They received an invoice from the supplier and considered that they had been charged for materials which had not been delivered. Furthermore, they consider that the quality and condi-tion of the timber made it unsuitable for the purpose for which it was

ordered. The firm (and the partners) have been sued by the suppliers for payment of the original bill after months of argument about it. A court writ has been served on the firm.

3. Mr X's firm did some building work for a customer and have rendered a bill but the customer has refused to pay it or has delayed to pay it. He has been unable to obtain any response from the customer to his repeated requests for payment. He now feels that they should sue for payment.

These would all be cases in which there would no doubt be many arguments about the substantive law and about the precise facts of each case. I am not going to dwell upon that. I am simply going to use them as real-life examples of cases from ordinary everyday civil practice.

In Scotland, we do have a relatively large number of distinct and distinctive types of procedure. When considering the different procedures, I have attempted to start each chapter with a simple narrative of what happens in plain language. This should give the reader an immediate appreciation of the main features of the procedure without becoming lost in its specialities. I have then considered what appear to me to be the more important rules in a little detail. Where there are cases which illustrate the application of the rules I have referred to some of these. The cases should only be regarded as an introduction to a fuller study of the points they illustrate. It is not my intention to explore any specialities in detail. I have also provided a flow chart outlining the main procedural steps in order to reinforce an appreciation of the basic structure of that procedure.

I hope this approach is user friendly. It is an attempt to demystify the procedures as far as possible. I have been reassured by many people that there would be a benefit in a "Beginner's Guide" to the variety of civil procedures existing in Scotland. Well, I hope that you now have it. I trust it will give readers a meaningful start and will continue to make sense when the experience of using the procedures in practice enables the reader to spot the deliberate mistakes and appreciate where the over simplification does not quite give the full picture.

Civil litigation is challenging. The more one knows about it, the more challenging it can become and the better one can use rules of procedure to handle cases efficiently and professionally. There is no substitute for experience and no shortcut to learning how best to conduct civil cases. I hope, however, that this introduction will be a first step towards meeting the challenge.

I have found to my regret that writing a book about it gives little opportunity for witty asides or facetious comments which have been known to pass my lips. A law book is far too serious for that sort of stuff. It is one omission for which I apologise in advance. I can guarantee you will not be rolling in the aisles—beyond which no admission is made, and no warranty is given (as we lawyers are always saying!).

I have tried to reflect procedure and practice as at April 1, 2008. Where possible I have included more recent developments and cases of significance and importance. It is appropriate at this point to advise readers that in the next few years there may be very substantial changes to the administration of the courts in Scotland and the procedures and practices which are detailed in this book. The Civil Courts Review under the chairmanship of Lord Gill, the Lord Justice Clerk, began its work on April 4, 2007 and is charged with the task of reforming the Scottish system of civil justice. Its terms of reference were as follows:

To review the provision of civil justice by the courts in Scotland, including their structure, jurisdiction, procedures and working methods, having particular regard to—

- *the cost of litigation to parties and to the public purse;*
- *the role of mediation and other methods of dispute resolution in relation to court process;*
- *the development of modern methods of communication and case management; and*
- *the issue of specialisation of courts or procedures, including the relationship between the civil and criminal courts;*

and to report within 2 years, making recommendations for changes with a view to improving access to civil justice in Scotland, promoting early resolution of disputes, making the best use of resources, and ensuring that cases are dealt with in ways which are proportionate to the value, importance and complexity of the issues raised.

Whilst certain reforms to some existing procedures and practices would be welcome, it is hoped that we do not lose sight of the fact that many of our procedures work extremely well. There are some fundamental shortcomings in the organisation and administration of our civil justice system as a whole, but many of our individual procedures and practices compare favourably with those of other jurisdictions in which large amounts of effort, time, and money have been expended introducing "modern" practices whose principal objectives seem to be to save money, and whose effectiveness, to my knowledge, has still to be demonstrated.

Charles Hennessy
August 1, 2008.

TABLE OF CASES

TABLE OF STATUTES

TABLE OF STATUTORY INSTRUMENTS

TABLE OF RULES

TABLE OF ABBREVIATIONS

ADR .... alternative dispute resolution
OCR .... Ordinary Cause Rules 1993
PBA .... proof before answer
PI .... personal injury
PN .... Practice Note
RCS .... Rules of the Court of Session 1994
SAR .... Summary Application Rules 1999
SCR .... Summary Cause Rules 2002

CHAPTER 1

RULES OF PROCEDURE AND PRACTICE

GENERAL INTRODUCTION

The good news is that the rules of procedure and practice in civil litiga- **1–01** tion actually make sense. The bad news is that it takes about 20 years to realise this. This book is going to try and provide a shortcut to that process. Some of the major obstacles which can prevent a clear under- standing of the subject are: (1) there are many different forms of civil pro- cedure in Scotland; (2) there are many rules in each form of procedure; (3) the terminology used in the rules can often appear obscure; (4) the rules only make complete sense when considered in practice; and (5) the practical application of the rules by the courts and by lawyers can vary widely. The approach of this book is to try and overcome these obstacles, and give the reader a general appreciation of what the rules do, without going too far into the intricate and esoteric details.

The main aims are: (1) to explain the reasons for having rules of pro- cedure in civil litigation and what they are trying to achieve; (2) to iden- tify and explain the major forms of procedure which do exist in Scotland; (3) to explain, in broad terms, what the rules of procedure and practice actually are; and (4) to give some preliminary guidance as to how the rules apply in practice, along with some pointers for further study.

This can be no more than a basic introduction to an enormous and complex topic. The reader only has to look at the leading textbooks on the individual procedures to appreciate the difficulties in distilling them to a concise version. When looking at all of the procedures dealt with in the book, the reader is asked not to lose sight of what procedural rules and practices are trying to achieve, namely an orderly, fair and economic method of facilitating the resolution of disputes between litigants.

We have an adversarial system in this country[1] which effectively means that both parties put forward their own arguments in support of their own position, and the judge decides who to favour. This can be contrasted with an inquisitorial system, in which the judge has the power and responsibility to make enquiries on his own initiative about the merits of both sides of any dispute. Such a judge would have a wide discretion to decide what procedure to follow himself. In any

---

[1] It can be argued that small claims are not entirely adversarial.

adversarial system, it is fundamental that the rules have to give each party to a litigation equal opportunities to explain and argue their position.

In some areas, practice is more important than rules of procedure. Practice can differ from time to time, from court to court and from judge to judge. Practice issues will be considered wherever they have an impact upon the application and interpretation of the formal written rules.

WHY HAVE RULES OF PROCEDURE AT ALL?

1–02 This deceptively simple question really has to be considered at the outset. In order to focus immediately on the practicalities, let us consider a case involving Mr X, one of our fictional clients for the purposes of this book. He is a partner in a firm of joiners and builders. He has ordered a quantity of furniture worth about £15,000 for his office but when it arrives, it is not what he thinks he ordered, he has already made various complaints about the order, and he refuses to pay for the furniture. The furniture company wants to take him to court for payment of their bill for supply and delivery of the furniture.

Why can the managing director of the furniture company (or his lawyers) not simply telephone the judge at his local court, arrange an appointment, turn up at court next week against Mr X (and his lawyers) to argue his case and have the court decide whether to order payment or not?[2] Why do we need any rules of procedure to enable this dispute to be canvassed and decided?

If the situation was very simple, and Mr X was delaying payment for no good reason, then there may be no convincing answer to those questions, apart from the practical difficulty of obtaining an appointment with the judge and securing the lawyers' services at short notice. However, as any practising lawyer knows, very few disputes are as straightforward as that. At the mythical hearing before the judge, the time available for preparation of the case will have been very short. The pursuer might not have brought along the invoice with details of what was ordered, when, and what type of furniture it was supposed to be. Mr X might not turn up for reasons unknown—was he told to do so and how? Mr X might have a plausible explanation for not paying—the judge does not know prior to the hearing if he has or what it is. The judge would probably like to be clear what the pursuer's response is to any defence put forward at the hearing, and would be assisted if he could be advised in advance what the parties are arguing about and what is not disputed.

---

[2] They probably did it this way in medieval times (probably without the phone call) after all.

He might think that there is a legal issue which would have to be resolved before he could decide the dispute,[3] and he might like to consult some law books or hear arguments about the applicable law. There might be documents or other pieces of information which would help him understand the problem better. He might think that he could not really decide the point until he had heard clear and credible evidence on oath from the parties and people who appeared to be relevant witnesses. He might even have some doubts as to whether his court had jurisdiction to deal with the case. He might wonder if the alleged debt was due by Mr X personally or by his firm.

The parties themselves might share these uncertainties and might want an opportunity to obtain documents and other evidence which would support their position in the light of what had been identified as the areas of dispute. The administration of the court, the lawyers' time, and the clients' time and business would be affected by the uncertainty about the nature and extent of the dispute, the length of time it might take to resolve, and the means of resolving it.

When they all turned up at the judge's office for the hearing, none of them might have any clear idea of what was about to happen. In a world of infinite resources there would be a surfeit of judges with limitless time and available courts. In that same world, lawyers would have plenty of spare time on their hands. Clients would have nothing to do but litigate all of their disputes to a rapid conclusion with no concern about costs and the possible disruption to their lives. If we had that world, the need for some well known and definite rules which create a structured regime within which civil disputes can be resolved, might be debatable. Individuals could drop everything to attend solely and exclusively to the dispute until, somehow, it was decided. In the real world, we prefer a framework, or indeed a number of different frameworks, within which various types of dispute can be canvassed and decided by methods which are tried and trusted and are known to lawyers and the public in advance. There are deficiencies in our civil court system, but few of the perceived deficiencies are caused by the terms of the rules of procedure themselves.

Rules as a means to an end

All civil procedure requires rules, but the rules should never be treated **1–03** as an end in themselves. They are a means to an end. The rules of any form of procedure essentially provide a structure in which a person who has a "legal problem", which cannot be resolved by agreement or compromise, can have that problem resolved by the court, which imposes its decision on the parties after hearing all of the relevant facts and arguments. All forms of procedure are likely to include rules which will provide the following:

---

[3] e.g. did Mr X order the furniture in his personal capacity or as an officer of the company of which he is director?

(1) provisions requiring the parties to conform with the organisation and administration of the court in which the procedure is to apply, e.g. prescribed forms and documents for particular types of case;

(2) a means of enabling a person to obtain an order from the court quickly if there is no defence to the action;

(3) a means of permitting a person to explain clearly to the court at the outset what the problem is;

(4) a means of bringing to the attention of the opponent[4] that an action has been raised, and allowing him time to respond;

(5) a means of allowing the defender to explain in detail what his response (defence) is;

(6) a means of focusing for the court, and for the parties, what the argument between the parties is really about;

(7) a means of choosing or deciding the process whereby the dispute can best be heard[5];

(8) various means for parties to enlist the aid or order of the court to have the dispute fairly and properly dealt with;

(9) various means of obtaining assistance from the court to obtain material essential to the proper conduct of the case;

(10) a means of hearing the dispute fairly so as to enable the court to reach a just and final decision on it;

(11) a timescale or timetable within which the various appropriate procedures should be carried out;

(12) various means of exercising any right of appeal against an adverse decision.[6]

We are going to look at a number of different types of procedure in this book. On the face of it, they might appear to be extremely unlike one another. Basically, however, they all have the same objective. The specific rules for individual procedures might emphasise some objectives rather than others. The economics of a particular form of procedure might be an important additional factor. When looking at the detailed rules under all of the different procedures, the reader should consider whether, and in what way, they are designed to assist the parties and the court in achieving the aims set out above. By focusing on the "end" they are trying to achieve, this will help to provide a universal approach to understanding them.

Different procedures and different rules

1–04   Anyone trying to understand our rules of procedure would be entitled to have doubts and misgivings as soon as he realised that we appear to

---

[4] Usually called the defender.

[5] Although it is arguable that this does not, strictly, apply to summary causes and small claims, see Chs 11 and 12.

[6] Note that the rules do not provide the right to appeal—this will usually be found in statute. They do, however, provide the administrative framework within which the right of appeal must be exercised.

have so many different ways of doing exactly the same thing. Scotland is a relatively small country. It is a relatively un-litigious country. Yet we have at least 10 principal forms of procedure for civil disputes. An action for a debt between £3,000 and £5,000 can only be pursued in the sheriff court under summary cause procedure. An action for a debt of more than £5,000 could be pursued as a sheriff court ordinary action, a sheriff court commercial action, a Court of Session ordinary action, or a Court of Session commercial action. The procedures and practices applying to these different types of claim would be significantly different.

For example, the way in which you would lodge a motion[7] in each of these cases would be quite different.[8] The time scales for conducting these various litigations could vary dramatically. The costs of doing so vary enormously.

As another illustration, imagine Mr X's car accident with four adults injured to varying degrees and each one wanting to sue the wrongdoer. In theory, depending upon the potential value of the individual claims, each one of them could quite properly and competently pursue his claim independently through the courts in Scotland under different procedures.[9] If the different actions were all started on the same day, their cases would finish at significantly different dates, and reach their resolution by significantly different routes. Each litigation would have exactly the same aim. Each would have the same broad objective. It is always a matter for discussion and debate whether such differences are justifiable and/or desirable.[10]

The rules in context

Most rules of civil procedure are intricate and detailed. They are full of qualifications, conditions and exceptions. In order to understand the rules properly it is necessary to consult the appropriate and accurate[11] set of written rules. You must look at their precise terms. A "shall" do something in a rule instead of a "may" do something, can make a world of difference. A comma here or there can alter the requirement in the rule significantly. The meaning of clauses, subclauses and sub-subclauses can depend upon their precise layout and order. One cannot understand or assess the rules, and ultimately in practice address the court about them, without having the precise terms of the rules available and without knowing exactly what **1–05**

---

[7] See Ch.15.

[8] Indeed, in a summary cause you do not call it a motion—although that is what it is.

[9] A very minor claim could be a small claim action. A not so minor claim could be a summary cause. A more significant claim could be a sheriff court ordinary action or a Court of Session personal injury action or ordinary action. It could end up being decided at a jury trial in the Court of Session. There is a vast range of procedural possibilities to resolve the issues arising from the same accident.

[10] In practice, if they were all raised around the same time, the major claim might proceed whilst the others would await the outcome of that claim.

[11] Make sure they are up to date—they change more frequently than might be imagined.

the rule says. However, whilst it is necessary to consider carefully the detailed terms of any particular rule, an overemphasis on this at the "learning" stage can be a source of confusion.

For example, in the sheriff court Ordinary Cause Rules (OCR), r.15.1(2)[12] states:

> "Subject to paragraph (3), a written motion shall be lodged with the sheriff clerk within 5 days after the date of intimation of the motion required by rule 15.2 (intimation of motions) with—
>
> (a) a certificate of intimation in Form G8; and
> (b) so far as practicable, any document referred to in the written motion and not already lodged in process.".

This makes very little sense in isolation. It has to be considered in the context of the terms of rule 15 as a whole. A reading of that whole rule will show what appears to be a complex arrangement for the preparation, lodging and intimation, not to mention hearing, of a motion in an ordinary action. What is Form G8? The rule contains the technical and administrative requirements for making a motion which have to be known but, in the major scheme of things it may not be that important, one does not have to memorise it, and one can always read the rule in detail as a guide. It may be more important to consider why it should be that a party would want to lodge a motion during the progress of a court action and what kinds of motion are competent or advantageous. This is not to say that the technical requirement is not important. If it is not complied with, then a party will not be able to proceed with the motion, whatever its merit. However, to use the rules of procedure to one's benefit in practice, it is important to identify the context in which the rule applies and to retain a wider perspective, rather than becoming bogged down in matters of form.

The rules in practice

1–06 When applying the rules in practice, the court is bound by the strict terms of the rules. However, there is still scope for different opinions about their meaning and intent. One can never be sure exactly what certain rules mean. They may contain inherent ambiguities with scope for differing interpretations. Sometimes these problems will not manifest themselves for years, and they may not be resolved until an authoritative decision is made regarding the application of the rule in a particular case. That in turn may give rise to an alteration of the rule if the interpretation of it is not what was intended or might itself give rise to further difficulties in other cases. In this way, the operation of the rules in practice can frequently depend upon the interpretation of the rule by a judge.

---

[12] See Ch.9.

The interpretation of the rule will always be done when the judge is considering the application of a rule to a specific set of circumstances. The system of rules is not devised as an academic exercise designed simply to confuse law students and practitioners alike. The rules provide the framework within which real litigations operate. They are influenced and supplemented by practice and judicial interpretation. Sometimes, the administrative practice of a court will be set out in a practice note which is an administrative document which will indicate how a particular rule ought to be complied with or how a court's business will be conducted under the rules.[13] There is no collection of "Rules of Practice", but there is a vast body of case law which has built up over the last 150 years or more, which shows how rules of procedure were applied at the time, and how some of our existing rules apply now. These cases often highlight the need for precise interpretation and understanding of the rules, and a study of these cases will illustrate situations where the qualifications and conditions in particular rules are interpreted. The practice of civil litigation is by no means rigid and inflexible. It develops in different ways and at different times. It may be different in different courts.[14] There are many grey areas and it is difficult, if not impossible, to appreciate the effect these nuances can have without experiencing them for some time in practice.

Changes in rules

The rules are susceptible to change at all times. At one level, changes **1–07** may be needed because of changes in legislation, changes in other rules of procedure, or changes in view as to the importance or significance of the objectives of particular forms of litigation. The rules can also change because the application of the rules in practice has led to an unsatisfactory result, or the terms of the rule are unclear. Sometimes the rules can change because the application of a rule has not conformed to what was intended by the draftsman of it.

At another level, rules are prone to major change in the light of changes in view about the nature, purpose and conduct of civil litigation generally. There is some current dissatisfaction with the way in which litigation is conducted. This dissatisfaction often focuses on the costs or length of litigation. It may simply be that people feel the procedures are not achieving the purpose for which they were intended.

One of the current issues under consideration is the question of whether there should be more active control of cases by judges. This is

---

[13] An example from the Court of Session would be Practice Note (PN) No.4 of 1994 which dealt with the practicalities of dealing with business by post or fax. An example from the sheriff courts (where each sheriffdom will have its own acts of court, practice notes or directions) would be the Act of Court (Consolidation etc.) 1990 No.1 which was issued by the Sheriff Principal of Lothian and Borders on April 4, 1990 and dealt with a number of matters including what was expected from an affidavit in a divorce action.

[14] This applies particularly to sheriff court practice.

known broadly as case management. Formerly, the parties had significant control over the conduct and pace of the litigation. Changes in procedural rules were brought in to alter that, because it was felt that if the
courts had control of the litigation, the litigation would move more
quickly and efficiently.[15] Dissatisfaction with the way in which existing
civil court procedures work and the desire to satisfy the needs of society
for an effective civil justice system can also prompt major change as the
Woolf reforms in England graphically show.[16]

For the first 70 years of the 1900s, the procedural rules in Scotland
were not significantly altered. Since 1970, however, we have had new
rules, new forms of procedure, new rules for old forms of procedure, and
updating of the sheriff court ordinary rules, summary cause rules and
small claim rules. We have new rules for commercial actions in the
sheriff court. In the Court of Session, the ordinary rules have been
rewritten, commercial actions have been brought in and, most recently,
there has been a whole new body of rules for personal injury actions.
Those responsible for the civil justice system are constantly keeping
under review the proper conduct of civil litigation. The Civil Courts
Review, which commenced in April 2007, may give rise to the biggest
changes ever seen in Scottish procedures.[17]

Failure to comply with procedural rules and the interests of justice

1–08   Parties must comply with the rules by spirit and by letter. The court
will usually apply them strictly, so any failure can be fatal to the outcome of an action. However, this itself can give rise to injustice where,
for example, a failure to comply with a technical requirement of the
rules could have a crucial impact on the outcome of a litigation, and prevent the merits of a genuine dispute being aired before the courts. It is
trite to say that the application of the rules of procedure and practice
ought to serve the interests of justice. The difficulty, of course, is in
determining what that means. There is considerable room for argument
between conflicting interests, e.g. in small claims, one can find a degree
of conflict between a quick resolution of a dispute and a fair resolution
of a dispute. In the rules relating to small claims, the emphasis is on
speed. This does not mean that fairness has been thrown out of the
window, but speed and economy are paramount and it might be argued
that in such cases the interests of justice are more in favour of minor

---

[15] Judicial control of the procedure in litigation is exercised in different ways and to
different extents in different types of action, but there is undoubtedly far more judicial direction of procedure generally than ever before and the trend is bound to
continue.

[16] After reviewing the way in which civil litigation was conducted in England, Lord
Woolf instigated reforms which effectively rewrote all of the civil procedure rules in
England.

[17] For details see the Scottish Courts website at *http://www.scotcourts.gov.uk/civilcourt-
sreview/index.asp* [Accessed August 15, 2008].

disputes between parties being resolved quickly as envisaged by the rules, than that there should be any elaborate and potentially expensive procedure which would focus the argument between the parties much more clearly prior to a hearing of evidence. Therefore, the courts might be more inclined to interpret the small claims rules in favour of advancing the litigation swiftly[18] and against allowing any default which causes delay.

A similar consideration applied in the case of *DTZ Debenham Thorpe v I Henderson Transport Services*[19] where, in an ordinary action in the sheriff court, the pursuer failed to lodge the record containing the parties' written pleadings in time for an options hearing and the action was dismissed because of this default.[20] This failure to lodge a document on time, which could have been regarded as no more than a technical administrative failure was in breach of the rules. The Inner House who heard the appeal against the dismissal expressed the view that it was not in the interests of justice to allow a breach of this rule. Their lordships were influenced by the fact that this was a cornerstone of the new, improved procedure brought in by the OCR 1993 and they apparently wanted to encourage the proper compliance with these new procedures. It was considered to be more in the interests of the public and in the interests of justice generally that these procedures were strictly complied with and enforced, than that an apparently valid action should be permitted to proceed where a formal rule had been breached. Since then, this approach seems to have been diluted somewhat for various (good) reasons, but the clear message given out at that time was that failure to adhere to the important procedural requirements of the rules would not be tolerated.[21]

At its worst, failure to comply with the rules means that a claim or a **1–09** defence can be thrown out. In other circumstances, it may mean that a party will lose some serious advantage or tactical benefit. In some cases, it may mean that the case will move quicker or slower. In some cases, it means that the case will simply cost more money because the failure to comply with the rules has caused further procedure and that has caused more expense. Lest it be thought, however, that the rules of procedure resemble, "a snakes and ladders board from which all the ladders had been removed",[22] it should be reassuring to know that all of the different

---

[18] See small claims case in Ch.12.

[19] *DTZ Debenham Thorpe v I Henderson Transport Services*, 1995 S.L.T. 553.

[20] See ordinary procedure in Ch.9.

[21] It should be noted that the pursuer would have been able to raise the action again, so perhaps there was no lasting harm done. A solicitor might feel duty bound to meet the costs of the abortive action or the costs of raising the new action if he felt that the failure was his fault.

[22] Sheriff Principal Graham Cox in *Strathclyde Business Park (Management) Ltd v Cochrane*, 1995 S.L.T. (Sh. Ct) 69.

sets of rules contain general provisions which permit a court to excuse parties from a breach or failure in observance of the rules.[23]

The "dispensing power", as it is known, is expressed thus:

> "[The court] . . . may relieve a party from the consequences of failure to comply with a provision in these rules which is shown to be due to mistake, oversight or other excusable cause, on such conditions . . . as thinks fit."[24]

This dispensing power must be treated with considerable reservation, however. It would be wrong to think that it is a cure-all for any failure to know or follow the rules, and it would be wrong to think that it makes the proper adherence to, and application of, the rules unimportant. It is a safety net for errors but one still has to walk the tightrope because it is the only way to get across—and the net is not always there! It is dangerous to mention this at the present stage because it might encourage people to think that the rules are there but they can be ignored. That is not the case. The dispensing power is a last resort.[25]

The danger of attempting to rely upon the dispensing power can be seen in a recent case in which, amongst other things, the nature of the dispensing power was authoritatively discussed. In *Brogan v O'Rourke Ltd*,[26] the Inner House said that r.2.1 must be interpreted in the context of the rules of court as a whole. The court observed that the rules of court are designed to serve the interests of justice by ensuring, inter alia, that cases are dealt with expeditiously, without undue expense, and without undue demands on the resources of the court: "The interests of justice are not well served by an approach which too readily excuses failures to comply with those rules".

Procedural rules and the public

1–10   We are going to look at the practical application and utilisation of the rules of procedure in the standard forms of litigation. Whilst these might

---

[23] e.g. Rules of the Court of Session ("RCS"), r.2.1; OCR, r.2.1; cover all actions in all procedures in both courts.

[24] There is an argument that the court always has a dispensing power in the interests of justice to excuse any party from a failure to comply with the rules. See Lord Young in *Boyd Gilmour & Co v The Glasgow and South Western Ry Co. Ltd* (1888) 16 R. 104.

[25] For an illustration of a variety of situations in which it was exercised—and not exercised—see *DTZ*, 1995 S.L.T. 553, above; *McGowan v Cartner*, 1996 S.L.T. (Sh. Ct) 10; *Crendon Timber Engineering Ltd v Miller Construction Ltd*, 1996 S.L.T. (Sh. Ct) 102; *Sutherland v Duncan*, 1996 S.L.T. 428; *X v Dumfries and Galloway Regional Council*, 1994 S.L.T. 1285; *Anderson v British Coal Corp*, 1992 S.L.T. 398; *Semple Cochrane Plc v Hughes*, 2001 S.L.T. 1121; *Canmore Housing Association Ltd v Scott*, 2003 S.L.T. (Sh. Ct) 68; *Will v Argyll and Clyde Acute Hospitals NHS Trust*, 2004 S.L.T. 368; *Greenwoods Ltd v ANS Homes Ltd*, 2007 S.L.T. 149.

[26] *Brogan v O'Rourke Ltd*, 2005 S.L.T. 29.

eventually become second nature to practising lawyers it is helpful to remember that for most members of the public, who are the parties[27] in those litigations, there is nothing everyday or routine about being involved in a court action. There are many real human problems which have to be resolved by litigation, and the personalities of the respective parties together with their expectations and interests have to be taken into account. The solicitor has to be able not only to understand the rules, but to utilise them to his client's advantage. Amongst other things, this involves selecting the competent form of procedure which best suits the needs of the client, and conducting the litigation in that procedure with a similar objective.

The solicitor will have to be in a position to explain to the client at each stage of the action what has happened, what is happening and what is likely to happen in the future. He may have to advise the client that going down one procedural road or another will serve his interests best. Frequently, there are several possible routes for the litigation to take. Because of the uncertainties of practice, he can never guarantee what a court will do in any case but he can give the client some indication of the prospect of what will happen in the case if he follows one procedure or another. He can then give the client various options and give him the consequences of each option.[28] The client will then give the solicitor instructions.

That is what conducting litigation in practice is all about and a solicitor cannot advise the client without being familiar with what he can achieve (or not) by using the rules. Explaining things like costs and timescales is part and parcel of the litigation solicitor's business and a thorough knowledge of the working practices and rules of every court is required to enable proper advice to be given. Regrettably, only experience and practice can give the depth of knowledge and understanding required, but it is hoped that this book will set the reader on his way and give him many of the milestones to look out for.

One final feature to mention is that there are usually two sides to the **1–11** story from which the litigation emerges. Each side is perfectly entitled to use the rules to the benefit of his client. Indeed, the solicitor on each side has a professional obligation to do so. However, there is also a professional obligation to the solicitor on the other side. He must be treated with courtesy and respect. One side should not try to take unfair advantage of oversights on the part of the other, especially those arising from simple inadvertence.[29] The clients may be at each other's throats, but there is not any real need for the solicitors to join them and adopt a similar approach to each other. Utilising the procedures firmly and fairly

---

[27] And the paymasters!

[28] Clients are rarely interested in the effect of r.76.8(1)(zz) on the drafting of a motion. They really want to know: "How much will my case cost?"; "How long will it take?"; and, "Will I win?". But not necessarily in that order.

[29] Especially where it is apparent that, regardless of the rights and wrongs of the dispute, there is a genuine dispute.

to the benefit of your client is the ideal. Handling the client's case to the best of the solicitor's ability and in the best interests of the client should be the aim, and that does require a significant degree of objectivity and professional detachment.

Similar considerations apply when dealing with a case in which the opponent has no legal representation, i.e. when he is a party litigant. It can indeed be argued that a solicitor engaged in litigation with a party litigant has an even greater responsibility to him, to the legal profession, and to the court not to take undue advantage. This could[30] extend to helping him positively to comply with procedural requirements, which most lay people will have difficulty understanding properly. This can undoubtedly be difficult in many cases. It is, however, a timely reminder that litigation involves real people and the rules of procedure are ultimately intended not to confound people but to give them an opportunity to have their disputes resolved fairly, economically and in an orderly way.

FURTHER READING

1–12 There have been a number of interesting papers, articles and reports on civil litigation of various types in Scotland over the last few years and the reader's attention is drawn to these. They are essential background reading for any person who wants to obtain a full understanding of our systems of procedure.

I.D. Macphail, *Sheriff Court Practice* 3rd edn (SULI/W. Green, 2006).
L. Foulis, "Sheriff Court Practice: Recent Decisions in Civil Procedure", 1997 J.L.S.S. 148 this article and many others since then by the same author, which are published on a regular basis are well worth reading and can be found on the Journal of the Law Society of Scotland website at *http://www.journalonline.co.uk* [Accessed August 15, 2008].
Lord Gill, "The Woolf, Cullen and Coulon Reports", 1997 J.L.S.S. 437.
R. Mays, "Barest of Bones", 1993 S.L.T. (News) 137.
R. Mays, "Case Management in the Scottish Civil Courts—whose case is it anyway?" (1998) 3 S.L.P.Q. 65.
N.M.P. Morrison, "Approximation of Judiciary Law in European Union", 1995 S.L.T. (News) 183.
N.M.P. Morrison, "The Cullen Report", 1996 S.L.T. (News) 93.
N.M.P. Morrison, "Reform of Civil Procedure", 1998 S.L.T. (News) 137.
R. Wadia, "Judicial Case Management in Scotland", 1997 S.L.T. (News) 255.
Scottish Civil Courts Review, The Scottish Civil Courts Review—a consultation paper (Scottish Civil Courts Review, 2007).

---

[30] And arguably, it "should".

CHAPTER 2

THE DIFFERENT COURTS AND THEIR RULES
OF PROCEDURE—AN OUTLINE

There are two levels of court in Scotland in which to conduct a civil **2–01** litigation, namely the sheriff court and the Court of Session. Each of these courts has a variety of different procedures depending upon factors such as the value and the nature of the claim. Often, the litigant can have an option to choose the court and the form of procedure in which to litigate.

There is a sheriff court in most population centres in Scotland, but only one Court of Session, which is located in Edinburgh. In very loose terms, they can be regarded respectively as our "local" courts (sheriff) and our "High" court (Court of Session). With certain exceptions, they can each deal with the same type of cases,[1] and, in particular, there is no upper financial limit on the value of cases which the sheriff court can handle. The Court of Session does not have jurisdiction in relation to claims totalling £5,000 or less. The sheriff court has "privative" jurisdiction over such actions.

Accordingly, the distinction between the types of cases they can competently decide is less than might be imagined. That is not to say that the differences in procedure and practice between them are slight—far from it. One of the major difficulties in understanding the various forms of civil procedure in Scotland is caused by the different ways in which precisely the same civil dispute between the same parties can be litigated upon in these two courts. There are significant divergences between them in, amongst other things, their tradition, rules, forms, terminology, practice and rights of audience.

This chapter contains an outline of all of the different forms of proce- **2–02** dure in the Scottish courts of first instance.[2] We will look briefly at their organisation, administration, jurisdiction, statutory regulation, how business might be allocated to one court as opposed to another, and how cases can be transferred from one court or one form of procedure to another. Certain cases must be litigated upon in a particular way, but,

---

[1] In which, they are said to have "concurrent jurisdiction".

[2] i.e. the courts in which action can initially be brought, as opposed to courts which hear appeals, for which see Ch.20.

where there is a choice, the choice can be governed by a variety of practical factors. The decision as to where and how best to pursue a case is often a matter of opinion and personal preference on the part of the solicitor instructed. There are interesting practical arguments about selecting an appropriate forum within the Scottish courts and we shall look at these after we have discussed what options are available in this country.

The forms of procedure which will be discussed in this book are the following:

Court of Session

Ordinary action
Petitory action
Commercial cause
Judicial review
Personal injuries procedure

Sheriff court

Ordinary action[3]
Commercial action
Summary cause
Small claim
Summary application

As a basic illustration of the options available to litigants in Scotland, let us take a simple action for payment of a debt owed by one person to another. If the value of the debt is £5,000 or less, then any action for payment would have to be raised in the sheriff court, for reasons we shall see later. If it was for (say) £150,000 then it could equally be raised in the sheriff court as an ordinary action or as a commercial action,[4] or in the Court of Session as an ordinary action or as a commercial cause. In personal injury actions, there are even more options available in pursuing a case. Some of the procedures we are going to consider are "privative", in other words, they alone must be used for certain cases, but many of them are alternative and it is for the pursuer, in the first place, to decide which procedure to use.[5]

---

[3] Including family actions—although we do not discuss procedure in family actions in this book.
[4] If the particular sheriff court had jurisdiction—see Ch.10.
[5] Either party can ask the court to "remit" a case from one form of procedure to another or from one level of court to another, after proceedings have been commenced. See paras 2–15 to 2–25, below.

COURT OF SESSION

History

The history of the development of the Court of Session rules of pro- **2–03**
cedure has been quite distinct from that of the sheriff court.[6] The Court
of Session jurisdiction and powers can be traced back to early times. The
original statutory power to make rules regarding the conduct of business
before it, go back to the College of Justice Act 1540. It can be argued
that the Court of Session has always had an inherent right, regardless of
statute, to regulate its own business.[7] In more modern times reviews
have been carried out in relation to the operation of the Court of Session
and its business. The Court of Session Act 1988[8] was passed followed
by the Act of Sederunt (Rules of the Court of Session 1994) 1994 (SI
1994/1443), which lays down the rules for procedure in any causes in
the Court of Session after September 5, 1994. The rules are extensive.
There have been some detailed changes by various Acts of Sederunt
since then, in which special rules have been introduced for particular
types of action. However, the 1994 Rules can be seen as the foundation
of the present procedures in the Court of Session.

Organisation and administration

Historically, all of the judges of the Court of Session sat as one court **2–04**
to hear cases. Then they were split into two divisions of equal status
where they sat, either all of them or a quorum of them, in the Inner
House. Then some judges from these two divisions were appointed to
hear cases individually in the Outer House of the court. The current
practice developed from there. Now, there are 32 Court of Session
judges[9] who all have equal status as Senators of the College of Justice.
There is also provision for appointing temporary judges to assist in the
conduct of business.[10] The Inner House is split into two divisions, the
First Division and the Second Division, each comprising four judges.
The First Division is presided over by the Lord President. The Second
Division is presided over by the Lord Justice-Clerk. The Inner House

---

[6] For details, see *The Laws of Scotland: Stair Memorial Encyclopaedia* (Edinburgh: Law
Society of Scotland/Butterworths, 1987), Vol.6.
[7] For a discussion of this see *Esso Petroleum Co Ltd v Hall Russell & Co Ltd (No.2)*,
1995 S.L.T. 127; in *Tonner v Reiach and Hall*, 2007 S.L.T. 1183, the existence of an
inherent power in the Court of Session, in the absence of a specific rule of court, to regulate procedure before it, was authoritatively recognised, although the circumstances in
which it would be exercised would be rare.
[8] Court of Session Act 1988 (c.36).
[9] At the time of writing. The number of judges can be increased by Order in Council.
[10] Law Reform (Miscellaneous Provisions) (Scotland) Act 1990, s.35(3); see *Clancy v
Caird (No.1)*, 2000 S.L.T. 546.

(either division) usually only hears reclaiming motions or appeals.[11] It usually sits as a court of three judges but there may be special cases in which they will have a larger court. There is power to form an Extra Division to cope with larger volumes of business. The senior judge of the Extra Division will preside and its decisions have the same force as judgments from the other two divisions.

Twenty two of the judges of the Court of Session sit as Lords Ordinary in the Outer House, in which they hear a variety of cases at first instance and also have certain limited functions in relation to some appeals. Certain judges are designated by the Lord President to deal with specific matters, as part of their judicial business. For example, there is an insolvency judge, and there are judges nominated to hear commercial actions.

The Court of Session sits in Edinburgh and all of the courts and administrative offices are located there. There is a hierarchy of staff responsible for the administration of business in the Court of Session. The Principal Clerk of Session and Justiciary is responsible for all matters of policy affecting the interests of the Court of Session (and the High Court of Justiciary) one of which concerns the constant conflicting demands of civil and criminal business conducted by the court. The Deputy Principal Clerk of Session and the Keeper of the Rolls are responsible for overseeing the daily working of all of the departments of the Court of Session. The Keeper of the Rolls will allocate civil business for disposal by the Inner House (in consultation with the Lord President) and in the Outer House. The First Division and Second Division each has its own depute clerk and other depute clerks are allocated to individual judges in the Outer House. There is a large administrative staff which is located in offices within Parliament House in Edinburgh. Documents relating to court actions in the Court of Session are lodged with officials of the appropriate departments and issued by them.

Jurisdiction

2–05   As has already been noted, there is very little limitation upon the jurisdiction of the Court of Session. By and large, all civil actions are competent in the Court of Session provided it has territorial jurisdiction. The court has no jurisdiction in actions at first instance for sums totalling £5,000 or less. There may also be particular provisions in specific statutes excluding its jurisdiction. The sheriff court and the Court of Session have concurrent jurisdiction in a number of cases, but there are a large number of cases in which the Court of Session has exclusive jurisdiction.[12]

---

[11] Although it does have some original, as opposed to appellate, jurisdiction, most notably for petitions to the *nobile officium*.

[12] e.g. actions of reduction, judicial review, patents, etc.

PRINCIPAL STATUTORY PROVISIONS RELATING TO
COURT OF SESSION PROCEDURE

Court of Session Act 1988 (c.36)

The main provisions in recent times are contained in the **2–06**
Court of Session Act 1988. This was an Act whose purpose was, inter
alia,

> ". . .to consolidate . . . certain enactments relating to the constitu-
> tion, administration and procedure of the Court of Session and pro-
> cedure on appeal therefrom to the House of Lords".

The principal features to note are:

s.1—relates to the number of judges;
s.2—confirms the details of the composition of the Inner House and
Outer House as explained above;
s.5—gives the court power to regulate its own procedure. This is to be
done by Act of Sederunt and the power extends to prescribing
procedural rules, forms of documents, etc. and including a general
power to make such regulations as are necessary to carry out the provisions of the Act;
s.6—the court is empowered to provide by Act of Sederunt for the
allocation of business into various categories, and for various
other measures designed with a view to securing that, "causes coming before the Court may be heard . . . with as little delay as
possible";
s.8—provides for the continuation of the Court of Session Rules
Council[13] which will comprise the Lord President, two judges, five
members of the Faculty of Advocates and five solicitors. The Rules
Council has power to frame rules regarding any of the matters relating to the court which the court is empowered to regulate by Act of
Sederunt, and submit these to the court for approval and for preparation of an Act of Sederunt;
ss.12 to 17 and ss.29 to 31—deal with provisions regarding jury trials
in civil cases, and application for review of jury verdicts;
ss.21 to 24—make special provisions for Exchequer causes,[14] which,
inter alia, "shall at all times take precedence of . . . all other causes
in the Court".

There are a number of provisions regarding the appellate jurisdiction of
the Inner House and matters incidental to this:

---

[13] Originally established 50 years before.
[14] These comprise special types of action, primarily actions by the Crown for recovery of
taxes and other duties.

ss.40 to 43—set out what interlocutors are appealable from the Inner House to the House of Lords and matters incidental to such an appeal.

The Act also took the opportunity to repeal in whole or in part numerous statutes which formerly had some bearing on the business conducted in the Court of Session which, "are no longer of practical utility."

Act of Sederunt (Rules of the Court of Session 1994) 1994 (SI 1994/1443)

2–07   This came into force on September 5, 1994 and states that the provisions of Sch.2 to the Act of Sederunt are to have the effect of providing new rules for the Court of Session. Schedule 2 is therefore the "rule book" for Court of Session procedure. It consolidated many of the provisions of prior rules and modernised the procedures to some extent. Other Acts of Sederunt since then have altered some detailed rules[15] and introduced other procedures, most notably, the commercial action procedure and the personal injury procedure. Consideration has been given to further wholesale review of the general rules of procedure for actions in the Court of Session but this has not found favour at the time of writing.

PRACTICE NOTES

2–08   Practice notes are administrative directions by the court itself which do not have the status of a rule and cannot amend or override a rule. However, the court can issue directions by way of a practice note which can explain how a rule is to be complied with, how it is to be dealt with for administrative purposes, or, indeed, to set out the practice of the court in a matter which might not be covered by a specific rule. When the new Rules of the Court of Session ("RCS") came into force in 1994, 54 practice notes relating to a variety of administrative matters[16] were revoked in order to clear the way for the new procedures. Since then, there have been many practice notes issued in relation to a wide variety of procedural and administrative matters. They include a practice note regarding the fixing of a hearing on the procedure roll[17] and even one which arguably overrides a specific rule.[18] These should be taken into account when considering Court of Session procedure and practice. The distinction between the practical effect of rules and practice notes in setting out

---

[15] e.g. a major amendment was contained in the Act of Sederunt (Rules of the Court of Session Amendment No.4) (Miscellaneous) 1996 (SI 1996/2168).

[16] See *Parliament House Book* (Edinburgh: W.Green), p.C2007 (as at Release 97).

[17] Practice Note No.2 of 2004.

[18] Practice Note No.4 of 1997 provides that notes of argument are to be lodged in every case which is appointed to procedure roll. The rule only says that the court "may" order such a note. See *Fairbarn v Vayro*, 2001 S.L.T. 1167.

procedure and practice has been somewhat diluted by the development of the commercial action procedure[19] and the new personal injury rules.[20]

SHERIFF COURT

History

The present sheriff court organisation was created by the Sheriff **2–09** Courts (Scotland) Act 1907. There has been one major statutory alteration to its provisions in the Sheriff Courts (Scotland) Act 1971. It has recently been stated that the sheriff has an inherent power to regulate procedure in any action before him,[21] but this power would not be used to override existing rules, rather it might cover the very rare situations where the rules are silent. There are five different basic forms of procedure in the sheriff court, each one of which has its own body of rules. The original rules for procedure in sheriff court actions remained substantially unchanged for well over 80 years but in more recent times they have undergone substantial alteration.

(1) The "rule book" for procedure in ordinary actions is contained in a Schedule to the 1907 Act, and this Schedule was altered by Act of Sederunt[22] in 1993 to effect a most significant change in the approach to litigation in ordinary actions in the sheriff court. The rules are called the Ordinary Cause Rules 1993.[23]

(2) Summary cause and small claims procedure did not exist as separate forms of action until 1976 and 1988 respectively. They were significantly altered in 2002 by Act of Sederunt[24] which provides the "rule book" for all such actions.

(3) Commercial actions in the sheriff court were created by Act of Sederunt[25] in 2001 and this provided a new Chapter in the existing sheriff court rules which gave alternative rules for commercial actions.

(4) Summary applications were given their new "rule book" by Act of Sederunt in 1999.[26]

The application of these sets of rules are kept under constant review and they are much more open to amendment now to take account of changes

---

[19] See Ch.7.
[20] See Ch.6.
[21] See *Newman Shopfitters Ltd v M J Gleeson Group Plc*, 2003 S.L.T. (Sh. Ct) 83.
[22] Act of Sederunt (Sheriff Court Ordinary Cause Rules) 1993 (SI 1993/1956).
[23] They will be referred to as the OCR throughout this book.
[24] Act of Sederunt (Summary Cause Rules) 2002 (SSI 2002/132).
[25] Act of Sederunt (Ordinary Cause Rules) Amendment (Commercial Actions) 2001 (SSI 2001/8).
[26] Act of Sederunt (Summary Applications, Statutory Applications and Appeals etc. Rules) 1999 (SI 1999/929).

in primary legislation and changes in views about the appropriate nature of, and mechanism for, civil litigation. In broad terms, actions must be brought as small claims if they have a total value of £3,000 or less, and must be brought as summary causes if they have a total value between £3,000 and £5,000.[27] The fact that the sheriff court has "privative" jurisdiction up to the summary cause financial limit means that any increase in that limit would exclude claims beneath that limit from the Court of Session and restrict them to the sheriff court.

Organisation

2–10   There are 49 sheriff courts in Scotland. For administrative purposes they are grouped into six "sheriffdoms" each one of which covers an area of Scotland.[28] For example, the local sheriff court for the town of Renfrew is Paisley Sheriff Court. Paisley Sheriff Court is within the Sheriffdom of North Strathclyde. That sheriffdom includes seven other sheriff courts, such as Campbelltown and Kilmarnock. A case heard at the court would be heard at the "Sheriffdom of North Strathclyde at Paisley".

Each sheriffdom is presided over by a sheriff principal, who is responsible for the administration of business within his sheriffdom. He may hear cases at first instance himself, although it is rare for him to do so nowadays, and he will hear appeals from the sheriff in civil cases where appeal has been taken to him.[29] The sheriff principal is required to see that the business of the sheriffdom is conducted with speed and efficiency.

Each sheriff court will have an appropriate number of sheriffs who will normally be permanently located there. Some sheriffs will also sit at other sheriff courts within the same sheriffdom. There are a few full time sheriffs who are not allocated to particular sheriffdoms or sheriff courts but can sit anywhere as required by the level of business. They are referred to as "floating" sheriffs. The total number of sheriffs in Scotland in 2008 was 142. To assist in the conduct of business within a particular sheriff court, the authorities can bring in a "part-time sheriff" who will be an experienced solicitor or advocate who is still in practice but could preside over any cases which a full time sheriff could hear. He is appointed as such[30] and can be called upon by the administration if necessary to sit at any sheriff court on any day or for any case where the volume of business demands it. In 2008 there were around 79 part-time sheriffs.

In each and every sheriff court, there will be a sheriff clerk's office. The office may be split into civil, criminal, commissary and other sections. It is not necessary to go into the organisation of the sheriff clerk's

---

[27] See Chs 11 and 12 for more precise explanation.

[28] The sheriff court districts.

[29] Certain appeals from a sheriff at first instance can be taken straight to the Inner House of the Court of Session thus leapfrogging the sheriff principal. See Ch.20 on "Appeals".

[30] Under the Bail, Judicial Appointments etc. (Scotland) Act 2000. There is a statutory limit of 80 part-time sheriffs.

service in any detail, but it should be realised that the sheriff clerk's office (civil) will perform a variety of functions of an administrative nature involving, amongst other things, the recording of information, the receipt of court documents, the issue of court orders, the allocation of hearings, and the daily organisation of business in the court. On a practical level, it should be remembered that any reference in the rules of procedure to the lodging of documents, etc. with the court or with the clerk, will mean lodging with an official in the sheriff clerk's office.

Up-to-date details of all of the sheriffs in post, all sheriff clerk's offices in Scotland and the sheriff court with territorial jurisdiction for any particular location can be obtained from the Scottish Courts website.[31]

PRINCIPAL STATUTORY PROVISIONS RELATING TO
SHERIFF COURT PROCEDURE

Sheriff Courts (Scotland) Act 1907 (c.51)

The purpose of the Act was, "to amend and regulate the laws and **2–11** practice of civil procedure in Sheriff Courts in Scotland". The important sections now remaining are:

s.6—provided an action is otherwise competent in a sheriff court, the principal grounds of jurisdiction of any particular sheriff court are:

- residence of the defender;
- place of business of the defender;
- where moveable property of the defender has been arrested in the sheriffdom;
- where the defender owns property in the sheriffdom which is the subject of the action;
- in interdicts where the alleged wrong was committed there;
- in contracts where the contract was executed or to be performed there;
- in multiple poindings where the fund "*in medio*"[32] is located there or the holder of the fund is subject to jurisdiction as above;
- where the proposed defender is already pursuing the proposed pursuer in an action raised there in delict;
- where the cause of action was committed there; and
- where the defender agrees to accept the jurisdiction of the court[33];

---

[31] At *http://www.scotcourts.gov.uk* [Accessed August 16, 2008].

[32] i.e. the sum of money, or the property, about which there are competing claims of ownership.

[33] In this connection, it should be noted that questions of jurisdiction generally are also dependent upon the Civil Jurisdiction and Judgments Act 1982. Reference should be made to that Act for details.

s.7—all causes not exceeding £5,000[34] in total value exclusive of interest and expenses which are competent in the sheriff court shall be brought in the sheriff court only;

ss.27 to 29—appeals to sheriff principal and to Court of Session[35];

s.38—summary removing; where tenants of property let for less than a year can be ejected under a summary (shortened) form of procedure;

s.39—the procedure in all civil cases in the sheriff court was to be as set out in the Schedule to the Act. The Schedule is, in effect, the rule book for ordinary actions in the sheriff court. The schedule was effectively rewritten in 1993 when a completely new set of rules was provided for actions commencing after January 1, 1994.

s.50—summary applications; these comprise a varied collection of different types of claim which, by statute or by common law, can be brought in the sheriff court. They have a special shortened or "summary" procedure[36] although some of the rules of ordinary actions apply to them.

Sheriff Courts (Scotland) Act 1971 (c.58)

2–12   This was an amending act which was concerned primarily with the administration of the sheriff courts rather than with the intricacies of procedure but again it is helpful to have an idea of the principal matters in the Act which have some practical significance for civil procedure.

ss.9 to 14—give the Secretary of State certain functions and powers relating to sheriffs, such as prescribing the number of sheriffs for each sheriffdom;

ss.15 to 17—give the sheriff principals certain powers and responsibilities within their own sheriffdoms and, inter alia, a duty, "to secure the speedy and efficient disposal of business" within the sheriff courts in his jurisdiction;

s.31—this section increased the privative jurisdiction of the sheriff court;

s.32—gives the Court of Session power to regulate the civil procedure and practice of the sheriff court by means of Act of Sederunt. Before making any changes, however, the Court of Session must consult with the Sheriff Court Rules Council;

ss.33 to 34—establish the Sheriff Court Rules Council, whose function is to, "review generally the procedure and practice followed in civil proceedings in the sheriff court (including any matters incidental or relating to that procedure or practice)". The council is empowered to draft alterations to the existing rules for consideration by the Court

---

[34] Originally this was £50 but it was increased over time.

[35] See Ch.20.

[36] The rules of which are now contained in the Summary Applications, Statutory Applications and Appeals etc. Rules 1999—*Parliament House Book*, p.D502 (as at Release 97). See Ch.14.

of Session who can decide to make such alterations by Act of Sederunt, as they think expedient;

s.35—introduced a completely new form of procedure to be known as a "Summary Cause" for use in cases where the value of the subject matter of the claim was below a certain amount. The first rules for that form of procedure were not provided until 1976, and completely new rules were provided in 2002;

s.35(2)—this section was inserted in 1985 and introduced a, "form of summary cause process" to be known as a, "small claim". The Lord Advocate was to prescribe what type of cases could be brought as a small claim and the Act itself did not prescribe financial limits.

s.36(2)—provided that a summary cause was to be commenced by way of filling in a printed form of "summons" in accordance with rules made under s.32 of the Act;

s.37—provided for "remits", i.e. the transference of an action from one form of procedure to another within the sheriff court, if and when this was considered appropriate. This introduced a degree of flexibility. It also provided that an ordinary action could be transferred to the Court of Session from the sheriff court in certain circumstances;

s.38—provided for appeals in summary causes.[37]

The Sheriff Courts (Scotland) Act 1971 (Privative Jurisdiction and Summary Cause) Order 2007 (SSI 2007/507)

This came into force on January 14, 2008 and provided that the limit of the privative (or exclusive) jurisdiction of the sheriff court should be £5,000, and the limit of the summary cause should be £5,000. The new limits do not apply to proceedings commenced before the order comes into force.

Small Claims (Scotland) Order 1988 (SI 1988 No.1999)

As provided in s.35(2) of the 1971 Act, the Lord Advocate duly made **2–13** this order, and he prescribed that "small claims" would be certain actions where the total value of the claim did not exceed £750. Two types of claim were specifically excluded, namely actions for aliment and actions for defamation.

The Small Claims (Scotland) Amendment Order 2007 (SSI 2007/496)

This substituted £3,000 for the £750 provided in the above order. It came into effect for all small claims after January 14, 2008.

---

[37] See Ch.19.

PRACTICE NOTES AND ACTS OF COURT

2–14 Only the Court of Session has power to make rules for regulating sheriff court procedures generally,[38] but the sheriff principal of any sheriffdom may regulate procedure in his sheriffdom in relation to certain matters by way of Acts of Court or practice notes.[39] He cannot alter the substantive law in doing so, and he cannot alter the terms of any rules contained in the Acts of Sederunt, but he can make administrative orders or directions regulating the way in which the court's business is conducted and regulating practice within his sheriffdom in the application of the rules. Individual sheriffdoms may well have their own practice notes.[40]

MOVEMENT OF CASES BETWEEN COURTS AND PROCEDURES

2–15 If an individual wants to pursue a claim in Scotland it is, to some extent, open to him to choose which court to utilise and what form of procedure best suits his purpose. Of course, he has to take account of the jurisdiction rules which may mean that certain types of claim have to be initiated in certain ways.[41] Where he has a choice of alternative competent procedures, he is free to pick whichever one he prefers. All actions commence by the preparation of an initiating document such as a summons or an initial writ. That document is then presented to the court officials (or, in special cases, to a judge) for them to give the authority of the court to the act of serving the document on the opponent. This authority will be in the form of a warrant in the sheriff court or signet in the Court of Session, attached to the principal writ or summons. If a prospective pursuer, having decided where and how to proceed, presents an initiating document under one of the various forms of procedure outlined above to the court, and if it is, on the face of it, competent, then he will be authorised to serve it on the opponent. The court will not express any view as to whether this form of procedure is desirable (as opposed to competent) for this particular case and obviously the opponent will have had no say in the choice which his adversary has made. By and large, there is likely to be a degree of consensus amongst those dealing with the case as to what court or procedure might be appropriate, but it is possible for the parties, either individually or collectively, or indeed

---

[38] Sheriff Courts (Scotland) Act 1971 s.32.

[39] His power to do so is based upon his common law power and s.15(2) of the Sheriff Courts (Scotland) Act 1971.

[40] A comprehensive and helpful collection of many (but not necessarily all) current practice notes is contained in the *Parliament House Book*, pp.D701–D1118 (as at Release 97).

[41] e.g. he could only seek a judicial review by virtue of the procedure available in the Court of Session. He could only sue for payment of a debt of £600 by way of a small claim action.

for the court of its own volition, subsequently to opt for a court, or a form of procedure, different from that under which the action was initiated.

This involves seeking a remit or a transfer[42] of the action to another level of court[43] or from one form of procedure to another form of procedure within the same level of court. We will look at some of the reasons why a party might want a remit or transfer later but, first of all, we should identify the rules which make it possible to exercise this option. As a matter of practice, it should be noted that motions to the court to remit actions are relatively rare. Because there are limited rights of appeal against the decision of a judge at first instance to grant or refuse a remit, there are very few decisions as to how and when the court will grant or refuse such motions.

REMIT/TRANSFER — CHANGING THE LEVEL OF COURT

Court of Session ordinary action

A case raised as an ordinary action in the Court of Session can **2–16** be remitted to the sheriff court provided the nature of the action is such that it could competently have been brought in the sheriff court. The remit can be done on the application of any party to the action or at the instance of the judge himself, and may be granted where, "in the opinion of the Court, the nature of the action makes it appropriate to do so".[44]

Sheriff court ordinary action

Provided that an ordinary action is not within the privative jurisdic- **2–17** tion of the sheriff court, i.e. for £5,000 or less,[45] the sheriff may on the motion of any party to the action remit it to the Court of Session. He has to be satisfied that, "the importance or difficulty of the cause" makes it appropriate to do so.[46] His discretionary decision to grant or refuse that motion is appealable to the Court of Session.[47]

---

[42] "Remit" and "transfer" are treated as interchangeable in this context.

[43] i.e. sheriff court to Court of Session or vice versa.

[44] Law Reform (Miscellaneous Provisions) Act 1985 s.14. See *McKay v Lloyds TSB Mortgages Ltd*, 2004 G.W.D. 37-757: also *Paterson v Advocate General for Scotland*, 2007 S.L.T. 846.

[45] This might apply to an action raised as a summary cause for (say) £4,000 and remitted to the ordinary roll.

[46] See *Butler v Thom*, 1982 S.L.T. (Sh. Ct) 57; *Data Controls (Middlesborough) Ltd v British Railway Board*, 1991 S.L.T. 426, but, note, this was overruled in *Mullan v Anderson (No.1)*, 1993 S.L.T. 835.

[47] See s.37(1)(b) and (3) of the 1971 Act as amended by the Law Reform (Miscellaneous Provisions) (Scotland) Act 1980 s.16(c) and the Law Reform (Miscellaneous Provisions) (Scotland) Act 1985 s.18(3)(b).

REMIT/TRANSFER—CHANGING THE FORM OF PROCEDURE
WITHIN THE SAME COURT

Court of Session

Ordinary action

2–18   A case raised as an ordinary action in the Court of Session can be transferred to the commercial roll of the Court of Session.[48] Any party may apply at any time to do this. The court cannot take that initiative. There are no particular provisions as to when such a transfer would be appropriate. The action would have to be one such as could competently be brought as a commercial action. The judge hearing the motion has a discretion as to whether to grant it or not. The motion would be heard by the commercial judge.

Commercial cause

2–19   An action raised as a commercial cause can be transferred to the ordinary procedure if a motion is made.[49]

Personal injury action

2–20   Any party may apply within certain time limits to have such a case proceed as an ordinary action.[50] However, there have to be "exceptional reasons" for such a motion. The court should have regard to the need for detailed pleadings, the length of time required for preparation of the action, and any other relevant circumstances.[51]

Sheriff court

Ordinary action

2–21   In an ordinary action, if both parties want it, the sheriff must direct that it be treated as a summary cause for all purposes.[52]
    A pursuer can elect to raise certain kinds of cases as a commercial action in the sheriff court,[53] but if he does not do so, and simply raises an ordinary action, then a defender can apply for it to be transferred to commercial action procedure.[54]

---

[48] See Ch.7.
[49] See Ch.7, for details of r.47.9.
[50] See Ch.6, for details of r.43.5.
[51] See *Tudhope v Finlay Park (t/a Park Hutchison Solicitors)*, 2004 S.L.T. 783, per Lord Cameron.
[52] Sheriff Courts (Scotland) Act 1971 s.37(1)(a).
[53] Provided that particular sheriff court has made the procedure available. See Ch.10.
[54] OCR r.40.5(1).

Commercial action

If both parties want a transfer from commercial action procedure to **2–22** ordinary action procedure then the court must do so. If one party only wants a transfer, then the sheriff has a discretion to do so and the criteria are extremely wide.[55]

Summary cause

In a summary cause, the sheriff may, on the motion of one of the par- **2–23** ties, transfer it to the ordinary cause. His discretionary decision depends upon him being satisfied that, "the importance or difficulty of the cause makes it appropriate to do so".[56] If both parties make the motion then he must do so. His decision on the remit is final.[57] In a summary cause, if both parties want to have it dealt with as a small claim then the sheriff must direct this. There is no power for one party to ask for this and the sheriff cannot, on his own initiative, decide to do so.[58]

Small claim

In any small claim the sheriff *ex proprio motu*[59] or on the motion of one **2–24** party may direct that it be treated for all purposes as a summary cause or as an ordinary action. The discretion which he has depends upon him being satisfied that there is either (a) a question of fact of exceptional complexity, or (b) a difficult question of law. If he is asked by both parties to direct that it be treated as a summary cause or as an ordinary action, then he must do so. His discretionary decision to remit or not is final.[60]

TRANSFER TO ANOTHER SHERIFF COURT

An action raised in one sheriff court can be transferred to another. This **2–25** can be done on the motion of either party, where the sheriff considers it, "expedient to do so having regard to the convenience of witnesses and parties." There are other provisions governing the transfer.[61]

EXAMPLES

In order to obtain some grasp of the factors which apply in practice to **2–26** the selection of an appropriate forum it is helpful to consider different

---

[55] OCR r.40.6(1)(a).
[56] See s.37(2) and (3) of the 1971 Act.
[57] See *Hamilton District Council v Sneddon*, 1980 S.L.T. (Sh Ct) 36.
[58] See s.37(2C) of the 1971 Act.
[59] Of his own volition.
[60] See s.37(2B) and (3) of the 1971 Act.
[61] See OCR r.26.1.

examples which reveal judicial thinking on the question of remits. A consideration of these cases will also give some insight into the relationship of the different procedures *inter se*.[62]

In *Mullan v Anderson (No.1)*[63] the pursuer raised an action in the sheriff court seeking damages from the defender who had allegedly murdered the pursuer's husband. The defender had been acquitted of the murder at the High Court. The defender sought to remit the case to the Court of Session. His motion to do so was refused and he appealed to the Inner House. The appeal was heard by a court of five judges. Their Lordships decided that the sheriff had misdirected himself and considered it would be appropriate to remit this very unusual civil claim to the Court of Session. Lord Penrose said, inter alia, that it was necessary to have in mind the characteristics of the two courts.

> "A court, in general terms, is defined not only by the characteristics of its judicial and other officers, but also, for example, by its forms of procedure, the classes of work it customarily deals with, its location relative to the residence or place of business of the parties appearing before it, the qualifications and experience of those who are entitled to practise before it, the expense incurred in using the court, and the efficiency of its programming for the disposal of work . . . The question . . . appears to me necessarily to require consideration of those factors relevant to the processing and disposal of the particular cause in the respective fora".[64]

2–27 In *McIntosh v British Railways Board (No.1)*,[65] the pursuer sustained an accident at work and raised an action in the Court of Session for damages. He sued for £3,000. Although the claim was admittedly of a low value the pursuer could have been awarded more than £1,500, which was the upper limit of the privative jurisdiction of the sheriff court. The defender enrolled a motion to remit to the sheriff court. The Lord Ordinary granted this. On appeal, the Inner House reversed the decision. Lord President Hope said:

> "The pursuer is entitled to avail himself of the jurisdiction of whichever court he finds more convenient or appropriate to his own circumstances. There may well be sound practical reasons for choosing one court as against another, and unless Parliament directs otherwise the court which is chosen must deal with the case which is before it . . . A remit (on grounds of modest value and

---

[62] We will consider later the practical factors which might influence a solicitor's choice of forum.

[63] *Mullan v Anderson (No.1)*, 1993 S.L.T. 835.

[64] *Mullan v Anderson (No.1)*, 1993 S.L.T. 835 at p.849.

[65] *McIntosh v British Railways Board (No.1)*, 1990 S.L.T. 637.

simplicity alone) . . . cannot be justified and the practical and procedural advantages to the pursuer of pursuing his claim in this court are such that it is not appropriate that he should be deprived of the benefit of having it decided here."[66]

In *Butler v Thom*,[67] Sheriff Macphail had to consider whether an action for damages for a young child who had suffered catastrophic injuries in a car accident should be remitted on grounds of importance or difficulty from the sheriff court to the Court of Session. There were no particular specialities in the merits of the claim but it was argued that the proof and assessment of damages were matters which made it appropriate to remit to the Court of Session. He decided that a remit would be appropriate because there might be difficulties in assessing damages as there was no comparable Scottish case dealing with similar types of claim. He took the view that:

> ". . . the judgment will be of such general importance that it is appropriate that it should carry the persuasive authority of a Lord Ordinary of the Court of Session."

A more recent case was that of *McKay v Lloyds TSB Mortgages Ltd*,[68] in which the pursuer was claiming £10,000 from the defenders who were the owners of a flat above the pursuer's property from which substantial water leaked, and caused the pursuer damage. The pursuer raised an action of damages in the Court of Session. The defenders sought a remit to the sheriff court. The judge granted the remit which was opposed by the pursuer. He commented that the Court of Session is under considerable pressure of business and that would be increased if:

> ". . . small value claims raising no difficulties of fact or law are permitted to proceed in the Court of Session . . . the effect might be that scarce judicial resources will be further stretched, to the detriment of pursuers in high value, difficult or complex cases which have been appropriately raised in the Court of Session."

He also granted leave to reclaim (appeal) his decision to the Inner House as he thought it might well be appropriate to have the decision in *McIntosh* reconsidered in the light of present circumstances.[69]

These cases are intended as purely illustrative guides to the way in which particular cases were dealt with at the time, and they should not

---

[66] See *McIntosh v British Railways Board (No.1)*, 1990 S.L.T. 637 at pp.640C–641B; as a contrast see what was said in *Hamilton v British Coal Corp*, 1990 S.L.T. 287.

[67] *Butler v Thom*, 1982 S.L.T. (Sh. Ct) 57.

[68] See fn.47, above.

[69] The appeal was allowed without argument so *McIntosh*, 1990 S.L.T. 637 has not yet been reviewed. See *Paterson v Advocate General for Scotland*, 2007 S.L.T. 846.

be regarded as demonstrating a trend or a general preference for one
form of procedure as against another. Personal views as to the appropriate forum for particular cases still conflict in practice. No general rule
can or should be advanced. If a particular procedure is adopted by a
party and, on final decision of the case, it appears that the action should
reasonably have been pursued in a court or under a procedure which
would have been more appropriate and cheaper, then the court can take
this into account when making an award of expenses.[70]

SELECTING A COURT

2–28 Assuming that it is competent to do so, then a pursuer and a defender[71]
(advised by their respective solicitors) have to decide which court suits
them best. It might assist the reader to understand some of the basics of
civil procedure and practice if we outline some practical considerations
which might be weighed in the balance when a decision is taken. These
observations are not exhaustive, they are not authoritative, and they are
not intended as stating any universal truths.[72]

(1) Practical convenience

2–29 There are a number of elements to this: convenience to the client; convenience to witnesses; and convenience to the solicitor.[73] One would
normally choose a court which was close at hand. On purely practical
grounds, litigating in one's local court, if it has jurisdiction, is highly
desirable. For people in Edinburgh, the Court of Session may be just as
"local" as the sheriff court. One might have a case which is going to feature a vital witness whom one wants to accommodate and encourage, by
making it easy to attend court to give evidence.

(2) Cost

2–30 Generally speaking, the higher up one goes, the more the case costs.
Small claims are the cheapest, followed by summary causes, sheriff
court ordinary actions, and actions in the Court of Session. The ability
to recover a party's expenses from the unsuccessful opponent may be a
factor.[74] The client may be reluctant to pursue a remedy in the higher
court if it will cost him more to do so and there is no obvious reason to
think he will achieve a more satisfactory result.

---

[70] See Lord President Hope in *McIntosh*, 1990 S.L.T. 637 at p.641B–D. Also see *Hunt v
British Bakeries*, 2004 G.W.D. 35-718.
[71] Although, in practice, the pursuer's position usually gives him more influence—he will
decide in the first place where he wants to litigate.
[72] Everyone has his own opinion on these issues.
[73] We will leave aside *forum non conveniens* considerations. See Ch.4.
[74] See Ch.21 on "Expenses".

(3) Speed

Small claims should be the quickest, followed by summary causes.[75]   **2–31**
A sheriff court ordinary action will generally finish quicker than a Court
of Session ordinary action. Procedures in the Court of Session which
are specifically designed with speed in mind, e.g. their procedure for
actions of damages for personal injury, can be worth using in particular
cases.

(4) Available competent procedures

If commercial action procedure is available in a particular case then it   **2–32**
might be a factor in the decision. If there is genuine doubt as to whether
a case can be brought under a specific procedure or not, then this might
be a reason for not using it. If the court had to decline jurisdiction at
some stage this might hold up the progress of the action—or indeed
mean that you have to start again.

(5) Finality

The lower down you start, the more appeal stages there are.[76]   **2–33**

(6) Standard of judgment

This is a matter of opinion and controversy. It is argued that one   **2–34**
receives a higher standard of judgment from a judge in the Court of
Session. Perhaps it would be fairer to say that there is a better chance of
receiving an authoritative analysis and assessment of a case involving
legal issues from a judge in the Court of Session. On the other hand it is
arguable that certain cases might be considered more effectively and
fairly in the sheriff court.[77]

(7) Importance, difficulty and complexity of case

All clients will think their case is important. Cases can be difficult and   **2–35**
complex for a variety of reasons relating to the law, the facts, the gath-
ering of evidence, the nature and expectations of the client, etc. As a
general proposition, a litigation solicitor might prefer to take such cases
in the Court of Session because, apart from anything else, he will have
the benefit of advice and representation from an advocate. Again that is
a matter of preference, and probably more dependent upon practical
experience than any general principles or accepted wisdom.

---

[75] Although that is not always the case for many reasons which are difficult to explain.

[76] Although there are only limited rights of appeal from small claims and restricted rights
of appeal from summary causes.

[77] Diplomacy and self preservation prevents any further comment but it is an interesting
debate.

(8) Novelty or legal uncertainty

2–36   It might appear that the courts have never before considered a particular matter of law which is central to the dispute in hand. Alternatively, the law may be unclear. A solicitor might want to take this in the Court of Session, but the authoritative status of a judgment from an Outer House judge at first instance is, strictly speaking, no higher than that of a sheriff. If a party did require an authoritative judgment on the point then the significant authority would come from a decision of the Inner House (or beyond) on appeal and, since both a sheriff and a Lord Ordinary can be appealed straight to the Inner House, it may make no real difference where you start.

(9) Value of case

2–37   Leaving aside low value claims,[78] the Court of Session and the sheriff court can equally competently deal with claims for substantial sums of money, although it is correct to say, as a generalisation, that claims for very large sums will normally be commenced in the Court of Session. In these circumstances, the client will often consider that the cost of adopting a more expensive procedure would be justified by the sum involved.

(10) Legal aid and funding

2–38   This is an insidious factor in the equation. If a party requires legal aid to raise proceedings, then he and his solicitor must persuade the Scottish Legal Aid Board that it would be appropriate for legal aid to be provided for the particular type of proceedings envisaged, and in the particular court requested. That does not always happen and if a party is only granted a legal aid certificate for particular proceedings this will effectively make his decision for him.

(11) Personal preference

2–39   Some people automatically raise actions in the Court of Session and some would rarely dream of doing so. There is an argument that there is less control over proceedings in the Court of Session by solicitors and that may or may not be regarded as desirable. On the other hand, there may be cases with a difficult client where a lack of direct and personal relationship between the advisor (counsel as opposed to solicitor) and the client would be helpful. Some clients also have certain preferences, prejudices and expectations and these may have to be taken into account when deciding where and how to proceed.

(12) Representation

2–40   A party can have a solicitor, a solicitor advocate or an advocate[79] represent him in any proceedings in the sheriff court. In the Court of

---

[78] Under £5,000 there is no choice.
[79] Junior or senior counsel, or both.

Session, only solicitor advocates or advocates can present cases. A solicitor outwith Edinburgh normally will, although he is not obliged to, use Edinburgh solicitors as his agents in a Court of Session action. With the necessary addition of counsel to conduct the case this can increase the costs to clients. The norm is for solicitors to appear in civil cases in the sheriff court, and for advocates to appear in civil cases in the Court of Session. The client might prefer to have his solicitor represent him in court personally or indeed he might prefer to have an advocate represent him. The cost of representation can play a part in this decision.

CIVIL JUDICIAL BUSINESS IN SCOTLAND

Contrary to popular perception, we are not particularly litigious in Scotland, nor are the civil courts inundated with substantially increasing volumes of cases. We may have one of the busiest criminal court systems but we only have a modest amount of civil business. If one left out of account actions for payment of debt in the sheriff court which are often actions raised by finance companies and the like on standard forms of writ, and which are rarely defended, we have relatively few contested litigations. **2–41**

There are limited official statistics. The latest available statistics are for the year to December 31, 2002, and doubt has been cast upon the validity of statistical information about the civil justice system in the public domain. In these circumstances, the figures noted here cannot be treated as representative of the present position.[80] The introduction of the special personal injury procedure in the Court of Session and the changes in the sheriff court jurisdiction limits in January 2008 may well have altered the spread of cases quite dramatically, but unfortunately one can only speculate about the impact these changes are having. Subject to these qualifications the principal statistics for the year to December 31, 2002 are as follows:

2–42

	Total Number of Court Actions Raised in Scotland							Total
	Court of Session			Sheriff Court				
	Inner House	Outer House	Total	Ordinary Cause	Summary Cause	Small Claims	Total	
2002	204	4,855	*5,059*	46,605	36,465	32,256	*115,326*	**120,385**
1998	228	4,173	*4,401*	48,423	35,094	52,527	*136,044*	**140,445**
1993	364	5,818	*6,182*	55,333	38,346	72,714	*166,393*	**172,575**

---

[80] See the foreword to Annex D, "Business of the Civil Courts" in *Scottish Civil Courts Review, The Scottish Civil Courts Review*—a consultation paper.

Type of actions raised

Court of Session

2–43

	Actions raised in the Outer House								TOTAL
	Actions raised in the General Department			Actions raised in the Petition Department					
	Per-sonal Injury	Other	Gen-eral Dept. Total	Sequestra-tion	Judicial Review		Other	Peti-tion Dept Total	
					Immigration	Other			
2002	2,419	1,144	*3,563*	561	68	92	571	*1,292*	**4,855**
1998	1,919	1,189	*3,108*	361	75	62	567	*1,065*	**4,173**
1993			*4,629*			158		*1,189*	**5,818**

Sheriff court

2–44   Of the 46,605 actions commenced in the sheriff court in 2002, 21,754 were for "debt", 6,422 were for divorce, 4,876 were for obligations due under mortgages, and 2,969 were for personal injury. In addition, there were 36,937 miscellaneous and administrative applications disposed of in the sheriff courts in 2002. Of these, there were a variety of types, e.g. adoptions, bankruptcy, child support, civil imprisonment, judicial factors and liquidations. Interestingly enough, this category of "case" appears to have increased substantially in numbers from the preceding years but it seems that this might largely be related to the fact that simplified divorce applications are now characterised as "administrative applications". There were 5,384 in 2002—more than the total number of actions of all types initiated in the Court of Session.

In 2002, there were 399 appeals from sheriff court ordinary, summary and small claim actions to the sheriff principals. There were 80 appeals direct from ordinary actions in the sheriff courts to the Court of Session.

CHAPTER 3

WRITTEN PLEADINGS

In most contested cases in Scotland there is a requirement for the parties to **3–01** set out in writing the details of their claim/defence in advance of any hearing of evidence about the case. These details are called their written pleadings. The system of written pleadings in Scotland is the process whereby, in the course of litigation, the parties will give each other and the court advance notice of the claim or defence. After the initial document detailing the claim is answered by a document containing the defence, the parties will adjust the written formulation of their respective cases in the light of their opponent's written response. The purpose is to focus for the court and for each other on what matters are agreed, what matters are disputed, and what matters might have to be proved in any hearing of evidence.

In simple terms, the pursuer might say in a writ: "I supplied you with goods to the value of £5,000 and you have not paid me for them."

The defender might respond in his defences by saying: "I only received £3,000 worth of goods and I did actually pay for them."

That response might prompt the pursuer to make some further enquiry and some alteration in his written case. That alteration might, in turn, prompt the defender to make some further alteration in his written case, and so on. At the end of that process of adjustment, the court and the parties should know exactly what is going to be argued at any proof in the action. Expressing the process in this way is perhaps a statement of the obvious, and yet it is remarkable how many procedural difficulties arise from the simple process of expressing the dispute between the parties clearly in writing.

In Scotland, we can be said to have a highly developed system of writ- **3–02** ten pleadings.[1] For some time there has been considerable emphasis on written pleadings and the court procedures which are required to enable the court to hear argument about what the written pleadings mean. Parties often appear to be more concerned with purely technical arguments about the written expression of a case or defence rather than about the merits of the case. This was particularly so in the field of reparation, where many personal injury cases were dismissed by the court for reasons which may have amounted to little more than that they were poorly

---

[1] This used to be a compliment but not so now. See *Gibson v British Insulated Callenders' Construction Co Ltd*, 1973 S.C. (H.L.) 15.

expressed in writing. Latterly, however, there has been a growing disen-
chantment with the utility of detailed written pleadings.[2] The new form
of procedure introduced in commercial actions in the Court of Session[3]
has reduced the significance of "technical" legal pleadings. The new
personal injuries actions procedure has taken the dramatic step of only
allowing abbreviated pleadings which are extremely brief. Summary
causes require no more than a brief outline of the claim, provided it
gives "fair notice" to the opponent. The view is that a party should normally be entitled to his day in court and should not be prevented from
having it because his legal advisers simply could not express his case
properly. It would be unfair, however, to say that the system only causes
problems. If the underlying principles are properly understood, observed
and applied then it can be of considerable assistance to the parties and to
the courts in understanding the precise nature and extent of the dispute
and adjudicating upon it.

It may be difficult for any reader coming to this topic afresh to understand why there should be problems arising from the written expression
of a party's case. It is outwith the scope of this book to provide a comprehensive guide as to how to plead particular cases or respond to words
and expressions used by an opponent.[4] The traditional "rules" of pleading[5] are often regarded as being a mysterious set of directions whose
sole purpose is to trap the unsuspecting litigant and which can, in
extreme cases, produce injustice.[6] It is important, however, not to allow
the intricate and detailed rules or practices of pleading to obscure the
fundamentals.[7] There are excellent books containing styles of written
pleading,[8] which can be of considerable assistance in enabling practitioners to crack the code.

In this chapter we are simply going to look at the function of pleadings generally. We will then discuss the factors which should influence
parties in drawing up their own pleadings, look at the practicalities of the
process of adjusting pleadings, and consider the court rules which dictate what must be pled in some cases.[9] Finally, we will consider some of
the better known pleadings issues which arise frequently. This will all be

---

[2] See Lord Coulsfield's *Report on Court of Session Procedure* on the Scottish Courts'
website at *http://www.scotcourts.gov.uk* [Accessed August 17, 2008].

[3] See Ch.7.

[4] See Hennessy, *Practical Advocacy in the Sheriff Court* (Edinburgh: W. Green, 2006),
Ch.3 for more detailed guidance.

[5] These are really practices of pleading which have developed and been sanctioned by the
courts in former days.

[6] See Lord Coulsfield's *Report on Court of Session Procedure*; also Thornburg, "The
Tyranny of Fact Pleadings", 2003 48(1) J.L.S.S. 19.

[7] For a far more specific introduction to the details, the reader can refer to two excellent
books, Macphail, *Sheriff Court Practice*, 3rd edn, pp.263–308 and *Greens Annotated
Rules of the Court of Session* (Edinburgh: W. Green, 2008), pp.C87–C95.

[8] See *Greens Litigation Styles* (Edinburgh: W. Green).

[9] There are remarkably few of them.

looked at in a practical context in order to assist a proper understanding of how the system works.

FUNCTION OF WRITTEN PLEADINGS

We are going to look at written pleadings in the context of Court of **3–03** Session and sheriff court ordinary actions only. An excellent exposition of the function of written pleadings can be found in the case of *ERDC Construction Ltd v H.M. Love & Co (No.2)*.[10] This was an appeal from an arbitration in which parties had expressed their positions in writing. Lord Prosser said[11]:

"Whatever machinery is used for the resolution of a dispute, there is likely to be some place for both written and oral material. A requirement that each party should formulate its position in writing at the outset has fundamental advantages not only as a means of giving fair notice to the other side and helping to focus and cut down the issues in dispute but also, and fundamentally, as an encouragement to each party to analyse the substance of the case, before trying to give it expression in writing. In my opinion, if a high quality of written formulation can be achieved at the outset, much expensive and time consuming oral procedure can often be avoided . . . Pleadings of the type currently used in ordinary Court procedure are frequently, and indeed normally, ill-suited to their true function. Failing to put essentials in sharp focus, and often putting in sharp focus inessential matters of detail which then become the subject of pointless procedural scrutiny . . . Arbiters will usually do better if they required in writing the kind of notice of issues which they in their own good sense feel they need, and which indeed any competent practitioner could set out in a relatively brief letter. If that were the practice in arbitrations, it may well be that the Court could learn from it."

To assist in these functions, pleadings should be expressed in plain language as far as possible. They should be brief, based on a common sense approach to the issues which are seen to arise, give fair notice of the issues, focus on the issues which are in dispute, and be confined to expressing simple matters of fact and basic legal propositions to justify the action or the defence. A reading of the pleadings in a record should enable anyone to understand the crux of the dispute between the parties and the kind of evidence which will probably have to be led to resolve these issues.

---

[10] *ERDC Construction Ltd v H.M. Love & Co (No.2)*, 1997 S.L.T. 175.
[11] *ERDC Construction Ltd*, 1997 S.L.T. 175 at p.180F–K.

FUNDAMENTALS

(1) Honesty or candour

3–04   One should only put in one's written pleadings those facts about which one has evidence, or which could be reasonably inferred from other facts about which one has evidence. For example, to say that work-man X had dropped a piece of timber from a scaffolding and caused an accident one might need: (a) direct evidence from a witness who saw him do it; (b) evidence of an admission by the workman to someone else that he did do it; or (c) any evidence which made it reasonable to infer that he was the only person who could have done it. Making allegations which are entirely speculative in the hope that evidence will turn up by the time of the proof is quite wrong.

By the same token, a defender pleading his defences to a claim should state his position honestly and clearly. The failure of defenders to do so[12] is often cited as one of the most obvious deficiencies of our system. Of course, it is not the system which is wrong; it is the way that some practitioners operate it that causes a problem. A defender can always put a pursuer to proof of his allegations, but where the defender knows that some or all of the pursuer's averments are true, he should admit them.[13]

(2) Clarity

3–05   It may seem obvious, but the pleadings ought to be clear. This will normally be achieved if the essential facts only are pled and if they are done in short, simple sentences. Difficulties can arise in practice in pleading a case clearly where the pleader does not have a clear statement or statements as his source material from which to draft a writ or defences. Other difficulties can arise in identifying what are the essential facts. This is a matter for the pleader who should try to analyse what facts are important and what facts he needs to prove in order to succeed with his case. Throwing in a jumble of facts from which the court or the opponent might be able to extract something sensible does not help any-one—including the pleader.

(3) The basic facts only

3–06   One difficulty which can arise is where a pleader allows his pleadings to become overcomplicated by "pleading evidence". What this means is that it is unnecessary and undesirable to put in one's written case the details of the evidence which support the basic essential facts. It can be difficult to decide where to draw the line, however. For example, in a case where a pursuer is suing for payment for goods delivered to a

---

[12] For fear of conceding there is no defence.
[13] For more on this point, see "Skeletal Defences", para.3–24, below.

defender it might simply be sufficient to say that goods were delivered to the defenders on a specific date. It might be quite unnecessary and "pleading evidence" to say that they were delivered, "... by the pursuer's employee, Mr S, who was driving a Mercedes Sprinter van registration no.XXX, and dropped them off at 6pm". Mr S might tell us this when he was giving evidence, but it may be that the only essential fact is that the goods were delivered, and not the person who made the delivery, nor the make of vehicle in which they were delivered, nor the time of delivery. If the defence was that they were not delivered, then it might be more appropriate to aver such details. What can be regarded as the "basic facts" is often a matter of opinion, and one of the dangers is that a party will plead an extensive description of events in case his pleadings might be criticised for lack of specification. Too much specification will never lead to an action being dismissed, but can often lead to the crux of the case being lost in a maelstrom of words.

(4) Fair notice

It is for each party to give fair notice of his case to the opponent. What **3–07** is "fair notice"? There is no simple answer to this question. It is suggested that fair notice means giving the opponent sufficient detail of the essential features of one's case[14] to enable the opponent (and the court) to understand what the case is, to investigate the allegations made and to give him an opportunity to contradict it with his own allegations, if appropriate. A complaint that an opponent's case did not give fair notice would be a complaint about lack of specification.[15] The fundamental argument would be that one party was likely to be prejudiced in his investigation of the case and in his preparations for the proof without factual information which is or ought to be within the knowledge of the other party.[16] In the example given above, it could in theory be argued by a defender that the pursuer failed to give fair notice of his claim by a failure to supply details of the driver of the vehicle and of the kind of vehicle which did the delivery. For such an argument to succeed, it would be necessary to demonstrate that there was some meaningful way in which the defence to the case would be affected in a practical sense by the lack of that information.

(5) Stating the basic legal justification for the case

This does not mean that a party should include in his pleadings an **3–08** argument or discussion about the legal propositions which underlie his case. In simple terms, it may be sufficient for him to say, e.g. that "It was an implied term of the contract between the pursuer and defender that

---

[14] Both on the facts and the law applicable to it.
[15] See Ch.4 on "Preliminary Pleas".
[16] Especially where it can be seen to be outwith the knowledge of the defender.

[. . .]. The defender was in breach of that contract because [. . .]."
Alternatively, "that the accident was caused by the negligence of the
defender . . . the defender had a duty to take reasonable care not to
emerge from a minor road on to a major road without giving way".

Problems can often arise with the expression of the legal justification
for a claim. There are "styles" of setting out the legal basis for a claim
which are sometimes copied without consideration of whether they necessarily apply to the circumstances of the particular case. Considerable
difficulties can arise where there may be complex legal issues involved.
If this is taken in conjunction with different allegations of what actually
happened between the parties then there could be a number of alternative
legal propositions which would justify a claim. It can then become
extremely difficult to formulate the claim coherently. There are often
complaints from one or other side that the factual pleadings of his opponent are not sufficient to justify the legal remedy which is being sought.[17]
These would be complaints to the relevancy of the written pleadings.

 PRACTICAL ILLUSTRATION OF THE FUNDAMENTALS

3–09 It might be helpful if we were now to go back and consider these general principles applied in the practical context of the claim against Mr
X's firm by the suppliers of timber mentioned in the preface. One would
normally expect the written pleadings in the writ to allege that certain
specific goods had been supplied if, and only if, the pursuer's solicitor
had prima facie evidence that this was so. One would expect the writ to
be set out briefly and clearly and to allege roughly that, e.g:

> "On (a certain date) the defenders ordered (certain specific) sup-
> plies from the pursuer. That (on a certain date), the pursuers deliv-
> ered (certain specific) goods to the defenders' premises and that the
> goods were (to the value of £X), etc. and that the defender has
> refused or delayed to pay for them".

For the purposes of the initial writ, those might well be the basic facts.
They would be expressed in numbered paragraphs with a little more
detail than that outlined above. There would be little need to say a great
deal about the basic legal proposition underlying that kind of claim. It
would simply be that the pursuers had supplied goods to the defenders
on their order and the defenders were, therefore, legally bound to pay for
them. It would be unlikely that the writ in a case of this type could be
criticised for lacking detail or for stating a legal proposition (the entitlement to payment) which was not supported by the facts alleged.

---

[17] Or the defence which is being advanced.

When we go on to consider possible defences to that claim we see the way in which the "system of pleadings" comes into operation. The defender ought to respond to the specific allegations in the writ fact by fact or sentence by sentence. The classic and correct approach is that he ought to:

(1) admit the matters which he knows to be true ("It is admitted that x, y, and z . . .");
(2) if there are matters which he does not know whether they are true or not, he would say so ("It is not known and not admitted that a, b, and c . . .");
(3) if there are matters he disputes or denies, then he would say so ("It is denied that . . ."). Often this is expressed as "*Quoad ultra* denied"—in other words, as for anything else alleged in the averments, apart from that which has already been admitted or is not known, that is denied;
(4) if he has an explanation or wishes to add something to the facts which are set out in the pursuer's allegations in the writ then he should say so ("It is explained that . . .").

He must respond honestly to the writ. He cannot take up the position that he is simply saying nothing about the claim. If he knows that the goods, or some of them, were delivered then he must admit that and he ought to respond succinctly to what the pursuer alleges. If he wants to add anything to the subject matter of the dispute then he ought to say so in his defences by putting in the essential features of the defence in sufficient detail for the pursuer to understand exactly what the defence is. Accordingly, the defender might admit that certain specific goods were indeed delivered. He might want to say that certain specific goods were not delivered. He might want to say that, of the timber which was delivered, it was not of the quality which was ordered and explain the discrepancy. He might want to say exactly what was wrong with the other (defective) timber and how much of it was affected.[18] The defender should then explain the legal propositions upon which the defence is founded. For example, he might say that, since certain goods were not supplied (according to the defender) then the pursuer obviously is not entitled to payment for these. In relation to the goods which were supplied, but which were defective, then he might argue in his written case that the pursuer was in breach of contract and is not entitled to payment in respect of these goods.

When defences like this are intimated to the pursuer then the pursuer **3–10** has an opportunity to respond to the defences. He may simply say there is no substance to anything said in the defences. He may say there is some truth in part of the defences but not in others. He may say, e.g. that

---

[18] For example: "Of the 40 wooden battens delivered to the defender, 24 of these were rotted by exposure to water and could not be used."

one or two of the battens were wet because they had been left out overnight prior to delivery but that this was superficial and they would have dried out. He might dispute that there was a breach of contract. The pursuer would do "adjustments" to his writ to enable him to respond to what the defender was saying and to start the process of narrowing down what the issues really were. These adjustments would be intimated to the defender and the defender in turn would have an opportunity to consider how to respond to them if he wanted to respond at all. It can be seen that, by this process, the parties should be able to narrow down exactly what facts are in dispute and define what legal issues arise between them. The pleadings taken as a whole might indicate that, if it can be proved that 24 wooden battens could not be used, there could be no dispute between the parties that the pursuer was in breach of contract to that extent. The dispute could simply be that, as a matter of fact, this was not true. If the battens were defective, the defender would win. If they were not defective, the pursuer would win.[19]

In the ordinary court procedures which we will consider, the parties would adjust their respective pleadings during a set period allowed by the court and then prepare a document called a record in which the allegations and counter-allegations[20] by the parties will be set out together. The intention is that the record will be one document which contains all of the essential facts setting out the final position of the parties on the facts and containing all of the conflicting legal propositions which both parties would wish to argue.

This simple model for the preparation of written pleadings shows how the system of written pleadings should enable disputes to be focused. As we have already indicated, the model often does not work and can give rise to difficulties which will complicate even the simplest of litigations and cause delay and expense. There is a skill involved in pleading a case clearly and precisely on both facts and law. That skill should not be underestimated. It has to be learned. It is not as easy as might have been suggested but if the basic principles outlined above are borne in mind that is a useful starting point. This chapter will not deal with the precise formulae for drafting good written pleadings. It is arguable whether this can be reduced to a formula and, even if some formulae do exist, it would be a mammoth task to try and explain the way in which they might be used.

We shall now go on to consider the rules of court which have some application to written pleadings in all the forms of procedure which we shall be discussing in later chapters. Generally speaking, the rules of court only provide a basic outline of the form which written pleadings should take and basic rules which apply to the written pleadings in the different types of procedure.

---

[19] We are leaving aside any questions about onus, etc. meantime.
[20] Otherwise, "averments and answers".

There are different rules regarding the format of written pleadings **3–11** under the different procedures which you will be considering later in the book. The rules relate largely to matters of form. They do not touch upon the content of the detailed pleadings in a case to any significant degree.[21]

Court of Session

Ordinary action

Rule 4.1—This prescribes the form, size and general appearance of a **3–12** court summons. The same provisions apply to any other written pleadings in a court action.

Rule 13.2—This contains provisions regarding the form of a summons. It is to be in Form 13.2-A. Generally speaking, the form prescribes which words must appear on the first page of the summons and what must appear on the backing of the summons. The opening words of the summons are largely matters of form and will be followed by the conclusion of the summons.

Rule 13.2(2)—This provides that the conclusion in the summons shall be stated in accordance with the appropriate style contained in Form 13.2-B. It is very helpful to look at the principal forms of conclusion provided. They can be used on their own or in combination and if there is no precise form of conclusion which is appropriate to the action in question then other conclusions may be drafted.

It is then provided that, after the conclusion, there shall be annexed to the summons a statement in the form of numbered articles of the condescendence[22] containing the averments of fact which form the grounds of the claim and appropriate pleas in law. It may be difficult to visualise the summons based simply on the description in the rules, but if one sees a Court of Session summons then it is relatively easy to identify the main features, as outlined above.

In the condescendence there will be averments[23] which will deal with **3–13** the domicile of the defender, the grounds of jurisdiction of the court, and other formal provisions regarding jurisdiction.[24]

---

[21] With the exception of personal injuries actions.

[22] Which really just means the statement of facts.

[23] Statements in written pleadings.

[24] This is to ensure compliance with the Civil Jurisdiction and Judgments Act 1982 but specialities of jurisdiction are outwith the scope of this book. No direction is given as to the contents of the condescendence or of the pleas in law, which will of course be entirely dependent upon the circumstances of each individual case.

Rule 18.1—This provides that defences to an action shall consist of numbered answers corresponding to the articles of the condescendence and appropriate pleas in law. An outline of the standard approach to drafting answers has already been suggested[25] but this is simply based on practice and the detailed content of defences is not circumscribed by any other rules.[26]

Rule 22.2—This provides that there will be an adjustment period of approximately eight weeks. The period can be extended in certain circumstances.[27] During the adjustment period the parties will intimate adjustments of their written pleadings to each other. At the end of the adjustment period the record will close. A closed record consisting of the pleadings of the parties and the interlocutors pronounced in the case shall be lodged. Further procedures will take place as will be noted in later chapters. It should also be noted that after the record is closed, further alteration of the written pleadings can take place but this will have to be done by way of amendment and not adjustment.[28]

Petition procedure

3–14   In actions raised by petition in the Court of Session[29] a petition must be in Form 14.4 of the RCS. This contains a simple format and reference should be made to the rules. By r.14.4(2) a petition shall include a statement of fact in numbered paragraphs setting out the facts and circumstances on which the petition is founded and a prayer setting out the orders sought. The appearance and outline content of a petition is therefore materially different from that of a summons although the general principles about expression of the substance of the written pleadings would still apply.

Rule 14.4(3)—This provides that if there is a petition presented under a statute then the statement of facts[30] shall expressly refer to the relevant statutory provision.

There are similar provisions to those in relation to summonses regarding averments about jurisdiction and reference should be made to the rules themselves.

---

[25] See para.3–09, above.
[26] There is no RCS rule equivalent to OCR r.9.7 discussed in para.3–18, below, perhaps because it is considered unnecessary to point this out to Court of Session practitioners.
[27] For more detailed provisions see Ch.5.
[28] There are certain special rules about amendment but, in simple terms, an amendment is simply an adjustment made after the record is closed. Parties can adjust as they like during the adjustment period. Parties can only amend after the record is closed with the leave of the court.
[29] See paras 13–09 to 13–12, above.
[30] Not called a condescendence in a petition.

Rule 14.4(5)—This provides that the prayer of the petition will contain certain particulars. Again, it is difficult to visualise the form of a
petition on the basis of the content of the rules but it is relatively easy
to identify the various basic requirements for a petition if one sees a
petition itself.

Rule 18.3—This makes provision for the form of answers to a petition.
It provides that the answers will consist of numbered answers corresponding to the paragraphs of the statement of fact in the petition to which it
applies together with appropriate pleas in law.

Personal injuries actions

There are special provisions regarding the form of summons and the **3–15**
pleadings.[31]

Rules 43.2(1)(a) and (b)—These provide for a form of summons containing abbreviated pleadings which are in stark contrast to the form and
content of "normal" pleadings, and the only special matter requiring
specific averment is the detail of any doctor or hospital who treated the
pursuer.

Commercial action

The form of summons is prescribed in rule 47.3.[32] In general terms, the **3–16**
written pleadings in a commercial action are intended to be "abbreviated"
to some extent[33] and reference should be made to Ch.7,[34] where the form
of summons and defences are discussed.

Judicial review

The form of petition in a judicial review is set out in r.58.6.[35] It should **3–17**
be noted that in any petition for judicial review there is a requirement for
the petitioner to state briefly in his pleadings the legal argument upon
which the petition is based. That is a unique exception to the rule that no
written pleadings should contain discussion, argument or review of the
legal issues upon which a case is founded. The norm is for the pleadings
simply to state the legal proposition which supports the case. Argument
about this and whether it does indeed support the case is usually confined to oral argument alone at debate or after proof before answer.

---

[31] See Ch.6.
[32] See Ch.7.
[33] Although not in the same way as personal injuries actions. The judge is more likely to
discuss and agree the form and content of the pleadings depending upon the specific
nature of the action.
[34] See paras 7–09 to 7–12, below.
[35] This is discussed in detail in Ch.8.

Sheriff court

Ordinary action

3–18   Rule 3.1—This states that an ordinary cause must be commenced by an initial writ in Form G1. Form G1 simply contains a very basic outline of what is required. The basic requirements are that on the first page one should state the sheriffdom and sheriff court in which the writ is being presented. The parties to the actions are stated. After that, one states the crave which is the request to the court for whatever order is sought. Thereafter, one will have the condescendence and the form requires the party to state in numbered paragraphs the facts which form the ground of action. Subsequently, there are the pleas in law which are to be stated in numbered sentences. Again it is difficult to visualise this in the abstract but it is easy to identify the different elements when one considers any example of a sheriff court writ.

Rules 3.1(3) to (6)—These contain provisions regarding the type and appearance of the document which is to comprise an initial writ. A writ must contain certain averments regarding jurisdiction.

Rule 9.6—This provides that defences shall be in the form of answers in numbered paragraphs corresponding to the articles of the condescendence and shall have appended a note of the pleas in law for the defender.

Rule 9.7—This provides that every statement of fact made by a party shall be answered by every other party.[36] It is also provided that if a statement of fact by one party which is within the knowledge of the other party is not denied by him then the other party shall be deemed to have admitted it. That is a rule which is taken for granted in the RCS and it is a statement of what would be regarded as a matter of fundamental principle in written pleadings.

In sheriff court ordinary proceedings, there is an adjustment period of approximately 10 weeks. The parties will adjust by sending each other[37] copies of the adjustments during the adjustment period. After the expiry of the adjustment period a record is made up for the options hearing.[38] There is provision for further adjustment for a limited period after the options hearing. Adjustment of the pleadings in the sheriff court after the record has been closed[39] must be done by way of amendment. The same general observations apply to amendment in the sheriff court as apply in the Court of Session.

---

[36] This applies to both pursuer and defender.
[37] But not the court
[38] See Ch.9 for more precise details of the procedure.
[39] Which will either be after the options hearing or a continued options hearing or a procedural hearing.

Commercial cause

Rule 40.4—This provides for the form of writ for a commercial action, **3–19** Form G1A, which is not dissimilar to the form of writ for an ordinary action.[40]

Rule 40.7(1)—This provides that there should be restricted pleadings if the action only relates to the construction of a document.

Rule 40.7(2)—This states that any documents founded upon or incorporated in the pleadings in the writ should be listed.

Rule 40.9—This provides for the style of defences which shall be, "in the form of answers that allow the extent of the dispute to be identified . . . and shall have pleas in law." The defences do not need to answer each specific article of condescendence. [41]

Rule 40.12—At the case management conference, the sheriff can make a variety of orders in relation to the need for, form of, extent of, or allowance of adjustment of both parties' pleadings. Again, this will depend on the nature of the action and the nature and extent of the dispute.

Summary cause

In this form of procedure, there is far less emphasis on written plead- **3–20** ings.[42] In essence, the pursuer will draft a statement of claim in order to initiate the action. The form of statement of claim is not prescribed in the rules but r.4.2 of the Summary Cause Rules ("SCR") provides that the statement of claim shall give the defender fair notice of the claim and shall, in particular, include certain details such as the details of the basis of the claim including any relevant dates and details regarding jurisdiction. This can be set out in any way but, by and large, solicitors will normally prepare a statement of claim in a summary cause action in very much the same terms as an ordinary action. There will be no pleas in law however. The same general principles about pleading should apply.

The defender must lodge a form of response to the summons which gives fair notice to the pursuer of the defence.[43] There are no special rules about the form and format of defences but again the general principles of written pleading are taken to apply to any written pleadings which might exist in a summary cause action especially where solicitors are instructed on both sides.

---

[40] Reference should be made to the two forms for details.
[41] This is not the usual form of defence although, in practice, most defences are framed in the traditional manner. It does, however, allow for more abbreviated pleadings if the dispute can be better focused in this way.
[42] Reference should be made to Ch.11 for details.
[43] See SCR r.8.1.

There is no period for adjustment of pleadings in a summary cause although a party can alter the terms of the summons or of a defence if allowed to do so.[44]

Small claims

3–21   There is even less emphasis on written pleadings in this procedure. The form of summons to be used in a small claim is provided for in r.4.1 of the Small Claims Rules 2002. The form prescribed is Form 1 which is a pre-printed form.

Rule 4.2 provides for what should be contained within a statement of claim in a small claim summons. The defender must be given fair notice of the claim and the details required are very much the same as required in a summary cause.

There is no provision for the lodging of written defences. The defender is simply required to state a defence orally. The sheriff, on hearing the defence, will ascertain what the disputed issues are and he is obliged to make a note of the disputed issues on the summons.[45] In a sense, the sheriff, when conducting this hearing, performs the function of the system of written pleadings by attempting to focus the matters in dispute on the basis of what is usually a brief statement of claim and an oral defence.

Rule 12.1 provides that the sheriff can allow amendment of the summons or a note of defence, and can adjust the disputed issues if that becomes necessary.

Looking at the matter generally, therefore, it can be seen that the rules of procedure mean that each different form of procedure has slightly different guidelines for written pleadings. The written pleadings will all look slightly different. It may not be obvious[46] but there can be quite significant differences in language, style and approach between Court of Session pleadings and sheriff court pleadings. That again is a detail which we will not explore.

SOME PRACTICAL PLEADING ISSUES

3–22   We shall now try to illustrate some of the main features of written pleadings which have given rise to comment or misunderstanding and explain what they are. We shall also try to explain the practical context in which they would come into play. It is outwith the scope of this book to canvas all the minute details or specialities of written pleadings. Particular complexity can arise where there is more than one pursuer and more than one defender. The existence of counterclaims or third parties in a case can further complicate matters because the interaction between the

[44] See r.13.1.
[45] See r.13(5).
[46] Nor justifiable.

pleadings for the various parties can be extremely complex. No two cases are alike and no two sets of pleadings are alike.

Words and phrases of style

Concentrating on using common sense, simple words and concise state- **3–23** ments of fact and propositions of law is likely to be far more worthwhile than wrestling with the intricacies of legal sounding words and phrases, whose meaning might be obscure to the pleader. Over the years, practitioners in the courts have developed special words and phrases[47] with the intention of simplifying or shortening the expression of their case in their written pleadings. In many cases, these are very helpful. If one understands exactly what they mean and exactly how they can be used then they are a convenient shorthand method of formulating one's case. Unfortunately, if their meaning and application are not properly understood they can simply confuse. There is a gradual move away from the use of Latin words and maxims and the use of expressions of style but no substance. It is a trend that is likely to continue. It is quite possible that abbreviated and extremely basic pleadings will be the order of the day in future but the existing system will be with us for some time. Where the court has the power and the responsibility under the rules to decide upon what would be the appropriate further procedure for the resolution of a particular case and/or to encourage parties to reach agreement on non-contentious matters, it may be appreciated that good written pleadings which focus clearly the matters in dispute are extremely helpful, if not essential. If this is done properly and if the standard words and phrases are used sparingly and appropriately, it can provide an excellent model for an efficient means of identifying and resolving issues in advance of any hearing.

SKELETAL DEFENCES

Skeletal defences are defences which basically deny most, if not all, of **3–24** the averments in the pursuer's writ without giving any substantive explanation of the defender's position. The defences often consist of the word "denied" in answer to each article of condescendence. This is regarded as one of the main drawbacks of our system of written pleadings. In the worst cases under our system, it is not possible for the court or the other party to go behind a basic denial of this kind and ask the defender to say anything more. If he denies it, then the pursuer must prove it and can only do so after proof. A proof will not, under the normal procedures in the sheriff court, e.g. take place for six or more months after the defences are lodged. A defender therefore can delay the resolution of the case by simply lodging a general denial in his defence.[48]

---

[47] Usually in Latin!

[48] A pursuer could force the issue by making a motion for summary decree (see Ch.19) but, for some reason, this is not done frequently in practice.

Let us go back to Mr X's case in which he is being sued for the cost of timber supplies. We should remember that, depending upon the value of the supplies, he could be sued under a variety of different procedures. We shall assume that the value of the timber is £10,000 and that he is being sued in an ordinary action in the sheriff court. That is the more likely forum for such a claim than the Court of Session[49] and although the format of a summons and initial writ are quite different, the substance of the written pleadings would be largely the same.

If we assume that the company who supplied the timber has sued Mr X's firm for payment and the firm are defending the proceedings, one of the first things they will have to do is lodge defences. It is open to them to lodge defences which simply deny everything that is said in the writ.[50] Of course, it may be that the pursuers are mistaken about the party with whom they were contracting. For example, they may have contracted with a limited company of which Mr X is a director but not with the partnership which they have purported to sue. In that case, a simple and general denial that there was any contract between the parties, that there was any delivery to the defender and that there was any obligation on the defenders to pay would be perfectly appropriate. That is perhaps unusual but not impossible.

It would also be open to a defender to make certain formal admissions and then make a general denial. For example, it could be admitted by the defenders that they contracted with the pursuer for the pursuer to supply timber but everything else could be denied. Alternatively, it could be admitted that the parties contracted for the supply of timber and admitted that, "some timber was supplied" but everything else denied, including a denial that any payment was due.

In these various examples[51] it could be argued that the written defences lodged by the defenders are skeletal defences. They may well be regarded as not stating the defender's position fully and honestly. The written pleadings are generally assumed to have some evidential justification and it would not be possible to go behind these defences and find out if they were true before there had been a hearing of evidence in the case. The hearing of evidence in the case might not be fixed for several months or even a year after the defences had been lodged.

3–25   Leaving aside the professional propriety of doing such a thing, the courts are critical of this approach by defenders and will tend to look closely at such a defence to see if there is a genuine defence. This will be done by, amongst other things, looking at the pleadings as a whole, construing the pleadings very strictly against the interests of the defender, and finding against the defender if there is any basis on which it might be suggested that their response to the claim is inconsistent with their denial.

---

[49] Although such an action would be perfectly competent in the Court of Session.
[50] Whether it would be proper for a solicitor to do so may be another matter.
[51] Which are by no means exhaustive of the possibilities.

For example, if the defender's response to the detailed averments by the pursuer of the contract for the supply of timber and the delivery of the timber is literally "denied" then the court might be dubious about this but could probably do little about it. However, if the response was to admit that there was a contract for the supply of timber and to admit that some timber was supplied but then to contain a denial of everything else alleged by the pursuer the court might take the view that the defence could be construed as an admission of the debt and, in the absence of any averment of payment, that the defences could be disregarded.

This can only be stated as a very general proposition and it is important to be careful when reading any cases about skeletal defences to pay attention to exactly what was said, or not said, in the written pleadings. Illustrations of the principle can be found in the undernoted cases.[52] A particular case in which the issue was discussed and the Inner House commented upon the honesty of the defences was *Gray v Boyd*.[53] The three judges in the Inner House expressed different views as to whether the defender's written pleadings could be regarded as skeletal and irrelevant.[54] With some regret, the majority decided that they could not go behind the dubious denial which was made in that case.[55]

 INCORPORATING DOCUMENTS IN PLEADINGS

Difficulties can often arise where a party wishes to plead his case by using the contents of documents to express his case rather than by setting out the words of the appropriate document in full or in part in the pleadings themselves. It may not be immediately obvious why that should cause a problem. Indeed, in pleadings in commercial cause actions[56] reference to documents and incorporation of other material outwith the formal written pleadings themselves is perfectly permissible. It is not possible to appreciate this fully in an abstract sense, but it is a source of confusion as we will try to explain. **3–26**

In practical terms, let us assume that the suppliers of the timber made averments in their written pleadings that they supplied, "certain timber to the defenders" but did not specify exactly what or how much. They simply lodged an invoice for the goods as a production. The invoice showed that they supplied 60 fence posts, 120 stakes and 40 battens of a certain length each of which had a specific value. A method of pleading this might be:

---

[52] *Ellon Castle Estates Co Ltd v MacDonald*, 1975 S.L.T. (Notes) 66; *Grampian Hydraulics (Buckie) v Dauntless Marine Engineering & Supply Co Ltd*, 1992 S.L.T. (Sh. Ct) 45; and *EFT Finance Ltd v Hawkins*, 1994 S.L.T. 902.

[53] *Gray v Boyd*, 1996 S.L.T. 60.

[54] The case was followed, again with regret, in the case of *Castleton Homes Ltd v Eastern Motor Co Ltd*, 1998 S.L.T. (Sh. Ct) 51.

[55] The case was distinguished in *Urquhart v Sweeney*, 2005 S.L.T. 442.

[56] Which might be regarded as the most modern model provided for a system of pleadings.

"The pursuers supplied the defenders with certain timber goods all as specified in the invoice no.0001 dated January 12, 1999 which is produced in process and is referred to for its terms which are held to be incorporated and repeated *brevitatis causa*[57] herein."

3–27 What that means is that the pursuer has not troubled to extract the information from the invoice and put it into words as averments in his written pleadings but is simply taking a shortcut by making the words of the invoice part of the pleadings themselves. The use of this type of phrase is in effect a formula for incorporating documents into the pleadings and it may be perfectly legitimate and acceptable in many cases. Indeed, it may be the most concise and sensible means of pleading the details of what was supplied. If the invoice was six pages long and made reference to numerous individual items supplied in various quantities and at various different prices then there may well be something to be said for not wishing to put all of that information into the actual pleadings.

However, difficulty can arise where that formula of words is not used, because a document which is not properly incorporated by reference in the actual averments cannot be considered by the court when considering the relevancy of the averments. In other words, if the pleadings simply said that the pursuers supplied goods and made no reference to the invoice or some other means of specifying the goods, then the pursuer's written pleadings could be said to be lacking in proper detail.[58] The precise application of this rule is not entirely clear, however, and there is some disagreement about the importance of it.[59]

The desirable approach is that when a party is founding on a document as constituting a part of his case then the document ought to be produced.[60] Ideally, the important parts of the document must be accurately repeated and transposed to the pleadings either by repeating them at length in the pleadings or incorporating them in the pleadings using the formula suggested above.

BREVITATIS CAUSA

3–28 The phrase, *brevitatis causa*, used in the above formula should also be noted. In written pleadings, many things can be referred to *brevitatis*

---

[57] Translated this means, for the sake of brevity.
[58] Even though the invoice is a production in the case.
[59] See the cases of *McIlwraith v Lochmaddy Hotel Ltd*, 1995 S.C.L.R. 595; *Eadie Cairns v Programmed Maintenance Painting*, 1987 S.L.T. 777; *Steelmek Marine and General Engineers' Trust v Shetland Sea Farms Ltd*, 1999 S.L.T. (Sh. Ct) 30; and *Royal Bank of Scotland Plc v Holmes*, 1999 S.L.T. 563.
[60] See OCR r.21.1 and RCS rr.27.1 and 2 regarding the need to lodge as a production any document founded on or adopted as incorporated in pleadings.

causa, this simply means "for the sake of brevity". In other words, there is no point and no need to repeat a document at length in the actual pleadings themselves. There is now something to be said for using the words "for the sake of brevity" in place of "*brevitatis causa*" but traditionalists might question this and prefer the preservation of the Latin phrase in this and other examples. In the interests of clear and simple expression which is understandable to all concerned, including the clients, there is some force in the argument that if an English word or phrase can be found which is equivalent to the Latin phrase then it ought to be used.

BELIEVED AND AVERRED

It was said at the outset of this chapter that one can only plead facts of **3–29** which one has direct evidence or which can be assumed as a matter reasonable of inference. In some situations, it may be helpful to plead matters when the inference is perhaps not quite inevitable but a distinct possibility. This would be done by saying that, "It is believed and averred that . . .". The difficulty, however, is that if the fact which the party believes to be true (but is not in a position to prove) is an essential part of the case then the case would have to be regarded as irrelevant because the pursuer would not be in a position to prove that essential fact. This, of course, involves assessment of what the essential elements of any particular case might be.

If Mr X's defences included an averment, ". . . believed and averred that the pursuers' agreed to discount the price by 50 per cent", that would be irrelevant. He could either prove that they did agree, in which case he could make a positive averment, or he could not prove that they did agree, in which case he could really say nothing.

Again it is difficult to express this in black and white. Because hearsay evidence is admissible in civil cases, there may be more scope for arguing that an averment that a party believes something to be true based upon hearsay at second or third hand might not be subject to such criticism as it has been before.[61]

---

[61] See the cases of *McCrone v MacBeth Currie & Co*, 1968 S.L.T. (Notes) 24; *Leslie v Leslie (No.2)*, 1987 S.L.T. 232; *Brown v Redpath Brown*, 1963 S.L.T. 219; *Partnership of Ocean Quest v Finning Ltd*, 2000 S.L.T. (Sh. Ct) 157 and *Burnett v Menzies Dougal W.S.*, 2005 S.L.T. 929.

CHAPTER 4

PRELIMINARY PLEAS

4–01 One of the most basic types of dispute in a civil litigation is between two parties who disagree about crucial matters of fact, e.g. whether goods were received or not, whether a job was done properly or not, whether a driver came through a red light or not, etc. Relatively few actions involve disputes which are as simple as this. In many cases, there are disputes about questions of fact and/or questions of law. The parties might agree on the basic facts, but argue about whether there are good legal grounds for a claim on those facts. The parties might be in dispute about the facts of what happened, and also be in dispute about what the law is if one or other version of the facts is established.

In the previous chapter we looked at written pleadings as the expression of a party's case and the means of identifying and focusing what is in dispute in any case. An important part of the written pleadings in most actions[1] is the preliminary plea. This can be described as any plea in law by a party which argues that the case should not go to a hearing of evidence about the facts of the dispute. Such a plea raises an issue which a party wishes to have resolved by the court as a preliminary to any evidence being heard about the facts of the dispute.

For example, a pursuer might sue for a debt which was admittedly incurred 10 years ago. The defenders might say in their defences that the debt has prescribed. They would argue that the court does not need to hear evidence about the circumstances in which it was incurred because the pursuer is not, as a matter of law, entitled to recover such a debt. They would insert a preliminary plea in their written pleadings that the obligation had prescribed and argue that the merits of the claim itself did not need to be explored in evidence. Another example might be a person suing for damages after a car accident who sues the grandmother of the negligent driver because she bought him the car. The grandmother would argue that, even if that was true, and even if the accident was caused by the fault of her grandson, there could be no legal basis for holding her liable for the accident and the court should not need to hear any evidence about the circumstances of the accident or the value of the claim. Her solicitors would take a preliminary plea to the relevancy of the claim as directed against her.

---

[1] Other than summary cause and small claim in the sheriff court and personal injury actions in the Court of Session.

Preliminary pleas can be contrasted with pleas to the merits[2] which only come into play once the facts of the case have been established.[3] It is not unusual for a party to have both preliminary pleas and peremptory pleas in an action. Preliminary pleas can be taken by both pursuer and defender[4] but they are taken more frequently by defenders.[5] There are a variety of preliminary pleas which can be deployed in written pleadings by either party and it is important to know what these preliminary pleas are, because if the preliminary plea is justified and is upheld by the court at a diet of debate[6] or procedure roll hearing[7] then that usually disposes of the whole case. The way in which preliminary pleas are taken by parties and dealt with by the courts can often be a very significant factor in the procedural progress of an action.[8]

It should be noted, however, that parties cannot take a preliminary plea in a sheriff court summary cause action or in a sheriff court small claim action where, generally speaking, all questions of law or legal principle are deferred until after evidence has been led. In theory, therefore, a summary cause action which is plainly time barred, and has no prospect of succeeding because of this, could still competently go to a summary cause proof[9] with detailed evidence being led before the parties and the court can address the legal issues.[10]

A defender will insert a preliminary plea in his pleadings with his **4–02** defences, or with his adjustments, or can even do so in an amendment after the record is closed. A pursuer can insert a preliminary plea in his pleadings by adjustment after he has seen what the defences are, or by way of amendment after the record is closed. There is no limit to the number of preliminary pleas which a party can take against an opponent.

The most common form of preliminary plea is what is known as a general plea to the relevancy. This is to the effect that the opponent's pleadings are "irrelevant *et separatim* lacking in specification". This could be seen as covering a multitude of possible defects in the opponent's

---

[2] Which can be termed "peremptory pleas".

[3] e.g. "The pursuer's averments, insofar as material, being unfounded in fact, the defender should be assoilzied", which means that the argument at the conclusion of the case will be along the lines that the pursuer has not proved it.

[4] And by a third party

[5] An example of a situation in which a pursuer might take a preliminary plea would be where a defender's explanation in his defences does not disclose any real defence. The pursuer would insert a preliminary plea in his pleadings to the effect that the defences were irrelevant and would not justify any hearing of evidence to decide the dispute— because there is no apparent valid dispute.

[6] Sheriff court action.

[7] Court of Session action.

[8] In the sheriff court and in the Court of Session. For a sheriff court action in which there was a detailed discussion of the nature of a preliminary plea see *Humphrey v Royal and Sun Alliance Plc*, 2005 S.L.T. (Sh. Ct) 31.

[9] Although the SCR 2002 make this less likely now. See Ch.11.

[10] Professionally, a solicitor who was well aware of the defect should not be raising or running such a case.

pleadings. It does not explain what exactly is wrong with those pleadings, but it can be regarded as including more specific legal arguments. In such a case, it is arguable that a plea that the pursuer's case is "irrelevant" could be regarded as including, e.g. the proposition that he had no title to sue. However, although not essential, it is desirable that the justification for any general plea to the relevancy should be given in more detail.[11]

If one or other party takes a preliminary plea against his opponent's pleadings in any case, then this usually, but not always, signifies that the party will want to have a legal debate[12] as an appropriate step in procedure for the resolution of the case. The general plea to the relevancy for a defender would normally be: "The pursuer's averments being irrelevant *et separatim* lacking in specification, the action should be dismissed."

This would mean that the defender would hope to demonstrate at a debate that the pursuer's written pleadings do not disclose sufficient facts to demonstrate that the pursuer has a stateable case and is entitled to the remedy which he seeks. The argument would be that the action should be dismissed without even allowing the pursuer to prove to the court the facts upon which he relies. There would be no point in having such a proof because, as a matter of law, the pursuer would be bound to fail.[13]

The general plea to the relevancy which a pursuer might take against a defender might be: "The defender's averments being irrelevant *et separatim* lacking in specification, the defences should be repelled and decree granted as craved [concluded for]".[14]

4–03 This means that even if the defender proves all that the defender says in his defences to the claim that would not, as a matter of law, amount to a good defence to a claim of this nature. The argument at debate would be that there is no point in hearing evidence about the case because the only evidence which the defender can bring to bear would not enable the defender to avoid the decree sought being granted against him.[15]

However, in practice, the disposal of preliminary pleas is not quite as easy as this. The most straightforward way of dealing with a preliminary plea is to have it argued fully at debate and for the court to uphold or sustain the plea, i.e. agree with it, or to repel the plea, i.e. decide there is no merit in it. There is, however, a third option for the disposal of a preliminary plea which regularly comes into play and that is to reserve the preliminary plea.

---

[11] Note that OCR r.22.1 and RCS r.22.4 effectively mean that the basis for the preliminary plea does have to be disclosed in some way. See Ch.17.

[12] In this Chapter, the word is used to cover both debates in the sheriff court and procedure roll hearings in the Court of Session.

[13] See, e.g. *Simpson v Ross & Morton*, 1992 S.L.T. (Sh. Ct) 33; *Duncan v Beattie*, 2003 S.L.T. 1243.

[14] This would be the Court of Session terminology.

[15] See, e.g. *Duncan Logan (Contractors) Ltd (in liquidation) v Royal Exchange Assurance Group*, 1973 S.L.T. 192.

What this means is that although one or other party has taken a plea to the effect that there is some "legal technicality" which ought to prevent the case proceeding to a hearing of evidence, the parties can agree, or the court can decide after hearing argument, that the strength or force of the "legal technicality" cannot be adjudicated upon until such time as the evidence about the whole case or at least the evidence about some aspect of the case has been heard.[16] If a defender took a plea to the effect that the pursuer's pleadings were irrelevant,[17] then the parties could agree, or the court could decide after hearing a debate, that it would not be possible to determine that question until the whole facts of the case had been established by proof.[18]

In certain circumstances, it is not appropriate to reserve a preliminary plea. Some pleas have to be decided by the court one way or the other before the case can progress to the next stage of procedure.[19]

There is the possibility of a preliminary plea giving rise to a slightly unusual form of procedure, namely a preliminary proof. For example, in a case in which the defender pleads a defence which includes a plea that the court has no jurisdiction, one would normally expect this plea to be adjudicated upon by the court after hearing legal argument from the parties at debate. The facts surrounding such a plea are often agreed. If, however, the circumstances surrounding the question of jurisdiction were not clear, or were not agreed, or not set out fully in the pleadings, then it might be necessary for the court to hear some evidence related solely to the issue of jurisdiction. In that case, if the plea was argued at a debate, the preliminary plea might be reserved for a proof to take place, and after the proof had been heard, the court would once again consider legal argument as to whether the preliminary plea should be sustained or not.[20]

The most common forms of preliminary plea are set out below, along with a style of plea and a brief explanation of what is involved. However, the vast majority of preliminary pleas take the form of a plea to relevancy or a plea of lack of specification or a combination of both. The other pleas arise infrequently.

---

[16] See, e.g. *Tilcon (Scotland) Ltd v Jarvis (Scotland) Ltd*, 2000 S.L.T. (Sh. Ct) 55.

[17] In this context, it would mean that they did not disclose a good basis for a claim as a matter of law.

[18] See *Smith v Carter*, 1995 S.L.T. 295. For more detailed explanation of this see Chs 17 and 18.

[19] See, e.g. *Edward Gibbon (Aberdeen) Ltd v Edwards*, 1992 S.L.T. (Sh. Ct) 86.

[20] The most common example is a preliminary proof on the question of time bar of a personal injury claim. Other examples can be seen in *Stanley Howard (Construction) Ltd v Davis*, 1988 S.L.T. (Sh. Ct) 30; *North Scottish Helicopters Ltd v United Technologies Corporation Inc*, 1988 S.L.T. 77; *Lowe v Grampian Health Board*, 1998 S.L.T. 731; *Irving v Hiddleston*, 1998 S.L.T. 912; *Wilkie v Direct Line Insurance Plc (No.2)*, 2002 S.L.T. 530.

(1) No Title to Sue

4–04 The usual form of the plea would be: "The Pursuer having no title to sue the action should be dismissed."

This means that even if the defender might be liable in the circumstances to have some form of decree granted against him, the particular pursuer(s) in the action has no legal entitlement to seek that decree.[21]

It should be noted that the pursuer must have a title to sue at the date when the action is raised and that title to sue must continue until final resolution of the case. If the pursuer doesn't have a title to sue at the commencement of the action then that cannot be cured by, e.g. a subsequent assignation.[22]

(2) All Parties Not Called

4–05 The wording of the plea would be: "All parties not having been called, the action should be dismissed."

The meaning of this plea is that there are other persons who should have been named as defenders in the case who have not been called as defenders and whose absence will prejudice the defender who has actually been sued, either in his defence or in his position after the defence has been repelled.[23] It is *pars judicis*[24] to take cognisance of the fact that all parties have not been called who should have been. This plea rarely appears in practice.[25]

(3) No Jurisdiction

4–06 This plea may be expressed in certain different ways to indicate that the court has no jurisdiction over the defender or that the court has no jurisdiction over that particular type of case.[26] One example is: "The court having no jurisdiction because . . . the action should be dismissed."

---

[21] See, e.g. *Macleod v Clacher*, 1993 S.L.T. 318. Also see *North Scottish Helicopters Ltd*, 1988 S.L.T. 77, in which the parties agreed that the question of title to sue should be decided after a preliminary proof of the facts pertinent to that issue. Also, *Thurso Building Society's Judicial Factor v Robertson*, 2001 S.L.T. 797; *Royal Insurance (UK) Ltd v Amec Construction Scotland Ltd*, 2008 S.L.T. 427.

[22] Although the matter is not quite as simple as that. See *Lanarkshire Health Board v Banafaa*, 1987 S.L.T. 229.

[23] See the case of *Lang v Ure*, 1994 S.L.T. 1235; *Arthur v SMT Sales and Service Co. Ltd (No.1)*, 1998 S.L.T. 1446.

[24] In other words, even if the defender does not take the plea, the judge hearing the case can and should take this deficiency into account.

[25] The latest reported cases appear to be *Royal Bank of Scotland v Home*, 2000 G.W.D. 29-1109 and *Thomson v Chief Constable, Grampian Police (No.1)*, 2001 S.L.T. 480.

[26] Examples are *MT Group v James Howden & Co Ltd*, 1993 S.L.T. 409 and *Clarke v Fennoscandia Ltd (No.2)*, 2001 S.L.T. 1311.

It may be that a plea to the effect that the court has no jurisdiction on either of these grounds ought to be included in the defences rather than be added by way of adjustment because it is arguable that once a party has lodged defences without taking a plea about jurisdiction he could be regarded as prorogating[27] the jurisdiction of the court.[28]

In the Court of Session, the rules provide specifically for cases where the defender contests jurisdiction, and they allow the defender to lodge defences solely relating to jurisdiction with a view to resolving that question before it becomes necessary to consider the substantive merits of the case.[29]

(4) FORUM NON CONVENIENS

This plea will normally be expressed by simply using the words: **4–07** "*Forum non conveniens*".

Where an action has competently been raised in the Scottish courts and the party (usually the defender) wishes it to be dealt with by the courts of another country then he can take a plea of *forum non conveniens*. It is a plea to the effect that the Scottish court in which the action has been raised and which does have jurisdiction, should not actually exercise its jurisdiction. This would normally be because it can be argued that there is some other court outside Scotland in which the case might be heard more suitably. It is not necessary to the success of such a plea that there is in fact another action already in existence at the time when the plea is taken, but the court is unlikely to sustain such a plea if there is no likelihood of the other action being raised soon.

The plea will not apply where identical proceedings are already in existence before another court of the contracting states as defined under the Civil Jurisdiction and Judgments Act 1982. The rule will then be that the first court has jurisdiction and the second court must give way to that. This does not mean that the second court must dismiss the action, and in these circumstances it would be quite competent for the second court to sist the action to await the outcome of the other action.

The justification for the plea is that the parties ought to litigate in the court which is:

"... the more suitable for the ends of justice and is preferable because pursuit of the litigation in that forum is more likely to secure those ends".[30]

---

[27] Accepting.
[28] See *Young v Evans*, 1968 S.L.T. (Notes) 57.
[29] RCS r.18.2. See *Lord Advocate v Tursi*, 1998 S.L.T. 1035.
[30] *Spiliada Maritime Corp v Cansulex Ltd* [1986] 3 W.L.R. 972; this was a House of Lords case which contains a very comprehensive analysis of the principles which would govern this issue.

4-08 In *De Mulder v Jadranska Linijska (Jadrolinija)*[31] the pursuer's yacht collided with the defenders' ferry in Yugoslavia. An action was raised in Aberdeen Sheriff Court and then remitted to the Court of Session.[32] There were already proceedings in Yugoslavia and aspects of those proceedings were under appeal in Yugoslavia. A preliminary proof was heard in the Court of Session to decide whether the court in Scotland was the appropriate court to hear the merits of the case. Evidence was led as to the circumstances which might or might not have a bearing on the appropriateness of the respective courts. The Court of Session sustained the plea of *forum non conveniens* by the defender, but sisted the action, because of the possibility that the Yugoslavian courts might ultimately give way to the Scottish courts.[33]

The plea can be decided on the basis of what is said in the written pleadings of the parties and/or the oral submissions when the plea is argued at debate, but it is perhaps more likely that the court will have a preliminary proof so as to determine whether the various factors which might justify the plea do exist. The burden would usually be on the defender to satisfy the court that the case should not be allowed to proceed in the Scottish court. If the defender can satisfy the court that there is a prima facie case for having the action heard by a court in another country, then the pursuer would have to argue that there were special circumstances justifying the hearing of the action in Scotland.

When the plea is taken it is usual to ask for the Scottish action to be dismissed, but the court has discretion about the disposal of the case if the plea is sustained and the court can sist such an action if there is a good reason for doing so.[34]

(5) LIS ALIBI PENDENS

4-09 The usual form of that plea would simply be: "*Lis alibi pendens*".

This preliminary plea can only be taken by a defender for obvious reasons and it is taken where the defender proposes to argue that the action is incompetent because the matter which is being disputed between the parties in the action in question is the same as a matter which is under dispute in a pre-existing, and still existing, action. The purpose of having such a rule and such a plea is to avoid a multiplicity of court actions arising out of the same set of circumstances.

Where the pursuer has reason to believe there are proceedings pending before any other court involving the present cause of action and between

---

[31] *De Mulder v Jadranska Linijska (Jadrolinija)*, 1989 S.L.T. 269.
[32] See Ch.2 on "Remits".
[33] See also *PTKF Kontinent v VMPTO Progress*, 1994 S.L.T. 235, this is one of the most recent Scottish cases dealing with the issue and in the judgement you will find a list of all of the relevant cases.
[34] See *L v L*, 2000 S.L.T. (Sh. Ct) 12.

the same parties to the action, he should put details of this in the initial writ[35] or summons.[36] It can be arguable whether another action is indeed "pending" at the time when the second action is raised, and there is scope for argument as to whether a subsequent action does indeed cover the same subject matter or cause of action as is being canvassed in the first action.[37]

If the plea is sustained then the action will be dismissed. In addition to inserting the plea in the written pleadings, the defender would also have to make averments to support the plea. These averments would no doubt contain details of the other (preceding) action, including its court reference number, so that it can be clearly identified. It should also be noted that the previous action should be an action which is pending in a court of competent jurisdiction in Scotland. The plea would not apply to proceedings which might exist before a foreign court because in that situation different rules come into play. These rules are complex and can be found in arts 21–23 of the Hague Convention. The rules do not impact upon situations where the other action has been raised in a Scottish court, or in another court in the UK, but they do mean that if an identical action has already been raised in the courts of one of the states which is a party to the Hague Convention then particular consequences will apply, which can include the Scottish courts declining jurisdiction, sisting jurisdiction or deciding that for some justifiable reason it should indeed exercise its jurisdiction.

(6) ARBITRATION

There could be a preliminary plea to the effect that the court should not **4–10** hear the case because the subject matter of the dispute is something which ought properly to be dealt with by arbitration, which effectively excludes the jurisdiction of the court. The plea would be along these lines:

"The dispute between the parties being one which falls to be resolved upon a reference to arbitration, (and such reference having been made) the action should be sisted."

It should be stressed that taking a dispute to arbitration is not an option which is open to parties in the normal course of events but it can be utilised if: (1) the parties have agreed to do so in the contract between them out of which the dispute arises; (2) in the absence of the above, where the parties have agreed to arbitration after the dispute has arisen by

[35] OCR r.3.1(4).

[36] RCS r.13.2(4)(c) and (d).

[37] Recent cases in which the plea was considered are *Stratmil Ltd v D & A Todd (Building Contractors) Ltd*, 1990 S.L.T. 493; *James M Sutherland & Sons v Pottinger*, 1989 S.L.T. 679; *Saudi Distribution Services Ltd v Kane*, 1985 S.L.T. (Sh. Ct.) 9; *Flannigan v British Dyewood Co Ltd*, 1971 S.L.T. 208; and *Levy v Gardiner (No.2)*, 1965 S.L.T. (Notes) 86. Also *Bank of Scotland v S.A. Banque Internationale de Paris*, 1996 S.L.T. 103 and *Bain v Bain*, 2002 S.L.T. 1177.

virtue of agreeing a contract of submission to arbitration; or (3) because there is some statutory provision which applies to the circumstances which are now the subject matter of the dispute and which compel or allow arbitration to resolve that dispute, e.g. under the Agricultural Holdings (Scotland) Act 1949 or the Trusts (Scotland) Act 1921 s.2.

Where the court is satisfied in any contractual reference to arbitration that (1) there was a valid contract between the parties; (2) the contract still exists and applies; (3) the dispute on the merits is covered by the arbitration clause; and (4) the contract clearly substitutes arbitration for court procedure, then the court has no discretion to refuse to sist the action for arbitration.

In a statutory reference to arbitration, provided the court is satisfied that the statute does apply and that the provision is imperative and not permissive, then, again, the court has no discretion to refuse a sist for arbitration.

It should be noted that the jurisdiction of the court is not ousted completely and for all purposes[38]. The court simply postpones the progress of an action and allows the arbiter to decide the merits of the dispute. Then the court can pronounce a decree to give effect to the arbiter's decision. Furthermore, the court can still deal with the case itself regardless of a prior sist for arbitration , if it subsequently emerges that the arbitration proves ineffective or abortive.[39]

The plea can be taken at any time before the closing of the record, but it is arguable that you may not be allowed to take the plea by way of amendment to your pleadings after the record has been closed.[40] If it is not disputed that the case should go to arbitration, then the parties can jointly move the court to sist for arbitration and there is no reason why that cannot be done prior to the closing of the record. However, the court would have to be satisfied on the pleadings and/or on the submissions by the parties at the material time that it would be appropriate for the case to go to arbitration.[41]

(7) INCOMPETENCY

4–11 The plea itself could take many forms depending upon the nature of the incompetency. In simple terms it might be sufficient to say: "The action being incompetent should be dismissed".

---

[38] For an illustration of sheriff court procedure surrounding such a plea, see *George Martin (Builders) Ltd v Jamal*, 2001 S.L.T. (Sh. Ct) 119.

[39] Although, see *Newman Shopfitters Ltd v M.J. Gleeson Group Plc*, 2003 S.L.T. (Sh. Ct) 83, where Sheriff Principal (now Lord) Macphail expressed some reservations as to whether the court could competently recall a sist for arbitration once it had been granted.

[40] See *La Pantofola D'Ora SpA v Blane Leisure Ltd (No.1)*, 2000 S.L.T. 105.

[41] On this plea generally, see, e.g. *Hill v Wildfowl Trust (Holdings) Ltd (No.1)*, 1996 S.L.T. (Sh. Ct) 46; *ERDC Construction Ltd v H.M. Love & Co*, 1995 S.L.T. 254; *Mendok BV v Cumberland Maritime Corp*, 1989 S.L.T. 192; and *National Coal Board v Drysdale*, 1989 S.L.T. 825.

But although that form has been used, it is suggested that the correct practice is to indicate in the competency plea the nature of the proposed attack on competency. It can be suggested, however, that provided the pursuer knows (in some way) of the basis of the argument, that might suffice in practice to give fair notice to the opponent.[42]

Even if the plea is not taken by the defender, it is open to the court to dismiss an action as incompetent on its own initiative if that seems to be appropriate and justified.[43]

(8) RELEVANCY

It has already been noted that the most frequently utilised preliminary plea **4–12** would be a general plea to relevancy and specification. Whilst the two are usually pled together, often as a matter of routine, they may be quite distinct. The usual form of a plea directed solely towards relevancy would be: "The pursuer's averments being irrelevant the action should be dismissed".

It is also possible to focus this further and direct it towards some distinct part of the pursuer's case by expressing the plea thus: "The pursuer's averments regarding . . . being irrelevant should not be admitted to probation".

This means that some distinct part of the pursuer's case, which could, in some meaningful and practical way, be separated from other parts of it, could be attacked quite specifically. As previously noted, a pursuer could take a similar plea to the relevancy of the defences which might be to the effect that the whole of the defences or some part of the defences should be repelled. In reparation actions, e.g. if the pursuer thought that the defences were irrelevant in that they failed to disclose a defence on liability for the accident, it would still be for the pursuer to prove to the court the value of his claim, so the plea might be expressed thus:

> "The defender's averments in relation to [common law/statutory liability] being irrelevant the defences should be repelled to that extent and proof restricted to quantum".

The significance of a plea to the relevancy and the disposal of pleas to the relevancy are dealt with in more detail in the chapters on proof before answer and debates.[44] The basic proposition is that the pursuer's written pleadings do not disclose a factual situation in which there is any legal

---

[42] See *Coxall v Stewart*, 1976 S.L.T. 275.

[43] Examples of incompetency are (1) a party seeking a remedy from the courts which the court had no power or authority to give. See *Jack v Jack*, 1962 S.L.T. 21; (2) where a statute provided for a specific method of recovering compensation but a pursuer sought to obtain compensation from the courts. See *Davie v Magistrates of Edinburgh*, 1952 S.L.T. 74.

[44] See Chs 17 and 18.

justification for the remedy which is being sought by the pursuer. In relation to the defender, the proposition would be that the defender's written pleadings do not disclose a factual situation where the defender has any real answer or defence to the claim against him which would be regarded, as a matter of law, as denying the pursuer the remedy which is being sought.

(8) SPECIFICATION

4–13 A preliminary plea can be taken to the effect that the opponent's pleadings do not contain sufficient detail to demonstrate either that there is a relevant case or that there is a relevant defence. In this case it can be, and invariably is, combined with the preliminary plea to relevancy which has been dealt with above. A preliminary plea to lack of specification can also be directed to the lack of detail in the opponents case which does not make the case easy to understand, does not enable the opponent to investigate or respond to the averments against him and which can be seen as causing some prejudice to the opponent in the proper preparation and presentation of his case at proof.[45] A plea to lack of specification may be directed to some specific aspect of the opponent's pleadings and might be expressed thus: "The pursuer's (defender's) averments regarding ... being lacking in specification should not be admitted to probation".

The argument would be that those averments should be deleted from the written pleadings and therefore it would not be possible to lead any evidence about the issue at a proof.[46]

(9) TIME BAR

4–14 A defender can take a preliminary plea to the effect that the claim by the pursuer is time-barred. In other words, the obligation (if any) on the defender to make any payment to the pursuer has been extinguished because the action has been commenced outwith the appropriate limitation period.[47] The rules regarding time bar and the impact of arguments about time bar on procedure are complex, especially in the field of personal injury claims[48] and beyond the scope of this outline.

---

[45] See *McMenemy v James Dougal & Sons Ltd*, 1960 S.L.T. (Notes) 84.
[46] e.g. an averment that, "Some time after the accident, somebody representing the defender phoned the pursuer and admitted liability" would be challenged as lacking specification by the defender, who would want to ensure that no evidence about this emerged at a proof without having an opportunity to find out in advance what this was about, and obtain evidence to challenge it.
[47] See the Prescription and Limitation (Scotland) Act 1973 (c.52) as amended.
[48] Where it is open to the court to extend the limitation period in certain circumstances.

The plea could be expressed in a number of ways. Examples are: "The action being time-barred should be dismissed"; "Any obligation on the defender to make payment to the pursuer having prescribed the action should be dismissed"; and, "The action not having been commenced timeously . . . should be dismissed".[49]

The action will be treated as commencing on the date when the proceedings are served on the defender,[50] and the period of limitation runs to midnight on the day when the limitation period ends. It may be thought that there would be little scope for dispute about whether an action was, in fact, time-barred or not, but the legislation is complex.[51] When the preliminary plea is taken there can often be preliminary proofs to enable the court to determine the issue before the merits of the action can be considered. This happens more frequently in personal injury cases where the legislation, inter alia, entitles the pursuer in an accident claim to ask the court to extend the time limit if the action is raised late. The court is asked to exercise its discretion as to whether to allow this or not.[52] A preliminary proof is sometimes heard on the factors which the court has to take into account when exercising its discretion but sometimes these factors are so intermingled with questions about the merits of the claim as a whole that the court can be persuaded to hear a proof on everything rather than try to deal with this as a preliminary issue.[53]

(10) PERSONAL BAR

A defender can take a plea to the effect that a pursuer has acted in such **4–15** a way as to make it reasonable to assume that he has waived his entitlement to pursue a claim. A pursuer can take a similar plea to the effect that the defenders have acted in such a way that they should not be allowed to insist on a defence.[54] The plea for the defender could be stated thus: "The pursuer being personally barred from insisting in the action, the action should be dismissed".

---

[49] See *Humphrey v Royal and Sun Alliance Plc*, 2005 S.L.T. (Sh. Ct) 31.
[50] *Miller v NCB*, 1960 S.C. 376.
[51] Prescription and Limitation (Scotland) Act 1973 as amended.
[52] See, e.g. *Ferla v Secretary of State for Scotland*, 1995 S.L.T. 662 and *Kane v Argyll and Clyde Health Board*, 1997 S.L.T. 965.
[53] However, in relation to the appropriate procedure see the case of *Clark v McLean*, 1995 S.L.T. 235, where the Inner House expressed authoritative views as to the appropriate procedure to be followed in such cases. Amongst other things they said, "it should seldom be necessary for the court in an action of damages for personal injuries involving only two parties to allow a proof with all pleas standing including those pleas relating to the question of time bar and those relating to the merits of the action". See also *McClelland v Stuart Building Services*, 2004 S.L.T. 1011.
[54] See *Gordon v East Kilbride Development Corp*, 1995 S.L.T. 62.

Such a plea is relatively rare but when it is taken it usually proceeds on the basis that the party has waived his rights,[55] and when it is taken it is often so closely linked to the merits of the claim that it will not be sustained at debate, but is likely to be reserved and a proof before answer fixed.

THE IMPACT OF PRELIMINARY PLEAS ON LITIGATION

4–16 In the last example mentioned above, the pursuer could take a preliminary plea in response to a plea of personal bar from the defender that the defender's pleadings and plea in law were irrelevant in that the averments did not disclose any conduct that could possibly amount to personal bar. It is not uncommon for parties to exchange preliminary pleas during adjustment of the pleadings whilst developing the arguments about the legal propositions which (they think) lie at the basis of the claim or the defence. It goes without saying that this can produce considerable confusion in pleadings and unnecessary complications if the meaning and significance of the respective pleas are not fully understood. The procedural implications of a variety of opposing pleas can also be difficult to understand and predict. A proliferation of opposing pleas can be a cause of confusion and delay in many litigations. If these matters are properly understood then they can simplify and focus disputes and contribute to the expeditious conduct of a case. If not, then the detrimental effect this could have upon the proper progress of a litigation would support the argument that they should be left out of the system entirely and a simple proof should be heard in every case so that all of the "technical" legal arguments would just "come out in the wash" after evidence had been heard. In this context, it is worth noting that in the most recent procedural regime introduced in Scotland, namely the personal injury procedure in the Court of Session, parties are not permitted to have preliminary pleas at all,[56] on the basis, presumably, that they might simply delay the proceedings unnecessarily, and their absence would not materially affect the conduct of the litigation. Where there is a genuine legal issue to be considered and resolved in other forms of litigation, however, an appropriate preliminary plea is necessary and should assist the parties and the court in focusing the genuine areas of dispute in any particular case.

---

[55] See, e.g. *Armia Ltd v Daejan Developments Ltd*, 1979 S.L.T. 147; *Scottish Life Assurance v Agfa Gevaert Ltd*, 1997 S.L.T. 1200; *Hoult v Turpie*, 2004 S.L.T. 308; *Moodiesburn House Hotel Ltd v Norwich Union Insurance Ltd*, 2002 S.L.T. 1069; and *William Grant & Sons Ltd v Glen Catrine Bonded Warehouse Ltd*, 2001 S.L.T. 1419.

[56] Although a party can still argue a purely legal issue and seek a procedure roll hearing (legal debate) in appropriate cases.

CHAPTER 5

COURT OF SESSION ORDINARY ACTIONS

The Court of Session is the supreme civil court in Scotland. Broadly, it **5–01** is divided into the Inner House, which is usually a court of appeal of three judges, and the Outer House, which is usually a court of first instance in which a judge will sit alone. The Court of Session comprises both "Houses". Its origins can be found in the fifteenth century, and in the nineteenth century its jurisdiction was reported to be, "universal as to extent and supreme in degree".[1] During the nineteenth century, a number of Acts were passed relating to the constitution, jurisdiction and powers of the Court of Session.[2] Whilst the evolution of the Court of Session is of little significance for present purposes, a basic understanding of that evolution does help to explain some of the names, terminology and procedures which still exist nowadays.

Various statutes in the early part of the twentieth century dealt with rules of procedure in the Court of Session culminating in the Court of Session Act of 1988. The modern statutory power of the Court of Session to make rules regulating its own procedure is contained in ss.5 and 6 of the 1988 Act. The current Rules of the Court of Session are in Sch.2 to the Act of Sederunt (Rules of the Court of Session 1994) 1994.[3] The Act of Sederunt came into force on September 5, 1994. These particular rules emerged as a consequence of a number of reports of the Rules Review Group which was set up by the Lord President of the Court of Session in 1984 to recommend changes in the layout of the rules as a whole, and changes in the rules themselves. The purpose was to simplify and improve the handling of civil business in the Court of Session. The main forms of procedure regulated by the rules are ordinary procedure and petition procedure, and they are set out fairly shortly in the 1994 Rules.

Section 8 of the 1988 Act continued the existence of a Court of **5–02** Session Rules Council[4] which meets from time to time and may frame suggested rules regarding the conduct of actions in the Court of Session for consideration by the court. Any suggestions or proposals for rule

---

[1] Commissioners on the Courts of Justice in Scotland, *First Report of the Commissioners on the Courts of Justice in Scotland*. 1816.
[2] A helpful and concise summary of the development of the Court of Session can be found in the *Stair Memorial Encyclopaedia*, Vol.6, paras 896–922.
[3] Act of Sederunt (Rules of the Court of Session 1994) 1994 (SI 1994/1443).
[4] Originally set up in 1933.

changes would have to be approved by the court and would then be incorporated in an Act of Sederunt.

In 1995, Lord Cullen was appointed by the Lord President of the Court of Session to carry out a review of the way in which the business in the Outer House was conducted. He was asked to consider, inter alia, what measures should be taken, by changes in the rules of procedure and otherwise, to simplify procedure and expedite the disposal of cases, achieve a greater degree of judicial control and management of cases, minimise delay in settlement of cases, and ensure that judicial time was used to best advantage. He reported in December 1995 with various recommendations for altering procedures. No significant changes were made at that time.[5]

In October 1997, the Lord President appointed a working party, under the chairmanship of Lord Coulsfield, to consider whether a system of rules could be devised for dealing with certain cases in the Outer House under a simplified procedure. Actions for damages for personal injury, which formed a significant proportion of the ordinary actions in the Court of Session, were identified as the type of case which might benefit from changes in procedure and ultimately a new procedure was introduced for these actions in the summer of 2004.[6] It should be noted that, apart from this change, the procedures in ordinary actions in the Court of Session have not altered significantly for many years and the recommendations by Lord Cullen have not been implemented.

5–03   If the court wants to make any change in its rules or procedures then it will do so by way of an Act of Sederunt. The court can also publish a practice note which would give some administrative direction indicating, for administrative purposes only, the way in which a rule or an administrative requirement may be complied with. Practice notes cannot alter, delete or add a rule because this can only be done by way of an Act of Sederunt, but it can sometimes be difficult to see the distinction between altering a rule by way of Act of Sederunt and altering the practical application of a rule by way of a practice note. In recent years, there have been a number of practice notes and, in order to understand the way in which the rules are being applied in practice, it is necessary to have some knowledge of the content of these practice notes.[7]

The Rules of the Court of Session are extensive[8] but in this chapter of the book we are simply going to concentrate on the rules relating to an ordinary action in the Court of Session. Before doing so, it is desirable to have a simple summary of the major topics covered by the rules as a

---

[5] The report is essential reading for anyone who would like to have a full understanding of the way in which the Outer House of the Court of Session operates in practice and the way in which the rules do, or do not, affect that practice.

[6] This is explained in more detail in Ch.6.

[7] See *Greens Annotated Rules of the Court of Session 2008/9* (Edinburgh: W. Green, 2008), pp.C2001–C2066.

[8] Around a thousand rules split into 85 "Chapters".

whole. Whilst the sheriff court rules relate largely to the conduct of an ordinary action in the sheriff court, the Rules of the Court of Session encompass rules relating to a number of different procedures. They include rules relating to the administration of the offices of the court and the organisation of the various departments in the court.

An excellent and detailed exposition of the whole body of these rules **5–04** can be found in *Greens Annotated Rules of the Court of Session 2008/9* to which reference should be made for the precise terms of each rule and a thorough commentary on the meaning and practical application of the individual rules.

The rules are divided into various chapters and for present purposes the following are the significant chapters:

Chapter 3—details of the general officers and offices of the court;

Chapter 4—the court process. In other words the form and description of the documents which are required in any court action;

Chapter 6—the rolls of court. This is a particularly significant feature of Court of Session procedure;

Chapters 13 to 37—these contain the main body of rules for the conduct of an ordinary action from its initiation until its conclusion, with the exception of Ch.14 which deals with petition procedure;

Chapter 38 to 41—rules regarding various appeals;

Chapter 42—rules regarding taxation of accounts and solicitors' fees in the Court of Session;

Chapter 43—rules for actions for damages for personal injuries;

Chapter 47—rules for commercial actions.

The remaining rules relate to many special types of action and make **5–05** provision for a variety of special rules or procedures in these cases. Most of them arise from statutory provisions which give the Court of Session jurisdiction in relation to particular matters provided by statute.[9] Reference must be made to the rules themselves for full details. For example, there are a number of rules relating to applications for the appointment of a judicial factor on the estate of a deceased. Basically, it is done by petition,[10] but there are special safeguards in the procedures to protect the interests of the creditors and the beneficiaries. The more notable chapters which comprise the remainder of the RCS[11] include:

Chapter 49—family actions;

Chapter 55—causes relating to intellectual property;

Chapter 58—judicial review[12];

---

[9] The separate rules regarding summary applications in the sheriff court (see Ch.14 of this book) can be seen to mirror some of the rules which are contained in the body of the Court of Session ordinary rules.

[10] See Ch.13 of this book.

[11] In no order of importance

[12] This is dealt with in Ch.8 of this book.

Chapter 61—rules regarding the appointment and control of judicial factors;

Chapter 62 to 93—rules regarding, e.g. the enforcement of foreign judgments, admiralty actions, actions relating to intellectual property, judicial factories, trusts, adoptions, companies, including winding up and receivership, references to the European Court of Justice, child abduction, procedures for the recovery of the proceeds of crime, proceedings in relation to the Human Rights Act 1998, the Terrorism Act 2000, and applications under the Protection from Abuse (Scotland) Act 2001.

We are not going to look at the detail of these later chapters here, but it is important to know that rules exist in relation to the exercise of many functions by the Court of Session, albeit cases involving the exercise of these various functions can be quite rare. A comprehensive index of all of the rules is contained in the "Arrangement of Rules" which can be found at the beginning of Sch.2 to the Act of Sederunt.[13]

In 1995 there were 26 judges in the Court of Session as a whole, 16 of these judges were Lords Ordinary sitting in the Outer House. In November 2004 there were 32 judges in the Court of Session as a whole, with 22 in the Outer House.

ORDINARY PROCEDURE NARRATIVE

5–06 If a party wants to raise an action as an ordinary action in the Court of Session then his solicitor would draw up a summons which is to be drafted in accordance with the style outlined in the rules. The summons is then given to a clerk in the general department of the Court of Session along with an appropriate fee.[14] If all of the basic requirements of the form have been complied with then the summons will be signetted. A signet is the authority of the court to serve the summons on the proposed defender. The summons will then be served upon the proposed defender.[15] Service will be done by post, sheriff officers or messenger-at-arms and, in a few cases, by newspaper. The defender will receive a service copy of the summons together with a copy of the warrant and a form of citation of the defender.

On receipt of the service copy summons, the defender does not require to do anything but he has a period of notice of 21 days to

---

[13] *Parliament House Book*, pp.C6–C32/5.

[14] From August 1, 2008 the fee is £170. For other fees see the Court of Session etc. Fees Amendment Order 2008 (SSI 2008/236). Most firms now have a credit charging arrangement which means that they are billed monthly for court dues such as this, rather than pay a cheque on each occasion when a document is lodged.

[15] It is, however, entirely up to the pursuer to decide when to serve it, although he must do so within a year and a day of signetting or the action will not be permitted to proceed.

consider the terms of the summons. In practice, any individual defender would be likely to pass this to his solicitor and his solicitor would in all probability contact the solicitor for the pursuer and advise him of his interest.[16] After the period of notice of 21 days has expired from the date when the summons was served, the pursuer, who will have the principal summons, can lodge the principal summons with the clerk for calling. It has to be lodged along with the certificate of service showing when service was carried out. "Calling" means calling on the rolls of court. The rolls of court are the list of cases in the Court of Session in respect of which some procedure is to take place. The rolls are published daily and any such action would appear on the "calling list" once the pursuer has lodged it for calling. If the pursuer serves the summons but, for some reason, decides not to lodge it for calling, then the case will not call.[17]

Assuming that the case has been lodged for calling and appears on the calling list, the defender then has three days in which to intimate formally to the clerk that he is entering an appearance in the action. He will do this by writing or faxing to the clerk or by attending at the clerk's office and having certain details noted on the principal summons. The defender then has seven days from the calling date to lodge written defences.

The defences must be in writing. They will respond to the terms of the principal summons. They will be in a particular format. The principal version of the defences will be signed and lodged with the clerk. A copy of the defences will be sent to the pursuer. The pursuer must then lodge the open record within 14 days after the date in which the time for lodging defences expired or on which the defences were lodged, whichever is the earlier. The open record is an amalgamation of the terms of the writ and the defences in one document, and is used for parties to write adjustment of their pleadings.

The case is then published on the adjustment roll of the Court of Session and the court will automatically allow a period of eight weeks for adjustment of the pleadings. The parties are free to adjust their written pleadings as appropriate during that time. Adjustments are written on the open record or attached to it and passed between the parties so that each is able to see the alterations or adjustments which have been made by the other. If a party wants to extend the adjustment period,[18] then he can make a motion to the court to do so.

At the end of the adjustment period, the record closes. The pursuer has **5–07** to make up a closed record which contains the pleadings as adjusted and any of the court interlocutors or orders which have been pronounced in the case to the date of closing of the record. The closed record must be lodged by the pursuer within four weeks of the expiry of the adjustment period. At the same time as lodging the closed record, the pursuer's

---

[16] There is no formal requirement to do so.

[17] A failure to lodge the summons for calling will have serious consequences. See *Brogan v O'Rourke Ltd*, 2005 S.L.T. 29.

[18] Or indeed if he wants to shorten it.

agents will enrol a motion to allow further procedure in the case. This will usually be done after there has been some discussion between the parties as to what the appropriate further procedure would be and there is often agreement between the parties about further procedure.[19] If there is a dispute about further procedure then the pursuer will enrol a motion to call on the by order (adjustment) roll at which the court will be asked to decide what further procedure would be appropriate. If the pursuer makes no motion, then the clerk will put the case on the by order (adjustment) roll for the parties to explain their position to the court and for the court to make an order for further procedure.

At this stage, there are four basic procedural possibilities: (1) the case can be sent to procedure roll for a debate on a matter of law which arises from the pleadings of the parties[20]; (2) the court can fix a date for a proof,[21] which simply involves the hearing of evidence about the disputed facts; (3) the court can fix a proof before answer; or (4) the court can fix a jury trial. These four eventualities are all dealt with in more detail in the chapters in this book.

If a party wants to amend his pleadings after the record is closed then there are rules whereby he can do so. The court has a discretion as to whether to allow amendment of pleadings or not.

There are specific rules regarding the procedure for lodging counterclaims[22] and specific rules regarding the procedure whereby a defender can bring another party (a third party)[23] into the action.

There are extensive provisions regarding the recovery of documents which might be evidence in a proof and the obtaining of evidence on commission[24] from witnesses who would otherwise be required to attend court to give evidence at a proof.

The rules make provision regarding the hearing of a proof which relate mostly to matters which are administrative or preparatory to the proof hearing itself. There are no rules which regulate the actual conduct of the proof. The right to have a jury trial in certain civil cases is unique to the Court of Session, and there are rules regarding the administration and preparation for the holding of a jury trial which requires more specific and detailed organisation than a proof before a judge.[25]

After the court issues a decision dealing with the merits of the case or, after certain other decisions during the progress of the action, an unsuccessful party can reclaim the court interlocutor to the Inner House.[26]

---

[19] This is positively encouraged by the court in Practice Note No.2 of 2004.
[20] If the case is sent to procedure roll, then the party who wishes to argue a point of law must lodge a note of his arguments in writing in advance.
[21] For completeness, this could be a preliminary proof on a particular aspect of the case as well as a proof at large on the whole merits of the case.
[22] See para.15–12, below.
[23] See para.15–08, below.
[24] See para.18–11, below, for a general explanation of this.
[25] See Ch.18 for "Jury Trials".
[26] See Ch.20 for "Appeals".

Once the action has been completed, the party who is found to be entitled to the judicial expenses of the case will either agree these expenses with the opponent or lodge his account of expenses with the auditor for taxation.[27] Judicial accounts are often agreed by negotiation without the need for taxation.

DETAILED RULES

Rule 2.1—This gives the court a dispensing power to excuse a party **5–08** from any failure to comply with the rules in certain circumstances.[28] The trend is towards a more liberal approach but it would be a serious mistake to assume the power is always likely to be exercised.[29]

Rules 3.1 to 3.7—The administration of the business of the Court of **5–09** Session is dealt with by different departments each of which is run by an officer of court. The departments and their officers are:

General department, run by a deputy principal clerk, dealing primarily with ordinary actions;

Petition department, run by a deputy principal clerk, dealing with all cases initiated by petition;

Rolls department, run by the Keeper of the Rolls and the Assistant Keeper of the Rolls, dealing with timetabling of cases and allocation of cases;

Extracts department, run by the principal extractor and his assistant, the extractor, dealing with the issuing of the formal decrees of the court;

Teind office, run by the clerk of teinds, dealing with church matters.

Two other posts which are mentioned are accountant of court, who has certain duties in relation to bankruptcies, liquidations, judicial factories, etc. and the auditor, whose major function is to tax solicitors' accounts in relation to litigation matters.

Rules 4.1 to 4.16—These rules relate to the form of court process. The **5–10** process is the collection of documents which comprise the paperwork required by the court in any case. Initially, it will comprise the principal writ and certain other (blank) documents including an inventory of process. As the action progresses, the number of documents will increase, the blank documents will be filled in as appropriate, and the inventory will be updated every time that an additional document is lodged in the case. By

---

[27] Which simply means an independent assessment of the charges being made in the account.
[28] See para.1–09, above.
[29] Examples from the Court of Session are *Brogan v O'Rourke*, 2005 S.L.T. 29, overruling *McDonald v Kwok*, 1999 S.L.T. 593. Also, see *McGee v Matthew Hall Ltd*, 1996 S.L.T. 399 and *Graham v John Tullis & Son (Plastics) Ltd (No.1)*, 1992 S.L.T. 507.

the end of a case, the process can comprise a very large bundle of documents. Each separate document is called a "step of process" and there is provision for the process to be kept in a particular type of document box. There are detailed provisions regarding the logistics of lodging, borrowing, intimating and returning steps of process. In practice, it is important to comply with all of the formal requirements of these rules, but their effect and significance can only be fully understood from experience of preparing and handling court documents on a regular basis.

5–11   **Rules 6.1 to 6.4**—These rules relate to the rolls of court and it is essential to a proper understanding of the way in which the Court of Session works to have some appreciation of the nature and significance of the rolls. The rolls are simply the lists of business of the court produced by the court administration on a regular basis. The general roll is the register of all cases of different types pending before the court. The daily rolls are the lists of business published by the rolls department[30] each weekday during term. They will show the names of the cases which are to be heard for specific categories of business on particular days. In cases in the Outer House, there will be a list of the cases which are "calling" on a particular day.[31] There will be lists of cases in which motions are to be heard on particular days. There are lists of cases calling on the adjustment roll,[32] and, e.g. cases calling on the procedure roll for debate.[33] If there are cases which require some intervention from the court because the parties cannot agree on procedure at the end of the adjustment period or because some intervention is required by the court to fix further procedure, then these will be published on the by order (adjustment) roll or the by order roll.

There are a number of such rolls and there are also a number of separate rolls for the different stages of business before the Inner House. Solicitors have to check the rolls carefully to identify their own case and to ensure that instructions are given for appearance before the court in relation to any case which is due to call in court as noted in the rolls. It is open to parties to make arrangement with the Keeper of the Rolls, in consultation with the opponent, for some cases to be heard at a time convenient to the parties and their counsel, but this cannot always be guaranteed. A case can suddenly appear on the by order roll for a variety of reasons and most firms will have systems in place to ensure the rolls are checked faithfully for their own cases.

The sufficiency of court resources for civil business and concerns about the proper allocation of court time to proofs and other substantial

---

[30]   And sent to those solicitors who pay for them.

[31]   This will enable a defender to know when to mark his appearance in the action.

[32]   Which will therefore give the starting date for the adjustment period.

[33]   Although there are special rules about this which mean that parties are given slightly earlier notice of the date for a procedure roll hearing.

court hearings gave rise to recent rule changes which require parties to give "certified" estimates of the duration of the hearing.[34]

Rules 10.5 and 11.1—The rules provide for the court to be in session **5–12** throughout the year, except for those periods which the Lord President shall designate as being in vacation. During vacation, there are certain sittings for some cases and solicitors will be given details of the days when the vacation court is sitting and details of cases calling then. The vacation judge[35] will usually deal with more urgent matters which could not wait until normal term time when the court is in session. However, he is not limited to this and may hear any motion which might be determined during session. He is not bound to hear or determine any matter if, in his opinion, it would be more appropriate for it to be dealt with when the court is in session.

Rules 13.1 to 13.13—These deal with the formalities of procedure **5–13** whereby an action should be raised, served on the defender, and defended by him. They also provide for procedure whereby a pursuer may apply for arrestment or inhibition on the dependence of an action.[36] If an action is being defended, the pursuer will normally arrange for it to "call", which means that he will return the principal summons with an execution of service, and the name of the case will be published on the calling list. The defender then has to take steps to indicate to the court that he is defending it and should lodge his written defences within seven days of the calling. The calling of the case is the trigger for this procedure. The pursuer does not need to lodge the summons for calling until he wants to, but if he does not do so within a year and a day after the expiry of the period of notice, the summons will be treated as at an end.

Rules 14.1 to 14.9—These deal with petition procedure which is **5–14** considered elsewhere.[37]

Rule 15—This rule relates to an application to the court by a document **5–15** known as a minute or, separately, a document known as a note. An application to the court in an ordinary action which cannot be by motion would be made by minute. A similar application in a petition would be

---

[34] Act of Sederunt (Rules of the Court of Session Amendment No.10) (Miscellaneous) 2007 (SSI 2007/548) which came into force on January 7, 2008. The amended rules were reinforced by Practice Note No.3 of 2007, encouraging parties to take care with time estimates and to keep them under review to assist in the orderly and expeditious conduct of court business.

[35] Who could be any judge and the term simply means that he is sitting in the vacation court.

[36] The rules about arrestment and inhibition on the dependence of an action have been altered by the Bankruptcy and Dilgence (Scotland) Act 2007, and the Act of Sederunt (Rules of the Court of Session Amendment No. 3) (Bankruptcy and Diligence etc. (Scotland) Act 2007) 2008 (SSI 2008/122).

[37] See paras 13–09 et seq., below.

made by note. They are difficult to categorise. Some minutes and some notes would be done by specific procedure as provided in the rules. This rule provides certain basic requirements for the content of a minute or a note. There may be circumstances where an individual who is neither a pursuer nor a defender in an action will have an interest in its outcome and would wish to make some representations to the court which is hearing the merits of the action. Where such a person is not a party to the action he can apply to the court by minute to be sisted as a party and he would be called a "party minuter".

5–16 **Rules 16.1 to 16.15**—These deal with service of proceedings on a defender. They include provisions regarding personal service, service by post, service abroad and service where a defender's address is unknown. Reference should be made to the rules for details. Recent rule changes have taken account of EC Regulations regarding the service in Member States of judicial and extra-judicial documents in civil or commercial matters.[38] They also deal with the execution of diligence. This generally refers to the way in which a party can lodge arrestments and inhibitions in connection with court proceedings. Again, reference should be made to the rules for details.

5–17 **Rules 17 and 18**—These provide for the way in which a defender will advise the court he is going to defend an action which has been served on him and the form of written defences he will lodge.[39]

5–18 **Rules 19, 20 and 21**—These relate to decrees in absence, decrees by default and summary decrees, all of which are covered in Ch.19 of this book.

5–19 **Rules 22.1 to 22.3**—These rules cover the formality of the procedure whereby parties will adjust their written pleadings in the court action. The Court of Session procedures and practice in this matter are quite different from the sheriff court. After the defender lodges written defences in a case, the pursuer must lodge two copies of an open record in process and, once he has a date for the commencement of the adjustment period, he must send a copy to the defender. An open record is one document which contains the pleadings of both parties in a set format and also includes the interlocutors pronounced in the case to the date of the open record. The lodging of the open record acts as a trigger for the commencement of the adjustment period and also fixes the end of the adjustment period which will normally be about eight weeks ahead. The adjustment period may be extended on a motion from one or other or both parties.

---

[38] Article 4(3) of Council Regulation (EC) No.1348/2000 on the service in the Member States of judicial and extrajudicial documents in civil or commercial matters [2000] OJ L160/37.
[39] These are dealt with in more detail in Ch.3.

Adjustment is done by writing on one copy of the open record any alteration to one's pleadings which is proposed and then sending this to the opponent for noting. The opponent will usually note that alteration on one of his own copies and intimate any adjustments in the same way. One particular copy of the record is usually used by both parties as the "base" document and will be passed back and forth between the parties as they make adjustments and note their opponent's adjustments. At the end of this process there will be an open record with numerous hand-written additions, alterations, extra printed additions, slips of paper, showing additions or alterations and a whole variety of annotations on the original open record. The copy of the open record which is used in this way is then available to allow printing of the pleadings as altered. This document is called the closed record. Both parties, by that time, will usually have their own copy of the open record with all of the adjustments and annotations, so that this can be checked against any closed record which is the product of this process. The process is far from sophisticated[40] and it can often be difficult to follow the pleadings in such an open record.

When the record closes, after the adjustment period or any continuation of it, the pursuer has to make up a closed record. Within four weeks of the closing of the record he must send a copy of the closed record to the defender and every other party and he must lodge three copies of the closed record in process. When lodging the closed record he will also enrol a motion for further procedure in the case. This will be either as agreed or, in the absence of agreement, to be fixed by order of the court.[41]

A party is entitled to insist on a case going to a procedure roll hearing if he wishes but, if so, that party must lodge a note of arguments[42] which should set out the details of the legal point(s) which he proposes to raise. There is no accepted style for this and no directions as to how brief or otherwise it must be.

Reference should be made to the rules themselves and to the other **5–20** chapters in this book for details of the following procedures:

Chapter 23—motions[43];
Chapter 24—amendment[44];
Chapter 25—counterclaims[45];
Chapter 26—third party procedure[46];
Chapter 35—recovery of evidence.[47]

---

[40] And compares poorly with the use of modern IT tracking facilities for document changes which are preferred in commercial actions.

[41] Hence, the case would, in these circumstances, call on the "by order (adjustment) roll".

[42] Normally within 28 days of the interlocutor appointing the case to the procedure roll.

[43] See para.15–03, below.

[44] See paras 17–12 and 17–13, below.

[45] See para.15–12, below.

[46] See para.15–08, below.

[47] See para.18–11, below.

5–21 Chapter 25A—*Devolution issues*: New rules were added, with effect from May 6, 1999, whereby a party who wants to raise a "devolution issue"[48] which arises in the pleadings of any action pending before the court can do so by virtue of certain special procedures. In essence, the rules provide that the party raising the issue must specify in the pleadings exactly what the issue is, so that the court can decide if an issue does indeed arise. If so, there is provision for intimation of the issue on the Advocate General and the Lord Advocate.[49] They can respond to the intimation by making written submissions on the issue if they wish. The matter must then be reported to the Inner House for a decision, and possibly thereafter to the judicial committee of the Privy Council. There are provisions for the sist (postponement) of the progress of the action until a devolution issue is decided.

5–22 Chapter 28—*Procedure roll*: The Court of Session name for the hearing at which the parties will debate preliminary pleas[50] is a hearing on the procedure roll.[51] The party who wishes to argue his preliminary plea at the procedure roll hearing will have lodged and intimated a note of arguments to give prior notice of the points which are being taken. In some cases, there will be a fixed date for this hearing arranged to suit the parties especially if it is likely to be complex or lengthy. Otherwise, the date will be fixed at relatively short notice and it is for the parties to organise the necessary appearance once the case has been published on the rolls as calling on procedure roll.

5–23 Chapter 29—*Abandonment*: After a pursuer raises an action, he may decide, for a variety of reasons that he does not wish to proceed with it. In theory, he could simply not comply with the necessary procedural requirements of the court and incur a decree by default. He might alternatively decide to take no steps to seek a diet for hearing of the case. That is regarded as an unsatisfactory way in which to signify that the case is not to be proceeded with. It may be significant (for the purposes of res judicata)[52] that an action has been raised, and is still in existence without being formally disposed of. It may be significant that a particular decree has been or will be granted in connection with the original proceedings.

These rules allow the pursuer a procedure formally to abandon an action whereby the pursuer can preserve his right to raise the action again if appropriate. The pursuer can lodge a minute of abandonment which is a written document lodged in process. He can consent to decree of absolvitor, in which case he is agreeing that he cannot raise these proceedings again, or he can ask the court for a decree of dismissal, in which case he could raise the action again. However, the court shall not

---

[48] As defined in, inter alia, Sch.6 to the Scotland Act 1998.
[49] In relation to Scottish issues.
[50] See Ch.4.
[51] Called a debate in the sheriff court.
[52] See para.19–24, below.

grant decree of dismissal unless full judicial expenses have been paid to the defender within a set time limit. The price of obtaining a decree of dismissal is the expenses of the first action.[53] If the pursuer does not pay the expenses within the time limit in the rules then the defender will be entitled to decree of absolvitor.[54]

Chapter 30—*Withdrawal of agents*: Sometimes the solicitors who have **5–24** been instructed to act for a client who is a party to an action in the courts[55] will have to withdraw from acting. This could be necessary for a number of reasons. For example, the client may have refused to follow advice given in the case, he may not have contacted his solicitor to give further instructions to enable the solicitor to deal with the case, or he may not be able to afford the cost of legal representation to take the case to its conclusion. Solicitors would not withdraw from acting for a client lightly but it does happen and often it happens close to a date for a hearing of the case at which it might be expected that the court would be likely to reach some significant decision about it.

It is necessary to have rules regarding the way in which a solicitor can advise the court that he is no longer acting so that no one will be expecting him to represent the client at callings of the case. It is also necessary to make provision for bringing to the notice of the client that the court is aware of the position and will be expecting the client to notify the court as quickly as possible if he still intends to proceed with the case. It would be unfair to the opponent if the case could be delayed and hearings postponed just because the opponent has parted company with his solicitor.[56]

These brief rules say that when a solicitor withdraws from acting in a case he shall write and advise the deputy principal clerk and all of the other parties in the action. If invited by the opponent to do so, the court will make an order allowing the opponent to write to the client with a standard form of letter[57] and advise him that he has 14 days to let the clerk know what he intends to do with the action, failing which the court can make a finding against the client. There is a standard form of response attached to the notice which the client is required to complete. A failure to intimate an intention to proceed as required will usually lead to the action being dismissed or the pursuer obtaining the decree sought.

Chapter 31—*Minutes of sist and transference*: This should not be con- **5–25** fused with a sist (postponement) of an action. If a party to an action dies, or comes under a legal incapacity, during the court action any person claiming to represent him can apply to the court to be sisted (i.e. added)

---

[53] See *Esso Petroleum Co. Ltd v Hall Russell & Co Ltd*, 1988 S.L.T. 33 and *Castlegreen Storage & Distributors Ltd v Schreiber*, 1982 S.L.T. 269.
[54] And can argue res judicata if any attempt was made to re-raise proceedings later.
[55] And whose details will inevitably appear on the court documents in the process.
[56] See *Munro & Miller (Pakistan) Ltd v Wyvern Structures Ltd*, 1996 S.L.T. 1356.
[57] See Form 30.2.

to the action as a party. In similar circumstances, where no one wants to be sisted as a party, another person[58] can apply to the court to have the case transferred and directed against anyone who is thought to represent the deceased or his estate.

5–26 **Chapter 33**—*Caution and security*: There are a number of circumstances in which the court can make an order for a party to find security, in the form of a guarantee or the like, for the costs of the litigation. Litigation is expensive and a person pursuing a claim who does not have the resources to finance his opponent's expenses (if the opponent wins) can put the opponent to considerable expense in defending a case of no real substance. In certain circumstances, the court can order that person to find security for the costs of the action and to satisfy the court that such security is in place before he is allowed to proceed with a case. The best recent example of such a case in which there was full discussion of the principles involved was *McTear's Executrix v Imperial Tobacco Ltd*,[59] a case in which the widow of a man who had died of lung cancer wanted to sue the tobacco company who sold the cigarettes. They said that they would be put to immense expense defending a claim which had little prospect of success and the pursuer ought to find caution before being allowed to proceed. The legal principles upon which the court's decision will rest are not as simple as asking if the party can afford to bring the litigation or pay the costs.[60] It is a matter within the discretion of the court and poverty is not the only issue.[61] It is rare to order a defender to find caution.

Caution can be found either by obtaining a bond of caution[62] or by consigning[63] a sum of money with the accountant of court. The rules deal with the administrative details of this. It is also provided that if a party fails to find caution as required then the opponent can apply by motion for decree as appropriate.

5–27 **Chapter 36**—*Proofs*: There are rules regarding citation of witnesses, lodging of productions, admission of written evidence and recording of evidence.[64]

5–28 **Chapter 37**—*Jury trials*: There are special rules for jury trials. Reference should be made to the rules themselves for details, and to Ch.18 of this book.

---

[58] Perhaps the opponent.
[59] *McTear's Executrix v Imperial Tobacco Ltd*, 1996 S.L.T. 530.
[60] See *Cairns v Chief Constable, Strathclyde Police* Unreported October 22, 2004 Ex Div. See also *Thomson v Ross*, 2001 S.L.T. 807 ; *Monarch Energy Ltd v Powergen Retail Ltd*, 2006 S.L.T. 743.
[61] See *Kennedy v Hamilton Brothers Oil and Gas Ltd*, 1986 S.L.T. 110.
[62] Often from an insurance company.
[63] i.e. depositing.
[64] See Ch.18 for details.

Chapters 38 to 41—These rules deal with the different forms of appeal **5–29** which can be taken in the Court of Session, usually to the Inner House. There are rules regarding appeals from a judge of the Outer House to the Inner House. It should be noted that such an appeal is called a "reclaiming motion". There are rules regarding appeal from the verdict of a jury in a civil case, properly called an application or motion for a new trial. There are extensive rules regarding appeals from an inferior court, primarily the sheriff court. There are detailed rules regarding appeals under certain statutes, which may be taken by a procedure known as a stated case. Furthermore, there are rules regarding appeals against the decision of a tribunal (other than those which can be done by stated case) in which a special simplified form of appeal is provided.

Chapter 42—*Taxation of accounts*: There are extensive rules regard- **5–30** ing the taxation of accounts of expenses incurred in Court of Session actions and regarding witness fees and solicitors' fees. Tables of solicitors' fees for particular types of litigation work are contained in the rules and are updated regularly as the scale of charges alters. Specific provision is made for the assessment of speculative fees to solicitors and counsel.[65]

Many of the remaining rules of the Court of Session (remember there are 85 Chapters of them) deal with some matters which are covered specifically in other parts of this book.[66] The other rules concern specific types of cases, which may have special rules that can be relatively short or quite detailed. Reference should be made to the other rules. There are not too many actions of these other types but it is necessary to know that different procedures do exist. For example, the Insolvency Act 1986 makes provision, inter alia, for the appointment of a receiver to a limited company. Rules 74.16–74.19 provide that application for appointment of a receiver should be done by a petition which ought to include certain specific averments designed to assist the court which is considering the petition to decide if it would be appropriate to do so. There are special rules regarding service and advertisement of the petition. There are rules regarding the procedure which would be appropriate once a receiver has been appointed and regarding other applications to the court in connection with the receivership.

Summary

The distinctive features of Court of Session ordinary procedure include: **5–31**

(1) There is no court generated timetable for the progress of an action through the different stages of procedure. There are rules providing timescales for various steps of procedure[67] but a careful study will

---

[65] These rules are explained in Ch.21.
[66] e.g. judicial review and commercial actions.
[67] e.g. lodging defences or adjusting pleadings.

show that these come into play only after there is some trigger from a party—usually the pursuer. For example, adjustment is to last eight weeks from the lodging of the open record. If the pursuer delays in lodging the record the adjustment period will not start to run until later than it should. That is not a criticism, but it has already been noted[68] that such practices will delay the progress of an action. There are many other examples, and in practice both parties are usually reluctant to complain about delays at these stages of procedure. Another example is the delay in lodging a closed record and a motion for further procedure after the adjustment period is completed. This may not be readily picked up by the court and there is unlikely to be objection from the opponent (the defender). This can easily extend the time taken by any court action without any obvious justification. In this way, the parties may exercise real practical control over the pace of the litigation;

(2) There is little case management of the procedures in an ordinary action by the judges themselves. This can be contrasted with the approach to procedure in commercial actions which we will see in Ch.7;

(3) The use of published rolls of cases as a means of drawing to the attention of parties any significant dates for their cases, can be contrasted with a system whereby the court simply advises parties directly of the date or dates fixed for each individual case;

(4) The rules contain very few provisions regarding the actual conduct of an ordinary action. These matters are covered by practice which has evolved over the years. One benefit of the Court of Session is that there is a degree of consistency of approach which assists practitioners. This can be contrasted with practice in the sheriff court which can vary quite considerably from court to court and between different parts of the country.

Further development and changes in the rules of procedure may be more likely in relation to individual types of action rather than a complete review of the standard ordinary action procedure for the generality of actions raised there. There are already separate and distinct rules for the many diverse types of actions dealt with there. There is no reason why there has to be one general form of procedure for all kinds of action,[69] and it is difficult to predict what changes are likely to materialise after the Civil Courts Review has taken place. There certainly seems to be resistance to the principle of judges in the Court of Session taking an active case management role in the progress of ordinary actions.

---

[68] See Lord Cullen, *Review of Business in the Outer House of the Court of Session* (Edinburgh: Scottish Courts Administration, 1996).

[69] Although a proliferation of different procedures may lead to confusion—for practitioners and students alike.

Flow charts of procedure

This flow chart shows the principle stages in the procedure of a stan- **5–32** dard action as envisaged in the rules. In practice, there can often be reasons why the action might be diverted from the standard procedure to be expected. A sist of action may delay matters considerably. A motion might have a significant effect on the procedural progress of an action. An amendment might also have a significant impact. However, it would be misleading to think that all cases will inevitably follow the flow of procedure set out in the rules. A random analysis of actual court cases will show various good reasons for the procedure going down a different path. For example, a successful motion to bring in a second defender in an action which is heading towards a proof might cause the progress of the action to go back to a point very close to the beginning and then further procedure in the action might go down a completely different route to what had already been planned.

Court of Session
Ordinary Action
Flow Chart of Procedure

5–33

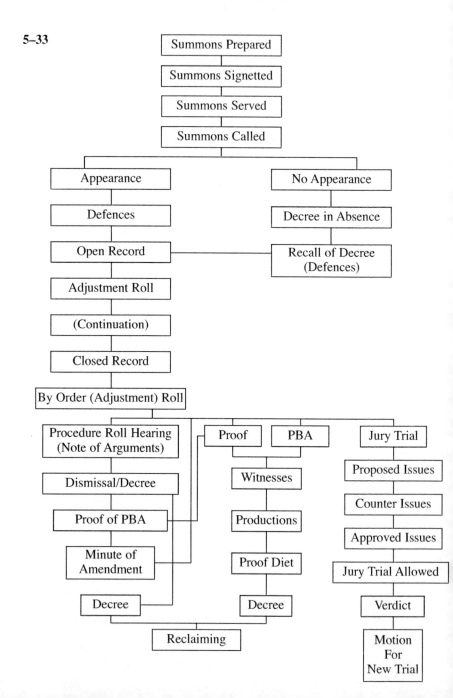

Summons Prepared

Summons Signetted

Summons Served

Summons Called

Appearance

No Appearance

Defences

Decree in Absence

Open Record

Recall of Decree
(Defences)

Adjustment Roll

(Continuation)

Closed Record

By Order (Adjustment) Roll

Procedure Roll Hearing
(Note of Arguments)

Proof

PBA

Jury Trial

Dismissal/Decree

Proposed Issues

Proof of PBA

Witnesses

Counter Issues

Minute of
Amendment

Productions

Approved Issues

Decree

Proof Diet

Jury Trial Allowed

Reclaiming

Decree

Verdict

Motion
For
New Trial

CHAPTER 6

PERSONAL INJURY ACTIONS IN THE COURT OF SESSION

As we have seen in the previous chapter, in 1995 Lord Cullen was **6–01** requested to carry out a review of the way in which the business in the Outer House of the Court of Session was conducted. He was asked to consider, inter alia, what measures should be taken to simplify procedure, expedite the disposal of cases, achieve a greater degree of judicial management of cases, minimise delays in settlement, and ensure that judicial time was used to best advantage. He reported in December 1995 with various recommendations for procedural changes in all cases in the Court of Session. These recommendations were not implemented at the time.

Thereafter, Lord Coulsfield was asked to monitor business coming into the Court of Session over a short period of time and see if it would be possible to identify, at an early stage, those cases which could be regarded as being of a, "more routine nature" and would benefit from procedural change. Many of the cases which came under review were personal injury claims which have always formed a large proportion of the ordinary actions raised in the general department of the Court of Session. Following this, on October 9, 1997 the Lord President appointed a working party chaired by Lord Coulsfield whose remit was to consider:

> ". . . whether, recognising that there is a group of cases, mainly cases of personal injury, which might reasonably be described as routine and which form a substantial proportion of the business of the Court, a simplified procedure could be devised which would eliminate unnecessary delay and unnecessary expense for these cases and make the most efficient use of the time of Judges and Court staff".

At that time, the Court of Session had a special procedure which was available, but not compulsory, for personal injury actions[1] which could reasonably be described as a simplified procedure, but it had not proved particularly popular or effective.[2]

---

[1] This was called optional procedure (for personal injury actions)—parties had an option whether to use it or not.

[2] See Hennessy, *Civil Procedure and Practice*, 1st edn (Edinburgh: W. Green, 2000), Ch.6 for an explanation of this.

6–02   The working party reported in 2000 and made three main recommendations regarding proposals for procedure in personal injury actions. These were that (1) there should be an automatic timetable laid down for personal injury cases which would be monitored by court staff; (2) that the parties should be obliged to produce and lodge in process justified valuations of the claim at an early stage in the proceedings; and (3) parties should be required to meet and discuss settlement at a defined stage in the procedure and make and lodge a minute of that meeting recording the points on which agreement had or had not been achieved.

It had been observed in the research carried out for the report that 98.2 per cent of all personal injury actions settled without proof. The detailed and elaborate procedures demanded of any Court of Session action could therefore, on one view, be regarded as somewhat academic and unnecessary. The report concentrated on proposals for procedural change which would bring forward the actual date of settlement of such cases.[3]

The report also made recommendations regarding the simplification of court pleadings in such cases and proposed that very simplified pleadings were all that were required. This recommendation did not initially find favour, but Lord Coulsfield was asked to convene a representative group of the original working party to re-examine the extent to which the original proposals regarding pleadings could be revised. The group made minimal changes to their original views and the whole proposals then went forward for the preparation of a comprehensive set of procedural rules to apply in all personal injury actions raised in the Court of Session. The procedures are a radical alteration to the way of conducting litigation in Scotland, and it will be seen that many of the standard features of our civil litigation procedures which are explained in this book simply do not apply to this kind of action.

The new rules for personal injuries actions were set out in the Act of Sederunt (Rules of the Court of Session Amendment No.2) (Personal Injuries Actions) 2002,[4] which came into force on April 1, 2003. The rules provide a completely new chapter, Ch.43, in the Court of Session Rules[5] and incorporate most of the recommendations made in the earlier reports. The rules do not apply to any personal injury action raised before April 1, 2003 but any personal injury actions raised in the Court of Session after that date must be raised and conducted under this procedure unless, in the course of the action, a motion is made to withdraw it from this procedure and have it proceed as an ordinary action.[6] As a

---

[3] Many of which settled on the morning of the proof itself and one-third of which were noted to have settled in the last week before the proof.

[4] Act of Sederunt (Rules of the Court of Session Amendment No.2) (Personal Injuries Actions) 2002 (SSI 2002/570).

[5] They replace all of the rules regarding optional procedure in personal injury actions. Optional procedure no longer exists.

[6] See r.43.5(1).

result of a practical problem with the terms of one of the rules, a further Act of Sederunt was soon issued. This was the Act of Sederunt (Rules of the Court of Session Amendment No.4) (Personal Injuries Actions) 2004.[7] It came into effect on June 29, 2004.[8]

An interesting feature of the introduction of this whole new regime **6–03** was the effort which was made to prepare, inform, and encourage participants to understand and embrace its provisions. Seminars were held for prospective litigators in anticipation of the rules coming into operation and it was recognised that they would constitute a significant "culture shock" for those involved. It was appreciated that the orderly and sensible adoption of the rules would be better achieved by explanation and consensus rather than by imposing sanctions on the users for any failure to observe them. Similarly, the continuing operation of the procedure is kept under review by the users of it, including solicitors, counsel, clerks and the judiciary. The practical operation of the rules is being monitored by a users group, comprising representatives of those principally involved in such actions, under the chairmanship of Lady Paton.[9] It meets regularly to keep matters under review.

The Scottish Courts website[10] has a dedicated site containing the latest information on the application of the rules. It also contains articles and other information about the rules and their application. It is intended to update the information on the website from time to time. Court decisions relating to the application of the rules can also be accessed on the Scottish Courts website,[11] and details will be given in this chapter. A useful snapshot of the operation of the procedures and issues arising from their implementation can be found in the Personal Injury User Group newsletter of September 2007.[12]

The precise nature, effect and meaning of the rules are being refined as they operate. Fairly significant practice notes have already been issued and this has been done in order to modify, expand upon or clarify matters arising from the operation of the rules. The rules provide the framework for the procedure but the practice notes, far more than in other forms of procedure,[13] contain details of the administrative and

---

[7] Act of Sederunt (Rules of the Court of Session Amendment No.4) (Personal Injuries Actions) 2004 (SSI 2004/291).

[8] For details see para.6–07, below.

[9] An Outer House judge.

[10] At *http://www.scotcourts.gov.uk* [Accessed August 18, 2008]. There is a dedicated page which contains the report of the working group, the rules, all practice notes affecting them, newsletters with minutes of meetings of the users group, articles about the procedure, and some of the forms used in the procedure. From time to time new advice and directives to users will be added.

[11] Relatively few of them seem to be reported.

[12] Which can be viewed per the Scottish Courts website at *http://www.scotcourts.gov.uk* [Accessed August 18, 2008].

[13] Although commercial actions in the Court of Session now have quite significant practice notes.

other requirements expected in the conduct of any litigation under this form of procedure. The underlying principle is that the rules should be interpreted in an enabling manner, i.e. with a view to achieving the aims and objectives of the procedure. It is relatively early in the life of the rules to make any detailed assessment of their benefits or otherwise. They have not produced the chaos which doubters predicted. Settlements seem to be occurring earlier than formerly. Teething problems appear to have been largely solved.[14]

NARRATIVE

6–04 The procedure in personal injuries actions in the Court of Session is quite significantly different from other forms of procedure in other types of action. However, reference should be made to the narrative of procedure in Court of Session ordinary actions[15] as a reminder of the terminology and the basic background. It should be noted that, where the specific rules in Ch.43 make no provision, the RCS will apply.[16] This summary simply contains the essentials of the personal injury procedure itself.

A party who wants to raise a personal injuries action in the Court of Session must do so under this new procedure. The written statement of the case in the summons will be much simpler than that required in an ordinary action. The summons will include a brief outline of the circumstances of the accident or other event which gave rise to the injury. It will give the briefest outline of the legal basis for the claim, i.e. a simple statement that there was common law negligence or breach of a specific statute. It will also include the amount of the sum claimed, but that figure will not be broken down or specified in any way at that stage. There will be no pleas in law.

At the time when the summons is presented for signetting, it is open to the pursuer's solicitor also to present a specification of documents in a standard style. The style is prescribed in the rules and would permit the pursuer to recover basic documents of a kind which would usually be needed in any personal injury claim, such as medical records, wage records and records of risk assessments in employers' liability cases. This specification will be automatically granted by the clerk at the outset of the case, provided that it is in the prescribed form.

After the summons has been signetted, it will be served on the defender in the normal way. The defender has the same time in which to

---

[14] For a detailed assessment of the operation of the rules see the report entitled *Managing procedure: Evaluation of New Rules for actions of damages for, or arising from, personal injuries in the court of Session (Chapter 43)*. Scottish Government, 2007.
[15] See Ch.5.
[16] e.g. the dispensing power in r.2.1 of the RCS applies to this procedure.

respond as in an ordinary action. After the expiry of the period of notice, the pursuer can then lodge the summons for calling. The defenders then have seven days after the calling within which to lodge defences. The defences should not contain any pleas in law and may be equally as brief as the summons.

Once defences have been lodged, the court will issue a timetable for **6–05** various steps of procedure in the action itself. In particular, the timetable will provide when the proof in the action is to be heard. This is expected to be around 12 months from the date of the lodging of defences. The parties will, accordingly, know at a very early stage when the case has been scheduled for a full hearing of evidence. Parties are expected to work towards that date which is unlikely to be adjourned or discharged easily.

The timetable issued to the parties also contains a period of time within which they will be allowed to adjust their pleadings but again it should be noted that the emphasis is on simplified pleadings so extensive adjustment is not expected. It is expected that the adjustment period will last for about two months after the date of defences and then the record will close. Two weeks after the record closes, the pursuer will enrol a motion for appropriate further procedure depending upon what issues arise between the parties.

It is expected that in most cases the further procedure will be a proof or jury trial. If a party wants another form of procedure (e.g. a procedure roll hearing) then that party has to enrol a motion in writing, seeking that particular form of procedure and justifying it. Such a motion will not be granted easily, because the intention of the court is to advance cases towards a proof with little opportunity for procedural delay.

Around the same time that the adjustment of the pleadings ends, the **6–06** pursuer has to lodge a statement of his valuation of the claim. This will be a detailed statement on a prescribed form which breaks down the claim into individual heads of claim and specifies the amounts sought under each head. This statement must be lodged in process and intimated to the defender. The defender will have a further eight weeks or so within which to lodge his statement of valuation of the claim, on the same prescribed form, in response. A failure to lodge the statement of valuation of the claim and a failure to comply with the timetable as required will lead to the court fixing a hearing on its own initiative and seeking an explanation for the failure. In extreme cases, a failure to comply with these requirements could lead to decree against one or other party.

Any productions for the proof have to be lodged eight weeks before the proof. Lists of witnesses for the proof also have to be lodged eight weeks before the proof. No later than four weeks before the proof, there must be a meeting between the parties to discuss settlement, and to discuss what matters of evidence could be agreed without prejudice to any questions of liability. The parties are required to complete and sign a minute in relation to that meeting, which has to be lodged in court. This is in a prescribed form and the parties have to confirm that certain specific matters were discussed at the meeting and record the important issues on which agreement was or was not reached. The minute has to be lodged at least three weeks before the proof. A failure to lodge such a minute will lead to the court ordering a hearing for an explanation.

Thereafter, the case will normally proceed to a proof or jury trial at which evidence can be led of most matters relating to the accident and the injuries, whether covered specifically by the pleadings or not. Arguments may also arise in relation to matters of law, albeit these may not be specifically focused in the pleadings. It is anticipated that any such legal issues will be identified and clarified at the pre-trial meeting. It will be something of a shock to parties who are used to conducting a proof with full and detailed pleadings on all of the points in issue, including a full description and explanation of the circumstances of an accident, to have to conduct it with no more than a basic outline of what allegedly happened and why there should be liability on a defender. Questions of whether a party has been given fair notice of the opponent's case will no doubt be interpreted broadly. It is expected that there will be an emphasis on what information has been made available to the opponent in some form or other prior to a hearing rather than focusing strictly on what information is provided in the written pleadings.

SPECIFIC RULES

6–07 Many of the RCS rules mentioned in Ch.5 will still apply to personal injuries actions. However, it may be apparent that some of the "traditional" rules have been disapplied to personal injuries actions and those which remain in place for such actions may not sit comfortably with the new procedures.[17] There have already been a number of decided cases on the application of the rules. The procedures and practices are still developing and there are regular illustrations of their operation in unreported cases on the Scottish Courts website.[18]

6–08 **Rule 43.1**—"Personal injuries action" means an action of damages for, or arising from, personal injuries or death of a person from personal injures. "Personal injuries" includes any disease or impairment whether

---

[17] A problem of this nature gave rise to Act of Sederunt (Rules of the Court of Session Amendment No.4) (Personal Injuries Actions) 2004 (SSI 2004/291) referred to in para.6–02, above, which disapplied the rule regarding pleas in law in defences in ordinary actions (RCS r.18.1(1)(b)).

[18] A search on the court judgments section of the Scottish Courts website (*http://www.scotcourts.gov.uk* [Accessed August 1, 2008]) specifying "Chapter 43" will produce more cases than the reader might appreciate!

physical or mental.[19] All claims for damages for personal injury raised in the Court of Session must be initiated by way of the personal injury procedure. However, it was soon recognised in practice that actions for damages for personal injury based upon allegations of clinical negligence would often be too complex and detailed, and unsuitable for this abbreviated procedure. Accordingly, r.43.1A[20] provided that a party raising such an action may apply to the court at the outset to raise such an action as an ordinary action. This is intended to avoid the delay and expense of raising the action in the abbreviated form and then redrafting it as an ordinary action.

Rule 43.2—This prescribes the form of summons to be used in personal **6–09** injury actions. Reference should be made to Form 43.2A containing the outline of the statement of claim for use in personal injury cases. The form is brief and the rule provides that there shall be annexed to the form a brief statement containing (a) averments in numbered paragraphs relating only to those facts necessary to establish the claim, and (b) the details of every doctor or hospital from whom the injured person received treatment for their personal injuries.

There is an emphasis on brevity, and reference should be made to the report of the working party in 2000 and the supplementary report on written pleadings.[21] The general approach by the working group was to suggest a method of pleading which encouraged brevity and simplicity and discouraged technicality and artificiality. It was also suggested that the pleadings should be couched in such a way as to require individual answers to particular averments of fact. It was recognised that there will be exceptional cases in which this approach might not be appropriate but, even in these cases, considerable simplification of "standard" pleadings would be desirable and expected. It was suggested that some guidance on acceptable styles of pleading might be provided in practice notes, but this has not materialised although there are "illustrations" in the supplementary report which can no doubt be adopted with some confidence.

In the case of *Clifton v Hays Plc*,[22] the court said that there was nothing in the rules which detracted from the basic principle that the defenders were entitled to be able to ascertain from the summons, without

---

[19] See *Tudhope v Finlay Park*, 2003 S.L.T. 1305, Lady Paton, and then 2004 S.L.T. 783, Lord Cameron. This was a claim against solicitors for failing to raise an action for personal injury within the triennium. Lady Paton considered that the summons should be presented as a personal injury action on the basis that it "arose from" a personal injury. Lord Cameron thereafter granted a motion to remove it from the procedure on the basis that the personal injury procedure was not appropriate or applicable to such an action.

[20] Introduced by Act of Sederunt (Rules of the Court of Session Amendment No.4) (Personal Injuries Actions etc.) 2007 (SSI 2007/282).

[21] See para.6–02, above.

[22] *Clifton v Hays Plc*, 2004 G.W.D. 2-23, per Lady Smith.

undue difficulty, the nature of the case against them. A pursuer ought not to raise an action against a defender except where he has information to make out a relevant case. This was quite an extreme example but drew attention to the requirement in the rule that the pursuer must (at least) state the facts necessary to establish the claim against the particular defender. That should include the facts from which any relevant legal duty against the defender could be inferred and an absence of such facts (whether omitted in the interests of brevity or otherwise) could lead to dismissal of the action.

In *Higgins v DHL International (UK) Ltd*[23] the court refused to allow a jury trial after consideration of the pursuer's pleadings which were considered to be lacking in the specification which would have been necessary for a fair trial to be heard. The pleadings were considered sufficient for a proof however and the judge, Lady Paton, said that:

> "I recognise that there is a degree of conflict between, on the one hand, the new personal injury rules (which encourage and indeed demand brevity in pleadings) and . . . the formalities and practicalities of a civil jury trial".[24]

There are other means, beyond the pleadings, for ascertaining the other party's position on various aspects of the claim and it is still open to defenders to seek a procedure roll hearing when a claim is plainly irrelevant. The practical application of the rule about pleadings will, undoubtedly, remain under review[25].

6–10 Rule 43.2(4)—A summons may include a specification of documents in a prescribed form (Form 43.2B). There are six separate types of documents which may be recovered in this way and the pursuer selects which of the documents is appropriate and necessary. If the summons contains a specification of documents as described, then once the summons is signetted the specification, "shall be granted". This is designed to give the claimant an automatic entitlement at a very early stage of the proceedings to recover what might be regarded as the "routine" documents which are often required in any personal injury claim. These include

---

[23] *Higgins v DHL International (UK) Ltd*, 2003 S.L.T. 1301.
[24] Other decisions about the allowance, or otherwise, of jury trials in personal injury cases include *Green v Chief Constable, Lothian and Borders Police*, 2004 S.C.L.R. 301; *Jones v M.K. Leslie Ltd*, 2004 G.W.D. 16-354; and *Patterson v Somerville* Unreported OH January 7, 2005.
[25] See *Slessor v Vetco Gray UK Ltd*, 2007 S.L.T. 400, and then Unreported OH July 13, 2007, per Lord Emslie. There is also a requirement for the defenders to give fair notice of their defence in their pleadings, abbreviated though they may be. See *Weir v Robertson Group (Construction) Ltd*, Unreported OH, July 11, 2006, Lord Glennie, and *McGowan v W. & J.R. Watson Ltd*, 2007 S.L.T. 169.

hospital and GP records, wage records of the pursuer's employers, any recoverable accident reports held by the defenders,[26] and risk assessments carried out by the defenders.

Rule 43.3—This provides for service and calling of a summons. If it **6–11** does not call within three months and a day from the date when it is signetted[27] then the instance shall fall. This is designed to ensure that if a pursuer raises an action, then he proceeds to serve and call the action without delay. Efforts to extend that time period by invoking the dispensing power in r.2.1 were authoritatively defeated by the Inner House recently and perhaps the stringency of this rule will be relaxed in the future.[28]

Rule 43.4—The specification of documents which may be attached **6–12** to the summons, if the pursuer chooses, will automatically be granted when the summons is signetted and the pursuer can then proceed to recover the documents under the normal procedures available in an ordinary action. If the pursuer (or the defender) wants to recover other relevant documents then they can both do so under the ordinary (RCS) rules and procedures.

Rule 43.5—Any party to an action may within 28 days of the lodging of **6–13** defences apply by motion to have the action withdrawn from this procedure and be appointed to proceed as an ordinary action. No motion shall be granted unless the court is satisfied that there are "exceptional reasons" for not following the personal injuries procedure. In deciding whether there are exceptional reasons the judge is directed to take into account the likely need for detailed pleadings, the length of time required for preparation of the action, and any other relevant circumstances.[29]

At present, there is only one general type of action identified[30] as usually inappropriate for the personal injury procedure. As we have noted, actions for medical negligence may avoid this procedure. Actions arising out of industrial diseases might be considered inappropriate[31]. Actions for sexual abuse might also be considered inappropriate.

---

[26] It should be noted that only certain specified accident reports are recoverable—see Allan G. Walker and Norman M. L. Walker, *The Law of Evidence in Scotland*, edited by Margaret L. Ross with James Chalmers, 2nd edn (Edinburgh: T. & T. Clark, 2000).

[27] As opposed to the date when it is served, as provided in the ordinary rules.

[28] See *Brogan v O'Rourke Ltd*, 2005 S.L.T. 29; overruling *Jackson v McDougall*, 2004 S.L.T. 770 and *Roberts v Chisholm*, 2004 S.L.T. 1171.

[29] In the case of *Broadfoot v Forth Valley Acute Hospitals NHS Trust* Unreported OH July 3, 2003, the judge considered that a case of alleged medical negligence at birth should be remitted to the ordinary roll. Reference has already been made above to the case of *Tudhope v Finlay Park* Unreported OH January 7, 2004, where a remit was made.

[30] Or prescribed in the rules.

[31] Special procedures were canvassed for certain cases involving claims by relatives of those suffering from mesothelioma following *Dow v West of Scotland Shipbreaking Co Ltd* Unreported OH, April 5, 2007, Lady Paton.

Actions involving a multiplicity of defenders and complex legal issues or novel legal propositions might also be inappropriate, but the judge has a wide discretion. The need to find "exceptional reasons" clearly means that actions will not easily be withdrawn from the procedure. It is difficult to predict what individual personal injury action, or type of personal injury action, might provide exceptional reasons and each case must be considered on its own circumstances.[32] A pursuer and defender in such an action would require to prepare pleadings in the abbreviated form before any such motion and then, if granted, the pleadings would have to be "converted" to the traditional form.

6–14 **Rule 43.6**—Once defences have been lodged, the court shall allocate a diet for the proof of the action.[33] The court shall also issue a timetable for various procedural steps in the action and set down specific dates for the following:

(1) when any application for a third party notice may be made;
(2) when the pursuer may execute a commission for recovery of documents;
(3) when the parties should complete adjustment of their pleadings;
(4) when the pursuer is to lodge a statement of valuation of claim;
(5) when the pursuer should lodge a record;
(6) when the defender (and any third party) should lodge a statement of valuation of claim;
(7) when the parties have to lodge a list of witnesses and productions upon which they wish to rely[34];
(8) when the pursuer is to lodge in process the minute of the pre trial meeting.

The timetable will state the last date upon which these steps should be taken. Parties are encouraged to take them sooner.[35]

If a party fails to comply with any requirement of the timetable then the case can be put out for a hearing before a judge by order, so that the court can have an explanation for the failure.

6–15 **Rule 43.6(5)**—Once the pursuer lodges the record as required by the provisions of the timetable, the pursuer must enrol a motion asking the court for one of the following:

---

[32] The most recent interesting example is *Cunningham v Glasgow City Council*, 2008 G.W.D. 26-407, in which the judge withdrew an action claiming damages for stress at work and harassment from the Chapter 43 procedure.

[33] The actual date is dictated by the court resources and volume of business.

[34] In *Quigley v Hart Builders (Edinburgh) Ltd* Unreported OH July 28, 2006, Lord Glennie, a party who sought leave to lead a witness not included on any list which had been lodged required leave of the court to do so. This could be allowed but on such terms as the judge thought fit. The terms imposed by the judge were designed to achieve fairness and the interests of justice. See the case for details.

[35] See *Zimmerman v Armstrong*, 2004 S.L.T. 915.

(1) to allow a preliminary proof on any matters specified in the motion;
(2) to allow a proof;
(3) to allow issues for a jury trial;
(4) to make some other order.

Where any party seeks a different order from one to three of the above then that party must enrol a motion specifying the order which is sought and giving notice of the reasons for seeking such an order.

An interesting issue arose in relation to the question of whether the allowance of a proof can also be taken as the allowance of a proof before answer.[36] In *Hamilton v Seamark Systems Ltd*[37] the defenders had a plea in law to the relevancy of the pursuer's pleadings.[38] The pursuer argued that it should be repelled and a "proof" allowed as provided in the above rule. The judge observed that the pleadings in the case did give rise to some questions of law which could only properly be resolved after the facts had been elicited. She allowed a proof before answer but observed that, once the rules about defences not having pleas in law came into existence, the allowance of a "proof" as stated in the rules would not prevent parties making submissions about points of law or mixed issues of fact and law arising from the evidence. In this sense, the allowance of a proof under personal injury procedure may, in practice, be indistinguishable from the allowance of a proof before answer. It was expected that parties would, however, give fair notice of any legal arguments upon which they might rely at a proof and it was suggested that this could be done[39] at the pre-trial meeting between the parties.

Rule 43.6(8)—Any production not lodged in accordance with the **6–16** timetable set out shall not be used at the proof unless both parties consent to this or the court allows it after hearing an explanation.

Rule 43.7—This contains provisions for enforcing the operation of the **6–17** timetable. Where a case is put out by order[40] under these rules, the parties will be given seven days notice of the date of the hearing. The party which is in default will be required to lodge with the court a written explanation as to why the timetable has not been complied with. A copy of that explanation has to be given to the other parties and this has all to be done within two clear working days before the hearing. At the hearing, the judge can make any order he considers appropriate in the light of the circumstances and explanation given, including an award of expenses against the defaulting party.

---

[36] For the distinction between these see Ch.18.
[37] *Hamilton v Seamark Systems Ltd*, 2004 S.C. 543, per Lady Paton.
[38] This was before the change in the rules which excluded pleas in law for the defenders.
[39] Presumably at the latest.
[40] i.e. at the court's instigation.

6–18 Rule 43.8—Any party can apply to have the action sisted by enrolling a motion. The motion can only be granted on "special cause shown". Any sist should be for a specific period and not for an indefinite period of time.[41] Similarly, individual provisions of the timetable issued by the court can be varied on the application of any party by way of motion. A variation of the timetable can only be granted on "special cause shown". This gives parties an opportunity in what, it is assumed, would be very special circumstances, to retain the framework of the procedure but to extend (or perhaps to restrict) the time limits. This gives the procedure a degree of flexibility if there is some good justification for a change.

6–19 Rule 43.9—Each party must lodge and intimate statements of their valuation of the claim and include a list of the supporting documents. At the same time, the party must lodge each of the documents bearing upon their valuation, and upon which they propose to rely. This is considered to be a central and critical feature of the new procedure, and is intended to promote an exchange of information and opinion about the valuation of a claim. This should minimise areas of unnecessary dispute, reduce evidence, and facilitate an earlier approach to settlement by indicating, regardless of the merits of any claim, what each party considers to be a reasonable valuation of the claim. There are some doubts whether reasonable and realistic valuations are always produced by the opposing parties in the course of this process. There is an inevitable temptation for the claimant to overstate the value of his claim and for the defender to understate it, thereby defeating the purpose of facilitating a reasonable approach to the claim.

The statement of the valuation of the claim is to be in a prescribed form, namely Form 43.9, and reference should be made to that form for the details. The form requires a party to break down the valuation of the claim into the component parts of the different heads of claim and ascribe a value to each. The opposing party should be given intimation of the list of any documents which are included by reference in the statement of valuation of claim. The opposing party can inspect those documents he has not had an opportunity to see.

The failure to lodge a statement of the valuation of the claim is given added importance by the terms of r.43.9(7), whereby it is provided that a failure to lodge the statement would automatically trigger a hearing on the by order roll. This could lead to the action being dismissed if the party in default is the pursuer, or alternatively lead to a decree for an amount not exceeding the pursuer's valuation if the party in default is the defender.

The status of the statement of valuation of the claim is not entirely clear. This was considered in *Millar v Watt*,[42] in which the judge consid-

---

[41] In practice it is understood that the court will only grant a sist for three months at a time.
[42] *Millar v Watt*, 2004 G.W.D. 25-530.

ered that it was perfectly competent to look at the reports produced with the pursuer's valuation for the purpose of deciding whether the case was suitable for a jury trial or not. In *Jones v M.K. Leslie Ltd* [43] the judge said that:

> "... a Statement of Valuation of Claim is not a Statement of Claim. This is underlined by a Practice Note referring to such matters which makes it plain that a Statement of Valuation of Claim does not bind the pursuer or defenders. Pleadings do."

In the absence of certain basic details in the pleadings, although very broad information was given in the statement of valuation, he refused a jury trial.[44]

In *Baird v Cowie*, the judge stated that:

> "[To consider whether sufficient specification has been given] the Court will, almost inevitably, now have to look outside the averments in the Statement of Claim to the content of the Statement of Value."[45]

Rule 43.10—Provides for a "pre-trial meeting" which is a unique **6–20** concept so far as our civil litigation procedures are concerned. It is a meeting between the parties to be held not later than four weeks before the date of the proof/jury trial which is to discuss settlement of the action and to agree the matters which are not in dispute between the parties. The parties are obliged to lodge a joint minute in a prescribed form (Form 43.10) which will confirm that certain specified issues were discussed and record the outcome of those discussions. This form must be lodged in process by the pursuer not less than three weeks before the date for the proof/jury trial and a failure to do so by the date specified in the timetable will lead to the case being heard by order. It is specifically provided that, during the pre-trial meeting, the representative of each party shall have access to the party or to another person who has authority to commit the party to settlement of the action. In other words, the meeting is intended to enable parties to reach an actual conclusion of settlement and not take refuge in speculative or possible agreements about settlement which were inconclusive and would neutralise its

---

[43] *Jones v M.K. Leslie Ltd*, 2004 G.W.D. 16-354.

[44] It may be noted that there have been many cases concerning the issue of whether a personal injury case under the new rules is suitable for jury trial or not, as predicted by Lady Paton in *Higgins v DHL International (UK) Ltd*, 2003 S.L.T. 1301. The reasons for this are explained in Ch.18. The most recent example noted is *Ramage v Scottish African Safari Park Ltd* Unreported OH May 8, 2008, Lord Mackay of Drumadoon.

[45] *Baird v Cowie* Unreported OH October 27, 2006, Lord Carloway. The case report contains a good example of a detailed statement of value and detailed observations on specification of a damages claim. He allowed a jury trial despite opposition.

effectiveness.[46] Modification of the information required to be included in
the pre-trial minute as originally prescribed has been dictated by practice.[47]

6–21 Rule 43.11—This contains provisions allowing a pursuer to apply for an
interim payment of damages. The terms under which such an application
can be made are substantially taken from the RCS and will be dealt with
in Ch.16 of this book.

6–22 Rule 43.13—This contains provisions regarding the application for a
payment of further damages following upon an award of provisional
damages. The rules are similar to those in the RCS and are dealt with
more fully in Ch.16 of this book.

6–23 Rule 43.14 to 43.19—These contain provisions regarding claims by an
executor or by relatives following the death of any person from personal
injuries and there are ancillary provisions to do with warrants and service very much as in the case of ordinary actions under the RCS. There
are special provisions for mesothelioma actions contained within a new
r.43.20.[48]

GUIDANCE FOR PRACTITIONERS

6–24 As already stated, the operation of these novel and unique rules
inevitably requires certain administrative directions and guidance as to
how they should apply. In one sense, the court has given up any direct
control during the course of the actions by laying down a timetable for
the parties to follow at the outset. This has been described as "case flow
management", as opposed to "case management". In a straightforward
case, this will mean that the action will not call in court from the time of
inception until the time of proof. On the other hand, the court has power
to supervise the procedure by calling on the parties to explain the position if they do not seem to be doing what they should be doing and when
they should be doing it. It was appreciated that this could give rise to
some doubts as to whether what the parties themselves were doing was
within the spirit and the letter of the rules. As the rules can be seen as
simply providing a basic framework, it was thought important and necessary to provide guidance to practitioners. This could take the form of
decisions, practice notes, and perhaps informal recommendations and
directions via the users group, the website, and experience. Whilst the

[46] For a case on pre-trial meetings see *Zimmerman v Armstrong*, 2004 S.L.T. 915.
[47] See the Act of Sederunt (Rules of the Court of Session Amendment No.4) (Personal Injuries Actions etc.) 2007 (SSI 2007/282).
[48] Introduced by the Act of Sederunt (Rules of the Court of Session Amendment No.4) (Personal Injuries Actions etc.) 2007 (SSI 2007/282).

rules of procedure are provided, the practice has to be shaped to enable it to function properly and effectively.

PRACTICE NOTE NO. 2 OF 2003

This is dated March 14, 2003 and was designed to explain how the **6–25** courts will approach the application and interpretation of the new Rules for Personal Injuries Actions, which were about to come into force in April 2003. As far as I am aware, this is the first time any such direction or guidance has ever been given in relation to the operation of new procedures. Formerly, rules were intended to speak for themselves.

Generally speaking, the practice note comments upon the rules and makes certain observations regarding the rules. These will not be repeated here. Certain specific points to note, however, are that motions to remove the case to the ordinary roll and for alteration of the timetable will not be granted, even if made of consent, unless information to justify such a motion in accordance with the terms of the rule is before the judge. It is also observed that if a case is regarded as suitable for procedure under this chapter, i.e. no motion is made to remove it to the ordinary roll or any such motion, having been made, was not granted, then it is, "most unlikely that a motion to extend a period of time under the timetable will be granted". Motions for acceleration of the timetable will be looked upon sympathetically especially in the case where the pursuer has a life expectancy which doesn't exceed the duration of the timetable.[49]

The practice note also emphasises that the periods and timescales within the timetable will be strictly insisted upon. The appropriate periods will "from time to time" be prescribed by the Lord President and the practice note set out the periods which, it was envisaged, would be prescribed. The more significant periods not specifically mentioned in the rules themselves are:

* The pursuer's valuation is to be lodged by eight weeks from the last date for defences being lodged;
* The adjustment period is to end eight weeks after the last date for defences;
* A motion is to be enrolled for proof or jury trial 10 weeks after defences;
* The defender's valuation is to be lodged 16 weeks after defences;
* The list of witnesses and productions for the parties are to be lodged eight weeks before the proof;
* The pre-trial minute relating to the pre trial settlement meeting is to be lodged 21 days before the proof;

---

[49] Fatal asbestosis and mesothelioma cases would be involved here.

- The proof or jury trial itself is to be assigned to a date approximately 12 months after the date for defences being lodged.

The practice note states that statements of valuation of claim are not binding on the parties who make them, but it will be open to either party to found upon the making of its own statement of valuation or upon that of the other party, presumably in relation to any question of expenses.[50] With regard to pre-trial meetings it is noted that a decision was made not to lay down formal requirements for such a meeting, but parties are encouraged to take steps as are necessary to comply with the letter and the spirit of the rule. There is an obligation to sign a minute of the meeting by counsel or a solicitor advocate on each side, and it is emphasised that by doing so the signatory is accepting responsibility to the court for the conduct of the meeting and the recording of what took place at that meeting.

PRACTICE NOTE NO.3 OF 2003

6–26 Parties are reminded that applications can be made to the court for an accelerated diet of proof or jury trial where there is good reason for doing so.

PRACTICE NOTE NO.3 OF 2004

6–27 All pleadings in personal injury cases should not have pleas in law. Defenders who wish to include in their pleadings an outline of their propositions in law should do so by inserting a brief summary of those propositions in the last answer of the defences.

PRACTICE NOTE NO. 1 OF 2007

6–28 This reminds parties that any productions on which they propose to rely should be lodged generally eight weeks before the proof or jury trial. It also reminds practitioners about the principle of early disclosure of evidence which underlies the procedures designed to facilitate early settlement. The practice of not disclosing expert reports until the last minute, "is to be discouraged". Parties are expected to lodge expert reports on which they intend to rely within a reasonable time of receipt and there may be a penalty in expenses if they do not do so, and fail to comply with the spirit of the personal injuries procedure.

---

[50] Presumably this covers a situation in which the leading of evidence of one or more witnesses about the value of some aspect of the claim could have been avoided if the parties had reasonably and genuinely complied with the requirements of the valuation—and reached some form of agreement on that matter.

Personal Injury Action 6–29

Flowchart

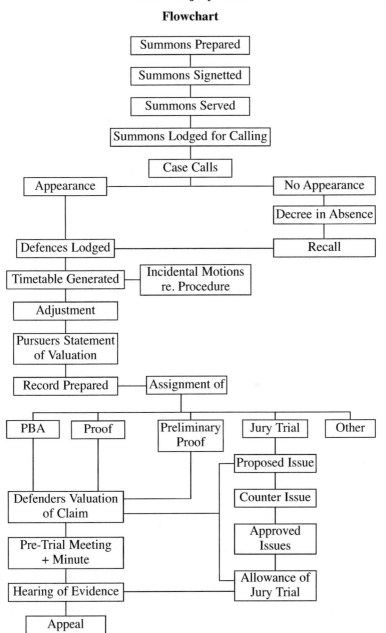

CHAPTER 7

COMMERCIAL ACTIONS IN THE
COURT OF SESSION

7–01 A commercial action in the Court of Session is the name given to certain
actions which can be raised there and which involve a "commercial or
business" subject matter. They are conducted by way of a procedure
which is significantly different to the ordinary procedure in the Court of
Session. There had been special rules of procedure in the Court of
Session for what were called "commercial causes" for some considerable time, but, when the current rules of procedure were introduced in
the Court of Session in 1994, they provided a distinct and unique procedural regime for what are now called "commercial actions".

The reason for having special rules in such cases was that it was felt
that the rules of procedure in an ordinary action were unacceptably formal, complex and slow. Litigating in the Court of Session regarding
commercial disputes was not regarded as a particularly attractive and
rewarding prospect for many business clients and their advisers. The
development of other forms of dispute resolution in business matters,
such as arbitration and alternative dispute resolution ("ADR"), suggested that the prevailing court procedures might not have been satisfy-
ing the requirements of the modern business world. This was apparently
reflected in the fact that relatively few actions were proceeding as commercial causes in the Court of Session in the late 1980s and early 1990s.
There was considered to be a real risk that parties doing business in
Scotland would be so discouraged from bringing their commercial disputes before the Scottish courts because of the perceived inadequacies
and delays in ordinary procedure, that the Court of Session would not be
involved in the ongoing development of Scottish mercantile law.

The new rules for commercial actions represented a radical departure
from the traditional rules of practice and procedure for actions in the
Court of Session. They contain many "modern" features which are significantly different from most other forms of procedure in any other
court. The procedure could be regarded, on the one hand, as representing some of the more advanced thinking in Scotland on the desirable
features of any modern system of civil procedure or, on the other hand,
as an unwelcome and unnecessary departure from accepted and understood procedures which have stood the test of time. The rules are not just
about speeding up court actions (although they are certainly intended to
do that) but they encapsulate a fundamentally different philosophy about

the role of the court in the management of litigation and the ways in which the courts can and should encourage and promote the efficient focusing and resolution of disputes.

The current rules for commercial actions followed upon the *Report of*   **7–02** *the Working Party on Commercial Causes* under the chairmanship of Lord Coulsfield in November 1993. When the general Court of Session rules were altered in 1994, they included specific rules for commercial actions in Ch.47. These rules were, however, amended very soon afterwards by the Act of Sederunt (Rules of the Court of Session 1994 Amendment No.1) (Commercial Actions) 1994[1] so that, with effect from September 20, 1994, the rules in commercial actions are contained within rr.47.1–47.16 of the RCS. The reader might appreciate that this appears to be a relatively small number of rules for what is in effect a completely distinct procedural regime.

However, the rules were to be read along with the terms of the Court of Session Practice Note No.12 of 1994 relating to commercial actions. That practice note was issued in order to explain the way in which it was intended to apply the new rules for commercial actions. In many ways, it was rather novel for the rules to be supplemented to such a significant extent by a practice note, but since the actual rules were fairly brief and the procedure unfamiliar, it was obviously felt that it would be helpful for there to be "guidelines" as to how they were expected to operate. It also made the regime more flexible, as it was, and is, much simpler to issue new practice notes about the way in which the rules of procedure were to operate, and what was expected of those litigators conducting commercial actions, than to change the formal rules themselves[2]. The practice note underlined a number of the unique features of the rules and it was made crystal clear to everyone involved in these actions that they were different, and were to be treated very differently by the court. The practice note also drew attention to the fact that the organisation and administration of commercial actions[3] depended heavily upon modern computer technology.[4]

There has been very little change to the rules since 1994, but recently   **7–03** the Court of Session published a new practice note, Practice Note No.6 of 2004,[5] which can be seen as a very significant development of the philosophy behind the rules and draws upon the experience gained from

---

[1] Act of Sederunt (Rules of the Court of Session 1994 Amendment No.1) (Commercial Actions) 1994 (SI 1994/2310).

[2] For a contemporaneous article on the changes see John MacKenzie, "A World of Change", 2005 J.L.S.S. 50(2) 19.

[3] e.g. court interlocutors produced on computer instantly, the court diary on computer, etc.

[4] It is worthwhile visiting the Scottish Courts website (*http://www.scotcourts.gov.uk* [Accessed October 1, 2008]) on which there is an area dedicated to commercial actions which contains useful information. The opinions in many complex and interesting commercial actions can also be seen on the website.

[5] Which came into operation on January 6, 2005.

the operation of this procedure over the last 10 years. This supersedes the 1994 Practice Note entirely but it repeats many of its original provisions. The most significant feature is that parties and their solicitors are now expected to have discussed and focused on the matters in dispute (and presumably found that, despite reasonable efforts, they cannot resolve their dispute) before commencing a commercial action.

During 1995 there were 130 actions initiated in the Court of Session as commercial actions. The numbers gradually increased and in 2002, there were 232 commercial actions. Since then there has been a reduction and in 2006 there were only 99 actions raised as such.

Narrative

7–04 Where proceedings can competently be raised in the Court of Session and where the type of action falls within the definition of a commercial action, a party can elect to raise an action in that way. He is not obliged to do so. It is assumed that the opposing parties will have been represented by solicitors prior to the raising of proceedings and the solicitors are expected to have taken all reasonable steps to focus on the precise nature and extent of the dispute and to have made genuine efforts to resolve it before going to the extent of raising of such an action.

The terms of the summons that initiates the commercial action can be less detailed than those of an ordinary summons and, if there are documents relied upon by the pursuer in the summons, then he ought to attach to the summons a schedule listing those documents. In practice, the pursuer is expected to lodge the pre-litigation correspondence demonstrating that they have discussed, focused and attempted to resolve the dispute.

The summons will be served in the same way as service for an ordinary action and the defender will indicate an intention to defend the summons similarly. The defences have to be lodged within seven days of the calling and are expected to be somewhat briefer than in an ordinary action, concentrating upon the real point at issue and lacking unnecessarily formal and technical pleadings. If the defender is going to rely upon documents in his defence, then he ought to attach a schedule of these documents to his defence.

Any callings of a commercial action will take place on the commercial roll and the procedure in the commercial action will be at the discretion of the commercial judge who is expected to work within a broad framework which is set out within the rules. The commercial judge will be one of a small number of judges specially nominated and with a special expertise in dealing with commercial actions.

It is open to a party to ask the court to withdraw a commercial action from this procedure at a relatively early stage. It is anticipated this will not lightly be done and there are certain criteria which the court has to consider before deciding whether it would be appropriate to withdraw the action.

The first calling in court of a commercial action is at the preliminary hearing, which will take place within 14 days of the defences being lodged. The parties are expected to lodge at the preliminary hearing a document containing details of the issues which they contend require judicial determination. Where possible this statement of issues should be agreed between them in advance. The commercial judge is given a wide range of powers at the preliminary hearing and, amongst other things, he can make directions regarding the expansion of the written pleadings, and regarding possible witnesses and productions in the case. Generally, he will prescribe what he considers to be the detailed procedure for the parties to follow in order to identify adequately and determine expeditiously the particular matter or matters in dispute. There is an underlying emphasis on disclosure of the position of the respective parties and a procedural mechanism for requiring the parties to agree as much as possible. The judge will take the lead in this and adopt an active role in what were formerly regarded as matters entirely within the province of the parties. He can fix a continued preliminary hearing, but the recent changes in the procedure[6] mean that parties are going to be discouraged from using the preliminary hearing as an opportunity to do no more than start thinking fully and properly about their claim or defence. Amongst other things, the judge can fix a date for the hearing of the merits of the case at the preliminary hearing.

The judge can continue the preliminary hearing for a period for good reason, but otherwise he will usually decide what further form of hearing would be the most appropriate to provide a legal determination of the issues in the case. On the assumption that he decides not to fix a hearing of the merits at the preliminary hearing stage, then, at the conclusion of the preliminary hearing, the judge will fix a date for a procedural hearing. This can be fixed at any time, and may be dependent upon the steps which the parties are required to take as a result of the judge's direction at the preliminary hearing. In any event, the procedural hearing will not be unduly deferred.

Three days before the procedural hearing the parties are obliged to **7–05** lodge a written statement of their proposals for further procedure in the case, and they must also lodge a list of witnesses and various other documents to give full disclosure and advance notice of their position on both facts and law. Accordingly, the judge's consideration of further procedure will not be restricted by the terms of the written pleadings alone, and, before deciding further procedure, the court should be given full material in one form or another to decide what further procedure would be appropriate.

Debates will proceed where a party has lodged a written note of argument setting out the basis of his preliminary plea and the judge is satisfied that debate is merited. The judge can order fuller written arguments to be submitted in advance of the debate.

---

[6] By the Practice Note No.6 of 2004.

If the case is sent to proof, the parties are encouraged to agree expert reports so far as possible, proceed by way of affidavit evidence if directed to do so, and should be prepared to have the proof restricted to certain specific matters which might not necessarily determine the whole case. It is expected that, once the case has passed the stage of the procedural hearing, the further procedure prescribed will actually take place, so that any possible settlement should have been discussed and negotiated extra-judicially between the parties by the time of the procedural hearing.

A pre-proof hearing will normally be fixed in advance of any proof hearing to ascertain the parties' state of preparation for the proof and to check the estimated length of the proof. Further documents may have to be lodged in advance of that hearing to enable the court to review the position. Any additional documents to be used as evidence in the case which have not already been lodged should be lodged for any proof not less than seven days before the proof and the judge is unlikely to allow them to be lodged late.

A commercial action can be judicially decided, in whole or in part, at debate or proof, and it is for the judge to provide what further procedure and what timescale should apply in relation to the progress of an action after a proof or debate which does not decide all of the conclusions of the summons (or counterclaim, where appropriate).

The judge has a discretion to decide matters of incidental procedure and he can have the case call for a hearing for further procedure at any stage if he thinks this necessary. He has very wide powers of controlling the course of the litigation which enable him to ensure the speedy progress of the action. He will set out specific dates for various procedures as seem appropriate to him and can enforce compliance with any time limits he imposes. A failure by either party to comply with a provision in the rules will entitle the judge to treat this as a default and to dismiss the action or grant decree as appropriate.

PARTICULAR RULES

7–06 For the reasons explained above, it is necessary to look at the specific rules provided in Ch.47 in association with the 2004 Practice Note. Traditionally, practice notes were regarded as no more than administrative directions to those using the particular procedures in our court system. They are not "rules" of procedure. However, it can be seen that the terms of the 2004 Practice Note are likely to be highly significant, and they must be taken into account in considering the rules so as to give a proper understanding of how this procedure is applied.[7] In this commentary, the rules

---

[7] Similar considerations apply to the new personal injury procedure in the Court of Session. See Ch.6.

and practice note are treated together where appropriate, and particular aspects of the new practice note which significantly impact upon the procedure are explained at the end of this section. Some of the cases given as examples pre-date the 1994 Rules, and the more recent unreported cases can be viewed on the Scottish Courts website.

Rule 47.1—This defines a commercial action as an action arising out of **7–07** or concerned with any transaction or dispute of a commercial or business nature.[8] Examples are provided in the practice note, such as the construction of a document,[9] carriage of goods, insurance,[10] banking, questions relating to commercial leases,[11] etc.

Rule 47.2—This provides for the nomination of "commercial judges" **7–08** by the Lord President and there are currently three commercial judges.

Rule 47.3—The pursuer may elect to adopt the commercial cause pro- **7–09** cedure and will do this by drawing up the summons in an appropriate manner.[12] The summons in a commercial action must:

(1) on the instance and on the backing of the summons contain the words "Commercial Action";
(2) contain conclusions, giving details of the orders sought.[13] It is also open to a pursuer to ask the court simply to adjudicate on the proper construction of a document—an important and useful remedy—and this would be done by stating in the summons the document in dispute and the pursuer's preferred construction of it[14];
(3) identify the parties to the action and the transaction or dispute from which the action arises;
(4) "summarise" the circumstances out of which the action arises;

---

[8] See, e.g. *House of Fraser v Prudential Assurance Co Ltd*, 1994 S.L.T. 416 (declarator of obligations in a lease); *Charisma Properties Ltd v Grayling (1994) Ltd*, 1996 S.L.T. 791 (construction of missives for sale of heritable property and declarator); *Unipac (Scotland) Ltd v Aegon Insurance Co (UK) Ltd*, 1996 S.L.T. 1197 (action for payment and rectification of insurance policy); *Rankin's Trustee v H.C. Somerville & Russell*, 1999 S.C. 166 (a dispute, "turning on an issue of the law of insolvency is likely to be a dispute of a commercial nature").

[9] *Forrester v Andrew Forrester Ltd*, 2003 G.W.D. 22-652, per Lord Clarke.

[10] *Aitken v Independent Insurance Co Ltd*, 2001 S.L.T. 376, per Lord MacFadyen.

[11] *West Castle Properties Ltd v The Scottish Ministers*, 2004 S.C.L.R. 899, per Lord Mackay of Drumadoon.

[12] Before doing so, however, he is expected to comply with para.11 of the 2004 Practice Note. See para.7–03, above.

[13] e.g. a declarator of irritancy of a lease and for the defender to remove from the property. See *Auditglen Ltd v Scotec Industries Ltd (in receivership)*, 1996 S.L.T. 493; declarator and implement of a contract. See *McCall's Entertainments (Ayr) Ltd v South Ayrshire Council (No.1)*, 1998 S.L.T. 1403.

[14] See *Barry D. Trentham Ltd v McNeil*, 1996 S.L.T. 202 and *Connelly v New Hampshire Insurance Co*, 1997 S.L.T. 1341.

(5) set out the (legal) grounds on which the action proceeds; and
(6) if documents are founded on or referred to in the summons, have a
    schedule listing the documents appended to the summons.

On one view, the requirement to summarise the circumstances out of
which the action arises is really no different from the requirement for
written pleadings in an ordinary action. However, it is suggested that the
pleadings should not be extended by lengthy recitals of contract documents, propositions of law or legal duties. Parties are encouraged to do
away with unnecessary verbiage such as words and phrases which are
largely matters of style and do not add anything of substance to an
understanding or clear expression of what exactly is in dispute. In one
sense, the pleadings should be regarded as abbreviated but it is probably
true to say that the nature of the dispute between the parties could well
dictate the amount of detail which is considered to be appropriate in the
summons.[15] The court is unlikely to take a formal and technical view of
the construction of the written pleadings and there are provisions in the
rules whereby any formal omission in the pleadings will be cured by the
lodging of documents, affidavits, and other background material so that
it may be difficult to argue a lack of fair notice based purely on what is
said or not said in the pleadings.[16]

It should be observed that, as a matter of practice and in connection
with the computerised recording and administration of commercial
actions, the pursuer has to complete and sign a special registration form
when the summons is lodged for signetting. This contains all of the basic
details that are required to enable a standard computer record to be
opened.

7–10 **Rule 47.4**—This is largely administrative and reference should be made
to the terms of the rule which require no further comment.

7–11 **Rule 47.5**—This provides that the procedure in a commercial action
shall be such that the commercial judge shall order or direct, provided
he keeps within the framework of the other rules in this particular chapter. The procedure in, and progress of, a commercial action is under the
direct control and supervision of the commercial judge.

7–12 **Rule 47.6**—This provides for the form which defences should take, and
there are similar requirements for the summons. There appears to be no

---

[15] A good illustration of this can be found in *John Doyle Construction Ltd v Laing
Management (Scotland) Ltd*, 2004 S.C.L.R. 872.
[16] But see *Johnston v W.H. Brown Construction (Dundee) Ltd*, 2000 S.L.T. 223, in which
it was observed that while in commercial actions it was acceptable, subject to the directions of the court, to give particulars of claims otherwise than by formal pleadings,
material adequate for the purposes of giving fair notice and enabling the court to determine whether or not inquiry was justified, required to be promptly presented.

need to stick to the traditional style involving formal admissions, denials, etc. provided the nature and extent of the dispute can be reasonably well identified from the defences. If the defences refer to documents, then they should contain a schedule listing the documents.

Again it should be noted that there is a requirement on the defender's agents to complete a registration form, so that their details will also form part of the computer records for the case.

Rule 47.7—This relates to the procedure to be followed if a party wants **7–13** to lodge a counterclaim or a third party notice. A defender who wishes to do so must apply by motion.[17] The judge can make any other directions regarding counterclaims and third party notices as he thinks fit, which simply reflects the very wide discretion he is given in relation to all procedure throughout commercial actions.[18]

Rule 47.8—Commercial actions call on the commercial roll on such **7–14** dates and at such times as shall be fixed. This is the roll for all of the procedural callings of a commercial action and the important point to note is that the roll makes reference to specific times[19] being fixed by the judge for the hearing of the case. This is designed to suit the convenience of parties and the court and to prevent excessive waiting. It is a welcome and a sensible innovation but it requires careful administration and enforcement. It might be difficult to organise this for other, more numerous, types of action.

Rule 47.9—Under this rule the parties can apply to the court to have the **7–15** action withdrawn from this procedure and have it proceed as an ordinary action.[20] The judge has a discretion to do so where one party makes the motion but he must take into account certain specific matters. He must be satisfied that the speedy and efficient determination of the action would not be served by the cause being dealt with as a commercial action because of: (1) the likely need for detailed pleadings to enable justice to be done between the parties; (2) the length of time required for preparation of the action; and (3) any other relevant circumstances. The judge himself can withdraw an action from the commercial roll if he considers it appropriate to do so, after hearing both parties. These are clearly matters of judicial discretion and opinion.

---

[17] It is not absolutely clear whether this is a motion which can be refused, but it is arguable from the terms of r.47.7(2) that the commercial judge's discretion does not necessarily extend to refusal of such a motion.

[18] e.g. he could decide that the existence of the counterclaim could make the case inappropriate for the commercial action procedure.

[19] Not just dates.

[20] This can arise for numerous reasons, e.g. a defender may consider that the case cannot be properly investigated or prepared in the restricted time scales which are applicable to this procedure.

Where one party makes a motion to withdraw the action from the commercial roll and this is consented to by all of the other parties, the judge must grant it.

7–16 **Rule 47.10**—Provided an action which has been raised as an ordinary action fits within the definition of a commercial action, then any party can apply by motion at any time to have it proceed as a commercial action. The motion is to be heard by the commercial judge and, if granted, there are provisions for appropriate procedure depending upon the stage which the ordinary action has reached at the time when the motion is granted.

7–17 **Rule 47.11**—This describes what is to happen at the preliminary hearing, which is the first significant hearing in the progress of a commercial action. The judge is required to consider the terms of the summons and defences and decide whether further details ought to be provided.[21] Furthermore, the judge has discretion to make a wide variety of orders as follows. He can:

(1) order a party to make more detailed written pleadings in relation to whole or part of the claim or defence;
(2) order a separate statement of facts to be made by one of the parties on all or part of the case;
(3) allow amendment of pleadings;
(4) order the disclosure of the identity of witnesses and disclosure of the existence and nature of any documents relating to the action, as well as giving authority to a party to recover relevant documents;
(5) order a relevant document to be lodged in process by either party within a specified time;
(6) order each party to lodge with the court and intimate to the opponent a list of witnesses;
(7) order reports of skilled persons or witness statements[22] to be lodged in process;
(8) order affidavits to be lodged in process in connection with any of the issues in the case;
(9) order the action to proceed straight to a hearing without any further procedure.

The judge has a discretion to put a time limit on any of the above orders, or to continue the preliminary hearing, or indeed to make any order which he thinks fit for the speedy determination of the action.

Assuming that the judge has not made an order for the case to proceed straight to a hearing on the merits without any further preliminary procedure, then he is obliged to fix a date for a procedural hearing.

---

[21] Reference should also be made to para.12 of the 2004 Practice Note.
[22] This does not mean "precognitions", but a statement of the evidence of a witness which should be signed by that witness.

Rule 47.12—This rule relates to the conduct of a procedural hearing, **7–18** which is the second significant step in procedure in a commercial action. The date for the procedural hearing will have been fixed at the preliminary hearing. The purpose of this hearing is to determine further procedure in the case on the basis of the parties' respective positions at that time, and, more specifically, to determine the form of inquiry into the facts or law which ought to take place and the extent of that inquiry. In essence, the court considers with the parties how the dispute, or at least a significant part of it, can best be decided by the court.[23]

The rule provides that each party has to give advance notice to the court and a copy to the opponent of his proposals for further procedure in the case. If the proposal is that the case should go to a legal debate, then he has to give details of what is to be debated and why a debate is appropriate.[24]

As well as giving advance notice of the above, each party has to give advance notice of a list of the witnesses he proposes to cite or call to give evidence and he must identify the matters to which the witnesses are going to speak. He must also lodge the reports of any skilled person upon whom he is intending to rely and, again, these additional documents have to be intimated to the other party.

At the procedural hearing, and after considering the different submissions and the submissions by the parties at the hearing, the commercial judge decides whether the case should go to debate or should be sent for proof on the whole or on any part of the action.[25]

If it goes to debate, he can order written arguments to be submitted in advance.[26] If the action is to go to proof, he can decide what method of proof (if any) would be appropriate, and give various directions as to the nature and scope of the proof. Finally, it is open to the judge to continue the procedural hearing to a date to be appointed by him.

These powers can be used in ways which traditionalists would regard as quite novel. The detailed powers given to the commercial judge cover most, if not all, of the conceivable options for dealing with the resolution of disputes on matters of fact and/or law. They also provide procedural mechanisms whereby parties are compelled to disclose their position, to agree evidence which is capable of agreement, and to face up to the steps which must be taken in order to secure the speedy judicial determination of a case. It should be appreciated that, in some cases, the judicial determination of one aspect of a case which does not deal with all of the matters in dispute between the parties can enable the parties to go on and reach a settlement extra-judicially on the merits of the whole case. We are

---

[23] It is assumed that the parties have discussed possible settlement and are not going to settle. See para.13 of the 2004 Practice Note.

[24] See *Highland & Universal Properties Ltd v Safeway Properties*, 1996 S.C. 424.

[25] See *Stirling Aquatic Technology Ltd v Farmocean AB*, 1993 S.L.T. 713.

[26] For an example see *Scottish Life Assurance Co Ltd v Agfa-Gevaert Ltd*, 1997 S.L.T. 1200.

accustomed to the court being presented with all of the contentious issues
at one time, and hearing evidence or debate about them all at the same
time. However, in certain actions, where a court is able to make a decision about some of the areas of contention authoritatively without having
to decide all of the issues, this can be more acceptable to the parties.
Apart from anything else, it will usually be quicker, simpler and cheaper
than a full-scale litigation on everything.

A good illustration of the range of options open to a judge in a commercial action is *British Aerospace (Operations) Ltd v PIK Facilities
Ltd*.[27] This complex action concerned the nature and extent of the parties' obligations towards each other regarding the provision of air traffic
control services at Prestwick Airport. There were seven conclusions in
the summons but it was agreed or decided that four of these were not to
be considered at the particular hearing of the merits concerned. The parties obviously narrowed down the areas of dispute and agreed to deal
with some of them separately. Affidavits from the principal witnesses
were lodged and accordingly no oral proof was required. This enabled
the court to consider the case as a question of the construction of a particular provision of a lease. After deciding that point (which may have
enabled the parties to review their respective positions on the whole dispute) the judge ordered the case to call again in order to determine what
further procedure would be appropriate for the case.

7–19   Another recent example is the case of *Ege Endustri Ve Ticaret v
Albion Automotive Ltd*,[28] in which a Turkish company was suing a
Scottish company for goods and services supplied. There were complex
contractual agreements and the main thrust of the defence depended
upon the terms of one agreement which was to be interpreted under
Swiss law. The judge allowed a preliminary proof restricted to the issue
of whether or not, "under Swiss law, a debt is due and payable to the
defenders under the . . . Agreement".

The procedural hearing and the preliminary hearing are designed to
enable parties to discuss realistically the issues involved in the action
and the best method of disposing of those issues. The hearing can be
heard in chambers. Persons attending may be seated, and wigs and
gowns may not be worn.

It should be noted, at this stage, that the 2004 Practice Note provides
for the fixing of a pre-proof hearing in advance of the proof diet itself.[29]

7–20 Rule 47.14—This provides that any documents required for proof,
which have not already been disclosed or lodged as per an order from
the court, or as part of a schedule with the summons or defences, should

[27] *British Aerospace (Operations) Ltd v PIK Facilities Ltd* Unreported OH August 6, 1996.
[28] *Ege Endustri Ve Ticaret v Albion Automotive Ltd*, 2004 G.W.D. 24-515, Lord Clarke.
[29] See para.15 of 2004 Practice Note.

be lodged not less than seven days before the date for the proof and parties are not encouraged to assume that the court will allow late lodging of productions—a fairly common occurrence in ordinary actions.

It is suggested in the practice notes that, as well as lodging productions, parties ought to prepare a "working bundle" in which all of the documents to be used in the case at proof are arranged chronologically or in some other order so that there is one central record of all of the documentary productions without any duplication. It may not be immediately apparent to readers with little or no practical experience of litigation, but this common-sense provision can prevent considerable confusion and delay at any proof.

Rule 47.15—This rule provides that a judge or a party can decide on his **7–21** own initiative to have the commercial action call before the judge for further procedure at any stage. This covers particularly unusual situations which cannot be anticipated and provided for in the rules.

Rule 47.16—This provides that any failure to comply with a provision of **7–22** the rules or any order made by the commercial judge can have fatal effects if the judge thinks this necessary. The purpose of the rule is to provide sanctions for the effective supervision and case management of the action.

Arrangements will be made to ensure that all appearances of an action in the commercial roll will be before the same judge and, although it is not necessary for the parties to use the same counsel for all appearances, it is expected that when the case calls the person appearing on behalf of either party will be the person responsible for the conduct of the case and will be authorised to take any necessary decisions on questions of procedure.

PRACTICE NOTE NO.6 OF 2004

Paragraph 11—It is assumed that, in commercial disputes, both parties **7–23** will have their own legal advisers. It is expected that, before the action is raised, the solicitors for both parties will have fully set out in correspondence the factual and legal grounds upon which the claim and the defence is based. They will have supplied to each other the documents upon which respectively they intend to rely, and they will have disclosed their expert report(s) (if any) to each other. They are expected to have had "considered and reasoned" correspondence on the issues. They are asked to consider whether all or some of the dispute may be amenable to some form of alternative dispute resolution. Other than in exceptional and urgent cases, action should not be raised unless and until it can be said to be "truly necessary".

Paragraph 12—The preliminary hearing will be conducted on the basis that the provisions of para.11 have been complied with, in other words, there is a genuine dispute which is properly understood and cannot otherwise be resolved. The hearing is not intended to provide the first occasion on which the parties seriously engage in formulating their claim and response. Parties should lodge prior to the hearing all correspondence, etc. which shows that they have complied with the requirements of para.11. A motion to continue the preliminary hearing to obtain information which should have been available if para.11 had been complied with may be refused. A failure to comply with para.11 which leads to a request for a continuation of the hearing may attract an adverse award of expenses. At the preliminary hearing, the parties should lodge a document which sets out concisely the issues which they contend require judicial determination. Where possible, this should be agreed between the parties. Time limits set for steps in the procedure as provided by r.47.11 will be realistic and dependent upon parties having a clear idea at the preliminary hearing of what will be required and when it can be achieved. Extension of the time limits will only be granted in certain circumstances.

7–24　**Paragraph 13**—It is normally expected that, by the time of the procedural hearing, the parties' positions will have been ascertained and identified and that all prospects for settlement have been fully discussed. It is expected that, once a case passes beyond the stage of a procedural hearing, it will not settle and consequently any hearing[30] allocated thereafter will actually proceed.

7–25　**Paragraph 15**—When a proof or proof before answer has been allowed, the court will normally also fix a pre-proof hearing to take place in advance of the diet, in order to ascertain the parties' state of readiness and to review the estimated duration of the proof.[31] The pre-proof hearing will consider, amongst other matters:

- any joint minute of admissions;
- any documentary productions;
- any expert reports—and whether the experts have had a meeting to agree the areas of dispute between them;
- in the case of a proof before answer, a statement of the legal arguments and list of authorities to be relied upon by the parties.

COMMERCIAL ACTION PROCEDURE—ADVANTAGES AND DISADVANTAGES

7–26　The rules of commercial actions represent a radically different approach to the regulation of procedure in civil litigation in Scotland and it is

---

[30] Proof or debate.
[31] The judge could have done this anyway under the provisions of r.47.15, if he had considered it appropriate, but the practice note makes it clear that all judges will "normally" do so in any case, and it's what he will be interested in at the hearing.

interesting to compare features of these rules with the traditional procedure. This may give some insight into current thinking about rules of
procedure in any civil litigation, what the objectives of rules of procedure ought to be, and the appropriate role of the courts in litigation procedure and practice. It may also provide some prediction of future
approaches to rules of procedure and practice in Scotland.[32]

Some of the unique features of commercial actions are as follows:

(1) **The role of the judge**. The judge is, in effect, the "case manager".   **7–27**
Formerly the parties were in control of the pace and procedure of the litigation to a large extent but the court has now assumed control of these features. The allocation of specialised judges to commercial actions generally
and the allocation of a specific judge to a case from start to finish so far as
possible may well be a desirable feature of any system. However, it has
implications for manpower and the utilisation of resources within the civil
justice system which may not be economically acceptable. Furthermore,
the judge or judges who are given a wide discretion by the rules of procedure might develop their own particular practices and unofficial "rules"
with a risk of procedural uncertainty and divergences between judges
which would be undesirable.[33] The judge's discretion extends to all aspects
of procedure and practice within commercial actions and he can take various initiatives regardless of the views and intentions of the parties.

(2) **The administration of cases on the commercial roll with the use**   **7–28**
of information technology. It seems inevitable that this will eventually
extend to all forms of procedure at all levels. There are economic implications. With the available technology the court can issue interlocutors
electronically to the parties and further extension of the use of IT is
expected and encouraged. Given that there are only a relatively small
number of commercial actions per annum at the moment, it could be suggested that the information technology is not justified on strict economics. In principle, however, court actions can be tracked, supervised and
administered very well by computer, and IT for the courts generally has
developed significantly since the commencement of commercial actions.

(3) **The allocation of times for the calling of cases as well as dates**.   **7–29**
In principle, this must be more desirable but again the administrative difficulty and cost implications of providing this facility cannot be left out
of account. The judge has to be taken off all other business so that he can
guarantee being available throughout the day when he is due to be hearing cases which are allocated to a specific time. He has to try to ensure
that cases stick to the time allocated to them.

(4) **The encouragement given to parties pre-litigation to focus and**   **7–30**
resolve their dispute. This development in 2004 can be seen as a real

---

[32] Similar considerations apply to commercial actions in the sheriff court. See Ch.10.
[33] In a sense, the practice notes might be seen as addressing any such uncertainties by
making it clear what is acceptable or not.

effort to emphasise the role of the courts[34] as a place of final resort for the resolution of disputes. Before a commercial action is commenced, in most cases, the matters in dispute should have been discussed and focused in pre-litigation correspondence between the parties' legal advisers. The procedure is intended for cases in which there is a real dispute which requires to be resolved by judicial decision. The procedure functions best if issues have been investigated and ventilated prior to the raising of the action. This helps to avoid delay and assists the court in securing an efficient and appropriate means of dealing with the particular dispute. These actions are expected to involve business people with access to legal expertise and advice. The court cannot prevent them litigating but can impose sanctions of a kind if it feels that they should not have found it necessary to litigate. The traditional view is that if a party raises an action, having intimated a claim which has been rejected, then he will recover his expenses from the opponent if his position is upheld by the court. Similarly, if a defender rejects a claim and is successful with his defence then he will recover his expenses. The new provisions mean that the court expects both parties, prior to litigation, to communicate with each other and to try meaningfully to understand their respective positions, strengths, weaknesses, etc. They should be able to ascertain what is truly in dispute and consider if that issue can be resolved. The court will not look kindly upon taking up court time and resources with hearings at which the prime function of the court seems to be to make the parties think seriously for the first time about these issues. If it appears that one or other party has by intransigence or unreasonable behaviour "caused" the litigation, or some part of the litigation could have been avoided by sensible actions on their part, then the court will take this into account. The 2004 Practice Note is an attempt to influence the conduct of the parties pre-litigation[35] and to make them think carefully about the function of the litigation and how it might help them, without imposing rules about what parties must do in every case. The courts cannot order parties to behave in any particular way before they come to court but, in these rules, the court can make it clear to the business community and to their advisors what is expected of them.

7–31   (5) **The difference of emphasis on written pleadings**. There remains a need for a written statement of the claim and written answers by the opponent. However, the procedure intends to encourage parties to concentrate on matters of substance and not on style. The idea of "pleadings" is extended in a realistic way. The pleadings are not just the formal words used in the summons and the defences. They can be amplified by documents. They can be further amplified by affidavits, witness statements, etc. The expression of the parties' respective cases is not confined

---

[34] Or at least this particular court.
[35] And during the litigation.

rigidly to the four corners of the condescendence and answers. The requirement of fair notice still exists, but fair notice is interpreted in a common-sense way rather than in a "technical" way. The court is not just looking at the precise words used in the writ but is asking if the other party really does not know what the opponent's case is. It is assumed that they are parties in a commercial dispute. It is assumed that they are intelligent. It is at least suspected that they may well have communicated about the subject matter of the dispute both before and during the litigation.[36] They may already, prior to litigation, have a very good idea of what the opponent has to say and, accordingly, to insist upon some formal notice of a position which is well known to the other party is unrealistic and unnecessary. The court adopts a wider approach to this than is apparent in ordinary procedure, although there is still the option for a party to say that he does not know what the opponent's position is and the court is obviously obliged to take this into account. If the complaint about the written formulation of the claim or defence does indicate that the opponent is prejudiced in dealing with the case or if it seems that there might be some basic legal argument which is of real significance to the success or otherwise of the case, then a party will have a perfectly good "pleading" argument.

(6) **It is specifically provided that there should not be wigs and gowns at the procedural stages of the action**. Traditionalists are unhappy about this development but it may herald the beginning of the end for a formality which is difficult to justify in modern times.   7–32

(7) **Parties give prior detailed written notice of their arguments and prior written submissions of their respective procedural position**. If the intention of the parties and the court should be to co-operate to bring the case to a resolution in the most appropriate way then this will assist. Parties would have to consider their position carefully well in advance of the procedural hearing and any debate subsequently fixed. It is one thing to stand up at a calling of a case and make oral submissions about it there and then, but it is quite another thing to have to state one's position clearly and accurately beforehand in writing. This obviously helps the court (and the opponent) to prepare for the hearing, but to some extent it also prevents a party from tailoring submissions at the hearing to the position adopted by the opponent, the views of the judge or the mood of the moment.[37] Similar provisions could be transposed to sheriff court procedures and supplement the options hearing rules to some advantage. One disadvantage might be the extra time and effort (not to mention cost) which would have to be expended on cases by solicitors to enable this to be done fully and properly.   7–33

---

[36] Indeed, the 2004 Practice Note makes it very important that they have communicated fully and sensibly pre-litigation.
[37] The last two are not necessarily unrelated.

7–34   (8) **The use of affidavit evidence and written witness statements as evidence**. In many systems this would be the norm but, until recently, it has always been rigorously opposed here. Other rules of procedure in other types of action now allow this to a limited extent[38] and the commercial actions rules take this a little further.[39] This might encourage a more extensive use of affidavits generally, but it must be said that they are still regarded as an unsatisfactory substitute for oral evidence and practitioners are wary of using the provisions in the other procedures. The use of "witness statements",[40] if they are found to be effective, might be developed in other forms of procedure. The procedure in commercial actions whereby the judge and the parties can discuss and agree in advance of a proof on the use of such evidence in the full knowledge of what is disputed, what that witness' evidence might be, and how important or otherwise it might be in the context of the dispute as a whole, cannot satisfactorily be replicated in any of the other traditional forms of procedure.

7–35   (9) **Disclosure**. The parties are encouraged, and can indeed be ordered, to provide disclosure of various matters which they could formerly have kept to themselves. This is intended to promote discussion between the parties about the true merits of claims and, consequently, settlement of cases. Traditionally, cases have been conducted with parties keeping their cards very close to their chests and disclosing as little as they can of any matters which might be prejudicial to their case. The rules and practice assisted in this, but parties tended to disclose less and less of their position if they felt it would assist them. Compulsory disclosure of specific facts or documents which have a real bearing on the outcome of the case may prevent attempts to confuse or complicate issues, but this must be balanced against rules about confidentiality and privilege which are desirable. The commercial action rules are the most significant formal breach in the traditional approach and may be a sign of things to come.

7–36   (10) **Speed**. The procedure intends to identify the issues quickly and resolve them judicially without delay. It can be argued that this is beneficial as being what the parties must be assumed to want and what is best for them. There is, however, a contrary view that the parties may not be unhappy about a case continuing for a reasonably lengthy period. They may have ongoing business or other relationships; they may require to come to terms with their prospective gains or losses; they may have other business to attend to which takes a priority over a court action. Some cases are complicated on facts and law and a delay to allow mature and sensible investigation or consideration might be quite appropriate. If the court imposes tight deadlines then parties' solicitors may have to drop every other case to concentrate on this one, which can

---

[38] e.g. evidence of written statements including affidavits in RCS r.36.8.
[39] It is not clear to what extent this is used in practice.
[40] A major feature of English civil procedure.

cause real practical difficulties.[41] Perhaps it can be suggested that "speed" of a litigation and "lack of delay" are not the same thing, and an emphasis on speed for its own sake could be a problem. It can, of course, be pointed out that the judge can take into account special features in any case which might justify an extended timetable.

An interesting recent case which illustrates many of the features of commercial action procedure and the tension which can exist between speed and justice can be found in *CSC Braehead Leisure Ltd v Laing O'Rourke Scotland Ltd*,[42] in which there was an action of some complexity between commercial property developers and their builders. The builders wished to bring into the action a number of other parties by way of third party notices.[43] This was opposed as it would delay the proceedings considerably. In allowing the third party notices, the judge said:

"When dealing with commercial actions under Chapter 47 of the Rules of Court, the court recognises the legitimate interests of business to obtain as speedy and efficient a determination of commercial disputes as is possible and attempts to meet that interest. However, commercial disputes are almost infinitely various in their nature, and it may be possible to determine one such dispute more speedily than another. A sharply focused dispute about the proper construction of a contractual term may perhaps be capable of a very speedy determination, and the Chapter 47 procedures are designed towards this end. By contrast, a complex dispute involving several parties and numerous issues of disputed fact and/or law may not be capable of being resolved as expeditiously—yet the active case management which the court is able to provide should nevertheless result in the speedier determination of the issues than would be the case on the ordinary roll. The aims of speed and efficiency cannot therefore be assessed in simplistic or absolute terms—the court will strive to achieve the speediest and most efficient determination of a commercial dispute in the particular circumstances of the case, and subject to what is in the interests of justice."

---

[41] The client may not want the action to interfere with the pursuit of more pressing commercial needs.

[42] *CSC Braehead Leisure Ltd v Laing O'Rourke Scotland Ltd* Unreported OH June 20, 2008, Lord Menzies.

[43] See para.15–05, below.

Court of Session

Commercial Action

Flow Chart of Procedure

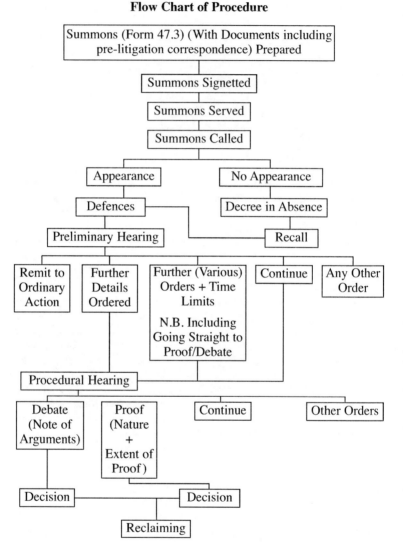

FURTHER READING

Scottish Courts website, *http://www.scotcourts.gov.uk*
R. Clancy, "The New Commercial Cause Rules", 1997 S.L.T. (News) 45 and 58.
"The New Commercial Action Practice Note, obstructing access to justice?", 2005 Civ. P.B. 61-1.

CHAPTER 8

JUDICIAL REVIEW

This book is concerned primarily with procedure and not with the substan- **8–01**
tive law. However, in order to understand why special procedural rules
were required for actions seeking judicial review it is necessary to know the
basics.[1] If someone who has power or authority over you makes a decision
which affects you, and which you do not like, you can, in certain circumstances, ask the Court of Session to examine the process whereby that
decision was made in order to see if that power or authority has been
abused. If the court agrees, then it can be asked to remedy the injustice.[2]
So, e.g. there might be situations in which the actings of a university
towards a student at the university might be susceptible to judicial review.[3]

A judicial review is a means whereby the Court of Session—and only
the Court of Session—can be asked to scrutinise, and, where appropriate, regulate the process by which decisions are taken by any decision-
making body whose powers are given to it by statute, agreement or any
other document. It is not the same as an appeal from that body, and it is
not for the court to put itself in the position of that body and substitute
its own view of the matter for that of the body concerned. The court can,
however, check to see that the person making the decision does not
exceed or abuse his powers or fail to perform any duty which has been
given to him which involves a decision-making process.[4]

Decisions of government departments are frequently subject to judicial
review. Decisions of the Scottish Football Association and the Criminal
Injuries Compensation Board have been subjected to application for
judicial review.[5]

---

[1] The substantive law is complex and this is simply the broadest outline. For a full discussion of the history of the remedy and an authoritative explanation of its application see
West v Secretary of State for Scotland, 1992 S.L.T. 636.

[2] The criteria for granting judicial review can be found in *Associated Provincial Picture
Houses Ltd v Wednesbury Corporation* [1948] 1 K.B. 223 and *Wordie Property Co Ltd
v Secretary of State for Scotland*, 1984 S.L.T. 345.

[3] See, e.g. *Carlton v Glasgow Caledonian University*, 1994 S.L.T. 549—a judicial review
of the refusal by a university to award an honours degree; *Naik v University of Stirling*,
1994 S.L.T. 449 and *Joobeen v University of Stirling*, 1995 S.L.T. 120.

[4] See *McTear v Scottish Legal Aid Board*, 1997 S.L.T. 108, and the cases referred to there.
See also *Boyle v Castlemilk East Housing Co-operative Ltd*, 1998 S.L.T. 56.

[5] Other examples of bodies against whom petitions for judicial review have been presented
are detailed in para.58.3.3 of *Greens Annotated Rules of the Court of Session 2008/9*.

The Court of Session has always had a supervisory jurisdiction over the decisions of inferior bodies exercising administrative, judicial or quasi-judicial powers. It was felt at one time that the sheriff court had a similar power of review but that is not so. The sheriff court can and does review certain decisions of certain administrative bodies but only where a specific statute provides for a specific right of appeal to the sheriff court.[6] Such a review, however, is not a "judicial review" as properly understood. There are many situations where bodies reach decisions and there is no right of appeal. It is against those types of decisions that the Court of Session's "super-eminent" jurisdiction applies:

> "It has long been recognised in Scotland that the Court of Session has jurisdiction to exercise a supervisory control over inferior courts and tribunals in cases where there is no right of appeal from those courts or tribunals and even in cases where appeal is expressly excluded by statute . . . a supervisory jurisdiction over inferior courts and tribunals is vested exclusively in the Court of Session as the supreme court."[7]

8–02 The seeds of the present procedure were sown in the case of *Brown v Hamilton District Council*.[8] This was an action raised by an individual against the local authority for refusing to put him on a housing list. The decision complained about was made in December 1978. After lengthy procedure and various appeals, the House of Lords issued their decision on the merits of the dispute on November 25, 1982.

In the House of Lords, Lord Fraser said:

> "It is for consideration whether there might not be advantages in developing special procedure in Scotland for dealing with questions in the public law area . . . They have advantages over ordinary procedures . . . by making available remedies which are speedy and cheap and which protect public authorities from unreasonable actions . . . Similar advantage might possibly be derived in Scotland from reviving . . . (certain procedures) . . . as methods of review of decisions in the public law field which are not subject to appeal to the court."

Following upon these observations and other observations in a similar case, a working party was set up in 1983:

> ". . . to devise and recommend for consideration a simple form of procedure, capable of being operated with reasonable expedition, for

---

[6] See Ch.14 on "Summary Applications".
[7] *West v Secretary of State for Scotland*, 1992 S.L.T. 636, per Lord President Hope.
[8] *Brown v Hamilton District Council*, 1993 S.L.T. 397.

bringing before the court for such relief as is appropriate, complaints by individuals."

That working party became known as the Working Party on Procedure for Judicial Review of Administrative Action.

After the working party reported, a new rule was made in 1985 (r.260B) in relation to proceedings commenced on or after April 30, 1985. It has now been replaced in the 1994 Rules, by Ch.58 rr.58.1–58.10. This form of procedure applies to all cases where an application is being made to the supervisory jurisdiction of the court and excludes the use of any other form of procedure.

The rules provide the judge with a quick and flexible procedure, in which he has considerable discretion. The precise procedure followed in any individual case may be dictated by considerations of the nature and complexity of the subject matter, the remedy or remedies sought, the issues involved, and the urgency of a decision. The rules try to balance the need to provide a speedy remedy against the fundamental entitlement of each party to have fair notice of his opponent's case. Furthermore, the rules of procedure attempt to encourage the parties to focus on the real live issues in dispute as early as possible by seeking agreement on all that can be agreed and avoiding unnecessary or irrelevant arguments.

Cases are heard by a single judge.[9] The kinds of issues which are normally determined in judicial reviews generally involve limited disputes on matters of fact. They can often be decided on agreed facts. This means that the actual hearing of the merits of a judicial review usually becomes a legal debate upon the powers of the body making the decision and the "decision-making process" which applied in any individual case, rather than a hearing requiring evidence from witnesses.[10]

In 1987 the total number of judicial reviews initiated in the Court of Session was 44. In 1996 there were 209 such cases. In 1998 there were 147 cases. A significant increase in the number of applications for judicial review was anticipated as a consequence of the adoption of the European Convention of Human Rights, but the statistics for this are not available. There certainly appear to be numerous cases on judicial review reported in the last few years.[11] In 2002 there were 160 petitions for judicial review—43 per cent of those related to immigration matters and 7 per cent related to housing. One hundred and one of those petitions were disposed of in 2002. In 41 cases the petition was not opposed, and in the remaining 60 cases, the petitioner was successful in 10 of them.

---

[9] There are six nominated judges who will hear judicial reviews.

[10] Although, in some circumstances, evidence may be heard to enable a decision to be reached.

[11] A search of 2006 to 2008 *Scots Law Times* will bear this out and will demonstrate the wide variety of circumstances in which the remedy has been invoked.

NARRATIVE OF PROCEDURE

8–03 An individual can apply for review of the decision of an appropriate body in the Court of Session by lodging a petition for judicial review. The petition has to be in a prescribed format which is set out in the appendix to the rules. At the same time as lodging the petition, the petitioner has to lodge documents or provide an affidavit from which it can easily and clearly be seen exactly what decision he is seeking to have reviewed.[12] The petition will be lodged with the petition department in the Court of Session and the department is then required to put this before one of the nominated judges for a formal calling.[13] When the petition along with supporting documents calls before him, the judge will hear submissions from counsel or a solicitor advocate regarding the petition and will be asked to make a first order. This will be an order by the judge setting out: (1) how and with what period of notice intimation of the petition ought to be made; (2) any documents which ought to be intimated along with the petition; and (3) a date for the first hearing; or (4) any interim order.

It is an important feature of the procedure that, at the time the petition is first lodged with the court, the petitioner can seek any interim order such as, e.g. an interim interdict.[14] This can give a party (the petitioner) a very quick and effective temporary remedy.[15]

8–04 When the opponent (the respondent) receives intimation of the petition which will of course tell him the date of the first hearing then, if he intends to appear, he has to give advance notification to the solicitor for the petitioner and to the Keeper of the Rolls who is the court official responsible for allocating and organising business in the Court of Session. It is also open to him to lodge answers and any relevant documents prior to or at the hearing itself and he should lodge these with the Keeper.[16] He would intimate copies of any answers and documents to his opponents.

An individual who has not been served with a copy of the petition but comes to know about it and considers himself to be affected by it, can take certain steps to protect his position. He can apply by motion to be allowed to enter into the process and, in that case, similar procedural provisions would apply to him. Furthermore, if a person or organisation believes that any issue in the proceedings raises a matter of public interest, he can apply

---

[12] e.g. the letter or documents containing details of the decision complained about.

[13] For a case in which there was detailed discussion of what is meant by "lodging" a petition and the administrative functions which surround the lodging of a petition, see *TOR Corporate AS v Sinopec Group Star Petroleum Corporation Ltd*, 2007 S.L.T. 552; overruled at 2008 S.L.T. 97.

[14] Obviously he has to satisfy a judge that it is appropriate. If such an order is to be sought, a copy of the petition is usually intimated (informally) to the respondent beforehand although there is no obligation to do so.

[15] Occasionally, at a hearing on the interim order, a judge can refuse to grant a first hearing if not satisfied with the merits of the petition.

[16] i.e. the officials in his department.

for leave to intervene, and may, in appropriate cases, be allowed to produce a written submission to the court bearing upon the issue concerned.

When the case calls for the first hearing the judge has to satisfy himself that the order for intimation has been properly complied with, and then he hears the parties who are present at the time. He has a wide discretion at the first hearing. He can decide the whole merits of the case at the first hearing if he wishes. Alternatively, he can make an order for further procedure, "as he thinks fit". In particular, he could:

(1) allow adjournment or continuation of the petition to another date;
(2) make an order for service on any other person not yet served;
(3) make an interim order (if sought);
(4) order answers to be lodged within a specified period[17];
(5) order the parties to give further information about the allegations in the petition or in the answers already lodged in relation to any particular matter which he considers appropriate;
(6) order any fact relied upon by a party at the hearing to be supported by evidence on affidavit which has to be lodged within a particular period prior to the next hearing;
(7) order any party to lodge documents relating to the petition within any specified period;
(8) appoint a reporter to report to him on such matters of fact as he wishes; or
(9) order a second hearing on such issues as he sets out.

The purpose of the first hearing is to enable him to ascertain what the parties' respective positions are and to determine any outstanding issues which can be disposed of at the first hearing. The idea then is for him to make an order which would be appropriate to secure the disposal at any subsequent hearing of any issue not disposed of at the first hearing. As a matter of practice, it is sensible for the parties to try and reach agreement between them on the subject matter to be covered by the first hearing and to put this before the judge so that the matters in dispute are narrowed down and focused. Most petitions are determined at the first hearing.[18] **8–05**

If the judge has decided that a second hearing is required, then the Keeper of the Rolls will fix a date for the second hearing as soon as reasonably practicable. Not less than seven days before the date of the second hearing the parties have to lodge all documents and affidavits which they are going to use at the second hearing together with copies for use by the court. Before the second hearing takes place, the case can be put out for hearing on the by order roll[19] for the parties to address preliminary matters, or for the judge himself to obtain such information from the

---

[17] Although a respondent may have lodged answers prior to the first hearing, there is no obligation on him to do so unless the judge orders it.
[18] See, e.g. *City of Aberdeen Council v Local Government Boundary Commission for Scotland*, 1998 S.L.T. 613 and *Henderson v Argyll & Bute Council*, 1998 S.L.T. 1224.
[19] On the instigation of either party or the judge.

parties as he considers necessary for the proper disposal of the petition at the second hearing.

At the second hearing the judge has three options: (1) he can adjourn the hearing; (2) he can continue it for further procedure, "as he thinks fit"; or (3) he can determine the petition.

The judge is to keep a tight control of procedure in order to avoid delay and to ensure that the matter is dealt with as expeditiously as possible.

As can be seen, the rules anticipate that normally there will be little need for a proof on matters of fact relating to the petition. For example, if a tribunal decided that the petitioner was "an unsuitable person" for some post or other, and this decision was open to judicial review, the court would not want to hear evidence about his suitability, but would probably only be interested in hearing how it was that the tribunal itself came to make that decision. In other words, what the "decision-making process" was. There is unlikely to be a disagreement between the parties as to the actual process by which the body made its decision. There is unlikely to be any significant disagreement between the petitioner and the respondent as to what was presented to, or said before, the tribunal or decision-making body. Accordingly, this form of procedure can often become simply a legal debate on agreed averments, documents and facts. The rules of procedure encourage this approach, but it is as well to remember that the procedural framework which operates in these cases is specifically designed for the types of disputes which come within its province, and probably could not be transposed to other types of dispute resolution successfully.

THE PARTICULAR RULES

8–06   Chapter 58 of the 1994 Rules relates to applications for judicial review. The rules relating to these applications are brief.

Rule 58.1—This starts with the general proposition that Ch.58 of the 1994 Rules relates to, "an application to the supervisory jurisdiction of the court".[20] One of the major issues which arise in petitions for judicial review is the competency of the petition, i.e. whether the decision complained against, regardless of its merits, can, as a matter of law, be subjected to judicial review by the court.[21] The petitioner also must have title and interest to sue.[22]

---

[20]   Reference should be made to the case of *West v Secretary of State for Scotland*, 1992 S.L.T. 636. See also the cases referred to in the *Annotated Rules of the Court of Session 2008/9*, pp.C473–C476; and, as a recent example, *Rooney v Chief Constable, Strathclyde Police*, 1997 S.L.T. 1261.

[21]   See, e.g. *Bell v Fiddes*, 1996 S.L.T. 51; *Ingle v Ingle's Trustee*, 1999 S.L.T. 650; and *Saunders v Royal Insurance Plc*, 2000 S.L.T. 597. Also see *Fotheringham and Son v The British Limousin Cattle Society Ltd*, 2004 S.L.T. 485.

[22]   *Bondway Properties Ltd v City of Edinburgh Council*, 1999 S.L.T. 127—petitioner had no interest to sue.

Rule 58.2—This provides that the standard procedure for petitions in the Court of Session, as set out in the 1994 Rules,[23] do not apply to petitions for judicial review.

Rule 58.3—This says that any application to the supervisory jurisdiction of the court, including an application under s.45(b) of the Court of Session Act 1988 (specific performance of a statutory duty), shall be made by petition for judicial review and this means that any such application to that jurisdiction must be made by petition for judicial review. However, a party cannot make an application for judicial review if he has made, or could have made, an appeal or review under or by virtue of statute.[24]

However, there might be circumstances in which the failure to use the statutory right of review was due to ignorance on the part of the individual, because of some irregularity of procedure on the part of the respondent, or because resort to the statutory remedy would, in the particular circumstances, be pointless or serve no practical purpose, or for some other special reason. In these special circumstances, an application for judicial review could be allowed.[25]

Rule 58.4—This sets out the powers that the court has in an application for judicial review. Its powers are wide ranging and the court has a complete discretion in dealing with the decision under review. It can:

(1) grant or refuse the petition or any part of the petition with or without conditions; and
(2) make any order, including an interim order, as it thinks fit, whether or not such order was sought in the petition, provided it is an order which could be made if sought. This includes an order for reduction, declarator, suspension, interdict, implement, restitution, and payment (of damages or otherwise);
(3) make any order in relation to procedure as it thinks fit.

Examples of different orders sought are: **8–07**

* Reduction of the decision to detain under the Immigration Act, along with suspension ad interim, and interim liberation.[26]
* Declarator, reduction, interdict, and an order for specific implement.[27]
* Reduction of a decision by a local authority that the petitioner had no priority need as a homeless person, along with an order to provide accommodation and damages.[28]

---

[23] See Ch.13 of this book.
[24] See *Ingle v Ingle's Trustee*, 1999 S.L.T. 650.
[25] See *MacKinnon v Argyll and Bute Council*, 2001 S.L.T. 1275.
[26] *Sokha v Secretary of State for Home Department*, 1992 S.L.T. 1049. See also *Ahmad v Secretary of State for the Home Department*, 2001 S.L.T. 282.
[27] *JDP Investments Ltd v Strathclyde Regional Council*, 1997 S.L.T. 408.
[28] *Mallon v Monklands District Council*, 1986 S.L.T. 347.

- A student failed to pay fees for a course and was excluded by the university. He sought judicial review of the decision, declarator it had been illegal, and damages.[29]
- Declarator of entitlement to a pitch in a travelling persons' site.[30]
- Declarator that a prisoner should not be removed from a particular prison, and interdict to prevent his removal.[31]
- Declarator that new regulations relating to the provision of criminal legal aid were ultra vires and incompatible with the European Convention of Human Rights.[32]
- Declarator and reduction of part of the Criminal Injuries Compensation Scheme.[33]
- Reduction of a decision of a local authority, declarator that they were in breach of the ECHR, and "such further orders . . .(including an order for expenses) as may seem to the court to be just and reasonable in all the circumstances."[34]

The most common remedy normally sought in petitions for judicial review is reduction of the decision or part of it and the court can reduce the decision and remit it to the decision maker to reconsider. The court can pronounce a wide variety of other orders as indicated in this section. It would be normal for the petitioner to seek in the petition the particular remedies which he wants the court to grant.

8–08 **Rule 58.5**—This provides that judicial review should be heard by a judge nominated by the Lord President or, if such a judge is not available, any other judge of the court. The idea is to have such petitions decided by a judge experienced in judicial review and administrative law matters.

8–09 **Rule 58.6**—This provides the form of petition which is to be used in any application for judicial review.[35] The form provides a very basic outline. The particular features of the form which set it apart from the normal form of petition or summons in the Court of Session are:

(1) There should be a clear and simple indication, in the instance, of the decision which is to be reviewed, so that the court has an immediate indication of what the case is about;
(2) In the body of the petition the petitioner seeks specific remedies, both interim and final, but also asks for anything else which the court thinks just and reasonable;
(3) There is a requirement for the petitioner to state briefly the legal argument on which he relies, and to refer to the act or judicial

---

[29] *Joobeen v University of Stirling*, 1995 S.L.T. 120..
[30] See *McPhee v North Lanarkshire Council*, 1998 S.L.T. 1317.
[31] *Beggs v The Scottish Ministers*, 2004 S.L.T. 755.
[32] *McCall v The Scottish Ministers*, 2006 S.L.T. 365
[33] *S v Criminal Injuries Compensation Board*, 2007 S.L.T. 575.
[34] *Bibi, Petitioner*, 2007 S.L.T. 173.
[35] Reference should be made to the form at this stage: Form 58.6 of the RCS.

authority on which he relies. This kind of petition will, unlike most other written pleadings, involve stating arguments and making submissions on law, rather than just narrating facts. This should have the beneficial effect of advancing the process of focusing the dispute and narrowing down the issues. It should be easier for the respondent to respond to a petition which is obliged to set out the basis of the petitioner's legal argument.[36] Note that the defender is not required to respond in similar terms.

The pleadings in such petitions are not to be construed too strictly[37] **8–10** and the court will look at other matters put before it but extraneous to the words of the petition, in order to understand the points in issue. However, it is still necessary for the petition and the associated documents to provide fair notice of the party's case and the legal arguments in support of it. A failure to do so may prejudice the success of the petition or the defence to it. In *McDonald v Secretary of State for Scotland (No.2)*[38] the court emphasised that the court had to look first at the pleadings to understand what the action was truly about. In *Whaley v Lord Advocate*[39] there was criticism of the lack of specification of the petition because of the paucity of the facts averred in the petition on the crucial issues. In *Phillips v Strathclyde Joint Police Board (No.2)*,[40] the judge commented that the arguments presented went beyond the terms of the petition and were reliant on documents which had only been lodged immediately prior to the (first) hearing. He allowed the respondent time to consider and formulate a response. In *Leighton v Lord Advocate*,[41] there was criticism of the fact that at the hearing on the merits of the petition, certain essential documents had not been lodged before the hearing although efforts were made to refer to them at the hearing itself. Whilst the traditional pleading requirements may be regarded as relaxed in this procedure, it is still essential, as a matter of fairness, that the court and the opponent have prior notice of any significant facts, documents or arguments which are likely to be deployed at the hearing.

With a view to ensuring that the matters in dispute are quickly identified and dealt with, the rules provide that not only should the arguments be made known at the outset, but also documents should be lodged and efforts should be made to identify any document which might be relevant and material. Furthermore, affidavits can be used to assist this process. The petitioner should attach to the petition a schedule detailing any documents upon which he proposes to rely when presenting and

---

[36] If so, should this approach be adopted in other procedures?
[37] Lord Cullen in *City Cabs (Edinburgh) Ltd v City of Edinburgh District Council*, 1988 S.L.T. 184 said that in proceedings for judicial review: "There is room for a more liberal construction of pleadings than applies in Ordinary Actions".
[38] *McDonald v Secretary of State for Scotland (No.2)*, 1996 S.L.T. 575.
[39] *Whaley v Lord Advocate*, 2004 S.L.T. 425.
[40] *Phillips v Strathclyde Joint Police Board (No.2)*, 2004 S.L.T. 73.
[41] *Leighton v Lord Advocate*, 2003 S.L.T. 800.

arguing the petition and details of the individual who has that document. This primarily relates to the documents which will set out what decision was made, and why the decision was made.

There may be cases, however, where the actual decision, and the reasoning for the decision will not be contained within any document, or at least intelligibly contained within any document or documents. In that case, it is provided that if a party cannot lodge documents which will give the court a reasonable idea of what is being reviewed, then he should lodge an affidavit which states the terms of the decision under review and why it is being challenged. Affidavits of witnesses can provide speed and flexibility and also minimise cost.[42]

8–11 Rule 58.7—This provides for the making of a first order, which is in effect the order which will specify the intimation of the petition which is to be made, the documents which are to be intimated along with the petition, and the date for the first hearing. At the hearing on the motion for the first order, a petitioner can also make motions for any interim orders as specified in the petition. The period of notice to be given to the opponent may be fixed at the making of the first order. The first hearing is not to be earlier than seven days after the expiry of the period of notice. This period is intended to give the opponent an opportunity to give reasonably full instructions to counsel and to be properly represented at the first hearing, once it has been intimated.

This rule also provides that any interim order can be made when the first order is made, but it is understood that interim orders at that stage are not particularly common. A petition can be disposed of finally at the hearing on the motion for the first order.[43] In a case where interim orders are sought by a petitioner and where a caveat has been lodged by the respondent, the court will hear both parties on the interim orders before dealing with the motion for a first order.[44] It is necessary for counsel, or a solicitor advocate, to attend at the first order. Sometimes the case can be determined at the first order stage by the judge, e.g. deciding a question of competency on his own initiative. A judge hearing the first order can express his own misgivings about the competency or otherwise of the action before any order for service is made, and counsel will have to be able to satisfy him that it is competent and that an order would be appropriate.[45]

8–12 Rule 58.8—This provides for intimation of appearance by the respondent. It is also open to a person who is directly affected by any issue

---

[42] Although they do not always achieve these aims. See *East Lothian Council v Lumsden*, 2002 S.L.T. 1141.

[43] See *Sokha v Secretary of State for Home Department*, 1992 S.L.T. 1049. Also *Fife Regional Council v Scottish Legal Aid Board*, 1994 S.L.T. 96.

[44] See *Millar & Bryce Ltd v Keeper of the Registers of Scotland*, 1997 S.L.T. 1000.

[45] A question of competency might, e.g. be whether the kind of decision being appealed against is one which is susceptible to judicial review.

raised in the petition to enter an appearance even though the petitioner has not been required to serve the petition specifically on him. There is no requirement to lodge any form intimating appearance, but the opponent and the Keeper of the Rolls should be told of the other party's interest. It is suggested that parties might want to lodge answers. Indeed, this now would seem to be regarded as highly recommended even for the first hearing.[46] The answers should be framed along the same lines as any answers to a petition such as are required under RCS r.18.3. They will include pleas in law.[47]

Rule 58.8A — Any person who believes that any issue raised in the peti-   **8–13**
tion raises a matter of public interest and considers that he has propositions to make about the petition which are relevant and will assist the
court is permitted to apply for leave to "intervene" in the petition by
lodging and intimating a minute of intervention (Form 58.8A). The court
can allow or refuse leave and must fix a hearing on the minute if any of
the parties requests it. The court can only allow the intervention if it is
satisfied that there is a matter of public interest, the intervention will
assist the court and it will not unduly delay or prejudice the rights of the
parties. The expense of allowing intervention has to be considered. If
intervention is allowed, this shall be done by way of written submission
restricted to 5,000 words although the court may in exceptional circumstances permit a longer written submission to be made or even allow oral
submission. The court's decision on any aspect of the proposed intervention is final and not subject to appeal.

Rule 58.9 — This sets out what the judge can do at the first hearing once   **8–14**
he is satisfied that proper intimation has been made and once he has
heard the parties. The judge has a wide discretion, and reference should
be made to the rules, in particular r.58.9(2), for the specific options
which are open to the judge at the first hearing.[48]

Rule 58.10 — This concerns the second hearing, where the judge has   **8–15**
ordered it. It is not always necessary and obviously the ideal is for cases
to be disposed of at the first hearing, if at all possible. This rule also provides for the lodging of any relevant document not less than seven days
before the date of the second hearing. Although the courts will normally

---

[46] See the case of *Blair v Lochaber District Council*, 1995 S.L.T. 407.
[47] For example, the plea of law in *Choi v Secretary of State for the Home Department*, 1996 S.L.T. 590 was: "The petitioner not having exhausted his statutory remedies, the petition is incompetent and should be dismissed".
[48] For examples of the way in which the court has dealt with procedure recently, see *Prestige Assets Ltd v Renfrewshire Council*, 2003 S.L.T. 679 and *Whaley v Lord Advocate*, 2004 S.L.T. 425, and then at 2007 S.L.T. 1209. See also *Somerville v The Scottish Ministers*, 2007 S.L.T. 1113. The reader should also consider the cases to which reference has already been made and note the particular stage of procedure at which the court has made decisions about relevancy, competency and the merits of the petitions.

be able to deal with the case without hearing oral evidence of any sort, that option is not excluded. Parties can have a proof at the second hearing if allowed by the judge at the first hearing.[49]

At any time before the second hearing, the case can be put out by order where the court wishes to check what the parties' positions are and what is likely to be happening at the second hearing. This will enable the judge to obtain any information which he considers necessary to help him determine any remaining issues and to maintain control of procedure to avoid delay and any unnecessary preparation. If parties are having difficulty in preparing properly in time for the second hearing, then they can use a calling on the by order roll to explain this to the judge, and also to discuss with their opponent whether any shortcuts might be taken or issues excluded.

Once matters have progressed to a second hearing, the judge can do a variety of things including adjourning the hearing, continuing it or deciding the petition. He has an extremely wide discretion in these matters and the court can effectively determine the procedure itself, within these broad parameters. If the nature of the dispute is such that there is an essential issue of fact which has to be resolved before a decision can be made on all or part of the remedies sought then it is open to the court to have a proof.[50]

---

[49] See, e.g. *Rooney v Chief Constable, Strathclyde Police*, 1997 S.L.T. 1261 and *East Lothian Council v Lumsden*, 2002 S.L.T. 1141.

[50] See *Rooney v Chief Constable, Strathclyde Police*, 1997 S.L.T. 1261; *Mallon v Monklands District Council*, 1986 S.L.T. 347; and *East Lothian Council v Lumsden*, 2002 S.L.T. 1141.

Court of Session
Judicial Review
Flow Chart of Procedure

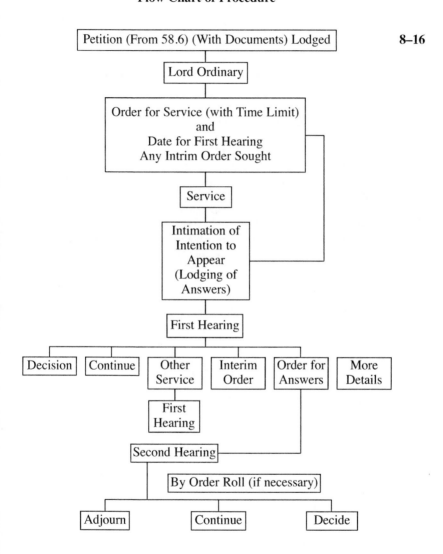

FURTHER READING

W. Stuart Gale, "Unreasonableness and proportionality: recent developments in judicial review", 2005 S.L.T. (News) 23.
Lord Clyde, *Judicial Review* (Edinburgh: SULI/W. Green, 2000).

CHAPTER 9

SHERIFF COURT ORDINARY ACTIONS

9–01 In this chapter we are going to look at the sources of the procedure and practice in what are termed "ordinary actions" in the sheriff court, consider a basic outline of the nature and content of the procedural rules which apply to such actions and then look at some of the more significant rules in detail.

A brief and concise history of the sheriff courts in Scotland can be found in the *Stair Memorial Encyclopaedia*.[1] The history of its development does not really assist an understanding of the practice of the present day sheriff court or its rules of procedure. The significant history for practical purposes starts in the early 1900s. The Sheriff Courts (Scotland) Act 1907[2] was passed for the purpose of regulating and amending the laws and practice relating to civil procedure in sheriff courts in Scotland. Whilst many of the sections of that Act no longer exist, it is still the basic starting point for a consideration of sheriff court procedures.

Sheriff courts deal with various types of action, and there are relatively few types of action which cannot competently be brought in the sheriff court. The sheriff court has privative jurisdiction for all claims up to and including £5,000 exclusive of interest and expenses. In other words, it is not possible to commence any claim for £5,000 or less in the Court of Session. An action for payment of a debt of, e.g. £15 million can competently be brought in the sheriff court because there is no upper limit to the value of actions which can be brought there. A party might prefer to raise such an action in the Court of Session for a variety of reasons[3] but there is nothing to prevent it being raised in the sheriff court. Of course, the particular sheriff court must have jurisdiction to deal with the case, and the grounds of jurisdiction for any particular sheriff court are set out in s.6 of the 1907 Act.[4] Reference should also be made in this context to the Civil Jurisdiction and Judgments Act 1982.[5]

---

[1] *Stair Memorial Encyclopaedia*, Vol. , paras 1022 to 1027.
[2] Sheriff Courts (Scotland) Act 1907 (c.51).
[3] See discussion in Ch.2.
[4] e.g. where the defender has a place of business within the geographical area covered by that sheriff court. The Scottish Courts website (*http://www.scotcourts.gov.uk* [Accessed August 1, 2008]) has a gazetteer which will show which sheriff court covers which areas.
[5] Civil Jurisdiction and Judgments Act 1982 (c.27). The precise provisions regarding jurisdiction are complex and beyond the scope of this book.

Section 39 of the 1907 Act set out the rules of procedure which were **9–02** to regulate the conduct of all ordinary causes raised in the sheriff court. These rules of procedure were contained within the first Schedule to the Act and, with the exception of certain matters,[6] there were remarkably few changes in the procedural rules for over 80 years.

Under the Sheriff Courts (Scotland) Act 1971,[7] provision was made to amend the law regarding sheriff courts in Scotland but most of those amendments were administrative and not procedural. By s.32 of the 1971 Act, the Court of Session[8] was given express power to regulate and prescribe the procedure and practice to be followed in any civil proceedings in the sheriff court. This was to be done by way of Act of Sederunt. Section 33 of the 1971 Act established a body to be known as the Sheriff Court Rules Council, whose function was to keep under review the procedure and practice followed in civil proceedings in the sheriff court, and prepare and submit to the Court of Session suggested draft rules for regulating sheriff court procedure and practice.

The most significant change brought about at the instigation of the **9–03** Sheriff Court Rules Council was the introduction of a completely new set of rules of procedure for Sheriff Court Ordinary Causes in 1993.[9] This was brought in after a lengthy review and consultation process, and the new procedure was intended to take account of criticisms which had been made of sheriff court practice under the former procedural rules. The criticisms were the familiar ones of delay, excessive formality and unnecessary complexity. The Sheriff Court Rules Council followed certain primary objectives for the new rules, namely:

(1) cases should only call in court when necessary;
(2) the number of times a case should call in court should be kept to a minimum;
(3) the rules should prescribe periods for completion of the various stages of procedure (in other words, a timetable);
(4) the control and management of cases should be vested in the court rather than the parties; and
(5) the procedures of the Court of Session and the sheriff court should be harmonised wherever possible.

These principles were the basis for the new rules for ordinary cause procedure which were brought into being as the Ordinary Cause Rules 1993 of the Act of Sederunt (Sheriff Court Ordinary Cause Rules) 1993 (SI 1993/1956) substituted a new first Schedule for the original Schedule in the 1907 Act. The 1993 Rules have in effect replaced the old

---

[6] Such as the development of family actions (including divorces) and the passing of primary legislation post-1907 creating new jurisdictions for the sheriff court in particular subject areas.
[7] Sheriff Courts (Scotland) Act 1971 (c.58).
[8] In its capacity as the supreme court in Scotland.
[9] Referred to as the OCR in this book.

rules as the rules of procedure for ordinary causes in the sheriff court. There have been further Acts of Sederunt since 1993, altering and refining the rules in the light of experience and practice, but nothing of any great significance and the general format and framework of the rules has remained the same.

The rules run to over 80 pages[10] excluding forms. Many of the rules apply to family actions in the sheriff court with which this book is not concerned. The rules provide approximately 30 different forms relating to ordinary causes and it is not easy to read and understand these rules and forms without some appreciation of the practical context in which they are used.

The rules of procedure in the 1993 Rules were in effect the first concerted effort to make a significant change in the way in which litigations were conducted in the sheriff court for over 100 years. Solicitors had to come to terms with these changes which demanded a different culture and a different approach to the handling of litigation. This was not an easy transition,[11] and the operation of the rules in practice has not yet had the full desired effect on the handling of sheriff court litigation. Generally, litigation in the sheriff court is faster. The number of times a case has to call in court has been significantly reduced. The effectiveness of the options hearing[12] has not been fully realised. The availability of administrative resources to support the operation of the rules, as in every set of procedural rules, is a factor in their effectiveness. The Sheriff Court Rules Council continues to keep the practices and procedures under review and propose alterations where considered appropriate, but whether the "new" rules will ultimately achieve their objectives in practice still remains to be seen.[13]

9–04   The number of ordinary causes initiated in 1996 in all the sheriff courts in Scotland was 45,660. About 50 per cent of these were actions for payment of debt. About 20 per cent were family actions, and about 10 per cent were actions by mortgage lenders seeking to recover arrears of mortgages and/or repossessing the mortgaged property. Around 5 per cent were actions of damages for personal injury or other losses. In 1998, there were 48,423 action initiated as ordinary causes. More than half of them were undefended. About 50 per cent of the actions raised were actions for payment of debt. There were just over 8,000 divorces (of which just over 6,000 were undefended). In 2002, there were 46,605 ordinary causes initiated. In 2006 there were 60,014 actions initiated.

---

[10] The rules can be found in the *Parliament House Book*, pp.D44/29–D44/112 (as at Release 97).
[11] This can be seen from the many cases about the operation of the "new" rules which were reported in the years immediately after their introduction.
[12] A pivotal feature of the new rules.
[13] See the report by the Central Research Unit of the Scottish Office 1995 HMSO (9501252) 3/95; the report by the Central Research Unit in 1997 on the implementation of the OCR 1993 J15424 11/97. See, also, Richard Mays, "Frying Pan, Fire or Melting Pot?—Reforming Scottish Civil Justice in 1990s", 1997 J.R. 91. Rachel Wadia, "Judicial case management in Scotland: indecision and indigestion", 1997 S.L.T. (News) 255.

NARRATIVE

If a party wishes to raise an ordinary action in the sheriff court, his **9–05** solicitor will draw up an initial writ which should follow a basic form outlined in the rules. The writ is lodged with the sheriff clerk along with an appropriate fee so that the clerk can issue a warrant for service of the writ. The warrant is the authority of the court to serve a copy of the writ on the proposed defender. Once a pursuer has the principal writ along with the warrant, he can then serve this on the defender by post or by sheriff officer. The defender will receive a copy of the writ,[14] along with a copy of the court's warrant, and a form of citation, together with a form (Form O7),[15] which he can use to advise the court that he is intending to defend the action.

The defender has 21 days[16] from the date of service of the writ on him in which to respond by lodging the Form O7. If he fails to do so, then the pursuer can ask the court for a decree in absence. If the defender lodges Form O7 signifying his intention to defend the case, then the clerk will issue to both parties Form G5.

Form G5 is a form which gives both the pursuer and the defender various dates of procedural significance in the action, and this effectively sets the timetable for the progress of the action.

Three separate dates are given in Form G5, and they are set by the clerk in accordance with the timetable provided in the rules:

(1) a note of the last day for lodging written defences. This will be 14 days after the expiry of the period of notice on the defender[17];
(2) the last day for making adjustments to the writ or the defences. This is the day up to which both parties can make adjustments to their written pleadings;
(3) a note of the date, time and place for the options hearing which must be fixed in the case. The options hearing is the most significant procedural hearing[18] in the action. The options hearing is to take place on the first court day occurring not sooner than 10 weeks after the expiry of the period of notice from the service of the writ.[19]

In a defended action, the pursuer must return the principal initial writ to the court, together with confirmation of the date when the writ was served on the defender, within seven days of the expiry of the period of notice.

The defences lodged to the initial writ should be in the form of answers in separate paragraphs corresponding to the articles of condescendence, i.e. the numbered paragraphs in the writ. A consideration of the writ and

---

[14] This is known as a service copy,
[15] There is an appendix to the rules which contains styles of numerous forms.
[16] Usually.
[17] i.e. 14 days after 21 days from the service of the writ.
[18] As opposed to hearing on the merits.
[19] i.e. more or less three months from the service of proceedings on the defender.

the defences at that time should give a basic idea of what the parties are disputing, although in practice, it is not uncommon for defenders to lodge brief (skeleton) defences if they have insufficient time or insufficient information to enable them to lodge detailed defences.

The parties are allowed a period of time up to 14 days before the options hearing to adjust the writ and to adjust the defences. If they have any adjustments, then they will simply intimate them to the opponent, and the adjustments are not formally recorded in any of the papers kept by the court.

If a party has included in his written pleadings a preliminary plea,[20] and if he wants to insist upon the preliminary plea, i.e. argue it at a debate, then he is obliged to lodge a note with the court explaining the basis of his preliminary plea at least three days before the options hearing. If he does not do so, then the preliminary plea will be repelled. At least two days before the options hearing, the pursuer has to lodge in court a record which will show the parties' respective written pleadings as adjusted as at the end of the adjustment period. By that stage, it is expected that the parties will have said all that they intend to say about the merits of their own case and of their opponent's case.[21]

9–06   When the options hearing takes place, the sheriff is obliged to, "secure the expeditious progress of the cause" and he has to do this by ascertaining from the parties the matters which are in dispute[22] and indeed any other information which may be relevant to the future procedure in the case. The parties are obliged to have sufficient information when they are appearing at the options hearing to enable the court to decide the appropriate order to be made.

The options which are open to the sheriff at the options hearing are:

(1) he can fix a proof on the whole or part of the case so that the issues can be decided following the leading of evidence in support of the parties' respective positions;

(2) he can fix a proof before answer, where there is a preliminary plea;

(3) he can fix a legal debate if he thinks there is a particular matter of law involved in the case which the parties want to have decided before evidence is led and which he considers ought to be decided before evidence is led;

(4) he can take the view, on his own initiative or on being persuaded by parties, that the case is complex enough to make it necessary that the parties be given further time to lodge adjustments to their written pleadings rather than fixing a proof or debate at that stage. He would order that the case proceeds under the "additional procedure";

(5) he can continue the options hearing for no more than 28 days if there is a good reason for doing so.

---

[20] See Ch.4.

[21] In practice this expectation is not frequently fulfilled.

[22] This should be apparent from the record but that is not always so.

It is also open to the sheriff, when allowing a proof or proof before answer at the options hearing, to order the parties to lodge a joint minute of admissions or agreement. Indeed, he can make any other orders in connection with the final hearing of the case as he might think fit.[23]

If the court decides at the options hearing to fix a proof or a proof before answer, then the following basic steps would have to be taken by the parties:

(1) a date would have to be allocated for the hearing of the proof. This would be done in accordance with whatever administrative arrangements were appropriate for that court. Some courts will allocate the date for proof at the options hearing itself, but other courts will have this dealt with administratively by the parties in consultation with the sheriff clerk;

(2) within 14 days of the proof being "allowed"[24] the parties have to exchange details of their respective witnesses;

(3) not later than 14 days before the proof itself, productions in the case have to be lodged and intimated to the opponent;

(4) a shorthand writer has to be ordered by the pursuer;

(5) witnesses have to be cited to attend court on the day allocated for the proof.

At the same time as fixing a proof the sheriff may[25] fix a "pre-proof hearing" which is a hearing fixed (usually) about two weeks before the proof itself at which the sheriff will ascertain if the parties are ready to proceed to proof on the date allocated and if they have complied with any preparations for the proof required by the rules or by the court at the options hearing.

If the court fixes a debate at the options hearing, then there are no **9–07** particular rules which govern procedure prior to the debate and the only matter of procedure and practice which might be of relevance would be the lodging of a note of authorities[26] in accordance with the administrative arrangements set out in any practice note for that particular court.

If the court decides at the options hearing to order that the case should continue under the additional procedure, then the sheriff continues the case for adjustment of the pleadings for a further period of eight weeks after the options hearing. This means that the parties can continue to adjust their written pleadings up to the end of that period.[27] When that period expires, then the record will automatically close. The court will fix a procedural hearing which will be on the first suitable court day not

---

[23] The practice on this point can vary considerably. Generally, sheriffs do not make "orders" at this stage but can often indicate to parties that they expect certain matters to be agreed in advance of a proof.

[24] Which is not the same as the date for proof being fixed.

[25] He is not obliged to.

[26] A list of the cases, legal texts and other authorities bearing upon the legal issues which are going to be argued at the debate.

[27] That period can, however, be altered in certain circumstances.

sooner than 21 days after the closing of the record. At the procedural hearing, the sheriff will be required to do very much the same as he was required to do at the options hearing. He will have similar options open to him but restricted only to the options of fixing a proof, proof before answer or debate. He cannot continue the action and he cannot allow any further time for adjustment of written pleadings.

The rules provide procedures for recovering documents which might be relevant to the case and which are held by the opponent or indeed by anyone else.[28]

The rules also provide that parties can make a motion to the court for a decree by default[29] if the opponent fails to comply with an order of the court or fails to comply with the timetable set down.

There are rules also which entitle a party to ask the court for a summary decree[30] where, at any time after the time allowed for lodging defences it appears that there is no real defence to the action, or part of it, disclosed in the defences. In this way, the pursuer does not have to wait until the options hearing or some other step in the procedure before seeking a decree from the court.

9–08   There are particular rules regarding amendment of pleadings,[31] counterclaims,[32] and third party procedure.[33]

There are also particular rules regarding the lodging, intimating and hearing of any incidental motions[34] which might be required by either party during the course of the action. The court will only require parties to appear before them to justify a written motion, where the opponent has indicated that he is opposing the motion, or where, even if the motion is not opposed, the court considers it appropriate to hear argument in favour of the motion. Otherwise, a motion will be granted without any appearance in court and on the basis of the information in the written motion itself.

The rules contain detailed provisions regarding the hearing of a proof which cover, amongst other things:

(1) procedure for requesting proof in whole or in part by affidavit evidence or for admission of a specified statement or document as evidence without calling the author;
(2) procedure for agreeing all of the relevant facts in a case to enable the matter to be resolved by a debate on agreed facts;
(3) hearing parts of the proof separately;
(4) citation of witnesses and compulsion of the attendance of witnesses;
(5) lodging of productions and copying of productions;
(6) notices to admit facts;

---

[28] See para.15–21, below.
[29] See Ch.19.
[30] See Ch.19.
[31] See paras 17–12 to 17–13, below.
[32] See Ch.15.
[33] See Ch.15.
[34] See Ch.15.

(7) instruction of a shorthand writer for the proof;
(8) recording of evidence;
(9) hearing argument on the merits of a case at the close of a proof.

The rules go on to deal with particular matters regarding decrees including the form of the decree, decrees in foreign currency, and "extracting" decrees.[35]

The rules make provision for appeals including provisions for leave **9–09** to appeal where this might be necessary, special provision for procedure in appeals to the Court of Session, special provision for procedure in appeals to the sheriff principal, and other incidental provisions regarding appeals.

The rules also provide procedure for the taxing[36] of expenses in any ordinary action by the auditor of court.

There is a separate Chapter of the rules dealing with commercial actions, a special form of procedure available in certain sheriff courts.[37]

Leaving aside family actions, the remaining rules deal with a number of miscellaneous matters, including special rules relating to actions of damages for personal injury, actions of presumption of death, actions of multiple pointing,[38] actions of removing and references to the European Court.

PARTICULAR RULES

We shall now look at some of the individual rules and explain the signif- **9–10** icant rules. The rules are split into Chapters and, e.g. r.1.1 is the first rule in Ch.1. Where possible, reference will be made to a decided case in which the rule has been interpreted or considered. Some of the specific procedures are dealt with in more detail in other chapters of the book. It should be possible to see the links between certain of the Sheriff Court rules and the Court of Session rules for similar forms of procedure.[39] Care must be taken, however, because there are differences of detail between the two which can have a significant practical effect. If in doubt, reference must be made to the precise terms of the two sets of rules.

Chapter 1

Rule 1.4—If the rules require the use of a form, such as are set out in the **9–11** appendices, then it is not necessary to use the exact form but a variation of it may suffice. In practice, it is preferable to use the form and it is rarely necessary to depart from the precise wording of the form.

---

[35] This means applying to the court for a certified copy of the decree which a party needs before he can take steps to enforce it.
[36] This means the "assessing" of judicial expenses. See Ch.21.
[37] See Ch.10 for details.
[38] See Ch.13.
[39] As set out in Ch.5.

Chapter 2—Relief from compliance with the rules

9–12 Rule 2.1—The court can grant relief from a failure to comply with the rules which is shown to be due to, "mistake, oversight or other excusable cause".[40]

Chapter 3—Commencement of cause

9–13 Rule 3.1—This provides that an ordinary cause shall be commenced by an initial writ in Form G1. This simply contains the broadest of outlines of a writ.[41] The writ should be written, typed or printed on A4 paper. The writ must say certain formal things regarding, inter alia, jurisdiction. The writ has to be signed. The writ is then sent to the sheriff clerk for the court to authorise service of the writ on the defender by providing a warrant of citation.

Rule 3.3—The warrant of citation for an initial writ should be in Form O1. This will be a standard printed form which the sheriff clerk will complete and sign when a warrant of citation is required.[42] In cases where a time to pay direction may be applied for,[43] then the citation is to be in Form O2.

Rule 3.6—The period of notice which has to be given to a defender for the service of proceedings on him is 21 days after the date of service provided the defender is resident or has a place of business within Europe and 42 days if he is resident or has a place of business outside Europe. It is open to the sheriff to shorten the period of notice.

Chapter 4—Caveats

9–14 Rule 4.1—This gives details of orders against which caveats[44] may be lodged and the form of caveat.[45] It will remain in force for one year from the date of lodging and will then have to be renewed.[46]

Chapter 5—Citation, service and intimation

9–15 Rules 5.1 to 5.10—These rules provide for the citation of defenders and service and intimation of proceedings on them. Reference should be made to the rules themselves for the details. There are specific forms which are to be used in particular circumstances depending upon the method of service used and the designation[47] of the defender.

---

[40] The "dispensing power". See Ch.1.
[41] For an interesting case on what is an initial writ, see *British Railways Board v Strathclyde Regional Council*, 1982 S.L.T. 55.
[42] See *Fitzpatrick v Advocate General for Scotland*, 2004 S.L.T. (Sh. Ct) 93.
[43] Under the Debtors (Scotland) Act 1987 s.1 the court may, on the application of a debtor, direct that certain types of decree against him should be paid by instalments. For the types of decree to which this would not apply see s.1(5).
[44] See para.13–08, below.
[45] Form G2.
[46] See *Stewart Nicolson (Caveat: Specification)*, 1995 S.C.L.R. 389.
[47] Address.

The simplest and most common form of service will be by first class recorded delivery post.[48] Service can be effected by sheriff officer, and service of documents on people residing outwith Scotland can be done by reference to the specific rules in r.5.5. Where the address of a defender is not known, then service can be done by publication of an advertisement in a newspaper or by displaying on the walls of court. If a defender carries on business under a trading or descriptive name, then he can sue or be sued in that name.[49] Rule 5.10 provides that if an individual appears in court in a case, then he will not be entitled to state any objection to the regularity of the service of the court papers on him and his appearance itself would remedy any defect in the citation or service upon him.

Chapter 7—Undefended causes

Rules 7.1 to 7.6—These relate to cases which are not defended and **9–16** primarily provide a procedure whereby, if an action is not defended, the sheriff can grant a decree in absence without anyone attending at court. The pursuer completes and signs a minute for decree on the initial writ. This minute is printed on the reverse side of the warrant for citation granted by the court when the initial writ is first presented. There are special provisions regarding decrees in absence against persons domiciled outwith Scotland. The minute is lodged with the sheriff clerk who will present it to the sheriff for the sheriff to grant decree if appropriate.

Chapter 8—Reponing

Rule 8.1—The defender may apply to be reponed against a decree in **9–17** absence[50] by lodging a reponing note with the sheriff clerk. This is a document which sets out his proposed defence and explains the failure to appear.[51] There is a specific procedure for hearing arguments on the allowance of a reponing note. This can often be hotly contested, especially if it appears doubtful that there is a genuine defence.[52]

Chapter 9—Standard procedure in defended causes

This is dealt with in some more detail here because this is the "core" **9–18** chapter of the rules which is intended to provide the framework of procedure for all defended cases.

---

[48] In the simplest case, the service copy writ, a copy of the warrant, Form O4, Form O7, and (where a time to pay direction may be appropriate) Form O5 will be sent to the defender by first class recorded delivery post.
[49] e.g. it is permissible to sue an individual called Mr N who trades as a shop called Food Stores, 1 Bell St, simply as "Food Stores, 1 Bell St"—although there might be good reasons to include his own name.
[50] i.e. ask the court to recall the decree.
[51] See *Thorn Security v Calders Mechanical Services Ltd*, 1994 S.C.L.R. 690; *Forbes v Johnstone*, 1995 S.L.T. 158; *Thompson v Jardine*, 2004 SLT 1214 ; and, more recently, *Russell v van Overwaele*, Unreported (Sh. Ct) March 2, 2005, Sheriff Principal Kerr.
[52] See Ch.19.

Rule 9.1—If a defender wants to defend the case, he will lodge with the sheriff clerk a notice of intention to defend (Form O7)[53] and send a copy to the pursuer.

Rule 9.2—When this has been done, the clerk will issue a form (G5) to both parties. That form will tell the parties:

(1) the last date for lodging defences;
(2) the last date for adjustment of pleadings; and
(3) the date of the options hearing.

The date of the options hearing will be the first suitable court date no sooner than 10 weeks after expiry of the period of notice.[54] If a second options hearing requires to be fixed after the first one has been given to the parties,[55] then the first options hearing is discharged automatically and the timetable altered to tie in with the new options hearing.[56]

Rule 9.2A—The sheriff and/or the parties may alter the date of the options hearing originally assigned in the Form G5.

Rule 9.3—The pursuer must return the principal initial writ to the sheriff clerk within seven days after the expiry of the period of notice.

Rule 9.4—If there is any type of hearing before the options hearing[57] each party should lodge a copy of his pleadings with the court two days before the hearing date.[58]

Rule 9.5—When an action is to be defended, the clerk prepares a process folder which includes a number of separate sheets or files as provided in the rule.[59] Any document lodged in connection with the case will be placed in the process folder.[60]

Rule 9.6—Defences have to be lodged within 14 days of the expiry of the period of notice.[61] The basic form of defences is outlined.

---

[53] Which will have been sent to him by the pursuer when the writ was served.
[54] Thus, the options hearing is likely to take place three to four months after the action was served on the defender.
[55] An example would be where the pursuer serves proceedings against a second defender some time after serving against the first defender.
[56] Rule 9.2A, which was added with effect from November 1996 to cure problems identified in *Blyszczak v GEC Marconi Avionics Ltd*, 1996 S.L.T. (Sh. Ct) 54.
[57] e.g. a hearing on a motion.
[58] In practice, this rule is not often followed.
[59] The idea is similar to the Court of Session system but the appearance and content of the two processes are quite different.
[60] e.g. a motion or an inventory of productions for a proof.
[61] Failure to do so could lead to the pursuer making a motion for decree by default—but this is rarely done unless it appears that the defence of the action is purely dilatory.

Rule 9.7—This contains express provision that every statement of fact made by a party in his pleadings should be answered by the other party. If that fact is within the knowledge of the opponent and is not denied then he shall be deemed to have admitted it.[62]

Rule 9.8—Each party may adjust his pleadings until 14 days before the date of the options hearing. The adjustments are exchanged between the parties and not lodged with the court. No adjustments after that period will be allowed except with leave of the sheriff.[63]

Rule 9.9—If a case has been sisted, any period of adjustment before the **9–19** date of the sist will be taken into account in calculating the timetable for the case and the new date for the options hearing when the sist is recalled. There has been concern that parties could take the control of the progress of the case away from the court by sisting the action if they required further time to do adjustments.[64] This provision preserves the timescales so far as possible.[65]

Rule 9.10—The sheriff can, during the adjustment period, order any party to lodge an open record showing the current state of the pleadings.[66]

Rule 9.11—At the end of the adjustment period and not later than two days[67] before the options hearing, the pursuer shall make up a record showing all of the pleadings in the case and lodge a certified copy of the record with the court. The aim is to ensure that the sheriff presiding at the options hearing can study a full record of the pleadings in advance of the options hearing. He is required to consider the pleadings and other relevant documents in advance of the hearing so that he can exercise the "case management" powers given to him in the rules. This rule gave rise to many cases in the early days of the OCR where parties had not lodged records on time (albeit some of them were lodged before the options hearing) and the court granted decree by default for the failure to do so.[68] Practitioners have now appreciated the importance of the time for lodging the record and the dire consequences of such an omission. The courts are probably more understanding now if there is some good reason for a

---

[62] This is simply a formal expression of what would be regarded as good pleading practice. See Ch.3.
[63] See *Taylor v Stakis Plc*, 1995 S.L.T. (Sh. Ct) 14.
[64] Or simply required further time to deal with the case.
[65] In this same context, r.15.6 provides that any motion for a sist must state the reason for the sist and the sheriff can, of his own volition, recall any sist. In practice, some courts will only sist for a specified period of time rather than indefinitely.
[66] This may be required if there is some incidental hearing, e.g. a motion, and the pleadings have become complex. It is rarely necessary.
[67] For what this means, see *Ritchie v Maersk Co Ltd*, 1994 S.C.L.R. 1038.
[68] See, e.g. *DTZ Debenham Thorpe v I. Henderson Transport Services*, 1995 S.L.T. 553 and *Group 4 Total Security v Jaymarke Developments*, 1995 S.C.L.R. 303.

delay in lodging a record.[69] The court can be asked to exercise the dispensing power in respect of any such failure but this certainly cannot be taken for granted.[70]

9–20 **Rule 9.12**—Options hearing: it is very important to understand what this hearing is designed to achieve, and how the rules attempt to support its objectives, because it is intended to be the pivotal hearing in the whole sheriff court ordinary cause procedure. This procedural calling of the case will take place automatically about three or four months after the action is raised. The court should, by this time, have an accurate record with details of the parties written pleadings and may have a r.22.1 note[71] for one or other or both parties too. The sheriff has an opportunity to study the papers in advance of the hearing and his function is to, "secure the expeditious progress"[72] of the cause. He is required to ascertain from the parties the matters in dispute[73] and seek further relevant information about the case. The parties attending the options hearing are obliged to supply sufficient information about the case to assist him.[74] He then has to decide which "option" for further procedure would be the most appropriate in the circumstances.[75] Before considering the procedural "options" available to the sheriff, it is necessary to explain the content and purpose of the r.22.1 note which will often be lodged by parties for the options hearing.

Rule 22.1—This rule provides that, if a party has a preliminary plea[76] in his pleadings and wishes to insist on that preliminary plea,[77] then he must lodge in process a note of the basis of his preliminary plea[78] not later than three days before the options hearing.[79] He must also send a copy of the note to his opponent. The aim is to give the sheriff and the opponent an opportunity to consider whether there is any substance in the preliminary plea and consider what effect this should have on further

---

[69] Not, however, if there is no record at all for the options hearing.

[70] A recent case in which such a failure was excused on appeal is *Mills v Chief Constable, Lothian and Borders Police* Unreported (Sh. Ct) April 25, 2005, Sheriff Principal A. Stewart.

[71] See next paragraph.

[72] See *Morran v GDCTA*, 1994 S.C.L.R. 1065 and *Mahoney v Officer*, 1994 S.C.L.R. 1059.

[73] These may or may not be apparent from the terms of the pleadings.

[74] See *Gordon v Mayfair Homes*, 1994 S.C.L.R. 862.

[75] The spirit of the rule was explained by Sheriff Principal Macphail in *East Lothian Council v Crane* Unreported (Sh. Ct) December 23, 2003, as requiring the sheriff to, "take an active part in focusing the matters truly in dispute" and the court has an overriding power to act in such a way as to, "do justice between the parties." This case involved a party litigant who could not reasonably be expected to be aware of the technical requirements of the rules for options hearings.

[76] See Ch.4.

[77] This means that he would want a debate or a proof before answer.

[78] An explanation or justification of the plea. The form of r.22.1 note is not prescribed in the rules and can vary quite significantly in practice.

[79] Or a procedural hearing under the additional procedure.

procedure for the case.[80] It is a vital part of the regime for case management provided by the options hearing.

If a party with a preliminary plea does not lodge a r.22.1 note, then he shall be considered to be no longer wishing to insist upon the plea and the plea "shall be" repelled.[81] The court would then simply fix a proof.

Where there is a preliminary plea and a r.22.1 note, a sheriff has no power at the options hearing to repel the preliminary plea either *ex proprio motu* or on the motion of the other party.[82] In these circumstances, even if the sheriff doubted the justification for the plea, he would have to fix a proof before answer.

Returning to the options hearing itself, the sheriff has power to fix a proof, proof before answer or debate. He can order that a difficult or complex case should proceed under the "additional procedure" provided in Ch.10 of the rules. Alternatively, he can continue the options hearing for no more than 28 days.[83] Where the options hearing is continued this is often done to allow a party to adjust his pleadings. If the adjustment adds a preliminary plea, then a r.22.1 note must be intimated and lodged three days before the continued options hearing. Any note in support of a plea taken at the original options hearing would suffice for the continued options hearing, but a further note can be done.[84]

If the sheriff allows a proof or proof before answer then he can make orders regarding the agreement about evidence which is likely to be uncontroversial, although, in practice, the sheriff will encourage this rather than make an order.[85]

Where the sheriff fixes a proof at the options hearing he may also fix a pre-proof hearing to take place some time before the proof and at which he can ascertain whether it is likely that the proof will actually be going ahead. He can enquire about the state of preparation of the parties and about other factors which will give an indication of the likelihood of the proof proceeding, e.g. if there are difficulties with witnesses attending or whether there are prospects of the case being settled. This is as much an administrative hearing as a judicial one and can be very helpful in the management of business in sheriff courts with limited resources.

---

[80] As a simple example, if a defender takes a preliminary plea to the effect that the pursuer's case is irrelevant, i.e. there is no good legal basis for it, the court might think that there would be no justification for fixing a proof (a hearing of evidence) because the whole case could be decided simply and solely by a legal debate which might well have the effect of disposing of the whole dispute.

[81] An oversight in failing to lodge the note on time could have a significant effect on the procedural progress of an action. See *Bell v John Davidson (Pipes) Ltd*, 1995 S.L.T. (Sh. Ct) 18 and *Dinardo Partnership v Tait*, 1995 S.C.L.R. 941.

[82] *Tilcon (Scotland) Ltd v Jarvis (Scotland) Ltd*, 2000 S.L.T. (Sh. Ct) 55.

[83] Often this is requested to enable further adjustment of pleadings. See *Strathclyde Business Park (Management) Ltd v Cochrane*, 1995 S.L.T. (Sh. Ct) 69.

[84] The rules were amended to take account of comments in *Hart v Thorntons*, 1995 S.C.L.R. 642.

[85] See *Weatherall v Jack*, 1995 S.C.L.R. 189.

There is no obligation to fix a pre-proof hearing which is entirely within the sheriff's discretion.

An important issue which often arises at an options hearing is whether the case should go to debate. The fixing of a debate will, inevitably, delay the progress of an action. In former times, defenders would take preliminary pleas as a matter of routine in almost every case and seek a debate in those cases. The rules meant that the defender could insist on having a debate even if there was no real substance to the point they wanted to take. Apart from anything else, this delayed the pursuer's remedy, and often caused substantial delay in the progress of the action. The OCR regime attempted to address that anomaly. The original rule required the sheriff to appoint the cause to debate at the options hearing after hearing submissions and considering any r.22.1 note, "if satisfied that there is a preliminary matter of law which justifies a debate". There were a number of interesting cases on this point which are well worth reading to give a good appreciation of the role of options hearings in directing the progress of an action in the sheriff court. The cases also give a further insight into the function of a debate in civil litigation which is not always properly understood.[86] The precise terms of the rule were changed recently[87] to the effect that, before fixing a debate, the sheriff must now be satisfied that there is a preliminary matter of law which, "if established following debate would lead to decree in favour of any party, or to limitation of proof to any substantial degree". There was some concern that parties were still obtaining debates too easily and this change emphasises the point that there has to be a sound justification for permitting the procedure in an action to be delayed by a debate.

Chapter 9A—Documents and witnesses

9–21 **Rule 9A.2**—Within 14 days after a proof or proof before answer has been allowed, each party must advise[88] the other of the documents in his possession or control which he is intending to use as evidence in the case so as to give the opponent the opportunity to inspect them. This rule was intended to give parties access at an early stage to the opponent's documentary evidence and the theory was that this would encourage disclosure of details of the case. This would, in turn, facilitate settlements or at least reduce the disputed evidence to be led at a proof. This rule is rarely followed in practice nor do opponents complain if it is not followed.

Rule 9A.3—Within 28 days after the proof or proof before answer has been allowed each party is obliged to intimate a list of his witnesses to

---

[86] See *Gracey v Sykes*, 1994 S.C.L.R. 909; *Blair & Bryden v Adair*, 1995 S.C.L.R. 358; *MacFarlane v Falkirk Council*, 2000 S.L.T. (Sh. Ct) 29; and, as a contrast, *Cyma Petroleum (UK) Ltd v Total Logistics Concepts Ltd*, 2004 S.L.T. (Sh. Ct) 112.

[87] By the Act of Sederunt (Ordinary Cause, Summary Application, Summary Cause and Small Claim Rules) Amendment (Miscellaneous) 2004 (SSI 2004/197), which came into force on May 21, 2004.

[88] This is distinct from lodging the documents as productions—which may be done later.

the opponent. This is intended to encourage disclosure again[89] and facilitate the reduction of the matters in dispute or promote settlement. Again, this is not followed often in practice and parties rarely complain about it provided they are given some notice of the details of the opponent's witnesses in advance of the proof. The rule provides that if a party seeks to call a witness at a proof who is not on the list which should have been intimated and the opponent objects, the sheriff has a discretion whether to allow this.[90]

Chapter 10—Additional procedure

If a sheriff decides at an options hearing that a case is difficult or complex and is unsuitable for the standard procedure envisaged for most cases, he can order that it proceed under the additional procedure. The case will then be continued for adjustment from the options hearing for a period of eight more weeks. That period can subsequently be varied in certain circumstances. Once that adjustment period ends, the record will close and the clerk will fix a procedural hearing.[91] That should be no sooner than 21 days from the closing of the record and the pursuer is required to lodge a closed record with all of the parties' pleadings with the court within 14 days of the interlocutor which closes the record. At the procedural hearing, the sheriff will deal with the case in the same manner as he would have done at an options hearing, although the options are more limited.[92]

9–22

Chapter 11—The process

Rules 11.1 to 11.8 contain provisions regarding the form of process, borrowing of parts of the process, lodging parts of process, etc. and other practical matters regarding the documents which comprise the process. The rules also provide for the manner of intimation of any adjustments, documents and motions to the opponent.

9–23

Chapter 12—Interlocutors

This contains administrative details regarding the content and signing of court interlocutors.

9–24

Chapter 13—Party minuter procedure

A person who has not been called as a defender or third party may apply by minute to be allowed to enter a process in which he claims he

9–25

---

[89] The opponent would be able to precognosce all of the other party's witnesses well in advance—if they were prepared to give him a precognition.

[90] He will normally consider if there will be any prejudice or unfairness to the opponent in allowing this.

[91] Not to be confused with a "procedure roll hearing" in the Court of Session.

[92] He cannot continue a procedural hearing.

has some title or interest. He is required to follow the procedure set out in this chapter. Reference should be made to the rules.

Chapter 14—Applications by minute

9–26 Rules 14.1 to 14.13 deal with the procedure where application is made to the court by minute. It is difficult to categorise or simplify the types of application which must be made to the court by minute.[93] Some applications by minute follow specific procedure, such as minutes of amendment, minutes of abandonment and joint minutes. They are used more often in family actions and it is rare for them to be used in other ordinary actions. Reference can be made to the rules, which generally provide for the form of minute, intimation of the minute to an opponent, opposition to a minute and hearing of a minute.

Chapter 15—Motions[94]

Chapter 16—Decree by default

9–27 Generally, a default exists if a party fails to lodge a document within the period required under the rules,[95] fails to implement an order of the sheriff within a specified period, or fails to appear or be represented at any diet. There were many cases regarding decrees by default in the period immediately after the introduction of the new rules.[96] If there is a default the sheriff can grant decree or dismiss the action or make such other order as he thinks fit to secure the expeditious progress of the action.[97]

Chapter 17—Summary decrees[98]

Chapter 18—Amendment of pleadings

9–28 Rules 18.1 to 18.8 give the sheriff power to allow certain amendments and make provisions for hearing parties on any amendment which is proposed. An amendment which simply alters the sum sued for in a defended action prior to the closing of the record requires no permission from the court. Otherwise, any amendment to a party's pleadings may, in the discretion of the court, be allowed if it is considered to be, "necessary for the purposes of determining the real question in controversy between the parties". A party who requires to amend may well be found liable for the expense of the amendment procedure.

---

[93] For an illustration see *Sleaford Trading Co v R.D. Norman*, 1994 S.C.L.R. 1093.

[94] See Ch.15.

[95] e.g. failure to lodge defences within 14 days. See *Muir v Stewart*, 1994 S.C.L.R. 935.

[96] See *Armando De Melo v Rezza Bazazi*, 1994 S.C.L.R. 564 and 1172; *McGowan v Cartner*, 1995 S.C.L.R. 312; and *Colonial Mutual Group v Johnston*, 1995 S.C.L.R. 1165.

[97] Rule 162(2)—a new rule replacing the rule which gave the sheriff no option other than to grant decree or dismiss the case.

[98] See Ch.19.

Chapter 19—Counterclaims[99]

Chapter 20—Third party procedure[100]

Chapter 21—Documents founded on or adopted in pleadings

Any document which is founded upon or the terms of which have been **9–29** adopted in a party's pleadings must be lodged at the time when it is referred to in the pleadings. If this is not done then the opponent can seek to recover it by specification[101] at the other party's expense.

Chapter 23—Abandonment[102]

Chapter 24—Withdrawal of solicitors

Where a solicitor withdraws from acting for a party, he must intimate **9–30** this by letter to the sheriff clerk and to the other party.[103] The sheriff shall[104] ordain the party to appear or be represented at court on a specific date allocated for that purpose. The party is informed that if he fails to do so the sheriff may grant decree or any other order against him. A copy of the court interlocutor fixing that date and a copy of Form G10 must be sent to the party by the opponent. The client must actually turn up or have new solicitors instructed to turn up at court on that date. There are special provisions if the withdrawal is made within 14 days of a fixed diet, e.g. a proof. See the rules for more specific details.

Chapter 25—Minute of sist and transference

Chapter 26—Transfer and remit of causes

Chapter 27—Caution and security

These rules are similar to the Court of Session rules which are **9–31** explained in Ch.5. Reference should be made to the precise terms of the rules.

Chapter 28—Recovery of evidence[105]

Chapter 29—Proofs

Rules 29.1 to 29.20 deal with a variety of procedural matters relating **9–32** to the preparations for and conduct of proofs in the sheriff court.[106]

---

[99] See Ch.15.
[100] See Ch.15.
[101] See Ch.15.
[102] See Ch.5 for an explanation of this in the context of the Court of Session rules. The rules are similar.
[103] Unless the withdrawal is made at the bar, i.e. in open court.
[104] On his own initiative or on the motion of the opponent.
[105] See Ch.15.
[106] Reference should be made to Ch.19 and to the specific terms of the rules.

Chapter 30—Decrees, extracts, and execution[107]

9–33   These rules contain largely administrative provisions regarding the form of decrees, the issuing of extracts (authenticated copies) of decrees, and other provisions regarding the enforcement of decrees.

Chapter 31—Appeals[108]

Chapter 32—Taxation of expenses

9–34   Taxation of judicial expenses is done in the sheriff court by the auditor. There are provisions for fixing a diet of taxation and objection can be taken to the auditor's decision on the account by lodging a note of objection.[109]

Chapter 33—Family actions and others

9–35   There are extensive and detailed rules (rr.33.1–33.95) regarding family actions, other actions to do with children, and other associated procedures. These are not dealt with in this book.

Chapters 34 to 38

9–36   It is not proposed to deal with these. Some are dealt with elsewhere in the book and reference should be made to the rules for the remainder which include actions for sequestration for rent, special provisions relating to actions of damages, actions of removing, and references to the European Court from the sheriff.

Chapter 40—Commercial actions[110]

Chapter 41—Applications under the Protection from Abuse (Scotland) Act 2001

9–37   This contains special provisions regarding the attachment of a power of arrest to an interdict and the intimation of any such interlocutor.

---

[107] Of decrees—not parties!
[108] See Ch.20.
[109] See Ch.21 and see the rules (32.1–32.4) for details.
[110] See Ch.10.

Sheriff Court   **9–38**
Ordinary Actions
Flow Chart of Procedure

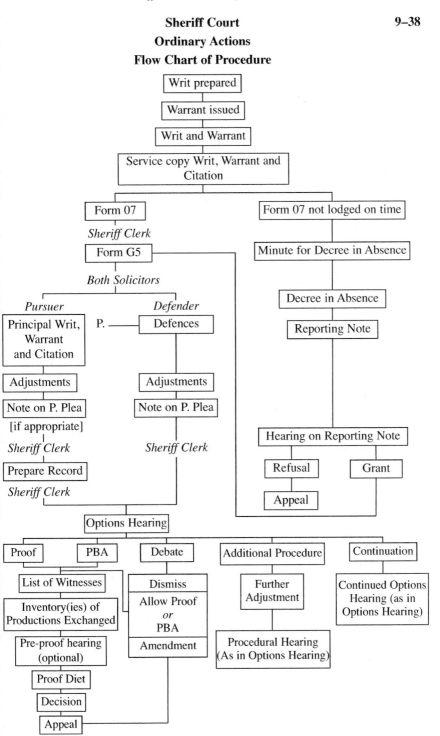

Writ prepared

Warrant issued

Writ and Warrant

Service copy Writ, Warrant and Citation

Form 07

Sheriff Clerk

Form G5

Both Solicitors

Pursuer

Principal Writ, Warrant and Citation

Adjustments

Note on P. Plea [if appropriate]

Sheriff Clerk

Prepare Record

Sheriff Clerk

Defender

P. — Defences

Adjustments

Note on P. Plea

Sheriff Clerk

Form 07 not lodged on time

Minute for Decree in Absence

Decree in Absence

Reporting Note

Hearing on Reporting Note

Refusal   Grant

Appeal

Options Hearing

Proof   PBA   Debate   Additional Procedure   Continuation

List of Witnesses

Inventory(ies) of Productions Exchanged

Pre-proof hearing (optional)

Proof Diet

Decision

Appeal

Dismiss
Allow Proof
or
PBA
Amendment

Further Adjustment

Procedural Hearing (As in Options Hearing)

Continued Options Hearing (as in Options Hearing)

CHAPTER 10

SHERIFF COURT COMMERCIAL ACTIONS

10–01 Following the apparent success of the commercial action procedure in the Court of Session[1] there was considerable interest in the introduction of a procedure with similar characteristics in the sheriff court. The sheriff court deals with many actions of a commercial nature, and it was felt that there would be benefits to court users in such actions if more streamlined court procedures were available in appropriate cases.

In 1999, a pilot scheme was run in Glasgow Sheriff Court whereby parties were given the option to conduct certain types of action in the sheriff court under procedures which were broadly similar to Court of Session commercial action procedures. This informal arrangement was considered successful enough to warrant adoption within the sheriff court rules. The Sheriff Court Rules Council thereafter prescribed a form of procedure which would be available for this type of action in the sheriff court in 2001. The rules were set out in the Act of Sederunt (Ordinary Cause Rules) Amendment (Commercial Actions) 2001.[2] This came into force on March 1, 2001 and applied to actions raised after that date. As the benefit of the procedure is dependent to some extent upon the availability of sheriffs who can be especially designated to deal with commercial actions, and upon the availability of administrative resources, an important practical consideration was whether any particular sheriff court would be able to provide the resources to support such actions. Glasgow Sheriff Court has been conducting commercial actions from the outset. The sheriff court at Jedburgh, Selkirk and Duns has done so for some time.[3] Aberdeen Sheriff Court has recently commenced actions under this procedure. The response from court lawyers to the use of such a procedure in the sheriff court has been very favourable indeed, to the extent that some parties will agree to prorogate the jurisdiction of Glasgow Sheriff Court in certain commercial disputes which would not otherwise have been capable of being raised and litigated upon in Glasgow, so that they can obtain the perceived benefits of this procedure.

The procedural rules are similar, but not identical, to the Court of Session rules for commercial actions. In some respects they could be

---

[1] See Ch.7.
[2] Act of Sederunt (Ordinary Cause Rules) Amendment (Commercial Actions) 2001 (SSI 2001/8).
[3] The sheriff there was one of the original commercial sheriffs at Glasgow.

said to be less detailed.[4] Some people would say that they have extended and developed the original model. Interestingly enough, there are few reported decisions relating to procedural issues arising out of the operation or application of the commercial rules. It seems that this is largely because the procedure usually emerges from a consensus between the parties and the sheriff.[5] Most parties involved in commercial actions are familiar with the ways in which the commercial sheriffs will approach certain types of dispute. Most parties can also see the benefits to their clients of adopting a business-like, pragmatic, and innovative approach to the conduct of litigation under the rules. Indeed, many lawyers will take an initiative in suggesting procedures to be adopted for the action which are tailored to the particular dispute and, importantly, can reduce the duration and cost of the litigation for their client.

There are no official statistics available for commercial actions in the sheriff court but it is understood that in Glasgow there are approximately 70 such actions raised every month. Just over 70 per cent of the actions raised are settled or decided within six months. Ninety per cent of those actions are settled or decided within nine months. These statistics are considered to be a very positive indicator of the success of the procedure in the expeditious resolution of disputes of a commercial nature.

NARRATIVE

There are relatively few rules and the sheriff can virtually do as he pleases **10–02** with an action once it is defended. A party must, first of all, choose to use the procedure, and he does so by drafting his initial writ accordingly. A party can elect to raise a sheriff court action as a commercial action in any sheriff court in Scotland provided that: (1) the sheriff principal for the sheriffdom has directed that commercial action procedure should be available there; (2) that the sheriff court concerned has jurisdiction over the defender; and (3) that the action falls within the definition of a commercial action.[6] In order to signify that the action is intended to be a commercial action, the initial writ will be in a prescribed form and the words "commercial action" will appear in the instance of the initial writ.

The pleadings in a commercial action may be less detailed and less formal than in an ordinary action, but they do not need to be. The writ should contain information in numbered paragraphs which is sufficient to identify the transaction or the dispute from which the action arises, include a summary of the circumstances which has resulted in the action being raised and set out the legal grounds on which the action proceeds. Technical words of form and style are not expected or encouraged.

---

[4] There are no practice notes such as those applying to the Court of Session actions.
[5] The "consensus" rarely appears to be imposed, although the sheriff is perfectly entitled to do so.
[6] The definition is interpreted very broadly.

Once a warrant has been granted on a commercial action then the writ will be served in the same way as for an ordinary action. The defender will have 21 days to respond and will respond by lodging a Form 07 as in an ordinary action. Once a notice of intention to defend has been lodged, the defender, without any further order of the court, must lodge defences within seven days of the expiry of the period of notice. In other words, the defences have to be lodged 28 days after service of the writ. The defences should be in the form of answers which allow the extent of the dispute to be identified, but each article of condescendence in the initial writ need not be admitted or denied. If it is possible to determine the details of the dispute from the defences then that will suffice.

If either the pursuer or the defender have documents upon which they propose to rely, or to which they wish to refer, then these documents should be lodged either with the initial writ or with the defences.

Once defences have been lodged, the sheriff clerk will fix a date for a case management conference and this will take place not sooner than 14 days nor later than 28 days after the expiry of the period of notice. Accordingly, the case management conference will take place no later than seven weeks after the service of the writ. In the meantime, parties can make a motion to the court for various orders in the same way as they could with an ordinary action. In particular an application can be made for summary decree.[7] This might well be done where defences are skeletal, or the defences simply do not explain the matter in dispute. In this way, the parties are not deprived an early remedy by having to wait for the case management conference before any meaningful order can be made.

At any time before, or at, the case management conference the sheriff must appoint a commercial action to proceed as an ordinary action on the joint motion of the parties or, provided the sheriff considers this would be appropriate, he may do so on the motion of one party. Once such a motion is made by one party and refused, no subsequent motion to the same effect will be allowed unless there is a material change of circumstances.

10–03   At the case management conference, the sheriff is required to seek to secure the expeditious resolution of the action. Parties have to give information to the sheriff regarding the case and the sheriff can make a wide variety of orders very much in line with the kind of orders which can be made in a Court of Session commercial action at a preliminary hearing or procedural hearing. For example, he can require the parties to undertake adjustment of the written pleadings in all or part of the case, he can require disclosure of witnesses and lodging of documents, he can fix a debate or a proof on any particular aspect of the action and make orders in relation to either. There are certain additional powers, such as giving the sheriff the power to record any admissions made on the basis of

---

[7] See Ch.19.

information produced to the sheriff at the case management conference. The sheriff can make any order which he thinks will result in the speedy resolution of the action, including the use of alternative dispute resolution, or he can require the attendance of parties in person along with the solicitors at any subsequent hearing. In practice, the parties and the sheriff will use the case management conference to identify the issues and agree upon a framework for their resolution. It is not uncommon, but it is by no means guaranteed, that the case management conference will be continued to a further case management conference at a specified time and on a specified date to allow parties to undertake further steps as timetabled and directed by the sheriff.

The practice in Glasgow Sheriff Court is for case management conferences to be allocated at a specific time of day. It is not uncommon for parties to communicate with each other and with the sheriff by email in relation to such callings and in relation to the action itself. It is also possible to have the hearing by way of telephone conference call so that solicitors are not required to attend court.[8] It is intended that the case management conference be conducted in the manner of a business meeting and similarly a case management conference by telephone conference call is to be conducted as a business meeting.[9] Whilst parties are given the benefit and convenience of email, conference call, etc. the calling of the case is nonetheless a court hearing and should be treated as such.

Any adjustments to the pleadings ordered by the court should be done by way of red lining, striking out or similar device. The parties are encouraged to exchange electronic copies of pleadings and to provide this to the court so that the pleadings can be fully and properly understood. There is often a requirement to produce an up-to-date record for the benefit of the court a few days before any continued case management conference.

It is open to the sheriff at any time to fix a hearing for further procedure or to make any other order which he might think appropriate in the action. Communication directly with the sheriff by way of email on matters relating to procedure in the action is encouraged within reason. The sheriff may also communicate directly with the parties' solicitors. A failure to comply with any rule or order of the sheriff would entitle the sheriff to refuse to extend any period for complying with the rules, dismiss the action (or counterclaim), grant decree, and make an award of expenses as he thinks fit. In this way, the sheriff keeps full control of the action and the procedure which is being managed by him.

---

[8] There is nothing in the rules to say that this can be done (or not) but it is a popular and helpful practice unless it is anticipated that the hearing will be particularly complex or difficult.

[9] Advising one's receptionist that the sheriff will be phoning and not to put him on hold for 20 minutes is a prudent practical precaution.

10–04   All of the rules for commercial actions in the sheriff court are contained within Ch.40 of the OCR. It should be noted that, in contrast to the Court of Session commercial actions, there is no practice note which accompanies the rules or is intended to explain or supplement them. This may be required in due course in individual sheriffdoms where the procedure is available. In Glasgow, where the procedure has been operating for some years, the sheriffs who deal with commercial actions have been very active in making their views known regarding procedure and practice. Most agents operating in Glasgow Sheriff Court have a very clear idea of what is expected of them in commercial actions and how it is intended that the rules should be operated. It can, however, be something of a culture shock for those agents who are unfamiliar with this procedure in sheriff court actions and are expecting a somewhat more leisurely and less inquisitive attitude from the court. Issues regarding the precise interpretation and operation of the rules have rarely arisen. Reference can be made to the Court of Session rules and practice notes, but although there are considerable similarities between the two procedures, the practical operation of commercial action procedure in the sheriff court has developed in its own way.

Rule 40.1

10–05   This contains a definition of commercial action and it is specifically stated that it does not include an action in relation to consumer credit transactions. The definition is usually interpreted broadly. A commercial action may be raised only in a sheriff court where the sheriff principal for that sheriffdom has directed that the procedure should be available. This qualification was necessary because it was not felt appropriate to introduce that procedure in every sheriff court where the administration, staffing and other resources would not be able to support the particular requirements of a commercial-type procedure.

Rule 40.2

10–06   All proceedings in a commercial action are to be brought before a sheriff of the sheriffdom nominated by the sheriff principal or if such a sheriff is not available any other sheriff of that sheriffdom. For example, there are currently three designated commercial sheriffs in Glasgow.

Rule 40.3

10–07   The sheriff can make any order that he thinks fit for the progress of the case. His discretion could be no wider than that. If any hearing is continued, then the reason for that continuation will be recorded in the interlocutor. In practice, most sheriffs will issue an interlocutor after a hearing, summarising the main matters discussed at the hearing and recording the steps that are to be taken by the parties. This will usually be emailed to the parties so that there is an accepted and accurate record of the hearing and the order.

Rule 40.4

A pursuer can elect to adopt the procedure in appropriate cases sim- **10–08** ply by drafting the writ in an appropriate form and adding the words "commercial action" above the word "initial writ" in the instance.

Rule 40.5

Provided any action fits the definition of a commercial action, any **10–09** party can apply by motion to have an action, which was originally commenced as an ordinary action, proceed as a commercial action. If such a motion is granted, then the interlocutor granting it will include a direction about further procedure.

Rule 40.6

At any time before or at the case management conference, the sheriff **10–10** may appoint a commercial action to proceed as an ordinary cause on the motion of a party where the circumstances warrant such an order being made. If there is a joint motion of the parties to do so, then the sheriff must grant it. If a motion by one party to transfer the case to an ordinary cause is refused, then no further motion can be made unless there has been a material change of circumstances. If the action is transferred to the ordinary roll then the sheriff will pronounce an interlocutor regarding the further procedure of the case as an ordinary action.

Rule 40.7

If the construction of a document is the only matter in dispute **10–11** between the parties then it is not necessary to have any pleadings or pleas in law in the initial writ. In this case, the pursuer would have a crave for declarator[10] as to how the document should be construed, and may have supplementary craves for what is requested from the court in the event of the document being interpreted as craved. The precise form of the pleadings in such a case is left largely to the parties and provided they make clear that the court has jurisdiction, what document or documents are under consideration,[11] and what their respective contentions are, the court can deal with the issue.

In any action, a list of the documents which are founded on, or adopted as incorporated in the initial writ, in a commercial action shall be appended to that initial writ at the time when a warrant is sought. The content of

---

[10] See Ch.13.
[11] Lodging the document or documents would suffice.

productions can be used to supplement the pleadings without undue formality.[12] Formal pleadings in relation to all or part of the case may be suggested or ordered by the sheriff in appropriate cases. This can often be done in relation to crucial aspects of any factual dispute as a means of narrowing down exactly what is in issue. In that situation, the sheriff could fix a proof restricted to the pleadings in that specific part of the case, on the reasoning that this alone might suffice to resolve the dispute.

Rule 40.9

10–12   Where a notice of intention to defend has been lodged, the defender shall lodge defences within seven days of the expiry of the period of notice. This is different from the rule in ordinary actions.[13] The defender shall append to the defences a list of the documents which are founded on or adopted as incorporated in the defences. The defender must append a note of his pleas in law. It is not necessary for the defender to answer each article of condescendence in the initial writ with admissions or denials, as is the case in ordinary actions. The defences are to be such that allow the extent of the dispute to be identified. As long as the defences make it clear what is in dispute, the precise form of the defences is immaterial. For example, it would be open to a defender simply to set out his version of events without reference to the precise terms of the writ.[14]

Rule 40.10

10–13   Once the defences have been lodged the sheriff clerk is to fix a date for a case management conference no sooner than 14 days after the expiry of the period of notice (five weeks from service) nor later than 28 days after that date (seven weeks from service). The clerk will intimate to the parties the date and time of the case management conference.

Rule 40.10(3)

10–14   The fixing of a date for the case management conference does not affect the right of any party to make an application by motion to the court in connection with the case. Very often, the motion will be dealt with at the case management conference but if there happens to be a degree of urgency then the motion can usually be accommodated in advance of that date. The same rules apply to intimation of motions in a commercial action as apply in an ordinary action. An application to dispense with or shorten a period of notice for such a motion would normally be heard by the commercial sheriff who has been allocated to deal with the case.

---

[12] Compare para.3–26, above.
[13] See Ch.9.
[14] Having said that, good pleadings, properly focused in the traditional way, might be preferable in particular cases. This is one of the things the sheriff can decide to order if he considers it necessary.

Rule 40.11

Where a party applies for a summary decree in a commercial action **10–15** then the period of notice for such a motion shall be 48 hours, as opposed to seven days in an ordinary action.

Rule 40.12

This is the rule which deals with the case management conference. **10–16** The case management conference effectively serves the same purpose as both the preliminary and procedural hearing in the Court of Session commercial action procedure. The purpose of the case management conference is to identify the issues between the parties and agree how these are to be resolved. Further factual information may be required to identify the issues properly, or for a variety of other reasons.

As previously mentioned, the conference can take place by way of telephone conference call initiated by the sheriff. On occasions, the conference can be dealt with by way of emails, e.g. where the parties and the sheriff agree in advance an appropriate course of action. If there is a hearing, then wigs and gowns would not be worn by the solicitors and parties remain seated during the hearing. Whoever does appear, in whatever form, at the case management conference, is expected to be properly briefed about the case and to be able to contribute fully to any discussions about the merits of the case and the further appropriate procedure.

There is little prospect of a defender maintaining a dilatory defence, or a pursuer continuing with a manifestly inept case, much beyond the first case management conference.[15] The parties must be prepared to provide such information as the sheriff may require to determine whether and to what extent further specification of the claim and defences is required and any orders which may have to be made to ensure the expeditious resolution of the action. That is the prime purpose of the case management conference.

Rule 40.12(3)

The orders which a sheriff can make at a case management conference **10–17** include but are not limited to:

(a) the lodging of written pleadings by any party which may simply be restricted to particular issues;
(b) the lodging of a statement of facts by any party which again may be restricted to particular issues;
(c) the allowance of an amendment to pleadings by any party;
(d) the disclosure of the identity of witnesses and documents relating to the action, or the granting of authority to recover documents;

---

[15] This is one of the real practical bonuses of the procedure.

(e) the lodging of documents in relation to the action including invoices, correspondence or similar documents;
(f) the exchanging of lists of witnesses;
(g) the lodging of reports of skilled persons or witness statements;
(h) the lodging of affidavits concerned with any of the issues in the action;
(i) the lodging of notes of arguments setting out the basis of any preliminary plea in cases where a party is seeking a diet of debate;
(j) the fixing of a diet of debate or a diet of proof or proof before answer without any further preliminary procedure;
(k) the lodging of a joint minute of admission or agreement;
(l) the recording of admissions made on the basis of the information produced at a case management conference[16]; or
(m) any order which the sheriff thinks will result in the speedy resolution of the action or requiring the attendance of parties in person at any subsequent hearing.

The sheriff can set a time limit for any orders made at a case management conference to be complied with and he may continue the case management conference to a specified date. In doing so, he can ordain the pursuer to make up a record of the relevant pleadings for that hearing and lodge that record in process in advance of the next case management conference.

As an illustration of how all of this works, and of how it differs from an ordinary action, consider the case in the preface in which there is a dispute over quantities of timber supplied. The pursuer claims payment for them. The defenders have a dispute regarding the quality of goods supplied. It may be averred by the pursuer that the parties contracted on certain specified terms and conditions. The defenders may dispute whether those terms and conditions applied, whether there was a breach of contract anyway, and what loss was caused or claimable as a result of that breach.

In an ordinary action, the timetable provided by the rules means that the parties would have adjusted their pleadings in the traditional way over a period of about four months without any intervention by the court until there was an options hearing. At the options hearing, the court would see the papers for the first time, and would have a limited opportunity to understand and assess the nature of the dispute. Continuations might be requested to amend pleadings or because the complexity of the issues demand it. This would inevitably give rise to delays. In an ordinary action, it is likely that all of these issues might ultimately go to proof with numerous witnesses being cited to speak to a variety of matters of fact.

In a commercial action it is more likely that the sheriff would have considered and discussed seriously the detailed circumstances of the

---

[16] These would be admissions made ex parte, during the case management conference, in relation to matters not specifically admitted in the pleadings.

dispute with the parties at the case management conference within about six weeks of the action being served. The sheriff might have asked the parties to expand their pleadings in relation to the constitution of the contract. He might have ordered the production of any relevant documents and the exchange of witness lists, etc. within three weeks to assist in his and their understanding of the case. He might have continued the case management conference for four weeks for specific things to be done and pleadings on some aspects of the case—but not others—to be expanded. It may be concluded that, if the terms and conditions of the contract contended for do not apply, then there would be no need to consider any other questions. A proof might be fixed, confined solely to the issue of what the contractual terms and conditions were. Alternatively, a debate could be fixed to determine whether, on facts which are not really disputed, there is any legal basis for the argument about the contract terms. This form of procedure, properly managed, would inevitably be shorter, less costly and more efficient than litigating the same dispute by ordinary procedure.[17]

Rule 40.14

At any time before final judgment the sheriff may on his own motion, **10–18** or on the motion of any party, fix a hearing for further procedure and may then make such order as he thinks fit.

Rule 40.15

A failure to comply with a provision in this chapter of the rules or with **10–19** any order made by the sheriff in a commercial action shall entitle the sheriff to refuse to extend any period for complying with the provision of these rules or with any order made by the court in the action. It would also entitle the sheriff to dismiss an action or a counterclaim in whole or in part and to grant decree in respect of all or any of the craves of the initial writ or counterclaim or to make an award of expenses. This rule provides the sheriff with the necessary sanction to achieve the aim which is an efficient resolution of any commercial action.

Rule 40.16

At the end of any hearing a sheriff may restrict his interlocutor to a **10–20** finding. This means that the sheriff may not have to make findings in fact at the conclusion of a proof and could simply narrate the circumstances of the case, a summary of the evidence of witnesses, and what his decision on the point or points at issue was. It is not clear, however, whether this rule would justify such an approach, although it has been pointed out

---

[17] That is not to say that the same benefits could not be gained from an application of the ordinary cause rules. In reality, however, the sheriff in case manager role in the commercial action is bound to be far more proactive.

that such an interpretation of the rule would enable the court to issue a more speedy decision. Technically this could give rise to procedural problems for the future of the action as we shall see later.[18]

Rule 40.17

10–21   All of the parts of process lodged in a commercial action should be clearly marked "commercial action". As it is, the case will be given a court reference number which will also identify the case as a commercial action. Parties are expected to include in any court pleadings details of the individual solicitor who is actually dealing with the case and that individual's telephone number and email address so as to facilitate communication throughout the duration of the action.

COMPARISON BETWEEN SHERIFF COURT ORDINARY ACTIONS AND COMMERCIAL ACTIONS

10–22 In the chapter on commercial actions in the Court of Session we have already discussed the advantages and disadvantages of a commercial action type of procedure as opposed to the more traditional type of procedure. Similar considerations apply to commercial actions in the sheriff court. It might be helpful to do a brief comparison of the major differences between ordinary procedure and commercial action procedure in the sheriff court.

(1) In ordinary actions, it is quite likely that different sheriffs will deal with the action at different stages of its procedure.[19] In a commercial action, one designated sheriff will be allocated to the case at the outset and he will retain control of the case throughout.

(2) In ordinary actions, the sheriff acts as the "referee" and the decision maker in the dispute. In commercial actions, the sheriff additionally acts as the case manager and directs the procedural progress of the action. He is expected to be proactive and take initiatives to promote the speedy resolution of the claim.

(3) In ordinary actions, there is one rigid framework for the procedure in all different types of dispute. In commercial actions, it is possible to have a more flexible range of procedural options depending upon the nature of the action, its complexity, and the disputed issues which seem to be important.

(4) In ordinary actions, the written pleadings are expected to be in the traditional formal style. In commercial actions the court's approach to the pleadings is somewhat more relaxed. As long as the issues in dispute can be identified in one way or the other, the pleadings are

[18] See *Jackson v Hughes Dowdall* [2008] CSIH 41.
[19] Although in smaller sheriff courts with fewer sheriffs, this is less likely.

not crucial. The court is more concerned with the reality of the dispute between the parties than the formality of its expression.

(5) Of necessity, an ordinary action will set out fixed timescales for various stages of procedure. In commercial actions, the court will allocate timescales which are appropriate to the nature of the dispute.

(6) In ordinary actions, the first real hearing of the issues between the parties may be at the options hearing[20] which is approximately four months after the commencement of the action. In commercial actions, the case management conference, at which there will be a real airing of the issues in the action, will take place no more than seven weeks after the commencement of the action.

(7) In ordinary actions, it is necessary for the parties to attend personally at court on the day when the action is to call without any specific time for the calling of the case. In commercial actions, the court can dispense with personal attendance of the solicitors and conduct the hearing by phone. The court will also allocate a specific time for the case to be heard.[21]

(8) In ordinary actions, there are limits to the way in which the sheriff can control the progress of the action. In commercial actions, the sheriff has very real control over the progress of the action and can adopt innovative steps unconstrained by rules, provided they are intended to achieve a speedy resolution of the case.

As can be seen, the flexibility afforded by the rules, means that it is **10–23** not possible to predict in advance how the court will deal with any individual case. That can be a drawback,[22] but a degree of familiarity with the practice in any particular sheriff court usually enables one to anticipate how the court is likely to approach a particular dispute. The commercial sheriffs have developed an experience and expertise in handling such actions and in the procedures which can be used in order to bring them to a satisfactory conclusion within a relatively short space of time. It is highly successful and popular with users. Parties have sought to use it because of its speed, flexibility, efficiency, and convenience.

However a very recent decision of the Inner House in an appeal from the commercial sheriff in the case of *Jackson v Hughes Dowdall*[23] has expressed reservations about some of the innovative procedures and practices adopted in commercial actions in the sheriff court and it is worth giving a brief summary of the concerns expressed by the appeal court.

---

[20] For practical reasons, the options hearing may not provide the rigorous assessment of the case as was intended. See para.9–20, above.

[21] At least, this is what happens in Glasgow. Other sheriff courts may do it differently, but you will not find any specific rules about this and it is necessary to check the practice of individual courts.

[22] It may be difficult to advise a client what is likely to happen in the case and how long it might take until the case management conference.

[23] *Jackson v Hughes Dowdall* [2008] CSIH 41.

The full details of the procedure followed are too complex to explain here but the court had some reservations about the practice of conducting most of the hearings by conference call. They considered it to be a general principle of constitutional importance that the administration of justice should take place in open court. They said that exceptions to that general principle, created by judicial practice, required to be considered with care, bearing in mind that convenience is not the only (or the most important) consideration. Whilst not expressing a concluded view, their disapproval was clear, especially when they gave an example of one such hearing at which they said that the pursuer was not represented because their telephone line was engaged. Fairness requires that both parties be heard and that requirement could not be dispensed with because of a difficulty in making contact by phone.

The court went on to comment upon the use of emails passing between the sheriff and the parties at various stages of the action. It was apparent that the discussions in those emails went beyond administrative matters of the kind which might otherwise have been dealt with by a clerk of court. For example, some of them contained legal submissions and arguments and it appeared that some of the communications were not copied to the opponent again raising the question of fairness. The court did not wish it to be taken that it tacitly approved the practice which was followed in the case regarding such emails.

The crux of the decision however was that the sheriff had heard a debate (on two occasions) and had apparently on the second occasion taken the view that the pursuer's pleadings were irrelevant as they stood. However, he thought that there could be a relevant claim somewhere in the pleadings and he allowed a proof before answer after deleting, on his own initiative, various irrelevant averments. It was agreed that this was incompetent.

The court emphasised that the sheriff was acting in complete good faith in doing what he did and with the best of intentions. They did not think that, just because this was a commercial action, the sheriff could do what he did. Although the sheriff was to manage the procedure in any such action to secure its expeditious resolution, the fact that he is actively involved in case management does not detract from the adversarial nature of such proceedings. The management of the case must not stray to the extent of making out a party's case for him (which the court considered the sheriff had done by identifying some possible basis for a claim) and should not involve the confusion of the role of a judge with that of an advocate.

Whilst it is easy to see that the sheriff appears to have crossed the line in some respects, the reservations about the way in which the case was "managed" in an administrative sense should be considered alongside the favourable verdict on the commercial action procedure given by its users in the research paper on commercial actions in the sheriff court published in 2005.[24]

---

[24] Scottish Executive Social Research. Elaine Samuel. *Commercial Procedure in Glasgow Sheriff Court*. The Scottish Government, 2005.

Whether commercial action procedure will be regarded as a blueprint for future procedure for other actions within the sheriff court remains to be seen. There may be good practical reasons for continuing to confine it to particular types of case and particular sheriff courts. Commercial actions have been regarded as a success where they have operated but, as has already been pointed out, they require expertise, resources, and administration which might not be readily available in all but the larger sheriff courts. However, at least some of the features of commercial actions could usefully be adopted and adapted in any ordinary procedure. The real difference is in the philosophy of managing and controlling litigation closely, fairly and efficiently at every stage. It may only be a short step from this development to the days when the sheriff will be seen as the administrator and case manager (and ultimately the decision maker) of a certain number of cases, with filing cabinets of his own which comprise his workload. Such an idea would have been unthinkable 10 years ago, but times and procedures change and will no doubt continue to do so.

10–24

Sheriff Court
Commercial Action

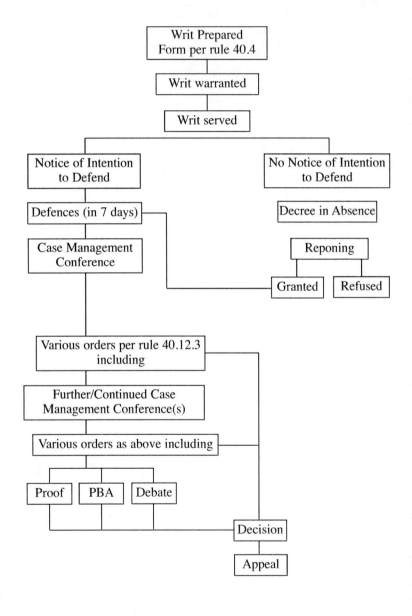

Chapter 11

SUMMARY CAUSES

Since 1976 there has been a relatively simple, cheap and quick form of **11–01** procedure in the sheriff court known as summary cause procedure. This procedure must be used for what can generally be termed minor claims. When this procedure originated, it applied to all claims for £1,000 or less. In 1988 the figure was increased to £1,500. At that time, a special type of summary cause procedure was introduced for all claims for £750 or less which is called a "small claim".[1] The rules of procedure for small claims are different so, although small claims are summary causes, we shall consider them separately in the next chapter.

On January 14, 2008, the financial jurisdiction limits for summary cause and small claims cases was increased substantially after many years of deliberation[2]. A claim, other than a personal injury claim, for up to £3,000 can only be raised by way of a small claim in the sheriff court.[3] A claim for between £3,000.01 and £5,000 can only be raised by way of a summary cause in the sheriff court. The sheriff court has exclusive or privative jurisdiction for all claims under £5,000 and proceedings cannot be raised in the Court of Session for an amount of £5,000 or less.[4] In certain circumstances, a party may apply to the sheriff to have an action which was originally raised as a summary cause treated as an ordinary action. On the joint motion of the parties an action raised as an ordinary action can be treated as a summary cause.[5]

It is generally considered that actions for smaller sums of money do not require to have the detailed procedures found in other forms of action. Such actions might be regarded as less difficult or important than others for higher value[6] and do not require the procedures and resources which may be needed for a fair and full resolution of the dispute. There

---

[1] Strictly speaking, a small claim is simply a special type of summary cause.

[2] For small claims there was the Small Claims (Scotland) Order 2007 (SSI 2007/496) and for summary causes there was the Sheriff Courts (Scotland) Act 1971 (Privative Jurisdiction and Summary Cause) Order 2007 (SSI 2007/507).

[3] However, any personal injury action below £3,000 must be pursued as a summary cause—in other words, there is no small claims procedure available for lower value personal injury actions which are regarded as too complex and difficult for small claims procedure.

[4] Sheriff Courts (Scotland) Act 1971 (c.58) s.31 as amended by SSI 2007/507.

[5] See para.2–23, above.

[6] Experience shows that this is not inevitably the case, however.

has always been a demand for cheaper and simpler court procedures which, in political terms, would be seen as improving affordable access to justice for the public. It has also been the view that individuals should be encouraged to litigate lower value claims without necessarily requiring legal representation. As part of that process, detailed work was done on the rules of procedure for such actions to make them clearer and simpler and to provide a "user-friendly" set of rules which would achieve some of the policy aspirations of the Scottish Executive for our civil justice system. In 2002, significant changes were made to the Summary Cause Rules.[7] In fact, a completely new set of rules was written although many of the features of the old procedures were retained.

This form of procedure applies to all actions of payment fitting within the narrow band of monetary claims between £3,000 and £5,000 and other specific claims such as claims for rent or recovery of possession of heritable property,[8] and actions for recovery or delivery of property of that same value.

STATUTORY PROVISIONS

11–02 The statutory foundation for summary causes as we now know them is the Sheriff Courts (Scotland) Act 1971 s.35. Section 36 of that Act gave the Court of Session power to make rules for summary cause actions. The detailed rules for summary cause procedure were then embodied within the Act of Sederunt (Summary Cause Rules) Sheriff Court 1976[9] which came into operation in 1976. The detailed rules were altered from time to time without any significant changes to the basic procedure. Then, following lengthy review and consideration by the Sheriff Court Rules Council, a completely new set of rules was provided by the Act of Sederunt (Summary Cause Rules) 2002[10] which came into force on June 10, 2002. Although the Act of Sederunt rewrote all of the Summary Cause Rules ("SCR"), the changes to the existing rules were not too dramatic. The underlying philosophy that relatively low value claims should have a simple speedy and inexpensive procedure remained. The new rules contain provisions intended to support those aims further. They provide one coherent document consisting of 35 Chapters which contains all one needs to know about the procedure. It is important to note that the rules contain a separate Chapter dealing with personal injury claims under £5,000, which shall be discussed separately at the end of this Chapter.

It will be appreciated that summary cause actions fit within a very narrow band for monetary claims. There have been very few reported

---

[7] And to the Small Claim Rules.
[8] Mostly housing authorities pursuing defaulting tenants.
[9] Act of Sederunt (Summary Cause Rules) Sheriff Court 1976 (SI 1976/476).
[10] Act of Sederunt (Summary Cause Rules) 2002 (SSI 2002/132).

cases on the procedure to date. It should be noted that many of the reported cases in this chapter relate to the former rules and care should be taking in reading any reported cases because the precise terms of the rules may well have altered from the date when the cases were decided.

During 1996 there were just over 30,000 summary cause actions initiated in the sheriff court. In 1999 there were 37,225. In 2002, there were 36,465 actions initiated. The majority of these actions are understood to have been actions for recovery of possession of property. The next highest category is actions for payment. In 2006 there were understood to have been 35,881 summary cause actions raised in the sheriff courts in Scotland.[11] It will be very interesting to see what impact the recent jurisdiction limit changes will have on the numbers of summary causes raised in the years to come.

NARRATIVE[12]

A person who wishes to raise a summary cause action first has to com- **11–03** plete a pre-printed form. Different forms are available for the different types of action which can be raised as summary causes. The individual forms are all called a "summary cause summons". Amongst other blanks to be filled in on the forms are those parts which require the party to provide a statement of the details of the claim. Once the form has been prepared then it is sent or taken to the sheriff clerk. A fee is payable and the sheriff clerk will provide a warrant for service of the summons by completing and signing one of the blanks on the pre-printed form. He will enter the details of the case in a register and he will provide the claimant with two dates:

(1) the return date, which is the date when the summons has to be returned to court after it has been served by the pursuer; and
(2) the calling date, which is the date when the case will actually call in court for the first time.[13]

The pursuer serves the proceedings by sending the defender a service copy of the principal summons. The service copy is on a pre-printed form and contains the same details as are on the first two pages of the principal summons. However, the form which comprises the service copy also includes a tear-off page which is to be used as the defender's

---

[11] Although this figure may not be exactly correct.

[12] The Scottish Court Service provides detailed guidance motes for lay persons involved in summary causes on the Scottish Courts website at *http://www.scotcourts.gov.uk* [Accessed August 22, 2008]. There are four separate booklets, running to a total of about 120 pages, explaining the procedures in ordinary language and including a glossary of the legal terms used in the rules.

[13] Assuming that the person upon whom the summons has been served intimates that he intends to defend it.

form of response. A defender can choose to do nothing in response to the summons, in which case it is likely that a decree will be granted against him. Alternatively, he can complete the form and indicate whether he is going to defend the claim, in whole or in part, or not. If he wishes to admit the claim, but wants to apply for payment of any decree which might be granted against him by instalments, then he can indicate this as well. More importantly, in defended cases, the defender is required to prepare a written note of his proposed defence which he has to lodge at the same time as his form of response. The sheriff clerk will then send a copy of the defence[14] to the pursuer.

If the defender fails to return the form of response, or indicates that he is going to admit the claim and would like to pay the sum due, then this will set in motion administrative procedures which lead to the court quickly granting an appropriate decree. Only a minority of summary cause actions are defended.

If the defender lodges a form of response indicating that he intends to defend the case, then this will set in motion the full procedure for a defended summary cause. The pursuer's solicitor must return the principal summons to the sheriff clerk and the case will then call in court on the calling date which was fixed when the summons was warranted. The pursuer and the defender (or their legal representatives) are required to attend court on the calling date. Failure to attend court by one or other or both may give rise to the court granting a decree either as sought or (where the pursuer does not attend) dismissing the claim. There is a procedure for recalling such a decree.[15]

Assuming that both parties attend court at the first calling of the case then, at that hearing, the court will have the principal summons with details of the claim and the written note of the proposed defence.[16] At the hearing on the calling date the sheriff can do a variety of things. The alternatives are:

(1) if one or other or both parties do not appear, he may grant a decree;
(2) if he is satisfied that the action is incompetent or the court does not have jurisdiction, he must dismiss the action;
(3) he must ascertain the factual basis of the action and any defence, and the legal basis on which the action and defence are proceeding;
(4) he is to seek to negotiate and secure settlement of the action between the parties; or
(5) he can continue the hearing to such other date as he considers appropriate.

---

[14] And any counterclaim, if stated by the defender.
[15] This can also be used where decree has been granted against a defender who failed to lodge the form of response.
[16] A defender could also have a counterclaim which would have to be detailed in writing along with the form of response but, for simplicity, we shall ignore such a situation.

It is worth pausing at this stage to emphasise that the primary role of the **11–04** sheriff is to ascertain if the parties are still in dispute, what it is that they are disputing, and whether there is any prospect that they could resolve the dispute without further action. Only once this stage has been passed and the sheriff is satisfied that there cannot be any settlement of the claim will he progress to the next stage which requires him to:

(1) identify and note the issues of fact and law which are in dispute;
(2) note any facts which are agreed;
(3) if he considers there is no good legal basis for the claim, or any defence, hear argument and decide the case immediately; and
(4) if he is satisfied that there is a valid dispute and that there are disputed issues of fact, fix a proof to hear evidence. However, if he is satisfied at the calling date that the facts are sufficiently agreed between the parties, he can hear them on the merits of the action on the basis of those agreed facts, and make a decision immediately.

If the sheriff fixes a proof the clerk is then required to make up a folder for the case papers for the proof. Once a proof has been fixed the parties will prepare for it in more or less the same way as they would prepare for a proof in an ordinary action. It is open to the court to hear parts of the proof separately and the sheriff has a discretion to do this of his own accord or at the request of either party. There are similar, but not identical, provisions for lodging documents and witness lists as in ordinary actions.

At the proof itself, the pursuer must lead unless the defender has made an application to the sheriff to direct otherwise. The sheriff will make a note of any facts agreed by the parties following upon the original hearing of the case and he may require the parties to lodge a written joint minute of admissions. Thereafter the sheriff will note the evidence himself, including any evidence to which objection has been taken during the proof, and he is required to retain the notes until after any appeal (if taken). Once the evidence has been led then the sheriff will hear argument. Thereafter he may pronounce his decision at that time or otherwise reserve judgment.

Any decision made by the sheriff dealing with the merits of the case, **11–05** either at the calling date or at any proof, must include a brief statement of the grounds of his decision including the reasons for his decision on any questions of law which might have arisen. If the sheriff pronounces his decision after reserving judgment, then he must issue a decision within 28 days and include a note regarding the matters mentioned above.

Any appeal against the decision of a sheriff must be lodged with the sheriff clerk not later than 14 days after the date of final decree. The appellant requires to lodge a form which requests the sheriff to state a case and specifies the point of law upon which the appeal is to proceed. The appeal should be heard orally and is to be confined to the questions of law in the written appeal unless the sheriff principal allows the question to be amended. In exceptional circumstances, the sheriff principal may grant a certificate that an action would be suitable for an appeal from his judgment to the Court of Session[17].

The rules include a large number of forms[18] for use in summary cause procedure and the length and variety of these forms can be quite intimidating. They are intended to simplify and standardise the procedures, and whilst they might seem difficult to digest in the first instance, considered reading of the forms will aid the reader's understanding of the rules of procedure. The rules also provide a glossary of legal terms in appendix 2 with an explanation for around 80 legal terms used in the rules.

One interesting and innovative provision in the rules is that any documents which have to be lodged with the sheriff clerk or intimated to another party may be sent in electronic or documentary form. There are one or two exceptions and qualifications to this but this is the first example of a general provision in procedural rules in Scotland which formally permits the use of email for such purposes.

COMMENTARY ON PARTICULAR RULES OF PROCEDURE

11–06 There are 35 chapters in the SCR 2002, containing about 150 individual rules. We will only look at the significant provisions here, and reference should be made to the full rules and the precise wording of the rules for a complete understanding of what they mean.

Rule 1.1(6)—The rules apply to a summary cause other than a small claim.

Rule 2.1—In certain limited circumstances and on certain conditions, an "authorised lay representative" can represent a party in the same way that a legally qualified person could. The most significant hearing at which he could do so is the calling date.

Chapter 4

11–07 This contains provisions regarding the form of summons to be used in summary causes (there are eight different forms), what the statement of claim should contain and the period of notice for intimation on the proposed defender. As the reader might see from the layout of the printed forms, there is little space provided for giving details of the claim. In practice, most solicitors will have the factual and legal basis of the claim typed out on a separate sheet of paper which is attached to the printed summons and headed "statement of claim".

---

[17] The reader is directed to read the judgment of the Sheriff Principal (Young) in the case of *Harris v Foubister* Unreported (Sh. Ct) July 14, 2006 in which he describes in detail the precise procedure followed in that particular claim. The significance of the precise terms of the defender's written defence was critical to the outcome of the case.

[18] Over 30.

It should be noted that the following must be included in the statement of claim with the summons:

(1) details of the basis of the claim including any relevant dates;
(2) in any claim for payment for the supply of goods or services, a description of the goods or services, and the date or dates on which they were supplied or ordered;
(3) in any event, and supplementary to the requirements of (1) and (2), the summons must, "give the defender fair notice of the claim".

There have been a number of cases on what is regarded as sufficient to give the defender the requisite notice in a summary cause action.[19] Generally speaking, the courts will not scrutinise the terms of the statement of claim at the outset of the case, but where it is plain that certain facts must be established in order to justify the remedy which is sought, and where it is plain that these facts are not set out in the statement of claim, the court is likely do something about it procedurally at the calling date. The clerk (and the sheriff) can, in theory, refuse to grant a warrant for service of a summons where they consider that the statement of claim does not comply with the requirements of the rules including the requirement of giving fair notice.

Chapter 5

This requires the sheriff clerk to keep a Register of Summary Causes **11–08** with certain prescribed details of all summary cause actions raised. There are also provisions regarding service of the summons and how it should be served in particular circumstances, e.g. where the summons has to be served outwith Scotland. Even if there is some technical difficulty with service on the defender this can be cured if the defender actually turns up at the calling.[20] If an appearance at court at the calling date is required, then the summons and the certificate of execution of service of the summons must be returned to the sheriff clerk not later than two days before the calling date.

Chapter 7

This relates to undefended actions. If a defender has not lodged a form **11–09** of response on or before the return day in an action for payment, the action does not call in court on the calling date, but the pursuer must complete a form (Form 17) and lodge it with the sheriff clerk on the second

---

[19] See, e.g. *GUS Catalogue Order Ltd v Oxborrow*, 1988 S.L.T. (Sh. Ct) 2; *Birds Eye Food Ltd v Johnstone* Unreported Cupar Sheriff Court February 3, 1977; *Gordon District Council v Acutt*, 1991 S.L.T. (Sh. Ct) 78; *Courtaulds Clothing Brands Ltd v Knowles*, 1989 S.L.T. (Sh. Ct) 84; *Gallacher v Chief Constable and Virgin Retail Ltd* Unreported Glasgow Sheriff Court March 22, 1996. These are all prior to the SCR 2002 but there is no reason to think that the general principles will be applied any differently.
[20] See *Ghani v Clydesdale District Licensing Board*, 1996 S.C.L.R. 648.

day before the calling date. The form requests the court to make a specific order (e.g. to grant decree for payment). A failure to lodge the form means that the sheriff must dismiss the action. If the sheriff is unwilling to grant the order sought, he can request the pursuer to attend a hearing. In other types of action, different procedures will apply in the event of a failure to lodge a form of response. For example, in an action for recovery of possession of heritable property, the action will call in court on the calling date, regardless of whether a response has been lodged or not.

Chapter 8

11–10   This contains a large number of rules relating to the procedure in a defended action. Reference should be made to the rules themselves for details but this is a summary of the important provisions.

Rule 8.1—If the defender intends to challenge the jurisdiction of the court or the competency of the action, or to defend the action in whole or in part, or to state a counterclaim, then he must lodge the form of response and a statement of his response (the defence) with the sheriff clerk by the return day. The statement must give the pursuer fair notice of his defence. If the defender does this, the action will call in court on the calling date for a hearing.

Rule 8.2—A failure by one or other or both of the parties to attend the hearing on the calling date may, and in certain circumstances must, lead to the action or the defence being dismissed and decree granted accordingly. The sheriff can continue the calling date in certain circumstances if he considers it appropriate to do so.

Rule 8.3—This rule sets out the purpose of the hearing at the calling date. It should be emphasised that the sheriff ought to have before him at the hearing a coherent and intelligible claim[21] and a clear and specific defence of some nature. These will be in writing. Each party ought to give "fair notice" of his position. Whilst "technical" pleadings are not expected in summary cause actions, the lack of advance notice of some details of the claim or of the defence might have an effect upon the issues which are allowed to go to proof.

The parties should both be present or represented at the calling date and should both be in a position to address the sheriff on the details of the dispute as disclosed in the statement of claim and defence and/or elicited from the parties at the hearing. In this sense, the hearing and the

---

[21] See *Dale v Lets Glasgow* Unreported (Sh. Ct) November 24, 2006, Sheriff Principal Taylor, where the claim was considered to be not "soundly based in law" and would no doubt have been dismissed but for the fact that the parties advised the court that it had settled!

calling date can be compared to an options hearing in the OCR procedures or a case management conference in commercial action procedures. However, the rules state quite specifically that in the first place
the sheriff is required to take an interventionist's role.[22] He must establish what the nature of the dispute, both in fact and in law, happens to
be. Then he has to go much further than any other form of procedural
rules require and must actively seek to negotiate and secure the settlement of the action. Accordingly, under the Summary Cause Rules, at the
calling date the sheriff is expected to adopt the role of mediator/arbiter/
facilitator to encourage settlement as well as the role of case manager.

Only if the sheriff cannot secure the settlement of the action in this way
is he required to focus on the nature of the dispute between the parties.
He is required to identify and note on the summons the issues of fact and
law which are in dispute. If the dispute happens to revolve around a question of law, he can immediately hear the legal submissions and decide the
case there and then. Otherwise, he could simply continue the hearing to
a further date to hear legal argument alone. If the claim or the defence
appear to have a sound basis in law but it appears that there is a dispute
between the parties on matters of fact, the sheriff can fix a proof in relation to the matters of fact which are in dispute. However, if all of the facts
are agreed and there is still an area of dispute between the parties, he can
simply proceed to hear an argument on the merits of the claim without
hearing evidence at a proof. He could hear the argument there and then
or alternatively could fix a later date to hear the arguments. The reader
will perhaps appreciate that these various options correspond to some of
the options which are available at an options hearing in the OCR although
an important feature is that the timescales are considerably shorter in
summary cause. The sheriff can continue the hearing rather than fixing a
proof or making any other order but he may be reluctant to continue
unless the purpose of the continuation is very clear.[23]

If sheriffs conduct the calling fully and exhaustively as required by   **11–11**
the rules then the hearing will be more than just a formality. The intention is that the case would only go to proof in cases after some definite
effort has been made to settle it. It will only go to proof where specific
factual issues had been identified. In deciding what is the appropriate
method of enquiry to resolve the dispute, the sheriff should have sufficient information from the calling date to make an informed decision

---

[22] See *Penman v Hunter* Unreported (Sh. Ct) February 13, 2008, Sheriff Principal Bowen,
in which the unsuccessful pursuer argued that the sheriff had gone "too far too quickly"
at the r.8.3 hearing. The sheriff principal concluded that the sheriff had been perfectly
entitled to decide the case there and then.

[23] e.g. at the hearing he may have identified for the parties various matters which might
resolve or focus the dispute. He might consider it would be sensible to allow the parties
time to consider these points. This might well apply especially where the hearing is
attended by the legal representatives of both parties and time for consideration with the
clients might be fruitful.

about what form of enquiry would be the most suitable. In practice, the calling is not frequently as rigorous as that.

Rule 8.5—Each party must within 28 days of the fixing of a proof intimate to every other party and lodge with the sheriff clerk a list of documents which he intends to use at the proof and the opposing party is entitled to inspect those documents.

Rule 8.6—Within 28 days of the fixing of a proof each party has to intimate to every other party and lodge with the sheriff clerk a list of the witnesses they intend to call to give evidence. A failure to do so may prevent any such witness being called.

Rule 8.7—Not less than 28 days before the proof a party must disclose to every other party in the form of a written report the substance of the evidence of any skilled person he intends to call as a witness and he must lodge a copy of that report.

Rule 8.8—The parties are encouraged "where possible" to agree photographs, sketch plans and any statements or documents which are not in dispute.

Rule 8.13—When the sheriff hears the proof he can make a note of any facts agreed by the parties since the hearing at the calling date and the parties may lodge a joint minute of admissions of any facts upon which agreement has been reached. Indeed, the sheriff can insist upon this if he wishes. During the hearing of the proof, the sheriff must make his own notes of the evidence led at the proof and he is required to retain his own notes until after the time for any appeal has passed and any appeal has been disposed of.

Rule 8.14—After all of the evidence has been led in the proof the sheriff must hear parties on the evidence and at the conclusion of that hearing the sheriff may pronounce his decision or reserve judgment.

Rule 8.18—Where the sheriff pronounces his decision at the end of the proof [24] the sheriff must state briefly the grounds of his decision including the reasons for his decision on any questions of law. If the sheriff does not pronounce his decision at the hearing itself and reserves judgment, he is obliged to provide the sheriff clerk, within 28 days of the date when he reserves judgment, with a statement of his decision and a brief note of the grounds of his decision. The sheriff clerk must send copies to each of the parties.

---

[24] Also, after any hearing at the calling date at which the sheriff is able to make a decision on the merits of the case.

It might be appreciated that this chapter of the rules contains all of the basic provisions for the full hearing of a summary cause in any defended action. The rules can be seen to be relatively brief and avoid undue technicality. They are, of course, designed to facilitate "the summary" disposal of the action.

Chapter 9—Incidental applications and sists

The name given to a motion in summary causes is an incidental application. The rules about incidental applications are broadly similar to motions in an ordinary action but the opponent only has two days within which to intimate opposition. The same rules apply to applications to sist a summary cause as apply to sists of an ordinary action. The reason for the sist must be stated in the application and the sheriff can recall the sist on his own initiative if he considers this appropriate.

11–12

Chapters 10 and 11—Counterclaim and third party procedure

The rules regarding counterclaims and third party procedure are brief and should be referred to for details. It is expected that a counterclaim should be lodged and a request for service of a third party notice should be made at the time when the defender lodges his form of response to the summons, although in third party procedure this can be done later if there is a good reason for the delay.

11–13

Chapter 12—Summary decree

A pursuer can seek summary decree by lodging an incidental application for summary decree on the ground that there is no defence to the action nor any part of it. This application can be made at any time after a defender has lodged a form of response. The pursuer has to give the defender not less than seven days notice before the hearing of the application. The same rules and principles apply to the grant, refusal or other disposal of an application for summary decree as apply in other forms of procedure.

11–14

Chapter 17—Productions and documents

Rule 17.1(1)—Provides that a party who intends to rely upon any documents or articles at any proof must lodge them with the sheriff clerk together with a list detailing the items no later than 14 days before the proof and he must at the same time send a copy of that list to the other party. Documents which have not been lodged in this way can still be used at the proof but only with the consent of the other party or with the permission of the sheriff. The remaining rules in the chapter relate to the provision of copy productions for the sheriff, borrowing of productions and retention of productions. There are certain special provisions which apply to party litigants or authorised lay representatives relating to the custody of productions.

11–15

Chapter 18—Recovery of evidence and attendance of witnesses

11–16   Similar provisions apply in relation to recovery of documents by way of commission and diligence as apply in ordinary actions. Reference should be made to the rules for the details. Witnesses must be cited to the proof on at least seven days notice and there are special provisions applying to actions in which party litigants wish to cite witnesses.

Chapter 22—Decree by default

11–17   If a proof is fixed in a summary cause and a party fails to appear at a hearing when he is required to do so then the sheriff may grant decree by default, although this does not necessarily apply to a failure to attend a hearing of an incidental application. If all parties fail to appear at a hearing or a proof where required to do so then the sheriff must, unless sufficient reason appears to the contrary, dismiss the action.[25]

Chapter 23—Decrees, etc.

11–18 **Rule 23.3**—This provides a procedure for the assessment of the amount of judicial expenses payable by one party to another in the event of a successful action. The amount of the expenses will usually be fixed by the sheriff clerk although, in certain circumstances,[26] the account of expenses may be taxed by the auditor of court. The details of how this will be done are contained in rr.23.3A and 23.3B.

Chapter 24—Recall of decree

11–19 **Rule 24.1**—Where a decree is granted in an undefended action or as a result of a failure to appear at the calling date, a party may apply for recall of that decree by lodging a form explaining the failure to appear.[27] The rules provide, however, that a party may apply for recall of a decree in the same action on one occasion only.

When a party lodges a minute for recall of decree then the sheriff clerk must fix a date, time and place for the hearing of the minute and the party must give seven days notice of that hearing. It is provided that, at that hearing, the sheriff *shall* recall the decree so far as not implemented and then the hearing shall proceed as if it was a calling date.[28]

Chapter 25—Appeals

11–20   One point to emphasise is that an appeal can only be taken in a summary cause from the decision of the sheriff on a point of law. In other words, a party can argue that a sheriff decided the case in the way that he

---

[25] Also any counterclaim.
[26] Especially where the account may be detailed or complex.
[27] Form 30.
[28] In other words, a party making an application for recall of decree is bound to have it granted—but once only.

did because he misinterpreted the law or because he failed to apply it properly to the facts which he decided had been proved. A party cannot appeal on the grounds that the sheriff ought not to have believed one body of evidence in preference to another. There is no opportunity to have a rehearing of evidence in an appeal. The appeal can only be taken in the first instance to the sheriff principal. This is done by way of requesting a stated case and specifying the point of law upon which the appeal is to proceed. Within 28 days of a note of appeal, the sheriff must issue a draft stated case and the draft stated case must contain: (1) his findings in fact and law or, where appropriate, a narrative of the proceedings which took place before him; (2) appropriate questions of law; and (3) a note in which he states the reasons for his decisions in law. The stated case is sent to the parties both of whom have an opportunity to lodge a note of suggested adjustments and there is a procedure whereby any such adjustments can be considered, accepted, or rejected. There is a tight timetable requiring the stated case to be adjusted (or not) so that the final stated case can be signed by the sheriff. It will then be forwarded to the sheriff principal for the hearing of the appeal and the parties will be sent a copy of the stated case along with a note of the date of the appeal hearing.

The rules make brief provisions for the hearing of the appeal and after hearing the appeal the sheriff principal can either pronounce his decision or reserve judgment whereupon he must issue his decision in writing within 28 days.

It is competent to appeal to the Court of Session in certain limited circumstances. A party can apply for a certificate from the sheriff principal that an action is suitable for appeal to the Court of Session. He must lodge this within 14 days of the date of the final decree. The sheriff principal is obliged to hear the parties or the solicitors on the application and he can grant or refuse the certificate. His decision to grant or refuse a certificate is final.

Chapters 26–33

These chapters contain specific provisions regarding the management **11–21** of damages payable to persons under legal disability,[29] actions of multiple poinding,[30] and other miscellaneous actions where the value of the subject matter is under £5,000.

Chapter 35

Rule 35.1—Provides that any document referred to in the Summary **11–22** Cause Rules which requires to be lodged with the sheriff clerk, intimated to a party or sent by the sheriff clerk may be in electronic or documentary form. If it is in electronic form then it may be lodged, intimated or

---

[29] Where the damages do not exceed £5,000.
[30] Again where the fund is £1,500 or less.

sent by email or similar means. The time of lodgement, intimation or the sending of the document shall be treated as the time when the document was sent or transmitted.

PERSONAL INJURY ACTIONS AS SUMMARY CAUSES — CHAPTER 34

11–23 It is necessary to deal with this in a little more detail because, although the practical impact of these rules has been minimal thus far, the increase in the jurisdiction limits for summary causes could well lead to a very significant increase in a number of such claims. This may focus considerable attention on the special provisions which were introduced for such personal injury actions. The rules have certain similarities with the rules for personal injury actions in the Court of Session.[31] It is worth observing that the Summary Cause Rules came into force on June 10, 2002[32] but there have been very few reported cases on the procedure in such actions. It is only possible to give an outline of what the rules provide and time will tell whether specific practices and procedures might develop when a greater number of actions are obliged to proceed under these rules. It should be noted that parties can elect to remit an ordinary action for personal injury to the summary cause procedure so that it can proceed under these specific rules. This is rarely (if ever) done in practice although there might well be advantages in doing so. The rules are as innovative as the rules for personal injury actions in the Court of Session,[33] and a brief outline of the procedure follows:

Narrative of procedure

11–24   The statement of claim in an action of damages for personal injury where the sum sued for is £5,000 or less should be in Form 10. This requires the pursuer to state briefly details of the parties, the grounds of jurisdiction, the facts of the accident, the injuries sustained, and the common law or statutory basis for liability. An outline of the facts of the case (and no more than that) will be sufficient. An outline of the allegations of fault or breach of statute should be all that is required. Obviously, there is no room or need for any pleas in law.

The pursuer is required to lodge along with the summons:

(1) all medical reports on which he is intending to rely; and
(2) a statement of his valuation of the claim in Form 10C with a list of supporting documents.

The pursuer may also include with his summons a specification of documents containing whatever calls are appropriate from those set out in Form 10E. On the assumption that the defender lodges a form of

---

[31] For which see Ch.6.
[32] i.e. long before the new personal injury rules in the Court of Session.
[33] Or even more so.

response the sheriff clerk must then grant the commission and diligence for recovery of the documents mentioned provided that they fall within the type of document contained in Form 10E.

These rules mean that by the time the defender receives the summons he should have a basic outline of the facts of the case, an outline of the common law or statutory case upon which the claim is based, and a reasonably good breakdown of the way in which the claim has been valued. The purpose is to give the defender an opportunity to consider all of this documentation and respond to it. The defender must respond fully and the rules make specific provision for a form of response which ought to prevent the defender from lodging skeletal-type defences.

The defender's form of response is one of the real innovations in the rules. The form is set out in Form 10B and requires the defender to state his position on a number of crucial aspects of the claim. The defender is required to answer certain specific questions. The intention is to encourage the defenders to show a degree of candour and where the defender is unable to answer or answer fully he would be expected to explain why he is unable to do so. Reference should be made to the form for the details.

The purpose of framing the rules in this way is that, in a defended case, **11–25** both parties should attend at the calling date by which time all of the above forms have been lodged and intimated, and the sheriff should then have a reasonably clear picture of the nature of the case and the nature of the dispute between the parties. He will also have a clear picture of what might be capable of agreement. It is not expected that a personal injury claim will be resolved by way of an argument about points of law at the calling date, nor is it expected that the sheriff would carry out a detailed analysis of the claim.[34] The sheriff will be encouraged to check that both parties understand what the arguments are and it would be open to the sheriff to make a decision about the whole merits of the case at the calling date. In the case of *Armstrong v Brake Brothers (Frozen Foods) Ltd*[35] this was actually done. This is the only case on these rules so far and it is worth reading for an explanation of what the rules were intended to achieve and how they were intended to operate.

It is open to the parties to amend the statement of claim or the form of response prior to the proof and this is likely to be allowed unless there was prejudice to one or other party in permitting such an amendment.

With regard to the quantification of the claim, as previously pointed out, the pursuer has to provide a valuation of the claim along with the summons. The defenders have to provide a valuation of the claim not later than 28 days before the proof. This does not mean that the defender must wait until 28 days before the proof, and if the defender is in possession of sufficient information to enable him to complete and lodge the valuation of the claim prior to the calling date then it is expected that

---

[34] Although that is quite possible.
[35] *Armstrong v Brake Brothers (Frozen Foods) Ltd* Unreported Glasgow Sheriff Court January 17, 2003, Sheriff Principal Bowen.

the defender would do so. As can be appreciated, the hearing at the calling date might be much more focused if the defender's quantification of the claim was available as well.

Apart from this outline of the procedure, the action itself is intended to be heard in accordance with the remaining summary cause rules although the general rules are not intended to apply where they are inconsistent with the provisions in this chapter relating to actions of damages for personal injury.

Summary Cause Procedure and Ordinary Procedure — A Comparison

11–26 The basic idea behind the creation of the summary cause procedure[36] was to provide a quicker and cheaper form of procedure for actions in which the amount or value of the claim was modest. Many such actions are for recovery of debts. Many such actions are not defended. That being so, it was necessary for there to be a relatively simple procedure for serving actions and obtaining undefended decrees. Furthermore, it was felt that actions for a modest amount of money which were being defended should not require an elaborate form of procedure, and would be unlikely to raise important and intricate factual or legal issues. It was considered desirable to do away with the more formal requirements of ordinary procedure for smaller value claims and the view was that this could be done without sacrificing the essential principle of doing justice to the parties. Finally, it was felt that the procedures ought to be user friendly so that lay people could understand and follow what was happening in any such case and would not necessarily require the services of a solicitor.

Some of the features of summary cause procedure which contrast with ordinary cause procedure are:

(1) **There is no requirement for detailed written pleadings in a summary cause**. This probably makes the procedure more "accessible" for a lay person. This may or may not be beneficial. There have been instances in the past of cases in which, because the parties and the court have not really identified the matters in issue, the hearing of the case has not produced a just result.

(2) **The procedure in a defended summary cause action is much simpler**. There is no time allowed for adjustment of pleadings in summary causes although there is a limited scope for alteration of pleadings. There is little room for debate on legal issues prior to the hearing of evidence, and this does away with one of the elements of ordinary procedure which is known to cause significant delay. There are very few technical procedural requirements and, in essence, once the court has been given the basic details of the claim and the defence to the claim it is likely to fix a proof within a relatively short time.

---

[36] Also the summary cause procedure of actions of damages for personal injury.

(3) **The procedure is less formal**. This makes it easier for a party or an authorised lay person to attend to any of the few technical requirements prior to a proof. It is considered desirable that people who are not legally qualified should be able to conduct the litigation themselves if they wish to. Whether that would still be desirable if the summary cause jurisdiction limit was substantially increased remains to be seen.

(4) **A defended summary cause action will go to proof and will be decided much more quickly**. Cases are likely to be allocated a date for a hearing of proof at the calling date. There is less prospect of a proof being discharged. Depending upon court timetables, a proof might be assigned within two months of the calling date. The calling date might take place about two or three months after the service of the summons. Accordingly, it is not unreasonable to expect a summary cause action to last for as little as six months from the date when proceedings are served until the date of a decision. The fixing of a diet of proof often encourages parties to consider settlement and in summary cause actions an early proof is likely to lead to a quicker resolution of the claim either by virtue of the court giving a decision or because the prospect of an imminent proof has "encouraged" the parties to negotiate and settle.

(5) **It is a cheaper form of procedure**. Some of the reasons for this are:

(a) the scale of fees which a successful party can recover from the other side, i.e. their judicial expenses, is significantly less than the scale which applies to ordinary actions;
(b) there is less formal procedure in a summary cause action and therefore less cost;
(c) the court dues are less;
(d) there is no provision for the recording of evidence in a summary cause proof by shorthand writers and this can represent quite a significant saving; and
(e) there is a practical disincentive to the parties to incur large costs and outlays in preparing and presenting a case at proof where the sum at stake in the litigation is quite modest and any such cost would be out of proportion.

The procedure can be criticised broadly on the basis that the mechanism for identifying and focusing upon the matters in dispute between the parties can be somewhat crude and unsatisfactory, although the sheriff has an important role in focusing, identifying and expressing these matters of dispute. It can also be suggested that the early and automatic fixing of a proof is not necessarily the best way of resolving every dispute. It is difficult to find a balance between the need to provide a simple and quick form of procedure which is accessible to all and a procedure in which the parties are given the time and the opportunity to digest, consider and prepare for a hearing of what might be a difficult case, albeit for a low value. A significant increase in the financial jurisdiction limits would be likely to bring this form of procedure into much greater prominence.

11–27

Sheriff Court

Summary Cause (Not Personal Injuries)

Flow Chart of Procedure

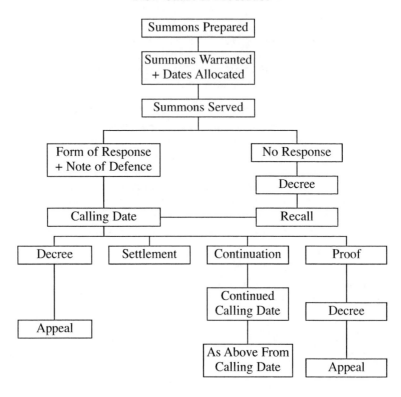

CHAPTER 12

SMALL CLAIMS

OUTLINE

As we have seen, the summary cause is a new form of procedure which **12–01**
was designed to be quicker, cheaper and more accessible to the public
than ordinary sheriff court procedure. Summary causes were first introduced in 1976 and after about 10 years it was decided that there should
be a special form of summary cause process to be known as a "small
claim". This was to be used for certain summary cause proceedings as
prescribed by the Lord Advocate. In 1988 it was provided that certain
types of cases would be small claims. Primarily, these were to be claims
for sums of money of £750 or less. The procedure in small claims was to
be even quicker, cheaper and more informal than summary causes. The
sheriff was also required to assist parties to identify and resolve their disputes if possible. In 2002, a further change in the Small Claim Rules was
introduced which was intended to simplify the procedure even further. In
January 2008 the small claims limit was increased to £3,000.

STATUTORY FRAMEWORK

The statutory framework for small claims can be found first in the Law **12–02**
Reform (Miscellaneous Provisions) (Scotland) Act 1985 s.18(1), which
provided new subss.(2)–(4) of s.35 of the Sheriff Courts (Scotland) Act
1971. In particular, s.35(2) of that Act, as amended, provided that the Lord
Advocate could prescribe what was to be a "small claim" by way of order.

By the Small Claims (Scotland) Order 1988[1] the Lord Advocate prescribed proceedings which would be small claims as: (1) actions for payment of money not exceeding £750 exclusive of interest and expenses,
but not including actions of aliment or interim aliment nor actions of
defamation; and (2) actions *ad factum praestandum*[2] and actions for the
recovery of possession of moveable property where the value of the subject matter does not exceed £750.

---

[1] Small Claims (Scotland) Order 1988 (SI 1988/1999).
[2] An action brought to enforce the performance by the defender of an act other than the
payment of money.

It was provided that no award of expenses was to be made in such small claims where the value of the claim did not exceed £200. Where the value of the claim was between £200 and £750 the sheriff was entitled to make an award of expenses but only to the extent of £75. However, this restriction on the award of expenses was not to apply in the case of a defender who (a) had not stated a defence; (b) had not proceeded with a defence once it had been stated; or (c) had not acted in good faith as to the merits of the defence. Nor would the restriction of expenses apply to either a pursuer or a defender on whose part there had been "unreasonable conduct" in relation to the proceedings or to the claim.[3] The provisions regarding expenses are one of the unique features of small claims actions.

By the Act of Sederunt (Small Claim Rules) 1988[4] a detailed set of rules was provided for small claims which came into effect from November 30, 1988. These rules remained in force until 2002.

By the Act of Sederunt (Small Claim Rules) 2002[5] a completely new set of rules was provided for small claims with effect from June 10, 2002. The rules are brief, and the procedure is intended to be easily understood, flexible, and informal.

On January 14, 2008 the financial limit for small claims was raised from £750 to £3,000[6]. All claims for less than £3,000 must be raised as a small claim unless they happen to be personal injury claims. A personal injury claim for any figure less than £3,000 has to proceed as a summary cause. The order also provided that, in a small claim, the court could make an award of expenses not exceeding £150 where the value of the claim was £1,500 or less and an award of expenses not exceeding 10 per cent of the value of the claim if the value was greater than £1,500.

STATISTICS

12–03 In 1987 there were approximately 74,000 actions raised as small claims in Scotland. In 1993 there were about 73,000 such actions. In 1998 there were 52,500 small claims, with most of them being actions for payment and about 60 per cent of them being undefended. In 2002, there were 32,256 actions raised during the year with all but about 400 of them being actions for payment. About 50 per cent of them were undefended. In 2006 there were estimated to have been 29,022 small claim actions raised throughout Scotland.

---

[3] Sheriff Court (Scotland) Act 1971 s.36B.
[4] Act of Sederunt (Small Claim Rules) 1988 (SI 1988/1976).
[5] Act of Serderunt (Small Claim Rules) 2002 (SSI 2002/133).
[6] The Small Claims (Scotland) Amendment Order 2007 (SSI 2007/496).

NARRATIVE

The procedure is intended to be simple and flexible. The procedure is **12–04** very similar to the procedure under the Summary Cause Rules so we will only deal briefly with the basic framework of the procedure.[7] We will not consider the rules specifically. They are relatively brief and can be easily read.[8]

If a person wishes to raise a small claim action then he prepares a summons in a form which is prescribed in the rules. He must insert a statement of his claim, which gives the defender fair notice of the claim and includes certain prescribed details.[9] The form is given to the sheriff clerk and it is then signed by the sheriff clerk. That signature is sufficient warrant or authorisation for the summons to be served on the defender.

When he signs the summons, the sheriff clerk will also assign two dates, namely the return day and the hearing date. The return day is the day by which the pursuer must return the duly served summons to the court and the defender must lodge his response with the court. The hearing date is the first date when the case will be heard in court, assuming, of course, that it is going to be defended.

The summons will then be served on the defender. There are circumstances in which it might actually be served by the sheriff clerk but, in most cases, the summons would be served by the pursuer in the normal way in a manner similar to what has already been described in summary causes.

If the defender wishes to appear and answer the summons either in whole or in part, whether it be on the merits of the claim or on the amount of the claim or where the defender seeks a time to pay direction, he has to intimate his position by completing the tear-off part of the form which is attached to the service copy summons and lodging it with the sheriff clerk before the return day. If the defender wishes to dispute the claim, or the amount due, then the form of response only requires him to give a brief indication of his position. There is no requirement for him to supply any more details until the hearing date.

If the defender does not lodge a form of response then the case will not call in court.[10] The pursuer must lodge a minute with the clerk in a prescribed form and this will usually ask the court to grant decree. There is no need to attend at the hearing date if there is no response. If the defender has not lodged a form of response and the pursuer has not lodged the prescribed form of minute for decree then the court will simply dismiss the claim.

---

[7] For a more detailed treatment of small claims see W.C.H. Ervine, *Small Claims Handbook,* 2nd edn (Edinburgh: W. Green, 2003).

[8] The Scottish Court Service provides detailed guidance notes for lay persons and others involved in small claims. This can be found on the Scottish Courts website at *http://www.scotcourts.gov.uk* [Accessed August 22, 2008].

[9] Chapter 4 of the Small Claims Rules.

[10] See Ch.8.

If the defender has lodged the form of response indicating that the claim is going to be defended, and if the pursuer has returned the principal summons to court as required, then the case will call for a hearing.[11] The hearing shall be held on the hearing date, which will be seven days after the return day. If the claim is not resolved at the hearing then the sheriff may continue it to such other date as he considers to be appropriate.

12–05   Assuming that the formal requirements have been complied with and that both parties are present at the hearing date, the sheriff is required to do certain things:

(1) if he is satisfied the claim is incompetent or the court plainly has no jurisdiction then he must dismiss the action[12];
(2) otherwise, he must ascertain the factual basis of the claim and any defence and the legal basis on which the claim and defence are proceeding[13];
(3) the sheriff must seek to negotiate and secure settlement of the claim between the parties if possible;
(4) only if the sheriff cannot secure settlement of the claim shall he identify the issues of fact and law which are in dispute, note these issues on the summons, and note on the summons any facts which are agreed; and finally,
(5) if it is possible to do so, he will reach a decision on the whole dispute on the basis of the information put before him at that time.[14]

However, where the sheriff determines that evidence has to be led for the purpose of enabling him to reach a decision on the dispute then he shall: (1) direct the parties to lead evidence on the disputed issues of fact which have been noted; (2) advise the parties of the matters of fact which require to be proved and indeed give guidance on the nature of the evidence which ought to be led; and (3) fix a hearing on evidence for a later date.

It can be seen therefore that the sheriff is required to take a very active part in trying to resolve the dispute between the parties and can indeed decide the whole case there and then if possible. The procedure whereby a defender can simply turn up at the first hearing and put forward his defence (verbally or otherwise) can cause problems. The statement of claim may not be particularly well focussed. The defence or defences may not be clear. The parties and the sheriff may be hearing various features of

---

[11] See Ch.9.
[12] For a small claim which was dismissed on appeal after consideration of fairly complex jurisdiction issues see *Niven v Ryanair Ltd* Unreported (Sh. Ct) April 15, 2008, Sheriff Principal Young.
[13] The expression of the statement of claim may not make either of these points clear, and in certain circumstances the defence as expressed at the hearing date might not be very clear either. The sheriff is obliged to assist the parties to clarify any such matters.
[14] See *SACL v Edinburgh City Council* Unreported May 29, 2008, Sheriff Principal Bowen.

the dispute for the first time. The process of identifying the disputed issues can often be a difficult one in these circumstances. Sometimes an apparently simple dispute can have hidden complexities of fact and of law which can impose a considerable burden on a sheriff in a busy court.[15]

There are general rules regarding the conduct of hearings[16] in a small claim.[17] The hearing of evidence has to be conducted as informally as the circumstances of the claim permit. The sheriff can adopt any procedure at the hearing which he considers to be fair, best suited to the clarification and determination of the issues before him, and provides each party with sufficient opportunity to present his case. The sheriff is obliged to explain to the parties the form of procedure which he intends to adopt before he proceeds to hear any evidence. In appropriate circumstances, the sheriff may, in order to assist the resolution of the disputed issues of fact, put questions to the parties and to the witnesses and may also explain any legal terms or expressions which might be appropriate to the case if he considers this is necessary for a fair conduct of the hearing. Evidence will normally be taken on oath[18] but the sheriff can dispense with that requirement if it appears reasonable to do so.

As will be appreciated, the sheriff is in complete control of the form, content and substance of any hearing required to reach a fair decision on the case. The formal rules of evidence do not apply.[19]

The sheriff is required to make notes of any evidence given at a hearing for his own use. Where practicable, he must give his decision and a brief statement of his reasons at the end of the hearing of the claim. He is permitted to reserve judgment, but within 28 days of the hearing he has to give his decision in writing together with a brief note of his reasons and the sheriff clerk has to send a copy to the parties. After giving his judgment, he must deal with the question of expenses and, if appropriate, make an award of expenses.

There are various provisions in the rules regarding miscellaneous procedural matters but, as previously explained, the rules and formalities are kept to a minimum.[20] In broad terms, the miscellaneous procedures are very much as explained in the Summary Cause Rules. For example, a motion in a small claim is called an "incidental application", and the rules about intimation and hearing of this are broadly similar. There are rules regarding the lodging and borrowing of productions and rules regarding the recovery of documents and the attendance of witnesses. Again, these are very much as provided in the Summary Cause Rules.

---

[15] See, e.g. *Experno Ltd v Banks* Unreported (Sh. Ct) June 14, 2007, Sheriff Principal Young, in which an issue arose at the hearing in relation to res judicata.

[16] This includes the hearing at the hearing date and the hearing on evidence.

[17] See r.9.3.

[18] Or affirmation.

[19] Although the sheriff could take the view that, if both parties are represented by solicitors, the hearing could and should be conducted in the traditional manner.

[20] See Chs 10–19 of the rules.

The court can grant decree by default if any party fails to attend or be represented at a hearing of evidence.[21] If all parties fail to appear or be represented at such a hearing then the sheriff must, unless sufficient reason appears to the contrary, dismiss the claim.[22]

There are special provisions regarding expenses.[23] If the court does decide it is appropriate to make an award of expenses on the summary scale, then the expenses will be assessed in accordance with the table of fees appropriate to a summary cause, and under the procedure applicable to such an action.

A party can seek recall of a decree in absence by lodging a minute in Form 20. The detailed rules are very similar to the rules for summary causes.[24]

An appeal can only be taken on a point of law.[25] A note of appeal has to be prepared in a form provided in the rules and lodged with the sheriff clerk not later than 14 days after the date of final decree. The sheriff will be requested to state a case and the appellant has to specify the point of law upon which the appeal is to proceed. There are similar provisions as apply in Summary Cause Rules for the adjustment, signing and presentation of a final stated case and the provision of a date for the hearing of the appeal.

Any document which requires to be lodged with the sheriff clerk, intimated to a party or sent by the sheriff clerk may be in electronic or documentary form. Documents in electronic form may be lodged, intimated or sent by email or similar means.[26]

THE SMALL CLAIMS PHILOSOPHY

12–06 The small claims procedure is intended to be flexible, informal, simple and easily accessible and understandable to all court users and particularly to members of the public. It can be argued that the informality and unpredictability of the procedure could possibly lead to an unfair result or an unfortunate approach to the attempted resolution of the dispute.[27] Not all claims of a low value are simple and straightforward and small claims may include actions in which there are complex legal principles to be resolved or in which there is extensive and conflicting evidence to be heard. The underlying philosophy of the small claims procedure can be taken from judicial pronouncements by three sheriffs principal as follows:

---

[21] See Ch.20.
[22] Also any counterclaim.
[23] See r.21.6.
[24] See Ch.22.
[25] See Ch.23.
[26] See Ch.5.
[27] See *Barlow v City of Edinburgh Council*, 2004 G.W.D. 27-574, Sheriff Principal Macphail; and *Registrar of Companies v Stonelee Developments Ltd*, 2004 S.L.T. (Sh. Ct) 116.

"Those who advocated the introduction of Small Claim procedure envisaged a happy land in which reasonable litigants would be assisted by friendly interventionist Sheriffs to reach fair and amicable solutions to their dispute free from the malign influence of confrontational lawyers".[28]

"In my opinion it is a most unfortunate aspect of Small Claim procedure that Sheriffs should be obliged to decide for themselves, and without any guidance from Parliament, how to resolve conflicts between the intended informality of that procedure and the normal rules of practice which are present in other forms of civil litigation".[29]

"While I support in principle the proposition that the Court should be prepared to adopt a liberal and enabling approach in the Small Claims procedure, I respectfully dissent from the proposition that this approach should be universally applied. In my opinion different considerations may apply where a party is represented by skilled advisers and where a party is an unrepresented party litigant. I do not consider that a liberal and enabling approach should be universally adopted so as to excuse insufficient identification of the disputed issues by solicitors or other skilled advisers".[30]

The flexibility and informality of small claims has been increased during its lifetime. This can cause problems where the court still requires to do justice between the parties although the consequences of a "slight" injustice in a small claim may well be worth incurring when compared with the perceived benefits of the procedure. It is arguable that, given the nature of small claims and the underlying philosophy of this form of procedure, solicitors should not be involved in small claims. The extensive guidance provided by the Scottish Court Service presupposes that many of the users of this procedure will be lay members of the public. However, the rules do not exclude solicitors and, in practice, parties are often represented by solicitors.

There is an argument that the parties should be left to present their own case with the assistance, advice and ultimately the conclusive decision of the sheriff. It can be said that the present financial limit is such that, even if the procedure could give rise to some injustice no major injustice is likely to be done that would cause any individual substantial financial hardship. The increase in the financial limits for small claims

---

[28] Sheriff Principal Risk in *Catto v Lindsay & Kirk*, 1995 S.C.L.R. 541; this has yet to be realised!

[29] Sheriff Principal Nicholson in *Kuklinski v Hassell*, 1993 S.L.T. (Sh. Ct) 23—the recent rules make it plain that Parliament does not intend to provide any guidance and the sheriff has the broadest of powers to deal with any small claim in such a way as he thinks fit.

[30] Sheriff Principal Hay in *McGregor v Strathclyde Motor Auctions Ltd*, 1991 G.W.D. 11-690.

may have a serious impact on the way in which many of the litigations in Scotland are conducted. Whilst a well intentioned decision by a judge at a flexible and informal hearing of a case might be socially acceptable where the sum at stake was no more than £750, it may not necessarily be acceptable where the sum at stake is significantly higher than that. In that situation an individual might well want—and be entitled to have—professional legal advice and assistance in putting forward his case. The relative informality of the procedure might, in some cases, frustrate the interests of justice. Of course, it should be borne in mind that, if one or other party, or both, consider that the small claims procedure is not suitable for the resolution of their dispute regardless of the fact that it is for a relatively small amount of money, it is open to them to seek a remit to summary cause procedure or even ordinary procedure. This would be warranted if there was a difficult question of law involved in the case or a question of fact of exceptional complexity.[31]

12–07 **Sheriff Court**

Small Claim

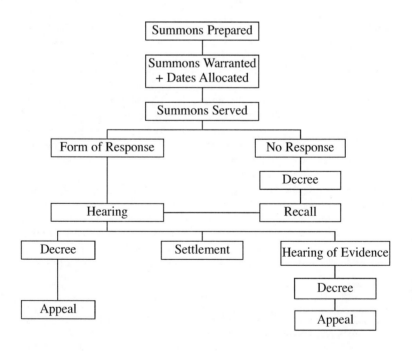

---

[31] See s.37(2B) of the Sheriff Courts (Scotland) Act 1971.

CHAPTER 13

DECLARATORY ACTIONS AND PETITORY ACTIONS

These two categories of action do not have any particular common fea- **13–01** tures, but are simply dealt with together in this chapter for convenience. Broadly speaking, declaratory actions request the court to state the nature of a person's legal rights in a particular situation. Petitory actions request the court to make some kind of order other than an order for payment of money. Most of the actions we have been considering thus far usually have, as their principal objective, recovery of a payment of money.[1] The pursuer will normally be craving the court to grant a decree against a defender to make a payment which the defender is legally obliged to make. In this chapter, however, we are going to consider these two different types of action whose principal objectives are somewhat different.

A crave or craves for payment can be made in these kinds of action. It is perfectly competent to ask the court for a declarator on its own, but a crave for declarator can often include other craves including craves for payment of money. The procedure in actions for declarator alone, or actions which include a crave for declarator with other craves, is generally no different from the procedure in an ordinary action.

Petitory actions are more likely to contain a single crave asking the court to do something than to be combined with other craves, such as for payment. The procedure in petitory actions in the sheriff court varies depending upon the precise remedy which is being sought. There is a completely separate set of procedural rules for petitory actions in the Court of Session.

It should be noted that the two types of claim, whilst described together in this chapter, are not significantly related to each other. They are distinct from other types of claim because of the nature of the remedy being sought from the court. Depending upon the specific nature of the remedy sought in actions of each type, there may be certain procedures in the case which will differentiate them from "normal" civil procedures. We are going to consider briefly what kinds of action declaratory and petitory actions are, what particular rules or procedures relate to them, and provide some brief examples of each.

---

[1] Judicial review is the obvious exception.

DECLARATORY ACTION

13–02 This is a name which can be given to any action in which the pursuer
asks the court to declare that he has some right or entitlement to something.[2] In this type of case the pursuer may crave the court for a declarator simpliciter[3] and for nothing else by way of payment or performance
by a defender. Equally, however, a crave for declarator can be combined
with other craves. For example, see the case of *Bank of Scotland v
Fernand*,[4] where the bank made a crave for declarator that they were
entitled to enter into possession of subjects over which they held a security, along with other craves including a crave for the defender to vacate
the property and a crave for ejection if he failed to do so. As demonstrated in that case, the term "declaratory action" as a category of action
has more to do with the nature of the remedy sought than with any speciality of procedure which was followed.

The courts will not entertain an action for declarator simpliciter where
the granting of a decree of declarator would have no legal or practical
consequence for the pursuer. The courts will not adjudicate on an issue
simply for academic interest and an action of declarator of that kind
would be incompetent.

Whenever a pursuer wants to pursue a claim of some kind, but the right
upon which he wishes to rely in order to found that claim is not clear,[5] then
he must preface any crave in his claim by a crave for declarator of the existence and definition of that right.[6] For example, in a claim for compensation for damage caused to property where there is a doubt that the property
damaged is actually owned by the pursuer then a declarator of ownership
would be required.[7] If an action has been raised without a declarator
and a declarator is required for the reasons mentioned above, then there is
no reason why a crave for declarator could not be inserted into the action.[8]
An interesting case where a petition for judicial review was adjusted
after the first hearing[9] so as to include, amongst other things, a crave for
declarator, is the case of *Shaw v Strathclyde Regional Council*.[10]

---

[2] Or that the court should declare that what appears to be a right does not exist.
[3] i.e. for a declarator and nothing else.
[4] *Bank of Scotland v Fernand*, 1997 S.L.T. (Sh. Ct) 78.
[5] e.g. whether he has a title and interest to sue.
[6] A recent example can be found in *Gaelic Assignments Ltd v Sharp*, 2001 S.L.T. 914, in
which the court discussed the essential nature of an action of declarator.
[7] See the case of *Macdonnell v Caledonian Canal Commissioners* (1830) 8 S. 81, where
a separate action of declarator was raised.
[8] This would be done by way of amendment. A good recent example of a case in which
an action for damages also included a crave or conclusion for declarator is the case of
Esso Petroleum Co Ltd v Hall Russell & Co Ltd, 1988 S.L.T. 874. Paradoxically, in the
case of *Gaelic Assignments Ltd*, 2001 S.L.T. 914, the claimant introduced by amendment a conclusion (crave) for payment in an action of declarator.
[9] See Ch.8.
[10] *Shaw v Strathclyde Regional Council*, 1988 S.L.T. 313.

Any crave or conclusion for declarator must be precise and clear in its terms.[11] The pursuer will crave the court to, "find and declare that . . . (for example) the defender has incurred the irritancy of the lease dated . . .". In the example suggested, the crave for declarator might be followed by a crave for a further declarator that the pursuer is entitled to enter the property, a crave for the defender to remove, and a crave for payment of arrears of rent.[12]

It may be difficult to decide in many cases whether a declarator is necessary or unnecessary and whether a declarator is competent.[13] It is difficult to generalise and perhaps it is more helpful to look at specific examples.[14]

The jurisdiction of the sheriff court to entertain an action of declarator is contained within s.5(1) of the 1907 Act. In essence, if a party could raise an action to enforce a right in that particular sheriff court, then he can raise an action of declarator of that right in that same sheriff court. The Court of Session has jurisdiction to hear all types of declarator to determine all rights which could competently be enforced in the Court of Session.

The defender in any such case would be the person who, or indeed all of the people who, dispute that right or would have an interest in doing so. There is a benefit in suing all of those who might have an interest in disputing the right because the decision of the court on the crave for declarator would be *res judicata*[15] against all those who were parties to the action but would not bind those who had not been sued.

There are no special rules of procedure in either the sheriff court or the Court of Session in relation to actions of declarator simpliciter or in relation to cases which include a crave or conclusion for declarator. There is, however, one notable speciality in both courts relating to an action under the Presumption of Death (Scotland) Act 1977 for declarator of the death of a person who has been missing for seven years. As can be appreciated, this is not a particularly common action, but there are special rules for such cases.[16]

---

[11] See the case of *Aberdeen Development Co v Mackie Ramsay & Taylor*, 1977 S.L.T. 177.

[12] Another example can be seen in the case of *Hill Samuel & Co Ltd v HAAS*, 1989 S.L.T. (Sh. Ct) 68 where the report details the different craves which were sought.

[13] See the case of *Clarke v Fennoscandia Ltd (No.2)*, 2001 S.L.T. 1311.

[14] In the sheriff court, see *Mears v Mears*, 1969 S.L.T. (Sh. Ct) 21; *Fraser v United Society of Boilermakers*, 1963 S.L.T. (Sh. Ct) 17; *Accountant in Bankruptcy v Butler*, 2007 S.L.T. (Sh. Ct) 200. In the Court of Session, see *Norwich Union Life Insurance Society v Tanap Investments UK Ltd (in liquidation) (No.1)*, 1998 S.L.T. 623; *Creswell v Colquhoun & Co*, 1987 S.L.T. 329; *Tiffney v Flynn*, 2007 S.L.T. 929.

[15] See Ch.19.

[16] Necessary because of the statutory provisions regarding such a declaration. See OCR Ch.37 and RCS Ch.50.

PETITORY ACTIONS

13–03 In a sense, all actions are petitory actions because they involve a pursuer seeking something (an order for payment or performance or whatever) from a judge. In this section, however, we are going to consider some petitory actions which have particular rules of procedure. These are different from, or at least involve procedures which are additional to, the existing rules for ordinary actions. Broadly speaking, in sheriff court cases there are a number of specific types of case which can be categorised as petitory actions and which have certain specific rules. In the Court of Session, there are special rules relating to petitions in general and other rules relating to particular applications by petition. Petition procedure in the Court of Session is a distinct form of procedure, and it is important to appreciate that there is a fundamental difference between Court of Session ordinary actions which are initiated by a summons and petitory actions initiated by a petition.

SHERIFF COURT PETITORY ACTIONS

13–04 It is difficult to define a petitory action in the sheriff court in a way which distinguishes it in principle from an ordinary action. What we shall do, however, is consider some of the more common petitory actions which might be encountered in practice. In these cases there are particular rules or procedures to be followed. As will be seen, the rules of procedure in these cases can be quite complex. They can be confusing to follow in practice, even with considerable experience, and accordingly concentrating over much on the details of the rules is likely to obstruct an understanding of the procedure. The intention therefore is to explain what the actions are, a very broad outline of the procedures and a basic narrative of how they work.[17]

ACTION OF MULTIPLE POINDING[18]

13–05 This is an action which can be raised in circumstances where a number of parties have a claim on some property or money which is in the possession of an individual and are in dispute as to how that should be disposed of or divided. A practical example might be a case where the police recover a stolen car some time after the theft and after the car has been sold on to others, altered, worked upon, etc. There might be a claim for recovery of possession of the car from the original owner, from his

---

[17] For full details reference should be made to the rules themselves. Don't expect to understand them readily!

[18] Pronounced "multiple pin-ding".

insurer, from intermediate buyers, etc. and in complex cases the police would be concerned about making any decision themselves as to who was the rightful owner. They might be concerned that handing over the car to the "wrong" party might give rise to a claim against them for doing so. An action of multiple poinding would enable the police to ask the court to adjudicate upon the competing claims.

It is necessary for the procedures in an action of multiple poinding to provide a means of identifying the property in dispute,[19] preserving the property, and adjudicating upon any competing claims for it. Because of the unusual nature of this claim, and the various legal rights and interests which have to be balanced between all of the parties involved in it, special procedures are necessary. The procedures are set out in OCR Ch.35 rr.35.1–35.18. The Court of Session rules are in RCS Ch.51 rr.51.1–51.15. There are differences between the two sets of rules but we will simply take an overview of the procedure which will apply in both.[20]

One of the first considerations is that an action of multiple poinding has to be competent in the circumstances.[21] The property or money in dispute is called the "fund *in medio*" and the person who is actually holding the fund, or any person with an interest in the fund, can raise an action of multiple poinding. In circumstances where the holder of the fund is simply holding it pending resolution of competing claims, then he will want to dispose of it as soon as possible because the final resolution of the claims may take some considerable time. One of the first stages of the procedure, therefore,[22] is to identify the fund and to make some order to ensure that it is preserved for safekeeping. The holder of the fund can then be discharged from any other responsibilities in relation to it. The parties with competing claims have an opportunity to lodge details of their claim in writing. Once details have been lodged the sheriff can make an order for adjustment of the claims. When that step is completed,[23] he will decide what further procedure is required, having considered the nature of the claims and the issues which the various claimants wish to raise. The adjudication of the claims could be resolved by hearing legal debate or by proof. Once the court decides the issue, the interlocutor ordering payment or transfer of the fund *in medio* to the claimant or claimants who have been successful, protects the holder of the fund from any claims against him.

---

[19] Which can sometimes be rather difficult.

[20] A detailed explanation of the procedures can be found in Macphail, *Sheriff Court Practice*, 3rd edn, paras 21.52–21.71 and *Greens Annotated Rules of the Court of Session 2008/9*, pp.C438–450.

[21] See the case of *Adam Cochran & Co v Conn*, 1989 S.L.T. (Sh. Ct) 27. Also see *McClement's Trustees v Lord Advocate*, 1949 S.L.T. (Notes) 59.

[22] Assuming there is no challenge to the competency of the action or jurisdiction of the court.

[23] In whatever time scale seems appropriate.

ACTION OF COUNT RECKONING AND PAYMENT

13–06 This is an action which was initially said to be based upon the relationship of principal and agent between two parties, whereby the principal was entitled to demand an accounting from his agent of the agent's intromissions.[24] That general definition was criticised as being too restrictive in the case of *Coxall v Stewart*.[25] Lord Maxwell attempted to analyse what were considered to be the essential features of an action of count reckoning and payment.[26] However, in the case of *Loretto School Ltd v Macandrew and Jenkins*,[27] Lord Kirkwood, who did not refer to *Coxall*, accepted the definition relied upon in the *Unigate* case. The matter has not been authoritatively decided, but it is clear that there is cause for some doubt as to the circumstances in which such an action is competent and as to the relationship between parties which could give rise to such an action.[28]

The procedure in an action of count reckoning and payment can be confusing and again we will simply look at the broad outline of the procedure rather than the precise details. There are no special rules for such actions in either the sheriff court or the Court of Session, but because of their unusual nature they do not fit very comfortably into the existing rules. The procedure which is followed in such cases tends to rely very much upon practice whereby the courts "fit" the specialities into the existing rules.[29]

In pleading such a case, the pursuer will normally crave the court to order the defender to produce a full account of his intromissions. He will usually also crave payment of any sum which appears to be the true balance due to him by the defender as disclosed by the accounting, and he will normally crave, as an alternative, that if the defender does not appear in the action or produce an account then decree should be granted for a specific sum of money.[30] The first issue which has to be decided in any action of count reckoning and payment is whether it is accepted or established that the defender has any liability to account to the pursuer at all. The initial question of liability to account is one which can be dealt with under the existing ordinary action procedures, and the existence of any such liability could be decided at debate or after proof or by admission.

---

[24] See *Unigate Food Ltd v Scottish Milk Marketing Board*, 1972 S.L.T. 137.
[25] *Coxall v Stewart*, 1976 S.L.T. 275.
[26] Reference should be made to that case for details.
[27] *Loretto School Ltd v Macandrew and Jenkins*, 1992 S.L.T. 615.
[28] For examples of cases where actions were raised see *Daks Simpson Group Plc v Kuiper*, 1994 S.L.T. 689; *Adam v McDonald*, 1990 S.L.T. 404; and *Hobday v Kirkpatrick's Trustees*, 1985 S.L.T. 197. A more recent example of a case in which the court decided that the relationship between the parties did not give rise to an obligation to account was *Ness Training Ltd v Triage Central Ltd*, 2002 S.L.T. 675.
[29] A case which did not "fit" into the rules very well is *Wylie v Corrigan*, 1999 S.L.T. 739.
[30] How this specific sum can be calculated may depend upon educated guesswork or not!

Once the case reaches that point, however, the procedural specialities would emerge. Once it has been accepted or established that the defender has a liability to account to the pursuer then the next step for the court to take is to order production of the accounts. The practice is for the defender to be ordered to produce an account within a specified period of time and for the pursuer then to be allowed to lodge objections to the accounting. The defender would then be allowed to lodge answers to any objections within appropriate time limits. In practice, therefore, the defender should produce a set of accounts of his intromissions which will show precisely what (if anything) he says is due to the pursuer. The pursuer will lodge objections in the form of a statement of facts in which he can dispute the accounting given. He may argue generally that the principles upon which the account has been produced are wrong or inappropriate. He may argue that specific items in the account are not proper entries.[31] He may argue a combination of both. The defender then has an opportunity to lodge answers to the statement of facts responding to the specific criticisms which have been made.

The procedure then would be that once the objections and answers had been lodged, and the parties had focused their dispute by adjustment, the record (a document containing the objections and answers as adjusted) would be closed. It is open to parties to take preliminary pleas in relation to the content of the accounts.[32] When the case calls before the judge after the record has been closed, consideration will be given to the nature and content of the objections and answers. A decision will be taken as to whether they can be disposed of by way of debate, proof or proof before answer or even by remitting to an accountant to report.[33] At the successful conclusion of any such action, the pursuer would be hoping to obtain a decree for the sum which the court finds to be properly due to him.[34]

ACTIONS AD FACTUM PRAESTANDUM

This is a type of action brought by a pursuer in order to enforce the performance by the defender of some act other than the payment of money. There are no special procedural features about the action of any great significance, but such actions often have a crave for performance supplemented by an alternative crave for payment of damages if the performance is not effected. Such actions can include an action for delivery of property **13–07**

---

[31] Mistaken, inaccurate or false, etc.

[32] e.g. there might be an argument that an item debited in the accounts is not something which is legally due to be debited.

[33] A helpful analysis and illustration of the basic procedures can be found in *Paterson v Paterson*, 2005 S.L.T. (Sh. Ct) 148.

[34] Some assistance may be gained from the reading of Guthrie v McKimmie's Trustee, 1952 S.L.T. (Sh. Ct) 49 and *Clarke v Clarke's Trustees*, 1925 S.L.T. 498, in which examples of specific objections and pleas in law can be found.

held by another, and in that case it may be combined with a crave to the court to grant warrant to officers of the court to search for and take possession of the particular articles for which delivery is sought.[35]

These types of actions can also be called actions for specific performance or specific implement.[36]

INTERDICT AD INTERIM

13–08 An action of interdict seeks to prevent someone from acting in a way which would breach the pursuer's legal rights. Interdicts are common in family actions and their use in such actions is well known. They are not very common in other litigations,[37] but they do occur and can often cause real concerns for solicitors and clients alike. A breach of an interdict could have serious consequences, so it is important that a breach can be clearly identified. Any crave for interdict should be clear and unambiguous. A crave for interdict can stand alone or be combined with other craves. Usually the crave for interdict will be combined with a crave for interim interdict. We are going to consider the special procedural provisions and practices regarding interim interdict.

Most parties seeking interdict will want to have an interim interdict as soon as possible. If one had to wait for the ordinary court procedures to run their course, and for a decision to be reached on whether the facts of the case established after proof could justify an interdict, this would obviously take considerable time. It might well defeat the original purpose of raising the action. An interim interdict, granted at the commencement of the action, which will remain in force pending the final outcome of the interdict action, will solve this problem. There are rules about the general considerations a court has to take into account in granting an interim interdict.[38] It can be granted by the court on the basis of allegations in the writ and/or oral representations[39] made by the solicitor at any hearing.

---

[35] See *Merchants Facilities (Glasgow) Ltd v Keenan*, 1967 S.L.T. (Sh. Ct) 65.

[36] See, e.g. *Postel Properties Ltd v Millar & Santhouse Plc*, 1993 S.L.T. 353; *Ford v Bell Chandler*, 1977 S.L.T. (Sh. Ct) 90; and *Retail Parks Investments Ltd v Royal Bank of Scotland Plc (No.2)*, 1996 S.L.T. 669, in which helpful observations were made on the general legal considerations to be kept in mind in assessing the relevancy of a plea for decree *ad factum praestandum*. A recent decision in such an action can be seen in *Highland and Universal Properties Ltd v Safeway Properties Ltd (No.2)*, 2000 S.L.T. 414.

[37] The masochistic reader can have some fun with the case of *Milmor Properties Ltd v W. and T. Investment Co Ltd*, 2000 S.L.T. (Sh. Ct) 2, in which the pursuer sought declarator, decree *ad factum praestandum*, and interdict.

[38] See S. Scott Robinson, *The Law of Interdict*, 2nd edn (Edinburgh: Law Society of Scotland/Butterworths, 1994) and Hector Burn-Murdoch, *Interdict in the Law of Scotland* (Edinburgh: Hodge, 1933).

[39] Known as "ex parte" statements.

An interim interdict can be sought at any time before the final resolution of the case, but it is commonly sought at the time when the writ is lodged with the sheriff clerk's[40] office for a warrant to be obtained for service on the defender.[41] The normal practice would be for the party who seeks the interdict to attend at the sheriff clerk's office and for arrangements to be made for the crave for interim interdict to be heard before the sheriff there and then. In cases of extreme urgency there are administrative provisions for dealing with interim interdicts out of normal business hours. The sheriff can grant an interim interdict if he is satisfied that it is competent and that the circumstances entitle him to do so. At that stage, he will only have heard one side of the dispute, and he may decide to limit the time for which the interim interdict remains in force by granting the interim interdict only until the defender has had an opportunity to be heard. In normal practice, he might grant the interim interdict, grant warrant for service of the proceedings and the interim interdict on the defender, and fix a specific date for a hearing at an early stage for the sole purpose of determining whether the interim interdict ought to be continued or not. The defender would then have an opportunity to appear and be represented at that early hearing. At that hearing, the sheriff would make a decision based on both sets of ex parte statements and any additional information which might be relevant. It is extremely important for a pursuer to intimate the grant of an interim interdict to the defender immediately. If the defender is unaware of its existence or of its terms then it would be ineffective against him.

A defender who suspects that a pursuer might wish to raise an action of interdict against him in which interim interdict will be sought at the outset can protect his position by lodging a caveat. Where a caveat has been lodged, its effect is to prevent a court granting an interim interdict unless the sheriff is satisfied that all reasonable steps have been taken to afford the person who lodged the caveat an opportunity to be heard in opposition to it. Any hearing on the granting of an interim interdict may have to be continued until the sheriff is satisfied that such steps have been taken.

Caveats are dealt with in the Act of Sederunt (Sheriff Court Caveat Rules) 2006.[42] This details the orders against which a caveat can be lodged. A particular form is prescribed for a caveat, and it is to be lodged with the sheriff clerk. It will remain in force for one year from the date on which it was lodged and can be renewed annually thereafter. In the Court of Session, caveats are dealt with in Ch.5. A form is prescribed and it is to be lodged in the petition department. Similarly it will remain in force for a period of one year and can be renewed annually.

---

[40] For convenience we will simply assume a sheriff court action but the same general procedures apply in the Court of Session under their administrative arrangements.

[41] A step which is required in any ordinary action.

[42] Act of Sederunt (Sheriff Court Caveat Rules) 2006 (SSI 2006/198).

13–09 In addition to raising an action by way of a summons in the Court of Session, a party can institute proceedings by way of a petition. Certain actions have to be raised by way of a petition. The general rules regarding petitions in the Court of Session are contained in Ch.14 but there are other rules which give special provisions for particular petitions. Broadly speaking, a petition involves a less formal procedure than a summons and the difference between a petition and a summons has been described as follows:

> "The object of the Summons is to enforce a Pursuer's legal right against a Defender who resists it or to protect a legal right which the Defender is infringing; the object of a Petition, on the other hand, is to obtain from the administrative jurisdiction of the court, power to do something or to require something to be done which it is just and proper should be done, but which the Petitioner has no legal right to do, or to require, apart from judicial authority."[43]

The rules provide that certain particular applications must be made by petition in the Outer House.[44] Certain particular applications must be made by petition in the Inner House. The rules prescribe a form of petition and the procedure whereby the petition may be intimated. There is provision for the lodging of answers to a petition and an opportunity to seek an early order for procedure which would enable the merits of the petition to be disposed of quickly.

PARTICULAR RULES

13–10 **Rule 14.2**—This details the applications which must be made by petition in the Outer House. They include an application for the appointment of a judicial factor,[45] certain applications to the *nobile officium* of the court relating to trusts,[46] a petition for breach of interdict, and an application for suspension and interdict. Also included are various applications to the court under the 1994 Rules or under, "any other enactment or rule of law". This includes a variety of statutory applications of which examples are given in the undernoted.[47]

Also included in such petitions are applications to the court to exercise its *"parens patriae"* jurisdiction. This is the jurisdiction of the court

---

[43] See pp.49–50, *Report of the Royal Commission on the Court of Session*, HMSO 1927.
[44] For an example of this see *Paterson, Petitioner(No.2)*, 2002 S.L.T. 1006.
[45] See RCS 1994 Ch.61 on judicial factors.
[46] See *Institute of Chartered Accountants of Scotland. Petitioners*, 2002 S.L.T. 921, in which the court decided that the petition should have been made to the Inner House under r.14.3.
[47] See *Greens Annotated Rules of the Court of Session 2008/9*, p.C118.

to take steps to protect the interests of those incapable of looking after themselves.[48] Included in this would be petitions to withdraw medical treatment from a hospital patient.

Rule 14.3—This details application which must be made by petition **13–11** presented in the Inner House. These include an application under any enactment relating to solicitors or notaries public, an application by petition which is incidental to a case which is already before the Inner House, an application to the *nobile officium*[49] not covered by r.14.2, and an application which has to be made to the Inner House by virtue of the provisions of a particular statute.[50]

Rule 14.4—This provides for a specific form of petition and the form itself is contained in the appendix to the rules at Form 14.4. The petition must include a statement of facts in numbered paragraphs setting out the facts and circumstances on which the petition is founded, and a prayer[51] which sets out all of the orders to be sought from the court in the sequence in which they are sought. If the petition is presented under a statute, then the statement of facts should refer to the relevant provisions justifying the presentation of the petition. The prayer of the petition must crave a warrant for such intimation, service and advertisement of the petition as may be necessary, and the name, address and capacity of each person upon whom service of the petition is sought must be set out in a Schedule annexed to the prayer of the petition. In particular circumstances, where it is sought in a petition to dispense with service or to shorten the period of notice, then this should be sought in the prayer, and the basis for such dispensation or shortening of notice must be stated in the statement of facts. No pleas in law are necessary at the stage of presentation of the petition.[52]

Rule 14.5—This provides that once a petition has been lodged the court will pronounce an interlocutor ordering intimation as appropriate. If the petitioner seeks an interim order, or to dispense with intimation, then he must do so by applying by motion along with the petition itself.

Rule 14.6—This provides the period of notice for lodging answers to the petition to be 21 days.[53] The period is reckoned from the date of service, intimation or advertisement, whichever is the latest.

---

[48] See *Law Hospital NHS Trust v Lord Advocate*, 1996 S.C. 301.
[49] See *Royal Bank of Scotland Plc v Gillies*, 1987 S.L.T. 54 and *London & Clydeside Estates v Aberdeen District Council*, 1980 S.C. (HL) 1.
[50] e.g. an application by petition under the Vexatious Actions (Scotland) Act 1898 to have an individual declared to be a vexatious litigant.
[51] The equivalent of a conclusion or crave.
[52] Although they apparently are stated in some cases.
[53] Or 42 days if the petition is to be intimated or advertised outwith Europe.

13–12 **Rule 14.7**—This provides that a petition shall be intimated on the walls of the court and in such other manner as the court thinks fit. It shall be served on every person specified in the petition by virtue of a form of citation. The form of citation is contained within the appendix to the rules at Form 14.7. Inter alia it advises the person upon whom the petition is being served that if he intends to lodge answers to the petition he must lodge them within 21 days[54] after the date of service.

If no answers are lodged within the period of notice then the petitioner shall make a motion to the court to dispose of the petition. This would normally involve the petitioner asking the court to grant the order sought. Once the order has been obtained, then it should be served forthwith on any individual against whom the petition was directed. The court may allow any such individual to have the interlocutor recalled and to lodge answers in certain circumstances. These include being satisfied that: (1) the person did not know of the petition in sufficient time to lodge answers; (2) there is a prima facie answer to the petition on the merits; and (3) the person has enrolled the motion for recall within a reasonable time after he knew about the petition.

Rule 14.8—If answers to the petition have been lodged, then the petitioner shall, within 28 days after the expiry of the period of notice, apply by motion for such further procedure as he seeks and the court will make an order for whatever further procedure seems appropriate. The hearing of the merits of a petition may be by proof, when evidence may be led, or alternatively by a "hearing" in which no witnesses will be led. In that case, the court can consider reports, affidavits and other documentary evidence along with the submission by the parties. It is for the parties and the court to decide by agreement if possible what form the hearing on the merits should take.

---

[54] Or, as noted above, 42 days.

CHAPTER 14

SUMMARY APPLICATIONS, STATUTORY APPLICATIONS AND APPEALS

These are the names given to three particular types of civil cases which **14–01** are dealt with in a summary manner[1] in the sheriff court.[2] Summary applications can be defined as all applications of a summary nature brought under the common law jurisdiction of the sheriff, and all applications brought under any statute which requires the application to be disposed of in a summary manner, but which does not define the procedure whereby that is to be done.[3]

For present purposes it is unnecessary to explore in detail the subtle differences between the three types of case because the form of procedure in each is virtually identical. Summary application is the generic name given to a form of procedure available in the sheriff court which can be used in a number of specific cases. Summary applications include certain civil applications made to a sheriff under his common law jurisdiction or by virtue of a specific enactment. They also include statutory applications,[4] although not all statutory applications are dealt with by way of summary application procedure.[5] They also include statutory appeals which are made to a sheriff by virtue of an enactment which confers a right of appeal[6] to a sheriff.[7] Invariably, statutory appeals proceed by way of summary application procedure. For the sake of simplicity we will concentrate on summary application procedure generally, and only touch briefly on any specific procedural requirements which might derive from particular statutory provisions.

It may be easier to understand summary applications and their procedure by giving some examples of what they might involve. An obvious and relatively common example might be a summary application to a

---

[1] Quickly and simply.

[2] The term is not to be confused with a summary cause (see Ch.11) nor with summary procedure in criminal cases.

[3] For full details, see George Jamieson, *Summary Applications and Suspensions* (Edinburgh: W. Green, 2000).

[4] i.e. where a particular statute gives a party a right to apply to the sheriff for some reason connected with the statute.

[5] It depends on the terms of the statute conferring the entitlement to make the application.

[6] As opposed to a right to "apply" to a sheriff.

[7] The differences between them were discussed in *Ward v DRM Driver Training Centre (Glasgow)*, 2002 S.L.T. (Sh. Ct) 108.

sheriff to review the decision of a licensing board not to grant a public house licence. The Licensing (Scotland) Act 1976 entitles any person aggrieved by a decision of the licensing board to apply to the sheriff to overturn that decision or to make some other order. That type of application to the sheriff would be done by way of a summary application. Another example would be an application under the Company Directors Disqualification Act 1986 for an individual to be disqualified from holding the office of director of a limited company.[8] That would be pursued by way of a summary application.[9]

The sheriff will have jurisdiction to deal with cases summarily at common law, particularly in cases where there is a degree of urgency.[10] More commonly, however, his jurisdiction arises because a statute specifically provides that a party is entitled to make an application to the sheriff under this procedure.[11] Indeed, even where the statute does not prescribe a procedure for such an application, it can often be assumed on the basis of established historical practice in the sheriff court, that it is to be dealt with by summary application procedure and rules.[12]

Many of the statutory appeals by way of summary application relate to the actions of local authorities and other decision-making bodies. However, these summary applications should not be confused with judicial reviews.[13] A summary application is a remedy which can be used in the sheriff court where the statute dealing with the subject matter specifically provides for a right of appeal to the sheriff. In such cases, and unless the statute provides a specific and alternative way in which the right of appeal is to be exercised, then the court procedure in any such appeal would be by way of a summary application.

STATUTORY PROVISIONS

14–02 Section 3(p) of the Sheriff Courts (Scotland) Act 1907 defines a summary application as:

> "All applications of a summary nature brought under the common law jurisdiction of the Sheriff and all applications . . . brought under

---

[8] See *Secretary of State for Trade and Industry v Stephen*, 2003 S.L.T. (Sh. Ct) 29.
[9] For a comprehensive list of the many statutes which contain provisions entitling persons to make an appeal to the sheriff by way of summary application see Macphail, *Sheriff Court Practice*, 3rd edn, Ch.26. See also Jamieson, *Summary Applications and Suspensions*.
[10] Examples are given in Macphail, *Sheriff Court Practice*, 3rd edn, pp.754 and 755, but common law applications are rare and rather obscure. There are very few reported cases dealing with summary applications at common law in the last 50 years.
[11] There are over 150 different types of such application.
[12] In the absence of any other procedural requirement in the statute itself.
[13] See Ch.8.

any Act of Parliament which provides, or, according to any practice in the Sheriff Court, which allows that the same shall be disposed of in a summary manner, but which does not more particularly define in what form the same shall be heard, tried and determined".

Section 50 of the 1907 Act provides that:

"In summary applications (where a hearing is necessary) the Sheriff shall appoint the application to be heard at a Diet to be fixed by him and at that or at any subsequent Diet (without record of evidence unless a Sheriff shall order a record) shall summarily dispose of the matter and give his judgement in writing".

These are the only statutory provisions which underlie the summary application procedure. There are, however, rules of procedure provided by Act of Sederunt.

In 1999, an Act of Sederunt was passed which consolidated all of the previous rules for various summary applications, and included specific rules for a variety of other statutory applications. This was the Act of Sederunt (Summary Applications, Statutory Applications and Appeals, etc.) Rules 1999.[14] It came into force on July 1, 1999. The intention was to regularise, as far as possible, the rules applying to all summary applications, etc. and to bring together in one document specific rules applicable to applications under particular statutes where it was considered necessary to make additional procedural provisions. The Act of Sederunt ("SAR 1999") provides that any application or appeal to the sheriff shall be by way of summary application unless otherwise provided in the Act of Sederunt or in the statute relating to the application itself.

The rules relating to summary application procedure generally are contained in Ch.2. The specific rules for applications to the court under specific statutes which require additional procedural provisions[15] are set out in Ch.3.[16] The 1999 Act of Sederunt also contains an extensive schedule which consolidates all of the forms required for summary applications generally and, where necessary, in relation to specific statutory applications which have their own specific rules.

The sheriff has an extremely wide discretion as to the procedure to be followed in summary applications and similar statutory applications. The Act of Sederunt does not in any way interfere with that discretion. The rules

---

[14] Act of Sederunt (Summary Applications, Statutory Applications and Appeals, etc.) Rules 1999 (SI 1999/929).

[15] e.g. in an appeal under the Licensing (Scotland) Act 1976, the specific rules provide for the parties to whom intimation should be made and oblige the pursuer to lodge the statement of reasons for the licensing board's decision along with the initial writ.

[16] Many of these additional or alternative provisions are minimal and the actual procedure followed in these other cases may, for all practical purposes be indistinguishable from the standard summary application procedure.

provide a very basic framework for the conduct of summary applications which is likely to promote a uniformity of approach. The number and variety of summary applications has increased in recent times. Lawyers working in local authorities, in particular, will be familiar with many different types of summary application, but otherwise this type of case will normally form a very small proportion of the cases handled in a typical civil practice. There are no clear statistics available for the number of summary or statutory applications raised or contested in the sheriff courts in Scotland.

NARRATIVE

14–03   The "application" is set out in writing in the form of a writ and it ought to contain details of the factual background and the order which is being sought from the sheriff. The general form of the pleadings will be broadly the same as in an ordinary action, but it is anticipated that the procedure as a whole will not be complex and will proceed with the minimum of delay. It is unlikely there will be any reason for complex legal pleadings or lengthy adjustment of pleadings. In essence, the court wishes to have a document which sets out the nature of the case (and any defences) and the basis for the application clearly and at an early stage. The court can immediately fix a hearing on the merits of the application with the minimum of procedure. In certain circumstances, a hearing on the merits of the application can take place as soon as the application first calls in court.[17] However, the sheriff is given a very wide discretion as to the appropriate procedure in summary applications, and there may be cases where, at the other extreme, the hearing of the application might involve taking a substantial body of evidence on matters of fact.[18] It may be necessary to establish the facts before the merits can be argued. In the normal course, however, it is anticipated that the procedure should be short, simple and quick.[19]

If it is competent to proceed by way of summary application,[20] and if the particular sheriff court to which the application is made has jurisdiction, then the action is commenced by initial writ in the form set out in the rules. The application has to be lodged with the sheriff clerk within 21 days after the date on which the decision appealed against, and which gave rise to the application, was intimated to the pursuer.[21] The party

---

[17] It is not necessary for there to be written defences or answers if the sheriff does not require them—although the interests of justice might dictate that some notice of the defender's position should be given before argument is heard.

[18] This is what happened in *Todd v Todd*, 2008 S.L.T. (Sh. Ct) 26.

[19] In *Anderson v City of Dundee Council*, 2000 S.L.T. (Sh. Ct) 134 it was anything but short simple and quick.

[20] See, e.g. the case of *Bradford & Bingley Building Society v Walker*, 1988 S.L.T. (Sh. Ct) 33.

[21] Unless the statute in question provides a different time limit or the sheriff can be persuaded to extend the time limit.

applying (who is called the pursuer) lodges the initial writ with the sheriff clerk to obtain a warrant. The warrant constitutes the authority of the court to serve the application on the opponent (who is called the defender). The warrant is in a specific form. It differs from the form of warrant which would apply in an ordinary sheriff court action in that it actually specifies a date and time when the application will call in court. When the defender receives service of such a writ and warrant, he is not obliged to do anything to advise the court or his opponent that he will be defending the case other than simply to turn up at the appropriate date and time.[22]

When the case calls in court on that occasion, the sheriff will normally ascertain the position of the parties and consider the best means of resolving the case. The sheriff has a wide discretion in deciding what further procedure will be appropriate. He can continue the case. He can order the defender to lodge defences. He can actually decide the merits of the application there and then, if he considers that this would be justified. The general purpose of the procedure is to keep delays to a minimum and avoid unnecessary or complex procedure. Often the order which will be pronounced at the first hearing of the case would be for a full hearing to take place on a specific date and for defences to be lodged within a period of time.[23] It is not necessary, and indeed it is usually considered inappropriate, to wait for defences to be lodged in writing before fixing a date for a hearing of the merits of the case but there may be circumstances which would justify that approach.[24]

Some consideration usually has to be given to the nature of the hearing which will be required in order to determine the case. Often the hearing will simply involve legal argument based upon the terms of the pleadings or any documents which form the background to the case. Sometimes it will be necessary for evidence to be led to clarify facts or indeed to reach decisions on disputed facts before hearing arguments on the merits of the dispute. If evidence is heard then it will rarely be taken down and recorded. The case should be determined as soon as possible after any hearing of evidence or any hearing of legal argument. There are rights of appeal against the decision of the sheriff on such an application, but these will often depend upon the nature of the summary application and upon the terms of the statute under which the summary application is proceeding. It is unnecessary to go into detail about this but the undernoted examples will provide an illustration of cases in which appeals were taken.[25]

---

[22] Although out of courtesy he might well do so and almost certainly should do so.

[23] Usually 14 days from the date of the hearing.

[24] e.g. it may not be possible to be sure about the type of hearing required until the defender's position is set out clearly in writing. The sheriff has a discretion to take this into account if he considers it appropriate.

[25] *Woolley v Strachan*, 1997 S.L.T. (Sh. Ct) 88; *Glasgow Airport Ltd v Chalk*, 1995 S.L.T. (Sh. Ct) 111.

Rules

14–04 As has been noted above, the sheriff has a wide discretion as to the procedure to be followed and this is reflected in the rules. There is little room for controversy about the procedural processes involved in summary applications. Although there are a large number of reported cases on summary applications over the last few years, the reports are mostly concerned with the merits of the dispute and procedure does not feature very significantly.[26]

We shall consider the principal rules briefly.

Summary Application Rules—Chapter 2

14–05 **Rule 2.3**—This contains the usual dispensing power allowing the sheriff to relieve any party from the consequences of failing to comply with the rules.[27]

Rule 2.4—This prescribes the form of initial writ (Form 1), and the form is very similar to the form of initial writ for an ordinary action. One significant difference is the writ should state at the top of the page that it is a "summary application under (the particular statute relied upon)".

Rule 2.5—If the sheriff thinks that some other party may have an interest in the application apart from the proposed defender then he can make an order for intimation to that person. This means that the application will have to be served on that person.

Rule 2.6—The summary application has to be lodged with the sheriff clerk within 21 days of the date of the decision complained of unless the particular statute under which the application proceeds provides otherwise. On special cause shown the sheriff may hear an application lodged outwith that period.

Rule 2.7—This provides for the form of warrant and certificate of citation. The details of the rules are largely similar to the rules for warrants and citations in ordinary actions subject to the specific difference that the warrant will contain a court date for the case to call in court and the defender will defend the action by turning up at court on that date rather than lodging a form of appearance in advance.

---

[26] This is not too surprising because the sheriff can effectively do what he likes.

[27] There are no reported examples of this but it is useful to read the case of *Saleem v Hamilton District Licensing Board*, 1993 S.L.T. 1092 in which, on appeal from the sheriff court, the Inner House took the view that it would not be appropriate to dismiss a summary application even where both parties failed to turn up at the first hearing and made certain brief comments about summary application procedure.

Rules 2.8 and 2.9—These relate to caveats in summary applications **14–06**
which would be relevant if the pursuer was seeking an interim order on
lodging of the application.[28] The form of caveat is Form 8, which is in
the Schedule to the rules.

There are extensive provisions regarding service (rules 2.10–2.17)
and reference should be made to the rules themselves for the details.
There are further rules regarding arrestments, transfer of cases to other
sheriffdoms and a variety of administrative matters (rules 2.18–2.29)
which are of no real significance for present purposes.

Rule 2.30—Any motion relating to a summary application[29] shall be
made in accordance with Ch.15 of the OCR 1993, unless the sheriff
directs otherwise.

Rule 2.31—This rule expresses the wide discretion conferred upon the
sheriff by s.50 of the 1907 Act and underlines the flexibility and informality of this procedure.[30] The sheriff may "make such order as he
thinks fit for the progress of a summary application in so far as it is not
inconsistent with section 50 [of the 1907 Act]".

RULES ON APPLICATIONS UNDER SPECIFIC STATUTES

Chapter 3 of the 1999 Act of Sederunt contains the rules for applications **14–07**
under specific statutes. They are termed statutory applications. Some of
the rules are relatively minimal and technical.[31] Some of them are complex and detailed.[32]

Schedule 1 of the Act of Sederunt contains a large number of forms
which are to be used in summary applications generally and in some of
the specific statutory applications noted above.

It may be helpful at this stage to set out some of the particular statutes
in respect of which specific rules are provided. They are:

- Administration of Justice (Scotland) Act 1972—for recovery of documents relevant to a court case prior to the raising of court proceedings.

---

[28] The provisions are largely identical to the provisions in the OCR 1993 for ordinary
actions.
[29] There should not be many but an example might be a motion to discharge a hearing of
the application for some good reason.
[30] See *Forsyth v Chief Constable of Strathclyde*, 1997 S.L.T. (Sh. Ct) 80; *Secretary of
State for Trade and Industry v Stephen*, 2003 S.L.T. (Sh. Ct) 29; *Capurro v Burrows*,
2004 S.L.T. (Sh. Ct) 51.
[31] e.g. Pt X rr.3.10.1 and 3.10.2 deal with appeals under s.6(5) or (5A) of the Rating
(Disabled Persons) Act 1978, and provide simply and solely that any appeal should be
lodged within 42 days from refusal by the local authority.
[32] e.g. Pt IX rr.3.9.1–3.9.17 contain specific provisions relating to the handling of property recovered under the Proceeds of Crime (Scotland) Act 1995.

- Betting and gaming statutes—dealing with bookmakers' licenses, gaming licenses and associated matters.
- Coal Mining Subsidence Act 1991.
- Conveyancing and Feudal Reform (Scotland) Act 1970.
- Copyright, Designs and Trademarks Acts.
- Drug Trafficking Act 1994—relating to the detention of cash seized by the Crown.
- Licensing (Scotland) Act 1976.
- Mental Health (Scotland) Act 1984—relating to applications for admission, guardianship applications and community care applications.
- Proceeds of Crime (Scotland) Act 1995—containing extensive provisions regarding the administration of property detained under the Act.[33]
- Rating (Disabled Persons) Act 1978.
- Representation of the People Act 1983—regarding elections.
- Requests for applications under the Model Law on International Commercial Arbitration.
- Sex Discrimination Act 1975.

In recent years, it has been necessary to provide by Act of Sederunt additional rules for statutory applications and appeals, including rules in relation to:

- Adults with Incapacity (Scotland) Act 2000.
- Proceeds of Crime Act 2002.
- Mortgage Rights (Scotland) Act 2001.
- Race Relations Act 1976.

Further statutory regulation in the future will inevitably give rise to further specific rules where the general rules for summary applications need to be supplemented to meet the requirements of the statute and to assist the summary disposal of the subject matter of the application or appeal.

---

[33] See *Ho, Petitioners*, 2003 S.L.T. 867.

Summary Application

Flow Chart of Procedure

14–08

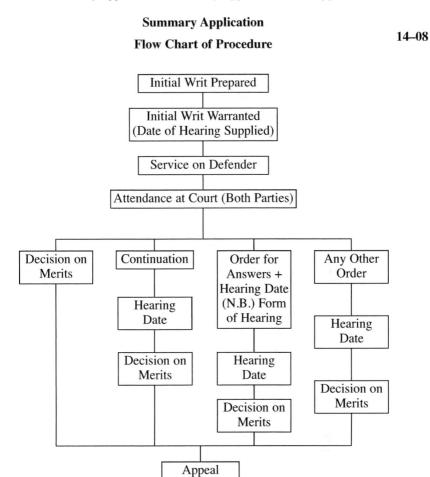

CHAPTER 15

INCIDENTAL PROCEDURES IN CIVIL ACTIONS

15–01 Any civil court action starts with an initiating document of some kind[1] and will usually end with a court order of some description. The obvious objective in raising an action is to have the court decide the merits of the claim contained in the initiating document[2] after a hearing of some kind between the pursuer and the defender. In reality, the majority of actions never go to a hearing. The rules can be seen as providing a framework for progressing the case to a fair hearing in a regulated way, but many of the rules of procedure and practice are concerned with what can be described as procedures which are incidental to that main purpose. That does not mean that they are unimportant, far from it, but their importance must be kept in perspective. There are numerous such incidental matters, and in this chapter we will concentrate on some of the more important procedures which the reader is likely to encounter in a civil litigation. Without the benefit of any practical experience, it may be difficult to appreciate when and why these procedures would be used. On some occasions, they can change the whole course of the action. Some of them will change the emphasis of the case. Some of them will help to make the action easier to win at the proof. We will deal with six particular matters in no order of importance or priority. There is no particular connection between them all.

By using Mr X's cases we can illustrate some of the practical circumstances in which they might come into play. In the action against Mr X's firm by the timber suppliers, let us assume that the proprietor of the timber company goes into hospital for major surgery two weeks after the court action is raised and he is the only person who can instruct his solicitors to do anything further about the action. He is going to be unable to give instructions for some time and he (and he alone) is also in possession of information which would be required for the purposes of adjusting pleadings or responding to any defences which might be lodged. The court timetable will be running but it is not going to be possible to handle the litigation on his side until he is fit again. The solicitor acting for him may well consider it appropriate to have the progress of the case halted until his client is available. In that event, he might make a motion

---

[1] A summons, petition or writ.
[2] Or some modification of it.

216

to the court to have the action sisted (postponed) until he can obtain proper instructions to enable him to deal with the litigation. After the pursuer recovers, the solicitor may then make a motion to the court to recall the sist and set the procedural timetable running again.

In the same case, Mr X's firm may have an insurance policy which gives them indemnity for claims of this nature. In other words, if anyone claims payment from them for unpaid timber supplies, the insurers will make that payment (if due) on behalf of their insured.[3] Unfortunately, in this case, the insurers say to Mr X that they do not consider that this particular claim is covered by the policy for some reason and they are not going to indemnify his firm for this claim if it happens to be due. Accordingly, although the principal action is an action for payment by a pursuer against a defender, and the defender may or may not have a defence to that action, the defender (Mr X) also has an argument that if he is found liable to pay something to the pursuer he is in entitled to be indemnified by another (a third party) with whom the pursuer has no relationship at all. The defender could, in that situation, lodge a motion with the court to be allowed to serve a third party notice on the insurer whereby the defender would involve the insurer in the ongoing proceedings. His position might be that he may or may not be due to pay something to the pursuer in terms of the contract between them but, if he is, then he is entitled to ask the court to grant a decree in the same action against the third party ordering the insurers to indemnify him. The court would hear all of the evidence about the case, i.e. the pursuer's claim against the defender and the defender's claim against the third party, in the one action, which might be the most economic and sensible means of resolving the whole dispute. The alternative would have been to wait for the outcome of the principal claim against the defender and then for the defender to institute a separate action against the third party.[4] This would not be in the defender's interests.

As a further example, take the case of Mr X's claim against the cus- **15–02** tomer for the building work which had been done on the customer's house. The customer might say in his defences that he has not paid the bill because the work was not done properly and the workman who did the work actually damaged a structural wall in the house which will have to be repaired at a cost far in excess of the bill. The customer might well lodge defences to the action against him and also lodge a counterclaim against the pursuer (Mr X's firm) for the cost of repair so that both claims would be decided in the one action. Mr X might take the view that this is a spurious defence and that the customer in reality has no money to pay his bill. His solicitor might suggest lodging a motion for the defender to find caution for expenses.[5]

---

[3] Admittedly this is a little unlikely in real life.

[4] In which they would respectively be pursuer and defender.

[5] Asking the court to order the defender to put up money or security for the costs of the court action which is competent in certain circumstances which will not be addressed here; but see para.21–12, below.

As a further illustration, take the court action raised by one of Mr X's passengers against the other driver who caused the car accident. The defender[6] might have no dispute about the accident being his fault and might be willing to settle the action but is unable to offer enough money to satisfy the pursuer. The defender in that case might decide to lodge a tender which is a judicial offer to settle the case at a certain amount and which might have adverse consequences for the pursuer in court expenses if it is not accepted.

Finally, in any of the examples given above, one or other party might consider it necessary or desirable to attempt to obtain access to documents which might be relevant to the claim or some aspect of it during the course of the action.[7] That party would lodge a motion and a specification of documents[8] asking the court to order the opponent or some other person to produce documents specified in the list.

These are just illustrations of practical circumstances in which the procedures to be discussed in this chapter can come into play. They are not restricted to the particular types of case mentioned and indeed it should be possible to appreciate that they can all be used in a variety of actions by both pursuer and defender. We are now going to look at them in some more detail.

MOTIONS

15–03 A motion can be described as any request by any of the parties to an action for the court to do something in relation to the procedure or merits of the action. As well as making a motion in writing, a party can make a motion orally at any time when the case happens to be calling before a judge in court.[9] Sometimes the reason for making a motion is simply based on practice. Sometimes the rules require a motion to be made. Before proceeding with a motion, you have to be satisfied that it is competent to make such a motion.[10]

Many motions are not opposed. A number of motions are for the benefit of both parties and, in that case, the parties can lodge a joint motion, which effectively advises the court of their agreed request.[11] In both the sheriff court and the Court of Session there are procedures whereby motions are intimated to the opponent in advance and in writing. Unless the opponent gives notice that he is intending to oppose the motion, then

---

[6] Who would in practice almost certainly be represented by an insurance company.

[7] There are provisions allowing recovery of documents before the raising of proceedings also and these are dealt with at para.15–21, below.

[8] Broadly speaking, a list or description of specific documents which is set out in writing.

[9] When it can be termed a "motion at the bar".

[10] In other words, that the court has power to grant your request and that the rules allow you to lodge a motion in those circumstances.

[11] Although the court may not necessarily be obliged to accede to it.

it will normally be granted without argument. There may, however, be occasions when a hearing on the motion would be fixed even when it is unopposed.[12]

The procedure for lodging, intimating, opposing and granting of motions in the Court of Session is set out in Ch.23 rr.23(1)–23(14) of the RCS.[13] Many of the rules are administrative in nature and there are provisions regarding the types of motion which require to call in court or can be dealt with by agreement.[14]

The procedure for the lodging, intimating, opposing, and granting of motions in the sheriff court are contained in the sheriff court rules in Ch.15 rr.15(1)–15(6). They are somewhat less detailed than the Court of Session equivalent and again they contain administrative directions regarding motions which are designed, inter alia, to minimise the necessity for a judge to hear motions which are not contentious. In summary causes and small claims, motions are called incidental applications. The way in which they can be made, lodged, intimated and heard, if necessary, are set out in rr.9.1(1)–(4) of the SCR. In small claims the rules are rr.10.1(1)–(5).

A party can always make an oral motion when the case is calling in court[15] for other procedural reasons. If it is not opposed, then it can usually be dealt with at the time.[16] If it is opposed, then the court might deal with it provided there is time to do so and the opponent has sufficient notice of the making of the motion to enable him to argue it fully if he wishes. In some situations, a judge will advise parties that he would not want to deal with a motion made verbally and at short notice and that a written motion to the same effect would be preferable.

SISTS

A sist is a stoppage or postponement of procedure in a case. It could more **15–04** fully be called a "sist of process". A sist is achieved by a party, or both parties, making a motion to sist.[17] The motion can be made orally or in writing. If a party requests a sist, and the request is opposed, the judge has a discretion as to whether to grant a sist or not. He has to decide what

---

[12] e.g. if the judge was not satisfied about its competency.

[13] The reader should refer to the detailed rules.

[14] Reference should be made to the *Parliament House Book*, p.C179–186 for details, which can be quite confusing for the uninitiated. Pre-printed forms of motion and opposition are used and the intention is to have motions call before a judge for a hearing and decision only where necessary.

[15] Strictly speaking, in summary causes, this requires "leave" of the sheriff under the rules, but that is really no different in practical terms from the position in other procedures.

[16] Although there is no obligation on the court to hear it—that compulsion only applies to written motions properly intimated.

[17] A judge can also sist an action "*ex proprio motu*", i.e. of his own volition or on his own motion, if he considers this an appropriate step in the procedure.

is in the interests of justice and he has to take into account whether there is any prejudice to the other party if the sist is granted. He also has to balance the suggested benefits of a sist to one party against the benefit of the action proceeding without delay or interruption to a final decision.

The most common reasons for sist of an action are as follows:

(1) for legal aid—both parties may want to do this. For example, if the pursuer has been obliged to raise an action to prevent the expiry of the limitation period on his personal injury claim[18] before his legal aid application has been lodged or decided then it would be normal for him to make a motion to sist until he had legal aid. On the other side, if a defender requires to apply for legal aid after the writ has been served upon him,[19] then he will seek a sist of the action. Neither party would want to incur the expense of court proceedings without the benefit of legal aid[20];

(2) for parties to negotiate settlement of the action.[21] Settlement might involve a delay in the payment of agreed damages or the carrying out of agreed obligations which might involve a delay of some months. The parties would want the action to remain in existence until matters were finally resolved but they would not want the expense and the further procedure of a "live" action;

(3) for arbitration to take place[22];

(4) to await the outcome of another case which has a bearing on the present case;

(5) for investigation of some aspect of the case which cannot reasonably be achieved within the time frame applicable to the litigation.[23]

Whilst an action is sisted, no interlocutor can be pronounced. The sist prevents the parties taking any step in the court process. It removes the action from the court rolls and suspends the operation of any timetable to which the action is bound. The parties can use a sist of an action to gain a breathing space. In the present climate of case management, there are two competing views about this. On the one hand, a sist of an action takes it out of the control of the court and prevents the court securing expeditious progress of the case. On the other hand, if the parties consider it is in the interests of their clients to have the action sisted, why should the court interfere? Sometimes a period of inactivity is helpful to a client. A pursuer may not be very sure if he wants to proceed with an action. Parties might want to negotiate or carry out investigations without any time compulsion and a sist would enable them to do this. A surprisingly large number of

---

[18] Usually three years from the date of the accident.

[19] He cannot apply for legal aid to defend it until the writ is served upon him.

[20] See the case of *Keel v Keel*, 1985 S.L.T. (Sh. Ct) 52.

[21] See *Graham v NCB*, 1964 S.L.T. (Sh. Ct) 53.

[22] See Ch.4 on "Preliminary Pleas".

[23] Often, in personal injury cases, the pursuer may still be undergoing medical treatment when the action is raised and it may be some time until his resultant condition will be known and appropriate damages can be assessed by anyone.

cases are sisted, and often for periods of six months or more. There was a concern that sists were perhaps more for the benefit of hard-pressed and overworked solicitors than for their clients, and this gave rise to specific rules which give the sheriff court some control over sists to ensure no unnecessary delays in litigation.[24] Rule 15.6(1) of the OCR provides that the reason for the sist should be specified in the motion for a sist. The court can sist for a specific period of time, rather than indefinitely, and, under r.15.6(2) the sheriff can, on his own initiative recall a sist after giving parties an opportunity to be heard on the matter. Rule 9.1(1)–(2) of the SCR make similar provisions for summary causes.

If a party wants to end a sist, then he will lodge a written motion for the sist to be recalled.[25] A motion to recall the sist can be opposed, and there can be arguments as to whether it is appropriate to recall or not.[26] In practice, such matters are often dealt with by way of joint motion, when the parties have agreed in advance that the case should be revived because the justification for the sist no longer applies.

THIRD PARTY PROCEDURE

Third party procedure is a procedural mechanism whereby a defender **15–05** can involve another party[27] (a third party) in the litigation which was initiated by the pursuer against the defender.[28] It can be used in cases where the defender claims a, "right of contribution, relief, or indemnity against any party who is not a party to the action."[29] At the beginning of the chapter, we considered a situation in which this might be appropriate.[30] There are circumstances in which it is regarded as desirable to have the issue of the third party's liability decided at the same time as the issue of primary liability.[31] Often the evidence in relation to both matters

---

[24] No specific rule was found to be necessary for Court of Session ordinary actions. However, in personal injury actions there are specific rules regarding sists, r.43.8(1)–(5) of RCS.

[25] The motion will usually contain a request for further procedure in the action as appropriate to the point at which it was sisted.

[26] See *McInally v John Wyeth & Brothers Ltd (No.2)*, 1997 S.L.T. 605.

[27] And indeed a number of other parties.

[28] Or even defenders. A pursuer could sue two defenders and one of them might want to involve someone else in the litigation. The other person would not be a "fourth party". To confuse matters further, you can bring into proceedings more than one "third party"—you can have a first third party and a second third party, etc.

[29] See RCS r.26.1(1)(a) and OCR r.20.1(1)(a).

[30] There are numerous other possibilities. One of the most common is in a personal injury case in which the pursuer sues a defender and the defender blames someone else (not the pursuer) for the accident.

[31] Although that does not always apply. See *Dormer v Melville Dundas & Whitson Ltd*, 1990 S.L.T. 186. For a good description of the procedure in a Court of Session action but note that the rules have changed since, see also *Tookney v Lafferty*, 1967 S.L.T. (Notes) 89, where it was considered appropriate to deal with the issues separately and take the third party's potential liability first.

will be similar and it will be convenient and economic to deal with it all at once.[32]

In a case in which a defender blames a third party for an accident, there is another procedural alternative to the defender bringing the third party into the proceedings. If the pursuer sees from the defender's pleadings that he says someone else was at fault and has caused or contributed to the accident, the pursuer can decide to rely on those allegations[33] and bring in that other person as an additional defender. He can ask the court to be allowed to amend his writ to include an additional defender, serve the amended proceedings against him as well and then proceed to seek damages from both defenders.[34]

There are often very subtle reasons why a pursuer would prefer to bring in someone as an additional defender rather than leave it to the defender to bring him in to proceedings as a third party, or even vice versa. It is extremely difficult to explain these reasons here, but they have to do with tactics and expenses[35] and other considerations which can only be properly understood from experience.[36] A major objection to the allowance of a third party notice can be the delay which it will cause to the progress of the action and the prejudice to the pursuer whose remedy will be postponed.[37]

The court has a discretion whether to grant a motion to be allowed to serve a third party notice or not.[38] The court can refuse it if there is no legal justification for it, and can also refuse it if the defender has apparently delayed for no good reason in attempting to involve a third party, especially when he may have been in a position to do so at an early stage of proceedings.

Once a defender has convened a third party into the action, it is open to the pursuer to amend his case at that stage and direct his claim against the third party as an additional defender. In that case, the party involved would be described as, e.g. "second defender and third party". There might be

---

[32] Although there can be cases where the court will not consider it appropriate to proceed in this way.

[33] He may not even know if they are true.

[34] This presupposes that the pursuer would, as a matter of law, have been entitled to raise proceedings directly against the third party if he had wished to do so at the outset of the action.

[35] For two recent illustrations from the sheriff court of the complexities of third party procedure and expenses see *Europools Ltd v Clydeside Steel Fabrications Ltd*, 2001 S.L.T. (Sh. Ct) 91; and *Erskine v Russell*, 2003 S.L.T. (Sh. Ct) 2, but do not expect to be particularly enlightened!

[36] See *Winchester v Ramsay*, 1966 S.L.T. 97. It was argued that, because of the existence of a third party notice, the court could not fix a jury trial.

[37] See *Halbert v British Airports Authority Plc*, 1996 S.L.T. 97, which has a good outline of the practical consequences of allowing or refusing a third party notice.

[38] See *Rogers v James Crowe and Sons Ltd*, 1971 S.L.T. 306; NB: older rules, but the case report contains a good example of the defenders' pleadings which were used to justify the third party notice.

appropriate cases in which this should be done or could be done but the reasons why this might happen[39] are outwith the scope of this book.

RULES — SHERIFF COURT

Ordinary action

These are contained in Ch.20 of the OCR 1993. Once the defender **15–06** decides to bring in a third party, then he lodges a motion asking the court to grant an order for service of a third party notice on the other person named.[40] Before lodging the motion, the defender's pleadings will have to show the basis on which he maintains the third party should be involved in the case.[41] The motion to be allowed to serve a third party notice can be lodged at any time.[42]

If the court grants the motion to allow the defender to serve a third party notice, then the defender will serve on the third party: (1) a third party notice in Form 010; and (2) a copy of all of the parties' pleadings in the case as at that date — sometimes a copy of the record will suffice but otherwise you have to send a copy of both parties' adjusted or amended pleadings. This must be done within 14 days of the grant of the motion.[43]

When the third party receives notice of the forms, he is obliged to lodge answers. This will usually be within 28 days and, in effect, these answers will be his defences to the third party notice.[44] Failure to lodge answers by the third party will usually lead to a motion from the defender for decree to give effect to the claim brought in the third party notice. If a minute of amendment which contains the basis for involving the third party has not been allowed[45] by the time a defender moves for decree, the defender must enrol a motion to have the amendment allowed before he can seek decree.[46]

One effect of a third party notice is that the progress of the case as it was originally timetabled will be delayed. When a third party notice is served, the last date for the lodging of answers by the third party is treated as the last date for lodging of the Form 07 in a normal case. Once answers have been lodged by a third party, then the clerk will fix a date and time for the options hearing and the adjustment period, etc. so that

---

[39] And the benefits or otherwise of following this course.
[40] See r.20.1(1).
[41] See r.20.2. If the basis is not shown in the pleadings by the time the record is closed, the defender must lodge a minute of amendment, per r.20.2(2).
[42] Even, in principle, shortly before a proof in the principal action.
[43] See r.20.4(1).
[44] The form of the answers is set out in r.20.5(2).
[45] As opposed to received.
[46] See r.20.5A.

the timetable will run as if the whole case was starting from the last date for lodging the answers.[47]

Summary cause

15–07   Until the SCR 2002, there was no provision for the service of a third party notice in summary cause procedure nor in small claims. A defender in these procedures was simply not allowed to bring in a third party.[48] Now he can do so.[49] He must do so by making an incidental application to that effect at the time when he lodges the form of response,[50] although the sheriff can allow him to do so later, on cause shown.[51] The other rules apply in the same manner as ordinary actions. There are specific forms for service on the third party as provided by the rules.

RULES—COURT OF SESSION

Ordinary actions

15–08   The rules of procedure are contained in RCS rr. 26.1–26.7. Broadly speaking, the procedure is similar to the sheriff court procedure described above, but there are small differences:

(1) the interlocutor allowing the service of a third party notice will specify the period within which it must be served[52];

(2) when the notice is served on the third party, it is necessary to send him, in addition to the documents already mentioned, a copy of the interlocutor allowing service;

(3) there is specific provision as to what is to happen if answers are not lodged by the third party[53];

(4) the course of procedure after answers are lodged is different, although this simply reflects the basic differences in standard procedures in the respective courts.[54]

---

[47] See r.20.6. See *Blyszczak v GEC Marconi Avionics Ltd*, 1996 S.L.T. (Sh. Ct) 54, in which there was some confusion over the procedure which should follow.

[48] The procedure will delay and complicate the case and these are intended to be short and simple forms of procedure.

[49] It was anticipated that the jurisdiction limit for summary causes would increase significantly so that more valuable and complex cases would be brought in this procedure. This has not happened yet.

[50] The standard form of response contains a page which the defender may complete if he wants to bring in a third party.

[51] See r.11.1(2).

[52] i.e. not automatically within 14 days.

[53] Although this is not particularly significant because the sheriff court consequences are similar without any specific rules.

[54] e.g. the defender has to make up open records.

Personal injuries actions

When the timetable is issued in such a case[55] it will contain a date by **15–09** which an application to serve a third party notice may be made. It would be possible to vary that date by motion[56] if a defender wanted to serve a third party notice later, but this would only be granted on "special cause shown".[57] The rules for service apply as in ordinary actions.

Commercial causes

This can be done by motion under r.47.7(1). The rules provide that the **15–10** judge shall make such an order, and then give such directions as he thinks fit with regard to:

(1) the time for service of the third party notice and the time for answers;
(2) a further hearing of the case following upon the lodging of answers; and
(3) any diligence which can be done on the strength of the third party notice.[58]

Counterclaims

Where one person (the defender) is sued by another person (the pur- **15–11** suer) and the defender wishes, in turn, to seek an order from the court against that pursuer for some justifiable reason, this can be described generally as a counterclaim. A counterclaim can be initiated by a completely separate action by the defender against the pursuer which could progress independently of the original action. In this section, however, we are going to consider a Counterclaim,[59] being the procedural device whereby a defender pursues his own claim against the pursuer without raising separate proceedings and within the pursuer's original action. This method of proceeding is positively encouraged in some situations, because it can avoid a multiplicity of court actions arising out of what is usually one core set of facts. It can prevent a duplication of time, cost and effort in court proceedings. One disadvantage is that it can lead to complexity and a degree of confusion when the written pleadings are developed. The main aim of the rules which are provided to deal with Counterclaims is to attempt to reduce potential for confusion between

---

[55] See Ch.6.
[56] RCS r.43.6(1)(b)(i).
[57] RCS, r.43.8.
[58] It will be apparent that, in keeping with the general approach of commercial actions, the judge has an extremely wide discretion in relation to matters which are specifically provided in the rules of other procedures.
[59] The capital "C" is mine and is intended to signify the procedural device known as a Counterclaim as opposed to describing any claim by a defender against a pursuer however it is raised procedurally.

the two distinct but associated issues.[60] It is arguable whether the rules have succeeded in this aim.

One of the major difficulties in this area is the substantive law and, in particular, the question of whether it is competent to put forward one particular type of claim as a counterclaim in response to another type of claim by the pursuer. Difficult questions arise as to whether a counterclaim (in the general sense) is available in certain circumstances[61] or should be regarded as allowing set off or retention rather than justifying an independent claim of its own, and difficult questions also arise in relation to the issue of whether you can counterclaim against a liquid debt with an illiquid debt.

It must be competent[62] to counterclaim before formal procedural issues come into play, but it is not possible to expand upon the substantive competency issues here, and readers are referred to the undernoted cases.[63] A word of caution, however, because some of the cases involve procedural rules which no longer apply.

Examples of the kinds of claim which might arise as Counterclaims are:

- A claim for payment of architects fees for work done on the defender's premises being met by a Counterclaim for damages for negligent design of part of the premises.[64]
- A claim for damage to a motor vehicle based on careless driving by the defender being met by a defence and/or Counterclaim by the other motorist.[65]
- A claim for payment of a quantity of whisky being met by a Counterclaim for damages for breach of contract in the course of a long-standing contractual relationship between the parties for supply of the whisky.[66]
- A claim for declarator that the defenders were in default under a standard security, being met by a Counterclaim that the defenders were entitled to have the standard security discharged.[67]

---

[60] The defender might say, in the example given at the start of the chapter, that the work was not done properly and that it caused additional damage. This would be a defence to the action raised by the pursuer, i.e. no payment is due because the pursuer was in material breach of contract, and also a claim for damages for the losses caused by the breach.

[61] See *Alex Lawrie Factors Ltd v Mitchell Engineering Ltd*, 2001 S.L.T. (Sh. Ct) 93.

[62] i.e. justifiable as a matter of law.

[63] *Armour and Melvin Ltd v Mitchell*, 1934 S.L.T. 90; *Halifax Building Society v Gupta*, 1994 S.L.T. 339; *Niven v Clyde Fasteners Ltd*, 1986 S.L.T. 344; *Governor and Company of the Bank of Scotland v John Baird*, 1987 S.C.L.R. 18; *Johnston v Robson*, 1995 S.L.T. (Sh. Ct) 26.

[64] See the case of *Wagner Associates v Joseph Dunn (Bottlers) Ltd*, 1986 S.L.T 267.

[65] See *Mayor v Simpson Motors Ltd*, 1966 S.L.T. 294.

[66] See *Barton Distilling (Scotland) Ltd v Barton Brands Ltd*, 1993 S.L.T. 1261, in which the distinction between liquid and illiquid debts involved in the supply of whisky does not seem to have caused any amusement at all. It must just be me.

[67] *J. Sykes & Sons (Fish Merchants) Ltd v Grieve*, 2002 S.L.T. (Sh. Ct) 15.

There are different procedural rules relating to Counterclaims in the Court of Session and in the sheriff court. The major distinction is that in the Court of Session a Counterclaim is prepared as a separate document, in other words, it is separate from the document comprising the written defences. In sheriff court ordinary actions, the Counterclaim is actually contained within the body of the written defences themselves.[68] This has been dictated largely by the different methods by which the respective courts deal with adjustment of pleadings.[69]

Court of Session rules

The rules are in Ch.25 rr.25.1–25.6 of the RCS. Reference should be **15–12** made to the rules themselves but a summary of the more significant rules is provided now:

Rule 25.1(1)—A defender may counterclaim in most forms of action and in respect of certain specified matters, such as anything, "forming part of, or arising out of, the grounds of the (principal) action".[70] It should be noted that questions of the competency of the Counterclaim may be concerned with whether it complies with the procedural rules, as well as whether it is justified under substantive law.

Rule 25.1(2)—The defender may lodge a Counterclaim in process at any time before the record is closed. After the record is closed the court may allow this but subject to conditions. After the record is closed, a defender would have to enrol a motion to have the Counterclaim received. This would have to be lodged and intimated along with the Counterclaim and the opponent could object to it. One of the most common objections and one which might well carry considerable force would be if the Counterclaim was so late that it was going to hold up the expeditious progress of the principal claim to the prejudice of the pursuer.[71]

Rule 25.1(3)—There is a format for a Counterclaim which has to be followed. It will be a document separate from the defences. It should be headed up "Counterclaim for the Defender". It should contain a conclusion similar to the conclusions which would be contained in a summons. It should contain a statement of facts comprising the facts upon which the Counterclaim is based.[72] It should also have appropriate pleas in law on behalf of the defender and counterclaimer. It must be signed on behalf of the defender.

---

[68] However, to confuse matters further, in summary causes the Counterclaim is a document distinct from the defences.

[69] There is no practical benefit in exploring this further.

[70] See *Borthwick v Dean Warwick Ltd*, 1985 S.L.T. 269.

[71] If the Counterclaim were not allowed, then the defender could always raise a separate action so his rights ultimately are not going to be prejudiced.

[72] Although reference can be made for the sake of brevity to the facts averred in the original writ and defences in the initiating action.

Rule 25.3—Answers to the Counterclaim "may" be lodged within certain time limits. Where the Counterclaim has been lodged prior to the closing of the record, then answers have to be lodged within 14 days of the Counterclaim. If a Counterclaim is allowed by the court after the record has been closed, then the allowance of the Counterclaim will also specify the time within which answers have to be lodged to the Counterclaim.

Rule 25.4—It is important to note that the pursuer can abandon the original action but this does not mean that the Counterclaim will fall. Once a Counterclaim is lodged, it is regarded as having a distinct life of its own and it is not dependent on the original action for its validity and continued existence.

Commercial action

15–13   A party seeking to lodge a Counterclaim in a commercial action[73] shall apply by motion to do so. In keeping with the philosophy of the commercial rules, the judge has a wide discretion to give directions as to when it can be lodged, and answers lodged to it. The form of Counterclaim may be somewhat less formal in keeping with practice in commercial actions pleadings.[74]

Sheriff court

Ordinary action

15–14   The provisions regarding Counterclaims in the sheriff court are contained in rr.19.1–19.4. The important features are:

Rule 19.1(1)—This provides for the cases in which a defender can counterclaim.

Rules 19.1(2) and 19.1(3)—The Counterclaim must be made in the defences.[75] This is where the sheriff court procedure and form departs from the Court of Session procedure quite significantly. The form of Counterclaim is not specifically prescribed but it is to be included in the defences and it is not a separate document. This can cause complexity and there has been a little confusion since the 1993 Rules came into operation about the proper way in which defences with a Counterclaim should be set out. They should include the following (in this order):

(1) a crave setting out what is being counterclaimed;
(2) the defences to the original action in the standard form responding to the pursuer's pleadings;

---

[73] See, e.g. *Euan Wallace & Partners v Westscot Homes Plc*, 2000 S.L.T. 327.
[74] See r.47.7.
[75] See rr.19.1(2) and 19.1(3).

(3) a statement of fact relating to the Counterclaim, i.e. explaining the basis on which it arises and the facts on which it is based;
(4) appropriate pleas in law which will be a combination of pleas in law directed at the pursuer's claim against the defender and pleas in law in support of the Counterclaim itself.

Similar considerations apply in relation to the timing of the Counterclaim in the sheriff court as have been mentioned in relation to the Court of Session. Where the Counterclaim is lodged after the closing of the record, this will have to be done by way of a minute of amendment amending the defender's pleadings. If that amendment is allowed, then the pursuer will usually be allowed time to answer the minute of amendment and, in essence, this means allowed time to answer the Counterclaim. It will be appreciated that Counterclaims generally, and especially after the record has closed, can cause practical difficulties in sheriff court pleadings. One aspect of this was the confusion as to how a record was to be set out in an action in which there was a Counterclaim. The rules[76] provide that a record should contain the following (in order):

(1) the crave or craves in the initial writ, i.e. the original action;
(2) the condescendence by the pursuer and answers by the defender to the writ;
(3) both parties pleas in law in relation to the writ[77];
(4) the crave or craves of the Counterclaim;
(5) the statement of facts by the defender in support of his Counterclaim and the answers by the pursuer to the Counterclaim;
(6) the pleas in law of the defender and the pursuer in relation to the Counterclaim.

Abandonment of the principal action does not affect the existence or validity of the Counterclaim. The sheriff is given specific power to deal with the counterclaim as if it had been stated in a separate action and regulate procedure as he sees fit. This gives the sheriff a wide discretion and a degree of flexibility which is helpful in circumstances where the more rigid timetables and procedures provided in the 1993 Rules are not entirely suited to some of the procedural complications which can arise with Counterclaims.[78]

Summary cause

The rules are fairly simple for Counterclaims. Every summons served **15–15** on a defender contains a standard form of response which includes a section which allows a defender to give details of his counterclaim (if any). If the defender wishes to state a Counterclaim then he must complete

---

[76] OCR r.19.2A.
[77] So far the record is just as it would be in any normal case.
[78] See r.19.4.

and return the form on or before the return date.[79] If a pursuer wants to oppose a counterclaim then he must lodge answers to it (and send a copy to the defender) within seven days of the lodging of the form of response. The intention is that when the case calls at the calling date all matters of contention are before the court. The sheriff can then deal with the case as appropriate at the calling date.[80]

Small claims

If a defender wants to counterclaim he must indicate this on the form of response and give details in writing on the form of response or orally at the hearing. The sheriff can allow a counterclaim to be stated later than the hearing. He can also allow a pursuer time to answer such a counterclaim.[81]

TENDERS

15–16 A tender is a form of offer by a defender to settle a claim by a pursuer. Before discussing the procedural aspects of making a tender it is necessary to provide an explanation of why tenders are significant and why they can have a very important effect on the practical handling of a case. It is notoriously difficult to explain this in the abstract, so the reader should remind himself of the brief practical illustration at the start of this chapter, which will be developed now in order to provide a practical framework in which to understand how they work. Tenders are often used in claims for personal injury where the value of the claim is difficult to predict,[82] but they can be utilised in a wide variety of claims.[83] Their effect is the same no matter what the subject matter of the case.[84]

A tender is a procedural weapon which can be used by a defender to protect his position about liability for the expenses of a case which he thinks he might[85] lose and could impose a liability for expenses on a pursuer. The defender may well accept that he is liable to pay something[86] and he may know that he is therefore going to "lose" the case. However, he may consider that the claim which is being pursued is overstated or that some deduction ought to be made from it.[87] He may be perfectly prepared

---

[79] The form simply requires the defender to, "state details of counterclaim".
[80] SCR rr.8.2 and 8.3.
[81] Small Claim Rules 2002 rr. 11.1(1)–(8).
[82] And where questions of liability, reductions for contributory negligence, and other factors are also difficult to predict.
[83] See *Ferguson v MacLennan Salmon Co Ltd*, 1990 S.L.T. 428 for a discussion about tenders.
[84] There are numerous recent reported cases about tenders, confirming the proposition that arguments about expenses are fought as keenly as arguments about the merits of an action.
[85] Or knows he will.
[86] Whether that is admitted to the other side or the court formally, informally, or neither.
[87] e.g. a deduction of a percentage for contributory negligence.

to pay an amount to the pursuer prior to any proof in order to stop the case being taken any further and more expense being incurred. If he offers money to settle it and it is rejected he may not want the court to know this.[88] In the absence of some form of procedural device, the defender would be unable to found upon a reasonable[89] offer which had been made to settle the case and would just have to let the court action continue, in the knowledge that he would almost certainly have to pay all of the judicial expenses as well as the principal sum awarded by the court.

A tender is a document lodged in court by a defender whereby he makes a formal offer to settle the pursuer's claim at a specific amount together with the pursuer's judicial expenses incurred up to the date of the tender. It is made without any admission of liability and, although it is made in writing and put in the court process, the judge who hears the case ultimately is not allowed to know what the offer is.[90] A copy is sent to the pursuer at the same time as the principal is lodged in court. It can be made at any time during the life of an action. More than one tender can be made. It can be withdrawn after it has been made and before there is any acceptance. It can have a very dramatic effect upon the amount of money a defender (who accepts that he is going to have to pay something) actually has to pay. It can have the same dramatic effect upon what a pursuer (who is bound to receive something in damages) will actually receive after a litigation. The crucial practical consequence of lodging a tender is that, if the pursuer does not accept the amount tendered, and a court[91] awards him a sum which is less than the amount tendered, then the pursuer will normally be found liable to meet all of the judicial expenses of the defender from the date when the tender was made.

This can represent a significant sum. A brief and simple illustration **15–17** might highlight its practical effect. A pursuer sues for £10,000 in an action for breach of contract. He is awarded £6,500 after proof, and, because he won, he is awarded the judicial expenses of the action against the other side of £4,000. His own lawyer's bill is (say) £4,500.[92] Therefore, the pursuer will actually recover £6,000 (£6,500 plus £4,000 from the defender minus £4,500 which he will have to pay for his own lawyer's fees). In the same case, with the same judicial decision, i.e. an award of damages of £6,500, assume that halfway through the progress of the action (when about half of the expenses had been incurred) the defender tendered £7,000 to settle. This was not accepted. The pursuer will receive £6,500 as an award but because he did not accept the tender and the sum tendered was higher than that awarded by the court, the defender can argue that the pursuer should only receive the expenses up

---

[88] Especially if he is apparently defending it on the merits.
[89] At least, in the defender's estimation.
[90] Although he will know that some offer has been made because he will be aware of the fact that a tender has been lodged.
[91] After hearing evidence and coming to a decision.
[92] See Ch.21 regarding the difference between judicial and extra-judicial expenses.

to the date when the tender was made (and should have been accepted). The expenses after that date have all been incurred because the pursuer refused a reasonable offer—as demonstrated by the fact that the court awarded less than the tender—and accordingly the pursuer should meet the liability for such expenses which would not have been incurred if he had acted reasonably. Let us say that the expenses of each party against the other will be equal and cancel each other out.[93] Therefore the pursuer will recover only £2,000 (£6,500 less £4,500) after settling his lawyer's bill. Although he won his case he has "lost" a substantial amount of money. In the same circumstances, the defender has lost the case but has probably saved an equivalent amount.

Procedure

15–18   There are no rules of procedure regarding tenders. The operation and effect of tenders is largely a matter of long-standing practice supplemented by decided cases.[94] The general principle applicable to tenders in the sheriff court and Court of Session is the same.[95] However, there are practical differences. For example, different scales of expenses apply in the respective courts and there are different methods of approaching the question of what is the "effective date" of the tender.

The terms of the tender

15–19   The defender will lodge a document, known as a minute of tender, in court and will intimate it to his opponent at the same time. The minute of tender is expressed in a particular form of words, and will usually run along these lines[96]:

> "X for the defenders stated and hereby states to the court that without admitting liability and under reservation of their whole rights and pleas the defenders tendered and hereby tender to the pursuer the sum of £YY[97] sterling together with the taxed expenses

---

[93] In reality, it would not be as simple as this. The expenses incurred at the end of a case—which would include the proof—are usually higher than those incurred at the beginning. A lengthy proof would be extremely expensive. The timing of the lodging of a tender can be very significant.

[94] There is a practice note applicable to tenders in cases in the Sheriffdom of Glasgow and Strathkelvin (*Parliament House Book*, p.D701 (as at Release 97)).

[95] There is a good, recent and authoritative case on tenders, with discussion about the nature of a tender and its effect upon expenses in *McKenzie v H.D. Fraser*, 1990 S.C.L.R. 785; see also *Bond v British Railways Board*, 1972 S.L.T. (Notes) 47. For a sheriff court case on tenders with a particular observation on the scale of expenses which might apply where the tender in an ordinary action is for a figure within the summary cause limit see *C.R. Perry Ltd v Connell*, 1981 S.L.T. (Sh. Ct) 90; but also see *Milne v Milligan*, 1991 S.C.L.R. 433 and *Walker v J.G. Martin Plant Hire*, 1995 S.C.L.R. 398.

[96] See Mcphail, *Sheriff Court Practice*, 3rd edn (Edinburgh: W. Green, 2006), para. 14.36; and *McKenzie v H.D. Fraser*, 1990 S.C.L.R. 785.

[97] Expressed in words and figures for the avoidance of any doubt.

of process to the date hereof in full of the crave(s) of the initial writ."[98]

This formula now has to be amended in actions of damages for personal injury in which recent legislation on the deductions of some social security benefits payable to an injured claimant has impacted upon the standard form of words.[99]

A judge hearing the case may well be aware of the fact that a tender has been made,[100] but under no circumstances will he be aware or made aware of the amount of the tender until some time after his decision has been issued.[101] The appropriate time at which to draw attention to the existence of a tender is the stage at which the court has decided the merits of the action and is going to decide on the question of expenses.[102]

The tender can be withdrawn at any time. It would be withdrawn by physically withdrawing the tender from process and also by advising the opponent. There is no limit to the number of tenders which can be made and withdrawn, nor indeed made and not withdrawn, with other tenders being made subsequently.[103]

The tender will specify a particular sum of money and this is intended to represent any principal sum plus interest down to the date of the tender.[104] The tender also must contain an offer to pay the expenses of the case to date to the pursuer.

The pursuer can accept a tender at any time before it is withdrawn.[105] He does so by lodging a minute of acceptance and by making a motion to the court for a decree in his favour in terms of the minute of tender and the acceptance. The decree will be for the amount contained within the tender and for expenses up to a date when the tender could reasonably have been accepted. An issue may arise regarding the appropriate level of expenses.[106] If a tender is refused and is then not beaten, then the court will normally award the expenses of the action in favour of the pursuer (assuming he succeeds in being awarded some amount by the court) up to the date of the tender, and award the remaining expenses of the action up to the date of its conclusion in favour of the defender.

---

[98] See *Brackencroft Ltd v Silvers Marine Ltd*, 2006 S.L.T. 85 in which the precise wording of the tender was subjected to scrutiny.

[99] Social Security (Recovery of Benefits) Act 1997 and the cases following upon this, e.g. *Mitchell v Laing*, 1998 S.L.T. 203; *Spence v Wilson (No.2)*, 1998 S.L.T. 959; *Wisely v John Fulton (Plumbers) Ltd*, 1998 S.L.T. 1026 and 2000 S.L.T. 494.

[100] Practice does differ between courts.

[101] See the cases of *Avery v Cantilever Shoe Co Ltd*, 1942 S.L.T. 275; *Ronald McDermid Ltd v Muir Crawford (Builders) Ltd*, 1978 S.L.T. (Sh. Ct) 17.

[102] See *Bryce v West Lothian District Council*, 1979 S.L.T. (Sh. Ct) 50.

[103] An interesting recent case on tenders is *Tait v Campbell*, 2004 S.L.T. 187.

[104] See *Manson v Skinner*, 2000 S.L.T. (Sh. Ct) 161 for an illustration of this.

[105] Even whilst waiting for a decision from the judge after a proof in the case.

[106] *Gillespie v Fitzpatrick*, 2003 S.L.T. 999.

Tenders with a multiplicity of parties

15–20 Where there are a number of pursuers and the defender wants to tender to all or any of them, then his tender must make it clear that a specific sum is being tendered in respect of a specific pursuer. One cannot tender one lump sum and leave it to the pursuers to split it amongst themselves as appropriate.

Where there are several defenders, one defender might want to tender so as to dispose of the case but this might have an effect upon another defender who may be quite happy to go ahead with the action. One defender might be quite prepared to accept that he is liable to a specified extent but cannot persuade another defender to agree the apportionment. Very clever[107] procedures might be open to them to protect their respective positions on expenses.[108]

RECOVERY OF DOCUMENTS

15–21 The courts have certain limited powers to allow one party to recover documents from another party[109] where these documents can be shown to have some bearing on the case which has been raised or upon a case which is likely to be raised in the future. However, it is important to appreciate that these powers are exercised very carefully and cautiously. There are very significant restrictions upon the circumstances in which the court can be persuaded to exercise the power. There is a general trend towards disclosure of information in litigation,[110] and it may be said that the recent cases suggest a degree of relaxation of the restrictions and widening of the circumstances in which recovery of documents might be allowed. Section 1 of the Administration of Justice (Scotland) Act 1972, as amended, has contributed significantly to this process, but it would be a mistake to assume that there is any automatic entitlement to recover any information which might be thought to be relevant to the case. The precise details of the principles applicable defy simple analysis and reference should be made to the undernoted works.[111] This section outlines the main issues which are of practical significance.

The court has a common law power to order recovery of documents and a statutory power to do so by virtue of the above Act. In order to

---

[107] And relatively incomprehensible!
[108] One is a "*Williamson* Tender", which is based on the case of *Williamson v McPherson*, 1951 S.L.T. 283, and used again in the case of *Morton v O'Donnell*, 1979 S.L.T. (Notes) 26. Another is a "*Houston* Tender" from *Houston v British Road Services Ltd*, 1967 S.L.T. 329; whether they worked in each case is unclear. See also *Associated Portland Cement Manufacturers Ltd v McInally*, 1970 S.L.T. (Sh. Ct) 9.
[109] Or from anyone else.
[110] Other systems have full disclosure as a fundamental right.
[111] Walker and Walker, *Evidence*, 2nd edn; Archibald MacSporran and Andrew R.W. Young, *Commission and Diligence* (Edinburgh: W.Green, 1995); Macphail, *Sheriff Court Practice*, 2nd edn, paras 15.50–15.83.

understand the parameters within which these powers can be exercised it is necessary to consider the many cases which have been decided both before and after the Act. The decisions by the courts in these cases often depend upon the precise circumstances and it might be difficult to appreciate the general principles which underlie the decisions. There is a broad conflict between the interests of justice and fairness in disclosure and the prevention of unnecessary and speculative "fishing" for information.

Putting the matter broadly, the court"s power at common law to order recovery of documents historically confined itself to documents which might be required by one party to enable him to prove the case which he had already made out by averment in his pleadings. It would only be exercised in an action which had already been raised and after a proof had been allowed in that action.

Section 1(1) of the Administration of Justice (Scotland) Act 1972 provided that the court shall have power to, "order inspection,[112] photographing, preservation . . . detention of documents and property . . . [in respect of which] . . . any question may relevantly arise in . . . existing civil proceedings . . . or in civil proceedings which are likely to be brought"; and s.1(2) provides, "unless there is special reason why the application should not be granted."

The interaction between that section and the common law powers and the move towards openness has led to further re-appraisal of the position. In essence, the court can order recovery of documents pre-litigation provided they satisfy the criteria in the Act. The person applying[113] must satisfy the court as to the substance and basis for the case which he proposes to make and that, on the state of the information produced, it is indeed "likely" that a case will be brought.[114] The court will assess whether it thinks such a case is "likely".[115]

Once litigation has commenced, the court's power to order recovery can be argued to be extremely wide, but there is some doubt as to whether this has made any substantial difference to the entitlement to recover documents at an early stage of an action. In the case of *Moore v Greater Glasgow Health Board*[116] it was said that recovery would be granted before a proof had been allowed provided this was necessary to allow the pursuer to make, "more pointed or specific that which is already averred, or to enable him to make adequate and specific replies to his opponents averments."[117] In practice, parties are more inclined to make applications for recovery of documents now than formerly and

---

[112] See *Cole, Petitioner*, 1993 S.L.T. 894.
[113] We will deal with the procedure shortly.
[114] See, e.g. *Parks v Tayside Regional Council*, 1989 S.L.T. 345 and *Dominion Technology Ltd v Gardner Cyrogenics Ltd (No.1)*, 1993 S.L.T. 828.
[115] A good recent illustration is *Harwood v Jackson*, 2003 S.L.T. 1026.
[116] *Moore v Greater Glasgow Health Board*, 1979 S.L.T. 42.
[117] This was quoted with approval in *Civil Service Building Society v MacDougall*, 1988 S.L.T. 687; this is an Inner House judgment which is essential reading.

more inclined to make the application earlier. In practice, the courts seem to be more inclined to grant them and not adopt a restrictive approach, but there remains binding authority against recovery except in the case of necessity.[118] The question is whether it is necessary for the documents called for by the pursuer to be recovered at this (early) stage in order to plead the case properly. It is also usually the case that the party seeking to recover the documents must have made averments in his pleadings which justify the order sought.[119]

The power to order recovery of documents is restricted to an extent by the nature of the documents which are being sought. For example, it is not possible to recover documents which are privileged or confidential.[120] A particular example of a document which cannot be recovered is one which was prepared *post litem motam*.[121] What exactly that means can often be a source of dispute.[122] Public interest immunity can be claimed by the Crown in relation to documents.[123]

Procedure

Recovery pre-litigation

15–22   In the sheriff court this is done by way of summary application. In the Court of Session this is done by way of petition.

Recovery during litigation

15–23   The procedure for recovery of documents at this stage is by way of a motion and specification of documents.[124] A "specification" of documents is a "list" of documents, or a description of the types of document, which a party wishes to recover.[125] It will be set out in numbered paragraphs[126] identifying particular documents or types of document.[127] The motion will ask the court first to approve of the specification of docu-

---

[118] However, see *McInally v John Wyeth and Brother*, 1992 S.L.T. 344, where the judge at first instance allowed recovery of various documents prior to defences being lodged but then, on appeal, reported at 1996 S.L.T. 1223, the Inner House refused it.

[119] See *Williamson v Advocate General for Scotland*, 2006 S.L.T. 811. There is a good discussion about the principles on which such orders may be granted in this case.

[120] See Walker and Walker, *The Law of Evidence in Scotland*, 2nd edn (Edinburgh: Tottel, 2000), pp.413–421.

[121] In connection with or in contemplation of litigation. See, e.g. *Ward v Marine Harvest Ltd*, 1997 S.L.T. 469.

[122] See *Young v NCB*, 1957 S.L.T. 266; *Hepburn v Scottish Power*, 1997 S.L.T. 859, which contains detailed comments on this issue and identified an exception to the rule.

[123] See *A.B. v Glasgow and West of Scotland Blood Transfusion Service*, 1993 S.L.T. 36; and contrast this with *Parks*, 1989 S.L.T. 345, where no immunity was apparently sought.

[124] This relates to both applications for commission and diligence for recovery of documents at common law and applications under s.1 of the 1972 Act.

[125] It may just be one, particular document, or extend to several pages.

[126] Usually termed "calls".

[127] e.g. "The letter dated . . . sent to the pursuer by . . ."; or, "Any letters notes, memos, faxes or other written communications held by the defender which show or tend to show. . .".

ments. The specification can be altered by agreement between the parties if some objection is taken, or by the court after hearing argument on the terms of the specification. The motion can be granted or refused in its entirety. Often the parties may agree to adjust the precise terms of the calls and agree that the motion to allow the specification as amended can be granted. The court can approve some parts or paragraphs of the specification and refuse others. The motion will also ask the court to, "grant commission and diligence" for the recovery of the documents which have been approved. Finally, it will ask the court to appoint a commissioner to recover the documents or, in other words, take possession of them.[128]

Commission

In normal practice, once a specification has been approved, a party **15–24** who is obliged to produce documents may well do so voluntarily without any further procedure.[129] There are procedures available if this is not done. The granting of the motion approving the specification entitles the party to hold a commission[130] to recover the documents but, as an alternative to this, there is a procedure available whereby a party can make a formal request to the "haver"[131] to produce them and certify that he has done so truthfully and fully. A person who holds the documents concerned but who is not a party to the action may be unaware of the granting of a court order and this procedure is often followed in relation to such a haver. If the documents are not produced in this way then the party can proceed to arrange for a commission to be held at which the haver or havers will be cited to appear.[132] The haver must bring with him any documents which might be covered by the calls in the specification.

The commission is heard by the individual who has been appointed as a commissioner by virtue of the motion approving the specification of documents or, if no appointment was made at that time, by virtue of a further motion to that effect.[133] He has all the powers of the court itself and his function is to conduct the commission, recover the documents and report back to the court with the documents concerned. The parties to the action will be represented by their solicitors or counsel at the commission and there will be a shorthand writer present to record the evidence given. The havers who have been cited will attend and will be put on oath. They will be asked certain limited questions by the party seeking the documents regarding the existence of documents sought in the specification. They will be asked to produce what they have or confirm

---

[128] As we will see, this is not always necessary and the court may decide not to grant that part of the motion at that time.

[129] Indeed, at any stage the party could do so.

[130] A special hearing which will be explained later.

[131] The person who holds the documents.

[132] Similar to the citation of a witness to a proof.

[133] This will normally be an experienced solicitor or advocate, or it could even be a judge.

they do not have a document.[134] If the records sought are within some
larger record then the commissioner may have to "excerpt" the relevant
details by, e.g. copying only the relevant parts. After the commission, the
commissioner reports to the court with a copy of the shorthand notes of
the commission and the documents recovered which he will list in an
inventory.

Optional procedure for recovery of documents

15–25   It may be appreciated that the procedure involved in a commission is
costly, inconvenient and time consuming. Sometimes it is absolutely
essential to proceed in this way in the interests of the client.[135] In most
cases, however, it is possible to avoid such a procedure and satisfy one's
self about the information provided by adopting the "optional procedure" for recovery of documents. This can be used if, and only if, the
court has granted the motion approving of the specification of documents. The rules for this procedure in the sheriff court are contained in
the sheriff court rules Ch.28 rr.28.1–28.8. The rules for this procedure in
Court of Session cases are in the RCS Ch.35 rr.35.1–35.8. The respective rules are virtually identical.

Reference should be made to the precise terms of the rules for details,
but, in essence, they provide forms for making an "official" request to a
person to produce documents detailed in the specification which will be
attached to the formal request. They also provide forms for the haver to
sign and certify that his response to the request is truthful. The "haver"
should send the documents, forms and certificate back to the court
within the time limit set forth in order to comply with the request. If he
does not do so then the party will no doubt proceed with the commission
if considered necessary. If the "haver" is claiming confidentiality then he
can enclose documents for which confidentiality is claimed in a sealed
envelope. In either procedure[136] a party would have to apply to the court
to have any documents for which confidentiality was claimed opened
up so as to adjudicate upon the question of whether they were indeed
confidential.

RECOVERY OF INFORMATION

15–26   As well as providing for the recovery of documents as described above,
the 1972 Act made other provisions regarding the recovery of other
information relevant to a litigation in existence or contemplated.

---

[134]   The purpose of the commission is to recover documents and not to ask questions about
the case itself. The range of permissible questions is limited.
[135]   The possibility of opponents or others trying to avoid producing prejudicial documents
cannot be ignored.
[136]   Commission or optional procedure.

Section 1(1A) of the 1972 Act gave the court power to order the disclosure of the identity of any person who:

"[A]ppear to the court to be persons who . . . (a) might be witnesses . . . in existing proceedings . . . or proceedings likely to be brought; or (b) might be defenders in civil proceedings which appear to the court to be likely to be brought".

The question of whether proceedings are, "likely to be brought" often becomes the crux of any argument regarding applications under these provisions prior to the commencement of any litigation.[137] The provisions have been used to order disclosure of the identity of prospective defenders.[138] They have also been used to order disclosure of the identity of potential witnesses.[139] The provision is not used frequently[140] and its utility was commented upon by the Justice 2 Committee of the Scottish Parliament in its report on the petition for civil justice for asbestos victims.[141]

It should also be noted that the rights to recover documents may be affected by the Freedom of Information (Scotland) Act 2002.[142]

---

[137] See *Pearson v EIS*, 1998 S.L.T. 189.

[138] In *Pearson*, 1998 S.L.T. 189, and *Conoco (UK) Ltd v The Commercial Law Practice*, 1997 S.L.T. 372, where there was discussion about confidentiality of communications between a solicitor and client.

[139] See, e.g. *Boyce v Cape Contracts*, 1998 S.L.T. 889, in which the court made an order in relation to the identity of employees of one defender but not in relation to another.

[140] Two unsuccessful examples are *Mooney v City of Glasgow District Council*, 1989 S.L.T. 863 and *Poterala v Uniroyal Tyres Ltd*, 1993 S.L.T. 1072.

[141] Justice 2 Committee, *2nd Report 2003: Petition PE336 on civil justice for asbestos victims*. 2003. SP Paper 734.

[142] Freedom of Information (Scotland) Act 2002 (asp 13), which came into force on various dates from September 2002 onwards. It is too early to say what effect this will have (if any) on the above procedures.

CHAPTER 16

SPECIAL PROCEDURES IN ACTIONS OF DAMAGES FOR PERSONAL INJURY

16–01 In recent years, attention has focused on the appropriate procedures for litigating actions of damages for personal injury.[1] They can proceed as personal injuries actions or ordinary actions[2] in the Court of Session. As we have seen already, they account for a significant proportion of court actions raised in the Court of Session. They can also proceed as ordinary actions or summary cause actions in the sheriff court. Within these actions[3] there are distinctive procedures which are required to deal with some of the specialities involved in personal injury claims. These features may be obvious as a matter of general knowledge to anyone with a basic appreciation of personal injury claims, namely:

(1) they frequently involve payment of large sums of money to an individual;
(2) most of the defenders are big organisations or insurers;
(3) they are frequently very hotly contested;
(4) the accidents about which the claims are concerned usually happened some time before the court case was raised or decided.

The desirability and appropriateness of a dedicated procedure for personal injury actions in the Court of Session was recognised in the new personal injury rules introduced in 2003, but for some time the courts have provided special procedures within the existing bodies of rules to accommodate some of the specialities of personal injury claims. Most of the incidental procedures which were discussed in the previous chapter in relation to court actions can apply in reparation actions.[4] However, the special nature of reparation claims has given rise to a number of specific statutory provisions which, in turn, have given rise to certain special procedures and rules of procedure which relate exclusively to reparation actions. To understand this more clearly, it is helpful to consider a detailed example.

---

[1] Known also as "PI claims" or "reparation actions".
[2] Albeit this may now be only in rare cases. See Ch.6.
[3] With the exception of summary causes for reasons which will be explained.
[4] Some of them, e.g. third party procedure, may well apply more often in reparation actions than in any other type of claim.

Let us assume that one of the passengers injured in the car accident in Ch.1 was Y (aged 14), and that he suffered a head injury in the accident. The evidence available suggests that the other driver was probably at fault and is probably liable to compensate him for his injuries. The other driver has car insurance and the insurers will deal with Y's claim. Unfortunately, even if they were willing to settle Y's claim, they might have a problem in doing so because the full extent of Y's injury and the future consequences of the injury are not known, and may not be capable of being ascertained for some time. He has already had one epileptic fit. There is a possibility he might have others in the future. He is having difficulty concentrating and this is having an effect on his schooling. Overall, the injury might affect his future career because he wanted to be an airline pilot, and it seems that the head injury might have affected his eyesight. The accident happened two and a half years ago. The insurers have not made any formal concession that they are liable to pay any damages at all to Y, although it is difficult to see what the defence might be. Y's solicitors cannot persuade them to make any payment pre-litigation and they are not absolutely sure what is best in his interests. If they raise a court action now, it might be another 18 months or so before there is a final decision on the case. Practical questions which might occur to anyone in such a case[5] might be:

- Why should Y have to wait all this time and, in particular, why should he have to wait for the court action to be finally completed[6] before he gets at least some money in settlement of his claim?
- How do you take into account the possibility of the injuries having very serious consequences for Y in the future (or, conversely, not really affecting him at all)?
- If the court does make a substantial award of damages, how would Y be able to look after the money?
- Were Y to die as a result of the injuries, would his relatives be entitled to claim damages for his death and, if so, would they all raise separate actions for their own claims?

The procedural responses to these questions are contained in special provisions relating to:

(1) interim damages;
(2) provisional damages;
(3) damages payable to children;
(4) intimation of the raising of an reparation action following death, to a relative[7] who might have a claim.[8]

---

[5] They are quite likely to occur to any client in such a case.

[6] e.g. 18 months later.

[7] In this context, known as a "connected person".

[8] In practice, these issues arise in relatively few cases but the desire to minimise the personal and financial impact of an accident upon an individual who may be severely disadvantaged as a consequence of his injuries has been a prime factor in promoting these particular rules.

INTERIM DAMAGES

16–02 In most reparation cases, the defender will be insured and will be represented by solicitors who are instructed by the defender's insurers rather than by the defender himself. Where a court action is raised against a negligent driver following a road traffic accident, then the action will be raised against the driver as an individual, and his name will be the only name on the writ as defender.[9] It is, however, common knowledge that any such claim is going to be defended and funded by an insurer.[10] Many larger companies and other institutions will have their own "insurance",[11] which means that, even though they are obliged to have insurance cover by law, they actually fund any payment themselves by reimbursing the insurer for any payment they have made. Alternatively, these institutions can sometimes have a very large excess on their policies,[12] which means that the institution has a very real and direct financial liability to pay damages. These insurance arrangements are normally made by bodies who can well afford to meet the liabilities for which others may have to insure.

Many personal injury actions will be settled by the defenders or their insurers before there is any need to commence litigation. Where litigation takes place, most of them will be settled before there is any proof. Even with the best effort and advice, an action might not be raised until sometime after an accident has occurred and a proof might not be fixed until some considerable time after the action has been raised. It is not uncommon for the court to be hearing proofs in cases where the accident occurred and the injury was caused four years or more before the diet of proof. During the period between the accident and the date of the final resolution of the claim, the injured person may want to have[13] at least some of the money by way of damages which he is likely to receive when the case is finally decided. Indeed, he may be suffering some considerable financial hardship or disadvantage whilst waiting for his case to be settled. It is not considered acceptable that he should have to wait until the whole action is dealt with in its entirety at the proof before he can enforce some payment of damages from the opponent[14] of what is probably going to be due to him.

---

[9] However, the European Communities (Rights against Insurers) Regulations 2002 (SI 2002/3061) provide that, as from January 19, 2003, a claimant may raise proceedings directly against the insurer of the vehicle, instead of, or in addition to, the allegedly negligent driver.

[10] Apart from car insurance, other types of insurance which come into play in accident cases are compulsory employer's liability insurance and public liability insurance. The best known examples of public liability accidents would be an accident caused by an individual tripping on the pavement or slipping in a shop.

[11] They would be described as "self insured".

[12] Although insured, they might have agreed with their insurer that they (the insured) will pay the first £100,000 of any claim.

[13] More significantly, he might need.

[14] Who can, by definition, afford it.

In many reparation actions, it is difficult to appreciate, from a reading of the written defences lodged, what the nature of the defence is.[15] There are circumstances where a general denial of the pursuer's allegations is entirely understandable, but it can be regarded as a device whose purpose is simply to delay the progress of the action (and the payment of money to the pursuer) until the last possible date. Last minute settlements of claims are all too frequent and a constant concern for litigants and their lawyers.[16] There are many cases where there is ex facie a perfectly valid but basic defence in the pleadings but the parties and the court can reasonably suspect that liability is not ultimately going to be contested. Admissions of liability by a defender in the pleadings are relatively rare.[17]

Apart from cases in which the defender is pursuing his defence because of a genuine dispute on the question of liability, there can be cases where there may be no dispute that the defender was at fault but a dispute as to whether that fault actually caused the accident or otherwise was the only or sole cause of the accident. In these cases, the defender might be reluctant to make any concession at all, because he feels there is another actual or potential defender who should be making the payment or should at least be contributing a large or small proportion of any damages. In that situation, where two or more defenders are really arguing amongst themselves as to who will pay the damages and in what proportions, the person who really suffers is the pursuer who may have to wait some time for the defenders to fight their own internal battle.

Finally, there is a situation where the defence to the claim is that the **16–03** pursuer himself was the sole cause of the accident or contributed largely to the accident. Even if the court says that the defender was at fault, a finding of contributory negligence against the pursuer would reduce the award of damages.[18] In that case, a defender might say that, whilst he was prepared to make some payment in settlement, he would not be prepared to do so because a court could make a significant reduction in any final award. If the parties could not agree this informally, then the pursuer might have to wait until the final decision of the case by the court before he received any damages.[19]

Formerly, the normal practice was that a pursuer raised his action and took it through to a conclusion,[20] whereupon he obtained an award by the court[21] of the whole amount of the damages which are due to him.

---

[15] It is regrettable, but not uncommon, for the defences simply to be a broad and general denial of the pursuer's allegations and little more.

[16] Also the courts.

[17] In this connection, they can often be regarded as a bad "tactical" move because they concede a bargaining counter which could be used to negotiate a settlement more favourable to the defender.

[18] A finding of contributory negligence to the extent of 100 per cent on the pursuer would negate any award of damages.

[19] Albeit there has never been any doubt that he is going to receive some damages.

[20] Unless the defender, on his initiative and entirely on his initiative, decided to make a payment in full or partial satisfaction of his liability.

[21] A decree.

Damages were usually assessed on a once and for all basis.[22] The decree created the compulsion on the defender to make a payment which, until it was granted, did not exist. These features, singly and collectively, gave rise to delay, hardship and unfairness and were regarded as unacceptable.

It has always been open to a defender to offer an interim payment of damages without any form of compulsion from the courts and even to offer more than one interim payment. However, this rarely happened in practice and it was felt desirable to give the pursuer some means of forcing a defender to make an interim payment. The means of achieving that was to bring in rules whereby an interim payment can be ordered by the court in a personal injury action, prior to the final conclusion of the case, subject to certain conditions. These rules were added to the Court of Session rules originally by statutory instrument in 1974.[23] They were deleted and effectively restated in the Act of Sederunt (Rules of the Court of Session Amendment No.2) (Personal Injuries Actions) 2002.[24] Similar rules were brought into the sheriff court by Act of Sederunt in 1988.[25] There are no rules regarding awards of interim damages in summary causes in the sheriff court. It may be apparent that the speed of summary cause procedure and the low value of personal injury claims raised there make it inappropriate and unnecessary to provide for interim payments of damages. If the limit on the value of summary causes is raised, a rule might be considered necessary.

NARRATIVE OF PROCEDURES

16–04 The court can make an award of interim damages when it is able to take the view that the pursuer is probably going to win his case and there is not going to be any significant reduction in any damages awarded to him by reason of contributory negligence on his part. An award can only be made where the defender making the payment can be regarded as able to afford it. In that way, there is unlikely to be any hardship to them and if it turns out that the making of an interim award and the assessment of an interim award at a preliminary stage is not merited on full enquiry in the case, then, in relative terms, no great financial hardship will result. There is indeed provision to pay back any over-payment or to make suitable adjustments in the light of any final award made in the case. As a safeguard, however, against manifest injustice or at least against procedural and administrative problems, the rules also provide that the interim award to be made has to be restricted to a reasonable proportion

---

[22] i.e. the judge, on the date of the judgment, assessed what all of the pursuer's past and future losses would be.

[23] Act of Sederunt (Rules of the Court of Session Amendment) 1974 (SI 1974/845).

[24] Act of Sederunt (Rules of the Court of Session Amendment No.2) (Personal Injuries Actions) 2002 (SSI 2002/570).

[25] Act of Sederunt (Amendment of Sheriff Court Ordinary Cause, and Summary Cause, Rules) 1988 (SI 1988/1978).

of the damages which might ultimately be awarded.[26] Once the court has decided that the pursuer will probably succeed on liability if the case went ahead to proof and has decided that there is not much of a chance of a significant finding of contributory negligence against the pursuer, then it is required to award a figure which it can be demonstrated at the time is likely to be somewhat less than it would probably have awarded assuming the matter had been dealt with fully at a proof.

PARTICULAR RULES

The rules are brief. The rules in the Court of Session are now rr.43.11 **16–05** and 43.12.[27] The rules for sheriff court ordinary actions are 36.8–36.10 of the OCR. The only difference is that the application for an interim payment is done by way of the different motion procedures in the respective courts. Reference should be made to the specific terms of the rules but we are only going to consider the Court of Session rules and cases under them in this section. There is no reason why they should be interpreted or applied differently in the respective courts.[28]

The rules apply to actions of damages for personal injuries or the death of any person from personal injuries. They do not apply to any other type of claim.[29]

Rule 43.11(1) and (2)—Application for an award of interim damages is made by the pursuer enrolling a motion for interim damages. The pursuer has to give written intimation with not less than 14 days notice.[30] In a case where more than one defender is being blamed for the accident, then the application can be made for interim damages against one or other of them or against both of them.[31]

Rule 43.11(3)—The court has a discretion whether to grant or refuse the motion but before it can exercise its discretion, it must be satisfied of three things:

(1) that liability is admitted[32]; or

---

[26] For a recent case illustrating this point see *Frank William Fletcher as guardian for Lisa Smart v Lunan* [2008] CSOH 55 in which the court awarded £500,000 as interim damages.

[27] In April 2003, these replaced the original rules in the Court of Session (rr.43.8–43.10). The authorities referred to in this section relate to the "old" rules but the significant terms of both rules are identical.

[28] There are few reported cases from the sheriff court regarding the application of that section in sheriff court proceedings although there is an interesting and detailed discussion of the rule in the case of *Calder v Simpson*, 1994 S.C.L.R. 27.

[29] See, e.g. *Mackenzie v Digby Brown*, 1992 S.L.T. 891.

[30] This somewhat extra notice will give the defender's solicitor the opportunity to take full and detailed instructions because if the motion is to be opposed, then it will undoubtedly be argued fully.

[31] See, e.g. *McNicol v Buko Ltd*, 1986 S.L.T. 12.

[32] This could be a formal admission in the pleadings or an admission at the bar. See *Nisbett v Marley*, 1988 S.L.T. 608.

(2) the pursuer would succeed in the action on the question of liability without any substantial finding of contributory negligence on his part; and, regardless of whether one or two apply;

(3) the pursuer would obtain a decree for damages against any defender in the action if the case went ahead.

Obviously it is not possible to say with any certainty when the motion is being heard that the pursuer will definitely succeed. In simple terms, he might not prove his allegations of how the accident happened and that might be enough to prevent an award. Whether there is going to be "substantial" contributory negligence is obviously a matter of opinion and that opinion will have to be reached on the basis of the information put before the court at the hearing of the motion. It is often difficult to predict what kind of cases will merit the making of awards of interim damages.[33] In this connection, a practical issue of some significance is whether the courts are bound or entitled to look at any material when considering the motion for interim damages other than the pleadings of the parties in the case.[34] There are slightly differing views about this but recent practice would tend to suggest that focusing rigidly on the pleadings alone might be regarded as too restrictive.[35] In the new personal injury actions in the Court of Session it will be interesting to see what impact the lack of detailed pleadings will have on motions for interim damages and how much extraneous material will be available for consideration by the judge.

It is very important to note that the court can make an award of interim damages against any defender in the action provided the court is satisfied at the hearing of the motion that the pursuer would obtain decree for damages against any defender.[36] It would then be left to the defenders[37] to adjust matters between themselves on the conclusion of the case. The intention is to avoid the defenders arguing against payment of interim damages because it is going to be difficult to determine which of them is actually going to win or lose. The court has a discretion to make an interim award against any of them. The court's powers are, of course, discretionary and, in particular cases, the court might decide not

---

[33] An explanation and analysis of the meaning of the rule is given authoritatively in *Cowie v Atlantic Drilling Co Ltd*, 1995 S.L.T. 1151, which should be considered fully.

[34] Making a decision about the merits of any case without evidence can be seen as unfair and unsatisfactory.

[35] See, e.g. the case of *Stone v Mountford*, 1995 S.L.T. 1279, where police photographs of a fence round a quarry where a child had an accident were lodged as productions in the case and were referred to and discussed by the court in the context of the motion for interim damages. See also the case of *Cleland v Campbell*, 1998 S.L.T. 642, where photographs of the condition of a road after an accident which were lodged as productions in the case by both sides, were discussed and referred to and appear to have carried considerable weight in the judge's assessment of liability.

[36] In other words, if there were three defenders A, B and C and it was patently obvious that C was going to be liable to the pursuer, the court could, in theory, make an award of interim damages against A or B or C or a combination of all of them.

[37] Each of whom, it is presumed, can afford to make a payment.

to make an award against particular defenders.[38] If the defender does not fit into the following categories, then no award can be made[39]:

(1) the defender is insured;
(2) the defender is a public authority; or
(3) the defender is a person who can afford to make an interim payment.

Rule 43.11(6) — Where there has been a change of circumstances, a pursuer can make a subsequent motion or motions for interim damages regardless of what happened to his first motion.

Rule 43.11(8) — This states that the rule about interim damages applies to claims for damages for personal injury which are pursued by way of a counterclaim and this simply avoids any doubt in interpretation of the rules.

Rule 43.12 — This rule provides for financial adjustments to take place once the case is finally disposed of by the court. When an interim payment has been made in any case and the court ultimately decides the question of liability in the normal way, i.e. after a proof, then the court has power to make any order required to give effect to that final decision and to take into account the interim damages already paid and order the necessary adjustments in order to give effect to the overall financial consequences of the court's final decision. This is really a matter of common sense and arithmetic and, amongst other things, the court can order the pursuer to repay to a defender an interim payment or part of an interim payment. The court can order one defender to repay some of the money to another defender.[40]

PROVISIONAL DAMAGES

In the normal course of events, any claim before the courts for payment **16–06** of damages for personal injury will seek all of the money properly due to the pursuer both now and in the future. Any award made by the courts will be made on that basis. In personal injury cases, where the long-term personal and financial consequences of an injury might not be known at

---

[38] See the case of *Herbertson v Ascosmit Co Ltd*, 1992 S.L.T. 1115; and for a case where a joint and several award was made against all of the defenders, see *Walker v Infabco Diving Services Ltd*, 1983 S.L.T. 633.
[39] See the case of *Ferguson v McGrandles*, 1993 S.L.T. 822.
[40] A good example of how this rule works in practice is the case of *Mitchell v HAT Contracting Services*, which is reported at various stages in the procedure and from which those of you with pen, pencil and calculator will be able to work out all of the financial implications of what happened during the lifetime of the case. A careful reading is required to follow the procedural steps in the action which is reported in 1992 S.L.T. 883, then at 1993 S.L.T. 734 and finally at 1993 S.L.T. 1199.

the date when the action is raised or even at the date when it is decided, the parties will effectively ask the court to make an attempt to predict fairly and reasonably what the likely consequences of the injury are going to be. The court will make an award on the basis of what could be described as an educated guess backed up by knowledge, experience and expertise and, of course, supported by proper evidence.

Some of the future consequences of an injury cannot be predicted easily, and it may be difficult to make a fair prediction because particular consequences might have a very profound effect on the award of damages. Consider an individual who has suffered an injury which might cause him to go blind in five years time, it might be just as unfair to award him damages on the basis that it is presumed that he probably will go blind, as it might be to award him damages on the basis that he probably would not. The court would undoubtedly address the task of balancing the future prospects with great care, but where the future consequences might be very serious indeed it is difficult to be satisfied that a speculative assessment will produce a fair result.

Section 12 of the Administration of Justice Act 1982 entitled a pursuer to ask the court for "provisional" damages in personal injury cases in order to address this difficulty. It provided that, in certain cases, the pursuer can ask the court to award damages on the basis that the future consequences of the injury which are not yet known can be left out of the equation entirely, with a right to come back to the court to obtain a further award if these consequences do in fact materialise. The future consequences have to be quite serious, and a time limit is to be imposed within which the pursuer has to come back to the court. This prevents the defenders being left with a completely open-ended obligation. Provisional damages can only be sought from certain financially sound defenders in the same way as in the rules about interim damages.

In practice, very few cases contain a crave for provisional damages. It can be sought in Court of Session personal injury actions and ordinary actions,[41] and in sheriff court ordinary causes and summary causes.[42]

NARRATIVE OF THE RULES

16–07 Provision is made in the Court of Session Rules, rr.43.2(2), (3) and 43.13.[43] Provision is made in the sheriff court rules 1993, rr.36.11–36.13. Again, as in interim damages, the rules are relatively similar and there is no real advantage in looking at them separately. In essence, the rules provide that it is for the party who considers it appropriate to seek provisional damages to ask the court for it in his summons or writ, to justify such an award in his written pleadings, to be prepared to lead evidence to

---

[41] This will only arise if a personal injury action has been transferred to the ordinary roll.
[42] See r.34.2(3) of the SCR.
[43] These substantially restate the prior rules.

support the appropriateness of making an award of provisional damages in that particular case, and to persuade the court to exercise its discretion to make such an award.[44] When that is all done and an award of provisional damages made, the pursuer will be given an opportunity to come back on the occurrence of a specific event in the future and ask for an additional award to be made. The court will not make such an award of provisional damages if it is not asked to do so and it is for the pursuer to persuade the court that the various factors required by s.12 of the Act apply in his case.[45]

PARTICULAR RULES

Court of Session

Rule 43.2(2) and (3)—This provides that any application for provi- **16–08** sional damages should be made by including in the summons a conclusion[46] for provisional damages and averments as to the matters referred to in the statute; namely: (a) that there is a risk that at some definite or indefinite time in the future the injured person will, as a result of the act or omission which gave rise to the cause of the action, develop some serious disease or suffer some serious deterioration in his physical or mental condition; and (b) the responsible person was, at the time of the act or omission giving rise to the cause of the action, (i) a public authority or public corporation; or (ii) insured or otherwise indemnified in respect of the claim.[47]

Rule 43.13—This applies to cases where a provisional award had been made and the event which was feared has in fact materialised. The rules set out the procedure for coming back to the court and obtaining a further

---

[44] These cases will provide a good illustration of the circumstances in which awards of provisional damages were made and not. In *Lappin v Britannia Airways Ltd*, 1989 S.L.T. 181, the risk of epileptic attacks in the future would have attracted provisional damages. In *Prentice v William Thyne Ltd*, 1989 S.L.T. 336, no award was made. In *White v Inveresk Paper Co Ltd (No.2)*, 1988 S.L.T. 2, no award was made. In *Robertson v British Bakeries Ltd*, 1991 S.L.T. 434, the risk of osteoarthritis following fracture dislocation of the ankle was appropriate for a provisional award. In *Bonar v Trafalgar House Offshore Fabrication Ltd*, 1996 S.L.T. 548, no award was made. Recent examples of such cases are *Duffy v Lanarkshire Health Board*, 1999 S.L.T. 906 and *Young v Scottish Coal (Deep Mining) Co. Ltd*, 2002 S.L.T. 1215.

[45] Even if they do apply, the court still has a discretion as to whether it makes the award or not and this was Lord Prosser's approach in the case of *Meek v Burton's Gold Medal Biscuits Ltd*, 1989 S.L.T. 338.

[46] In the sheriff court this would be a "crave" rather than a "conclusion".

[47] In the sheriff court rules, a suitable plea in law is also required, but pleas in law have been dispensed with in personal injury actions in the Court of Session.

award. The application is made by minute and the minute will include the following information:

(1) a conclusion in a specified form;
(2) written averments to support that conclusion.[48]

Rule 43.13(2) to (4)—These set out the procedure once the minute[49] has been lodged. After the minute is lodged in process, the pursuer lodges a motion at the same time for warrant to serve on the other party and his insurers if known. The warrant will include a notice to the recipient that he has 28 days from the date of service of the notice to lodge answers to the minute. The rules do not provide what procedure there will be if and when answers are lodged.[50]

COURT MANAGEMENT OF MONEY PAYABLE TO CHILDREN

16–09 Where an award of damages is made in favour of a child, i.e. someone under 16, there is legitimate concern that in some cases this money might not find its way to the child or it might be dealt with or invested on behalf of the child inappropriately so that the child does not, in the short term and in the long term, obtain the full benefit of the money. Formerly, this concern was met by leaving it to the good sense of the child's parents and their legal advisers. In some cases a *curator ad litem* was appointed to look after the interests of the child in such an action.[51] The situation has altered radically and the relevant rules have altered radically since the advent of the Children (Scotland) Act 1995.[52] Section 13 of that Act provides that where damages become payable to, or for the benefit of, a child under 16, the court can make such order relating to the payment and management of that sum as it thinks fit. The court may, without prejudice to this wide discretion, appoint a judicial factor to look after the money, or order the money to be paid to the sheriff clerk, the accountant of court, or the parent or guardian of the child, or simply order that it be paid directly to the child.[53] There were formerly detailed provisions in the rules regarding the management of money payable to children but these are no longer required either in the Court of Session or the sheriff court.

---

[48] Again in the sheriff court, a plea in law is required.

[49] For an additional award.

[50] I am not aware of any reported or unreported case in which this has actually happened yet. The sheriff court rules actually provide a rule about this but simply leave it to the sheriff to decide how to proceed.

[51] It may be of interest to consider some older cases dealing with this issue under the old rules. See *Riddoch v Occidental Petroleum (Caledonia) Ltd*, 1991 S.L.T. 721 and *Scott v Occidental Petroleum (Caledonia) Ltd*, 1990 S.C.L.R. 278.

[52] For a summary of the history of the rules and practice governing this issue in the Court of Session see *I v Argyll and Clyde Health Board*, 2003 S.L.T. 231.

[53] This would be unusual unless it was a small sum.

COURT OF SESSION

The court is empowered to make orders dealing with awards of damages **16–10** to children by virtue of the 1995 Act and accordingly no detailed rules are required. The terms of s.13 of the Act are sufficient to enable the various alternatives to be reviewed by the court[54] and there is considered to be no need for specific procedural or administrative rules to support the statutory provisions. The only surviving rule of court is r.49.88,[55] which relates to the procedure whereby an individual seeking an order for administration of the child's property[56] can apply to the court for such an order and this would be done by way of a minute in the process of the cause in respect of which the s.13 order was made.[57]

SHERIFF COURT RULES

There is only one rule in the sheriff court dealing with this matter. This **16–11** is r.33.95 which came into effect on November 1, 1996. It is to the same effect as the Court of Session rule detailed above and it provides that, where the sheriff has made an order under s.13 of the Children (Scotland) Act 1995, any person who is entitled to do so by virtue of s.11(1)(d) of the Act can make application in the process of the cause in relation to the administration of that property.

INTIMATION TO CONNECTED PERSONS IN CERTAIN ACTIONS OF DAMAGES

In a case where damages are being claimed for death caused to an indi- **16–12** vidual, then various relatives[58] of the deceased are entitled to claim damages. There was some doubt as to whether there was any obligation on one individual claimant who was pursuing his claim in court to advise the others that he was doing so or intending to do so. Some relatives may not want to and some of them may resent any approach along those lines. However, failure to let other relatives know that a claim was being litigated upon might lead to situations where they were simply unaware that they themselves were entitled to pursue a claim. Once they realised that a claim could be maintained, they might want to take steps to raise

---

[54] A useful outline of the alternatives available and the appropriateness of each option open to the court is contained in *Greens Annotated Rules of the Court of Session 2008/9*, pp.C436/14–C436/16.
[55] Which came into effect when all of the other rules were revoked on November 1, 1996.
[56] Sometime after an award has been made and paid.
[57] e.g. a request to have money invested differently could be made by an individual with an interest notwithstanding that an order had been made appointing some other person to invest the funds.
[58] The phrase used in the rules is "connected person" rather than "relative" but we will use relative for simplicity.

proceedings themselves. This could lead to a proliferation of actions arising out of the one accident. It was considered desirable to devise rules to ensure so far as possible that all of the people who had, or might have, an interest in pursuing a claim for damages for the death of a relative should be aware of that entitlement, and, if they wished to pursue a claim, should do so in the one action or at least should be given the opportunity to do so in the one action.

Rules were brought in whose purpose was to identify the individuals who might require to be informed of the existence of a court action[59] and whereby the terms of the writ were intimated to these people at the time when the action was raised. This would give them the opportunity to become involved in the action as an additional pursuer without raising separate proceedings themselves. It is equally open to them not to become involved in the action. It is particularly provided in the rules that, if someone who has been advised of their entitlement to raise an action does not become involved as a party to the action which has already been raised,[60] the court should not award him any expenses in any action which he might subsequently pursue himself.

The rules regarding intimation to these relatives are contained in rr.43.14–43.20 of the RCS,[61] in rr.36.1–36.7 of the OCR and rr.34.6(1)–(15) of the SCR.

The general content of the rules are very similar, but not identical as there are slight procedural variations. Reference should be made to the respective rules for precise details.

COURT OF SESSION

16–13 **Rule 43.15**—Where the pursuer does make averments about the existence of connected persons then he seeks a special warrant for the writ to be intimated to them.

Rule 43.16—Where the pursuer wants to dispense with intimation to connected persons for the reasons set out above, then he applies by motion for an order to dispense with intimation. The rule provides that the court ought to have regard to certain factors in deciding whether to order intimation or not and if the court is not satisfied that intimation should be dispensed with, then it can make certain directions to the pursuer's agents.

Rule 43.17—This provides that where the court dispenses with intimation for the reasons given and subsequently the address of one of the

[59] i.e. those who would have a title to sue if they wanted.
[60] Although he does not lose his right to pursue the claim for damages.
[61] Special rules apply to mesothelioma cases. See para.6–23, above.

connected persons becomes known to the pursuer, then the pursuer shall apply by motion for a warrant for intimation on that person.

Rule 43.18—This provides that if a connected person wants to become involved in the action then he does so by applying to the court by minute in the process of the action craving leave to be sisted as an additional pursuer. The crave will also crave leave of the court to adopt the existing grounds of action and to amend the written pleadings as appropriate. Alternatively, it can set out separate grounds of action, etc. Before lodging this minute in the process, the minuter has to intimate to every other party a copy of the minute and any other party may lodge answers to the minute.

Rule 43.19—This provides that where intimation has been made on a connected person and he does not apply to be sisted as an additional pursuer to the action but subsequently brings a separate action against the same defender in respect of the same personal injuries, then the court will not award him the expenses of that separate action except "on cause shown".

SHERIFF COURT

Rule 36.1—This is the definition section. A "connected person" is **16–14** defined as a person who has title to sue the defender in respect of the personal injuries from which the deceased died.

Rule 36.2—This provides that in any claim for damages for death, the pursuer has to make averments in the condescendence to one of the following three effects:

(1) that there are no connected persons; or
(2) that there are connected persons and the pursuer is going to ask the court to order intimation of the action on these persons; or
(3) that there are connected persons that the pursuer is going to ask the court not to have the action intimated to them either because they cannot be found with any reasonable effort or because they are persons who are unlikely to be awarded more than £200 each.

Rules 36.3 to 36.7—These are similar to the Court of Session rules, rr.43.15–43.19, detailed above.

In summary causes the rules are similar and the reader is referred to the rules themselves (rr.34.6(1)–(15)) for details.

CHAPTER 17

LEGAL DEBATES

17–01 In every day language, all disputes in court involve a "legal debate", and there are a number of stages during a litigation when the law applicable to the merits of the case or some part of the case might be argued before the courts. However, when solicitors in the sheriff court talk about a case going to debate, or when solicitors in the Court of Session talk of a case going to a procedure roll hearing,[1] they are referring to a very specific step in the procedural progress of an action. It can be a very important, and indeed conclusive, step in the procedure. It can, in particular cases, cause the court to dismiss the pursuer's claim, or repel the defender's defences entirely, without any hearing of evidence about the facts of the dispute.

WHAT IS A DEBATE?

17–02 Putting the matter broadly, it is an argument between the parties after the closing of the record:

(1) before there has been any hearing of any evidence in the case;
(2) based entirely on the written pleadings of the parties at the time the record closes;
(3) concerning the law applicable to the merits of the case or the way in which the written case has been pled;
(4) canvassing with the court whether the written pleadings—and only the written pleadings—justify any hearing of evidence (either for the pursuer or the defender) in order to decide the merits of the case, and/or whether, if evidence is to be heard, what type of hearing it should be, and the extent of evidence or argument which can be advanced at that hearing.

Unfortunately, whilst it is possible to explain the purpose of a debate in these theoretical terms, the range of matters which can be argued at a debate, the legal and tactical reasons for proceeding to debate or not, and the wide range of possible outcomes of a debate, do tend to give the procedure an air of mystery. The practical purpose and utility of a debate, as a step in procedure in any individual case cannot be easily explained

---

[1] Which is exactly the same thing.

or understood. Some lawyers would say that all debates prior to the hearing of evidence should be abolished. Some say they are essential to the proper conduct of a litigation. However, it is unwise to generalise about this. The recent trends in procedure[2] and changes in procedural rules[3] reflect the continuation of a determined move away from the former notion of debates on demand in every case, towards the principle of debates only if they can clearly be justified and may be seen as making a significant difference to the course or conduct of the litigation.[4]

Debates can cover a wide range of issues in a case. Some debates can last for 20 minutes. Some can last for days. Some arguments at debate have no apparent effect on the outcome of the case. Some are vitally important. The fixing of a debate can add considerably to the duration and expense of some cases and it will impact on the speed of progress of an action. The court administration has to make specific arrangements for hearing debates which are often expected to take up significant court time, and this means that it can often be several weeks or months from the date when a debate is allowed in an action to the date when it can actually be heard.

It is not possible to explore the whole mysterious world of debates in this chapter. More so than in many other procedural steps, the benefits of a debate and the practical implications of debates can only be fully appreciated with direct practical experience of individual cases. Putting the matter very crudely, however, there are three good basic reasons for having a debate:

(1) because the opponent's pleadings are such that, if that is all they can prove about the circumstances of the dispute, they do not have a, "snowball's chance in hell"[5] of winning;
(2) because there is so little detail and explanation of the opponent's case that a party's ability to prepare for a proof is seriously prejudiced in a practical way;
(3) because some material aspect of the opponent's case which would cause parties to make significant additional investigations and preparations for a proof has no real chance of succeeding.

A practical example could concern one of the X claims following the road accident. Assume that Mr X's accident is caused by the fault of a young driver of a sports car who was drunk at the time. If we assume, as an extreme case, that Mr X sues the garage which sold the sports car on the basis that they were obliged to check that their customers were teetotal before completing the sale, it would be likely that the garage would

---

[2] Such as personal injury actions. See Ch.6.
[3] Such as the OCR regarding options hearings. See Ch.9.
[4] The contrasting views can be understood in a practical context from a reading of *Cyma Petroleum UK Ltd v Total Logistics Concepts Ltd*, 2004 S.L.T. (Sh. Ct) 112 and the cases referred to in it.
[5] As it was put by an eminent and distinguished sheriff who knew what he was talking about!

take a preliminary plea in their defences to the effect that there is no legal basis for attributing liability to them in the circumstances stated in the pursuer's pleadings. There would be no point in having a proof about the circumstances because the court could not possibly decide in favour of the pursuer. The garage would argue at a debate[6] that the action should be dismissed against them. There would be no point in wasting time and expense having a hearing about the facts of the case because the pursuer could not possibly succeed with his claim against them. On the other hand, if Mr X sued the owner of the car, who was not driving it at the time of the accident, on the basis that he specifically allowed the car to be driven by a man he knew to be drunk, then there might be an argument at debate as to whether legal liability attaches to the owner in these circumstances. The action could be dismissed at debate if the judge was persuaded that there could not possibly be liability. The case could alternatively be allowed to go to a proof[7] on the basis that there could be such a liability and evidence ought to be heard to decide the issue. Alternatively, there could be arguments that, although there can theoretically be some circumstances in which such a claim could be pursued, the pursuer has not said enough in his written pleadings to show that his case is relevant.

Despite the apparent importance of debates,[8] the statistics tend to show that of the debates and procedure roll hearings fixed, considerably less than 25 per cent of them ever go ahead. That does not mean to say that they should never have been fixed in the first place. There can be many cases, however, when it is reasonable to ask whether the fixing of a debate is anything more than a time-wasting tactic on the part of a defender, and where it appears that there is really very little that the debate can achieve in focusing and helping to resolve the dispute.

Debates are discouraged but not incompetent in personal injuries actions in the Court of Session in which the court is likely to look very critically at the issue of whether a debate should be allowed. It should be noted that there is no provision in the rules of summary causes in the sheriff court for there to be a debate, as such. It is possible, however, to argue at the calling date in a summary cause that the claim is not competent or that the claim/defence, "is not soundly based in law in whole or in part" which is tantamount to making the kind of submissions about fundamental relevancy which might be made at a debate.[9] It is also open to the parties to agree evidence in a summary cause (and indeed in any case) at the calling date or subsequently and then effectively have a debate on the law applicable to the agreed facts.[10]

---

[6] It could possibly argue this at a motion for summary decree, although this would be rare in practice.
[7] Which would be a proof before answer. See Ch.18.
[8] Demonstrated by the vast number of cases sent to debate.
[9] See Ch.11.
[10] This happens rarely but see, e.g. *MacColl v Hoo*, 1983 S.L.T. (Sh. Ct) 23, where the parties effectively conducted a debate in a summary cause action. There is now a specific provision to this effect in the SCR 2002, namely r.8.3(3)(c).

As we shall see, most of the remainder of this chapter relates to debates (sheriff court) and procedure roll hearings (Court of Session) in ordinary actions, in which full pleadings will normally be provided.

WHEN CAN A DEBATE BE FIXED?

The basic point to grasp is that the court can only be asked by the par- **17–03** ties to fix a debate, and may only fix a debate, where one or other of the parties has a preliminary plea[11] in their written pleadings. The court can be asked to fix a debate once the parties have completed the adjustment of their pleadings under the procedural rules applicable to that kind of action. In a case where there has been amendment of pleadings (after the closing of the record) then the court can be asked to fix a debate after the completion of the amendment procedure.

PROCEDURAL RULES

There are few rules of procedure relating to the actual conduct of **17–04** debates. The only procedural rules which apply relate to the giving of advance justification for a debate, or the giving of advance notification of the arguments to be put at a debate. These have developed relatively recently because of shortcomings in the existing procedures, and with the intention of preventing unnecessary debates. It is worth explaining why these recent changes have taken place because it helps to give an appreciation of the procedural function of a debate.

The most common preliminary plea which you will find in a court action is a plea to the effect that the pursuer's or defender's pleadings are, "irrelevant *et separatim*[12] lacking in specification".

It is often pled as a matter of routine in defences and in practice it is usually taken by a defender against a pursuer's pleadings rather than by a pursuer. The basic propositions are that the pursuer's pleadings are irrelevant—in other words, even if the pursuer establishes all of the facts contained within his averments, these facts would not justify the remedy which the pursuer is seeking, and/or that they are lacking in specification—which means that the pursuer has failed to give sufficient details in his averments to enable the defenders to understand what facts or law the pursuer proposes to rely upon in order to justify his claim. It would usually be argued that the defenders were prejudiced in their ability to prepare for any hearing of evidence in the case by the failure to give full details or "fair notice" of the case which they have to meet.

Whilst this is most usually viewed from the perspective of the defender seeking a debate regarding the pursuer's pleadings, it is equally

---

[11] See Ch.4.
[12] i.e. "and separately".

open to the pursuer to seek a debate regarding the defender's pleadings. The pursuer could argue that the defences do not disclose a relevant defence in law. He could argue that the facts averred by the defenders do not give him fair notice of what the defender's defence is going to be. In any case, both the pursuer and the defender could have preliminary pleas directed against each other's pleadings.[13]

Formerly, there was no obligation on either party to disclose to the other or to the court, the argument or arguments which justified their preliminary pleas, prior to the hearing of the debate. The general terms of the "routine" preliminary plea quoted above gives no hint of what particular aspect of the other side's pleadings is under attack. There may be many cases where the plea is not justified at all, or where it relates to some small or technical pleading deficiency which does not go to the heart of the case nor should seriously affect further procedure in the case. Cases were routinely sent to debate in the past and parties were entitled to insist on them being sent to debate if they wished,[14] whatever the merits or otherwise of the plea. If a defender wanted to argue, on the one hand, that the whole legal basis of the pursuer's claim was a statute which was not in force at the material time or, on the other hand, that a sentence in the pursuer's pleadings was not very clear, he could do this by taking the same "routine" and general preliminary plea. The procedures which were brought in to deal with this were:

(1) in the Court of Session, r.22.4 of the RCS, supplemented by various practice notes;
(2) in the sheriff court, r.22.1 of the OCR.

COURT OF SESSION

Ordinary actions

17–05 The name for a legal debate in the Court of Session is a procedure roll hearing. This will be allowed by the court where:

(1) the record has closed; and
(2) parties have agreed this step in procedure; or
(3) in the absence of agreement, where the court sends the case to procedure roll after a calling on the by order (adjustment) roll.

---

[13] At the risk of over complicating this already, it should be noted that, as well as being open to the pursuer and the defender in any action to request a debate, it is open to a third party to request a diet of debate by way of a preliminary plea. This would be on the strength of criticism which he might make regarding the factual and legal basis on which it is thought that the third party is involved in some obligation to the defender. He can also take a preliminary plea or any other plea directed to the pursuer's claim against the defender.

[14] It was this entitlement to insist on debate which really caused the problem and enabled the party taking a preliminary plea to dictate the pace and direction of the litigation to a considerable extent.

Accordingly, if any party has a preliminary plea(s) and wants a legal debate then the case will be sent to procedure roll.

Initially, by Practice Note[15] No.3 of 1991 it was indicated that the court "expects" parties to discuss certain matters prior to fixing a hearing on procedure roll. These matters would include informing the opponent of the nature of the proposed argument and finding out if the point at issue can be resolved without resorting to a hearing. It was perhaps a more flexible and civilised approach than to lay down specific rules, but a rule was not long in coming and it was provided in r.22.4 of the 1994 RCS that the court may, at its own instance or on the motion of either party, order a party to lodge in process a concise note of argument stating the basis of his preliminary plea and send a copy to the opponent. The time scale for this is not specified in the rule. The note of proposed argument should be in numbered paragraphs and it is suggested that it does not need to be detailed but should be concise and contain any relevant authority. It should be appreciated, however, that these provisions and sanctions only come into play after the case has in fact been appointed to procedure roll and they do not, as per the sheriff court rule, prevent an action being sent to a "debate".

Commercial actions

Three days before the hearing at which the court is going to decide **17–06** further procedure, the parties have to give notice of their proposals for such procedure and, if they want a debate, they have to lodge a note of argument which should include the principal authorities and statutory provisions founded upon. In this way the judge can make an informed decision as to whether the action should be allowed to go to debate.[16] There is a slight difference in emphasis in the rules of each of these procedures, although the net effect is similar.

Personal injury actions

The rules require the pursuer to lodge a motion for further procedure **17–07** once the record is closed.[17] Debates are discouraged. If a party seeks a debate then full notice of the grounds will be required and must be given in writing. Any complaints about specification[18] will be dealt with on the hearing on the motion for further procedure. "A motion for Procedure Roll will not be granted lightly".[19]

Sheriff court

The court will fix a date for the hearing of a debate at the options **17–08** hearing, or at the continued options hearing, or at the procedural

---

[15] i.e. not a rule.
[16] See rr.47.12(1)(a) and 47.12(1)(d).
[17] See r.43.6(5).
[18] As opposed to relevancy.
[19] Practice Note No.2 of 2003.

hearing[20] under r.10.3 or, where there have been amendments after the closing of the record, at the hearing on the amendment under r.18.3. This would be done:

(1) if one or other or both of the parties want to insist on their preliminary plea or pleas; and
(2) if they have lodged a note in support of the plea(s) under r.22.1; and
(3) if the sheriff is satisfied at the hearing that: "[t]here is a preliminary matter of law which, if established following debate would lead to decree in favour of any party or to limitation of proof to any substantial degree".[21]

If they have not lodged such a note, regardless of the apparent merit of such a plea, then the plea is automatically repelled[22] and no debate can be fixed to argue it.[23] The note has to be lodged not later than three days before the relevant hearing and a copy intimated to the opponent.[24] All the note has to contain is a, "note of the basis for the plea" (r.22.1(1)(a)) and there are differences of opinion and practice as to how detailed that should be. It is open to the sheriff at the hearing at which the note is considered to examine the merits of the note and consider any oral submissions made in expansion of it. There are differences of opinion as to how rigorous that examination should be. It is important to realise, however, that this does not mean that the debate point itself is to be argued fully or decided upon at that particular time The sheriff should be satisfied that the argument justifies a debate having regard to the criteria in the rules, not that a debate would be successful, nor that the proposed arguments at debate were good or bad.[25] There is considerable scope for different application of these rules in practice.[26]

At any debate parties may, on cause shown, raise matters in addition to those set out in the r.22.1 note,[27] and practice varies between the courts as

---

[20] Not to be confused (as it can be) with the procedure roll hearing, the Court of Session equivalent of a debate.
[21] This wording was introduced by Act of Sederunt (Ordinary Cause, Summary Application, Summary Cause and Small Claim Rules) Amendment (Miscellaneous) 2004 (SSI 2004/197) effective from May 21, 2004.
[22] See *George Martin (Builders) Ltd v Jamal*, 2001 S.L.T. (Sh. Ct) 119. It is not possible to reinstate the plea following amendment unless there is new material in the amendment which justifies a preliminary plea.
[23] *Bell v John Davidson (Pipes) Ltd*, 1995 S.L.T. (Sh. Ct) 18.
[24] The court can exercise its dispensing power to allow late lodging of the note if there is good reason. *Colvin v Montgomery Preservations Ltd*, 1995 S.L.T. (Sh. Ct) 15.
[25] Inevitably, given the constraints of time, resources and practice, the arguments at an options hearing would be less detailed than at the debate itself.
[26] That is a masterpiece of understatement! The most helpful sources for understanding the operation of this important rule are the decision of the various sheriffs principal in the cases of *Cyma Petroleum UK Ltd v Total Logistics Concepts Ltd*, 2004 S.L.T. (Sh. Ct) 112; *Gracey v Sykes*, 1994 S.C.L.R. 909; *Blair and Bryden Partnership v Adair*, 1995 S.C.L.R. 358; *Dinardo Partnership Ltd v Thomas Tait and Sons Ltd*, 1995 S.C.L.R. 941; and *MacFarlane v Falkirk Council*, 2000 S.L.T. (Sh. Ct) 29. However, it should be noted that these all preceded the recent change in the terms of the rule.
[27] OCR r.22.1(4).

to the extent to which this will be allowed. In the Court of Session a party who fails to give notice of an argument can often be penalised by an adverse finding of expenses. For example, if the opponent requires time to consider a novel argument and the case has to be adjourned to give him a reasonable opportunity to consider and respond to the unexpected point, the court might find the defaulting party liable for the expenses of any such adjournment, regardless of the merits of the argument. There have been cases in which the judge has found the defaulter liable for the expenses of the whole debate, even where the opponent accepts there is merit in the argument of which he has not had notice and requires to amend to respond to it. It would be open to a sheriff to do likewise, but practice varies.

The intention behind all of these procedures preliminary to a debate is to ensure that trivial or insignificant arguments are not taken to debate and also to ensure that, if there is a good and substantial point, the other side can have an opportunity at an early stage to consider it and, if appropriate, seek leave to amend their pleadings to take it into account. Amendments will usually, but not automatically, be allowed, and the whole procedure then starts to appear rather slow and pointless. It is difficult to explain to a client why the progress of his case has been held up for three months or more by a "technical" defect in the pleadings which should have been avoided, and was not particularly significant in any event. That is not to say that all debates are about trivial and unimportant issues nor that all cases are easy to plead on facts or law—far from it—but there is a view that no harm would be done to our system if you could only have debates in very clear cases where they were vital to the success or failure of the action as a whole. The more recent changes in the rules and practices of the court tend to promote that objective.

WHAT HAPPENS AT A DEBATE?

Pre-debate

There are no written rules of procedure regarding the conduct of a **17–09** debate in the sheriff court or in the Court of Session. Practice is all that comes into play. The only written provisions which might have any bearing upon a debate might be the practice notes of a particular sheriff court. These will normally deal with matters such as the lodging with the court of a list of authorities, i.e. the cases or statutes which you intend to use and rely on to advance your argument at debate, and the intimation of that list of authorities to your opponent. This presupposes that the arguments need to be supported or justified by reference to authority. That should usually, but not always, be the case, e.g. a plea directed towards lack of specification might simply look at what the other party is saying in his pleadings and argue that the case is obviously not clear or understandable.[28] In theory, of course, such simple and fundamental points ought to have been

---

[28] Simply as a matter of common sense.

ironed out before parties proceed to a "substantial" argument at debate.[29]
A consideration of the cases on your list of authorities might give the court
and the other party some more detailed advance notification of the points
you are going to take but there is no obligation, apart from the rules
already mentioned, to provide further details in advance. As a matter of
courtesy and practice a party might do so and an opponent might ask for
more details in advance which can be given or not.[30] The opponent should
also be intimating a list of the authorities which support his position.

The debate diet

17–10   For present purposes we shall consider what happens at a diet of
debate in the sheriff court.[31] Similar considerations apply in procedure
roll hearings in the Court of Session, although there are certain differences which are largely matters of form.

There have been adverse criticisms about the system of written pleadings in Scotland and debates have become regarded by some as a central
pillar of that system, with parties concentrating on matters of form and language rather than substance and fairness. So-called "technical" arguments
about written pleadings can be frustrating and irritating, but there is a balance to be struck in considering the role and usefulness of debates. The
other side of the coin is that often debates are helpful in focusing minds and
factual issues. They can prevent cases proceeding to proof which really
have little prospect of being successful.[32] The problem with that is that this
might well be seen as depriving a party of his day in court when he has a
chance to put his case across.[33] Clients can perceive that the case has been
thrown out at a debate because of some strange legal technicality which
really has very little to do with the strength of the claim, and think this is
plainly unfair, not least because they cannot understand it. The rules about
prior notice of arguments mean that no solicitor should be taken completely
by ambush and miss the opportunity to consider and deal with valid criticisms of substance relating to the written formulation of the claim. Other
basic principles which are crucial to a proper understanding of debates are:

(1) the pleadings under attack—well, badly, or indifferently expressed
    —have to be read as if they were completely true, and should be inter-
    preted broadly and in favour of the pleader[34];

---

[29] Unfortunately life's not like that.
[30] There should be no good reason for not giving this information, and if the point or
points which you are taking are good ones there is no harm in advising your opponent.
[31] For further explanation of what happens at a debate in the sheriff court see Hennessy,
Practical Advocacy in the Sheriff Court (Edinburgh: W. Green, 2006), Ch.6
[32] A case which illustrates different views as to whether the pleadings in a particular personal injury claim should be allowed to go to proof or should be dismissed at debate is
Mitchell v Glasgow City Council, 2008 S.L.T. 368. It is understood that this decision
has been appealed to the House of Lords.
[33] It has been suggested, unsuccessfully, that debate deprives a party of a right to a fair
trial, or his "day in court".
[34] See *Jamieson v Jamieson*, 1952 S.L.T. 257.

(2) an action can only be dismissed at a debate if, reading the averments as if they were true, the claim was bound to fail even if the pursuer proved all the facts stated by him in his averments[35];
(3) in personal injury cases, a claim should only be dismissed on relevancy and/or lack of specification, in rare and exceptional cases.[36] Consequently, such a pursuer should usually be allowed his chance of his day in court to tell his story, provided the story (in the pleadings) might remotely justify a claim against the proposed defender.

When the case calls before a sheriff for debate, it is quite likely that the sheriff will not have had an opportunity to study the pleadings in the record in advance of the debate and may have done no more than read the pleadings quickly once. He is not required to do otherwise and so he comes to the case and to the arguments completely cold. He may not have the legal propositions at his fingertips and, if the arguments are complex and involve detailed review of the law and the facts, he will require to have the whole justification for the debate and the plea explained fully to him. It is important to appreciate this when proceeding to conduct a debate. If we assume that, in a sheriff court ordinary cause, the defender has a preliminary plea directed against the pursuer's pleadings which states the general plea that the case is irrelevant then, in broad terms, he might proceed at the debate as follows:

(1) advise the sheriff of the preliminary plea which he intends to argue;
(2) advise the sheriff of what he wishes the sheriff to do with the case if he sustains the preliminary plea;
(3) read the record to the sheriff or at least confirm that the sheriff has read the record prior to hearing argument;
(4) make submissions in support of his plea expanding upon the arguments advanced in the r.22.1 note. This may well involve an analysis of the material facts contained within the opponent's averments and a discussion of the law applicable to these particular facts or some other explanation as to why the party thinks that the action should be dismissed or that it would be inappropriate and inadvisable for the case to proceed to a full hearing of evidence without certain matters being explored, explained, canvassed or otherwise detailed in the opponent's pleadings.

When responding to this, the solicitor for the opponent would normally: **17–11**

(1) explain in broad terms what he would like the court to do with the case, e.g. fixing a proof;
(2) advise the court what he considers the court should do in relation to his opponent's preliminary plea;

---

[35] See *Miller v SSEB*, 1958 S.C. (HL) 44 and *Mitchell v Glasgow City Council*, 2008 S.L.T. 368.
[36] See *Miller and McGeouch v Strathclyde Regional Council*, 1985 S.L.T. 321.

(3) address the comments or criticisms made by the opponent in support
of the plea. For example, he could point out that the factual averments can be interpreted broadly, or are capable of being understood
as stated. He could argue that the law is not as suggested by his
opponent, or argue that it is simply not possible to determine any
questions of law until such time as the evidence has been heard
regarding the whole circumstances of the case.[37]

Difficulties can arise in deciding whether one party has given "fair
notice" of his claim to another. The court should not hear evidence at a
proof about matters which are not outlined[38] within the parties' pleadings.
The purpose of the pleadings is to give the opponent advance notification
of your case. Accordingly, it can be argued that it is not good enough to
respond to a criticism at debate of a lack of detail in the pleadings by saying that the detail will all emerge at the proof. If the detail is crucial to the
relevancy of the case, then it ought to be averred. However, if a matter of
fine detail is sought by the opponent, then he will have to explain why he
requires the fine detail. He may well be able to do so on the basis that the
law regarding a particular situation is so clear and precise that particular
facts would need to be pled (so that evidence of them can properly be led
at the proof) or alternatively that, in the absence of some detail, the
defender is prejudiced in his attempt to prepare the case for a proof.

If the opponent also has a preliminary plea,[39] then he will proceed to
argue his own preliminary plea after responding to the opponent. In arguing his preliminary plea he will proceed as above and then, when he has
finished his argument, his opponent will have to respond to that. Logically,
the person arguing for dismissal of the action[40] on the basis that his opponent's pleadings are irrelevant or lacking in specification, would normally
have his argument dealt with first. If his argument is successful, then it
does not matter that the pursuer has criticism of the defences. If there is no
relevant claim, then the question of the defences becomes academic.

Possible outcomes of debate

17–12 These are the normal procedural consequences of a debate:

(1) the sheriff could sustain the preliminary plea and dismiss the action;
(2) the sheriff could sustain a preliminary plea by a pursuer against the
defender's averments and repel the defences, i.e. say that the defences
are not defences at all. This could give rise to him granting decree
de plano[41] or fixing a proof on quantum;

---

[37] In other words, that the court should fix a proof before answer.
[38] An "outline" is sufficient but often questions arise as to whether the outline is clear
enough.
[39] There is no reason why both parties could not have a preliminary plea against each other
and quite often they do.
[40] The defender.
[41] See Ch.19.

(3) the sheriff could repel the preliminary plea for a defender which basically means that he does not agree with the defender's argument and he considers there is no question of law arising either on the pleadings or in the circumstances of the case. The case would go to proof;

(4) the sheriff could repel the preliminary plea or pleas for the pursuer and state that the defences are quite relevant and sufficiently detailed, so that the case would then proceed to a proof on the basis of the defences as stated;

(5) the sheriff could reserve the preliminary plea or pleas for the parties. This means that he does not decide the issue at the debate but he leaves the preliminary plea(s) standing and fixes a proof before answer.[42] For example, he might take the view that he cannot decide the question of law which might arise in the case until such time as he has heard evidence about it, or that he is not satisfied there is insufficient detail pled in the writ or in the defences, which would be prejudicial to the defenders and prevent a case going to proof. This does, of course, give rise to a problem when people start to lead evidence at a proof which is not strictly in conformity with the averments. If a party has criticised the lack of detail in his opponent's averments, and the sheriff considers the criticisms are not material, then there might be a problem for the pursuer if he comes along to the proof with evidence which is substantially broader (and significantly different) from that contained in his averments. The defender might be able to object to the leading of this evidence and, if that objection was sustained, that might be fatal to the whole or part of the pursuer's case;

(6) either of the parties can ask the court for leave to amend. Leave to amend can be sought (a) before the debate actually starts; (b) once the opponent's argument has been put; or even (c) after a reply is made to the opponent's argument and it appears that the reply is not commending itself to the sheriff.[43] It might be prompted (unofficially) by the sheriff, especially where he indicates that he is not finding your response to the other side's arguments rivettingly attractive. It cannot be ordered by the sheriff if not sought by the party whose pleadings are being criticised.[44] Nor can the court be asked to give a view on the merits of the opponent's argument before deciding whether to seek leave to amend. It would be done by way of a verbal motion at the bar asking the sheriff to allow a specific amendment of the pleadings there and then, or to allow the lodging

---

[42] See Ch.18.

[43] An experience which cannot be missed and is usually quite easy to recognise!

[44] See *Barton v Wm Low & Co*, 1968 S.L.T. (Notes) 27; also *Lord Advocate v Johnston*, 1983 S.L.T. 290.

of a minute of amendment.[45] The sheriff has a discretion to allow immediate amendment. He would confirm if the opponent was objecting to an amendment of the pleadings. If not, then amendment will often be allowed. If he was objecting, then the sheriff would have to consider the arguments advanced at the debate and in support of the motion to amend, and make a decision. The major principle governing amendment is the principle that an amendment should be allowed at the discretion of the sheriff, "if it is necessary for determining the true matters in controversy between the parties".[46] On that approach, leave to amend will often be allowed, especially where it seems that the criticisms are matters of technicality or matters of pleading which could be cured if the case was simply framed better or expressed differently. The court would be reluctant to prevent a party amending if the solicitor said that he felt that an amendment could be done, i.e. there was evidence to justify making an amendment which would cure any criticisms made by the opponent. It is always a matter for the discretion of the court whether to allow leave to amend, and it cannot be taken for granted that leave will be allowed.[47] There can also be problems with seeking leave to lodge an amendment materially affecting the basis of the claim outwith the appropriate limitation period for the purposes of time bar.[48] Some sheriffs may seek to confirm what the nature of the amendment would be, in order to satisfy themselves that a person is not simply looking for leave to amend as a means of buying some time, but that they actually have or can produce something more relevant and will be able to make an amendment which will have a material effect on the case and move it on procedurally.

17–13 If amendment is sought and granted, then the court will pronounce an interlocutor to the effect that the court has heard the parties in debate, that the pursuer has sought leave to amend, that there has been no objection from the defender[49] and that the pursuer has been allowed a specified period of time[50] within which to lodge a minute of amendment. The defender would usually then be allowed time to answer the amendment and then the case would be continued to a

---

[45] There is an important and significant difference between allowing a party an opportunity to lodge a minute of amendment and actually allowing the pleadings to be amended. The court can allow a party an opportunity to lodge a minute of amendment and then, after further consideration and argument, can decide not to allow the pleadings to be amended.

[46] OCR Ch.18; RCS Ch.24.

[47] e.g. if you have amended on a number of occasions at earlier diets of debate or even before debates had taken place, then there might come a time when the court would consider that you had already had sufficient opportunity to put your pleadings into a proper state and it was too late to amend now.

[48] See *Pompa's Trustees v Edinburgh Magistrates*, 1942 S.C. 119; also *Sellars v IMI Yorkshire Imperial Ltd*, 1986 S.L.T. 629 and *Cork v GGHB*, 1997 S.L.T. 404.

[49] Or otherwise.

[50] Usually 14 or 28 days.

specified hearing on the amendment,[51] so that the court could consider whether to allow the pleadings to be amended as proposed, and what to do with the action after the amendment procedure has taken place. That is the theory but, in practice, the amendment procedure can last considerably longer than the period initially set down by the courts. If the amendment is complex and difficult, and if it requires further information and further enquiry, then it can take some time for amendment to be prepared. If a detailed amendment is prepared, then it may take some time for the defender to answer it and obtain the necessary information to enable him to do so. After the defender has responded to an amendment made by a pursuer, then the pursuer himself might want to come back with further alterations to his pleadings. The court can often order a further period for adjustment of the amendment to give the parties time to redraw their pleadings in the light of the earlier debate, amendment, and answers. There is no obligation on the court to do this but it usually makes sense. It is not uncommon for actions to undergo a fairly lengthy amendment procedure. Strictly speaking, the rules do not contemplate this but, in practice, there can be very good and sensible reasons for allowing such a period;

(7) it should also be noted that as well as dealing with the whole of the merits of a case or of a defence the sheriff can, in the context of a diet of debate, deal with some part of the pursuer's pleadings or the defender's pleadings and exclude parts of them from proof. If he does not allow a part of the case to go to proof, then this is called, "excluding it from probation". It can sometimes be a worthwhile exercise where there is a distinct part of the case which would require quite detailed and time-consuming evidence but which is irrelevant, and therefore there would be no benefit in wasting court time in hearing evidence about it. It is also open to argument at debate that if a claim proceeds on a number of distinct legal bases, e.g. breach of contract and breach of statute, then a debate can lead to a decision that one of these bases is not relevant and if there are any facts in the case which are only relevant to that ground of action then there is no need to hear proof of them. It is difficult to understand the implications of this fully in a theoretical context.[52]

Debates and expenses

The party who "wins" the debate should obtain an award of the **17–14** expenses of the debate. Difficult questions might arise in particular cases where it is not clear who, if anyone, has "won" the debate. Quite significant amounts can be involved where a debate takes place followed by amendment and amendment procedure. The theory is that parties should

---

[51] See r.18.3 of OCR 1993.
[52] However, see *Stillie v Wilson*, 1990 S.L.T. 145 for an example.

have their pleadings in order by the time the record has closed on the first occasion. This means that if, as a result of unsatisfactory pleadings which give rise to the need for amendment, amendment procedure has to take place, then the party who is responsible for this should pay the expense of same. This in turn means that if a party is successful in having their criticism of the other side's pleadings upheld, it is quite likely that the court will make an award of expenses in favour of the successful party for the debate. Furthermore, the court may also make an award of expenses in favour of the successful party in respect of any subsequent amendment procedure. This means that the lodging of an amendment, and the lodging of answers and further procedure in the case necessitated by this, will all be done at the expense of the party who was responsible for having to do the amendment. This represents quite a significant penalty on expenses. It is, of course, in the discretion of the court to make an award of expenses and it is not necessary for the court to do so. It may be that during the amendment procedure the successful party has taken the opportunity, when answering the averments made in the amendment lodged by the other party, to make additional averments of their own unrelated to the amendment. This can sometimes lead the court to say that the expenses of the amendment procedure, or all of those expenses, should not be the responsibility of the amender, but there are no hard and fast rules about this. Often the court will reserve the question of expenses[53] until the final conclusion of the case because it does not want to make any decision on the rights or wrongs of the amendment until it sees how the action eventually resolves.

The expense of the debate and subsequent amendment is one of the most significant practical aspects of this stage of procedure. In an ordinary action in the sheriff court, an adverse finding of expenses in respect of a diet of debate and subsequent amendment procedure could easily total as much as £400 or £500.[54] Indeed, if it is a very lengthy debate, the liability for expenses could total significantly more than that. In the context of a relatively simple ordinary cause in the sheriff court for payment of (say) £5,000 that can very significantly affect the economic benefit to the client of pursuing the litigation.[55] On the other hand, if an amendment is necessary in order to preserve the existence of a claim which would otherwise be dismissed, then an amendment may just have to be done, regardless of cost.

---

[53] In other words defer the decision on liability for expenses of the amendment and any necessary procedure connected with it.

[54] i.e. the client would incur a liability to pay the opponent this amount, not to mention that he would have to pay you, his own solicitor, a similar amount for having to amend—a double penalty in effect and one which might well be difficult to justify to a client if the only reason for the amendment was some deficiency in the presentation of the case. The cost of comparable procedure in the Court of Session is substantially greater.

[55] See Ch.21.

APPEAL

It is open to either party to appeal against certain decisions taken at a **17–15** debate.[56] Leave may well be required.[57] There is an important and subtle distinction between appealing against the dismissal of an action (or of defences) after a debate, and an appeal against the refusal by a sheriff to allow a party leave to amend his case following upon an acceptance by a party that the criticisms of his opponent at the debate were valid. In the first example, the appeal would argue that the judge was not entitled to dismiss the action or defences on the basis of the written pleadings as they stood. In the second example, the appeal would argue that, although the pleadings did indeed merit dismissal of the action or repelling of the defences, the sheriff ought to have exercised his discretion and allowed the party an opportunity to rectify the defects. It would consequently be an appeal against the sheriff's exercise of discretion in refusing the proposed amendment.[58]

JUDGMENT FOLLOWING DEBATE

In the absence of concession or motions to amend, the court will be **17–16** required to adjudicate on the arguments advanced at the debate. If the point is a simple one, then the court could issue a decision there and then. It is more usual in cases of substance for a decision to be reserved,[59] so that the sheriff can consider the averments, the arguments, and the authorities to which he has been referred and then issue a written judgment. The written judgment will normally contain a note which should record the arguments presented by the parties to him, his decision on the legal issues raised before him and state the sheriff's order with regard to the further procedure in the case (if any). There is no time limit within which the judgment must be issued.

---

[56] See Ch.20.
[57] This is a complex subject. See Ch.20.
[58] See Ch.20.
[59] The sheriff makes avizandum.

CHAPTER 18

PROOF, PROOF BEFORE ANSWER AND JURY TRIAL

18–01 These are the three types of hearing at which evidence about the merits of a case will be led. These are proofs, proofs before answer ("PBA") and jury trials. They can be regarded as the civil equivalents of a criminal trial. Of course, the rules of evidence and procedure in a civil proof are significantly different from those in a criminal trial[1] and the conduct of a civil proof is quite distinct from the conduct of a criminal trial.[2] There is a subtle difference between a proof and a proof before answer which we will consider shortly but, from the point of view of procedure before and during the hearing, the distinction between the two is not particularly significant.

Almost all hearings of evidence in Scotland are by way of proof/PBA.[3] Only very rarely do cases go to jury trial, and it should be noted that jury trial is only available in some types of action in the Court of Session. Apart from giving a brief outline of the circumstances in which a jury trial might be available and a very short description of the basic procedures, we will not dwell upon the particular specialities of jury trials.[4]

What these hearings all have in common is that they are the stage of procedure at which the parties will present to the judge (or to the jury) the evidence which they wish to lead in order to prove their case. Generally speaking, this will comprise the evidence of witnesses who will testify on oath about the material facts in dispute in the case and evidence in the form of any documents which might be relevant to the case. It is worth re-emphasising that the primary purpose of pleadings and procedure from the commencement of the action to the date of the proof is to focus the matters which are in dispute between the parties and to assist the parties in determining what evidence to place before the court in order to support their case.

---

[1] To confuse matters further, in England and America a civil proof is called a "trial".

[2] The same applies to civil/criminal jury trials.

[3] Unless otherwise indicated, reference to proof from now on includes PBA.

[4] Reference should be made to Andrew M. Hajducki, *Civil Jury Trials*, 2nd edn (Edinburgh: Avizandum, 2006).

PROOF AND PROOF BEFORE ANSWER

The court will decide, after hearing evidence at a proof, whether one or **18–02** other party has established to the satisfaction of the court the facts of which prior notice has been given in the written case.[5] If one looks at it this way, one can see that most of the procedure leading up to any hearing of evidence can be viewed as little more than a preparation for the proof by identifying with some degree of refinement what the respective parties are arguing about, what they will have to try and establish, and what the court may hear evidence about.

Relatively few cases actually go to proof.[6] Most of them settle, although many of those which settle do not do so until shortly before the hearing of the proof itself. Many settle on the morning of the proof, "at the door of the court".[7] Although we will consider the procedural aspects of proof it should be appreciated that the simple fact of allocating a date for a proof[8] is an important psychological trigger. The fixing of a date for proof is a powerful incentive to the parties to ensure that their preparations are full and complete. An imminent date for proof concentrates the mind because the proof is the hearing at which the case will be won or lost. The prospect for witnesses of actually having to appear in court becomes much more real and immediate. Thoughts of settlement may start to come to the fore even amongst the most determined of clients or their legal representatives.[9] In this connection, the assigning of a proof date in personal injury actions in the Court of Session at a very early stage of the procedure might help that process and there are other procedural devices in place to encourage settlement.

For example, in a claim for damages following a road accident, if it is alleged that a defender's car crossed the centre line of a road and caused an accident which injured the pursuer, and this is contradicted by the defender, the respective position of the parties should be easy to establish from the written pleadings.[10] The proof could be concerned with hearing evidence from a variety of different people talking about their perception of the circumstances, their view of the accident, their recollection of the movement of the vehicles, the length of skid marks, scientific evidence about the nature of the collision, evidence about comments

---

[5] Although usually the primary onus is on the pursuer to establish his case, we shall leave aside more complex questions about onus of proof, etc. for the time being.

[6] No reliable statistics are available but it is thought that about 95 per cent of Court of Session ordinary actions settle without proof and sheriff court actions are probably about the same.

[7] The reasons for this are complex and not entirely objectionable, although it is difficult to justify last minute settlements.

[8] Usually a few months ahead, although there can be wide variations on this.

[9] Of course, all of these points should have been considered before the later stages of the case but, in reality, they often are not.

[10] The defender may be saying that the pursuer actually crossed the centre line or he may have some good explanation for why he did so.

made immediately after the accident by one or other driver, etc. Sketch plans of the location, photographs of the vehicles and medical reports on the injuries could all be lodged as productions and used as evidence at the proof. All of this evidence taken together would be intended by the respective parties to satisfy a court on the balance of probabilities that their version of events has been established as being more likely. The court may be required to decide no more than that.[11] There are risks of success and failure for both sides. Could one or other side be certain of succeeding? Compromise of some kind might be highly desirable for both in these circumstances.[12] This is just the kind of case which might well settle as it comes up to a proof diet. A settlement would save the court expense of both parties, which could be considerable.

The decision of the court will be dependent upon the evidence which the parties choose to put before the court and which the parties are allowed to put before the court at the proof, so as to satisfy the court that they have established the facts on which they are relying. The court itself has no power to seek out proof from any other source and the court must decide the case solely on the evidence led by the parties. The court might like to determine the absolute truth of what happened, but in the real world can only decide what is proved by the evidence it has heard. The type and amount of evidence led by either party at such a proof would depend upon various considerations. Obviously each party has to make a judgment as to what he considers has to be proved to make out the claim as a matter of fact. A party has to decide what facts have to be established in order to demonstrate that there is a good legal basis for a court granting decree in its favour or refusing to grant a decree. In any proof, after the evidence has been led, the parties would make arguments to the court as to what facts they considered had been established by the evidence and, therefore, whether the pursuer or the defender should succeed with the claim and obtain a decree.

DIFFERENCE BETWEEN PROOF AND PROOF BEFORE ANSWER

18–03 Two of the most difficult questions which confront any court practitioner are, "What is the difference between a proof and a proof before answer?", and "Is it in my interests to agree a proof or a proof before answer, or should I insist upon taking a legal issue in the case to debate?"

This is an attempt to answer those questions but, although they can be explained in an abstract way, the explanation may not make any sense until it can be seen in operation in an actual litigation. Indeed, it is probably necessary to experience the problems in a number of litigations which have been taken to a conclusion before their practical significance is appreciated.

---

[11] Leaving aside questions of onus again.
[12] The cynical practitioner's definition of a settlement is a compromise which leaves both sides equally unhappy.

A proof is a hearing of evidence of the material facts in a case in which the only real issue the court is asked to decide is which evidence or body of evidence is to be preferred. Once it has decided that issue the result of the case will follow. In other words, once it has decided, e.g. in Mr X's case regarding the timber supplies where the parties are disputing what the price of the goods was to be, that the evidence establishes that the parties agreed the price was £10,000, then that is sufficient for the court to reach its "verdict".

A working definition of a proof before answer would be a proof in a case in which the court considers it necessary to hear the evidence of both parties before deciding any legal questions which may have to be resolved in order to make a final decision in the case. Using a similar analogy, Mr X might say that the goods were faulty and the faults were such as to entitle him to repudiate the contract. The other party might argue that the goods were not faulty but, even if they were, the faults were not so material as to entitle the opponent to repudiate. The court would have to decide, as a matter of fact, exactly what faults there were and would do so by considering the factual evidence. Once it had made that decision on the facts, it may then have to decide whether the precise defects which it found to have been established were such as to amount to a material breach of contract. That is a question of law but it could not really be assessed until the court had resolved the disputed facts upon which the legal decision would depend.

The court and the parties would have to face up to the question of what **18–04** procedure would be appropriate for resolving this particular dispute at the time when the record was closed and the written pleadings of the parties were available for consideration. Each party would have to analyse his respective position. In the second example quoted above, the pursuer would be facing a preliminary plea to the relevancy of his claim (and may also have a plea himself against X's pleadings). The pursuer might not understand the basis for X's legal argument. He might simply think that all the court required to do was decide whether the goods were faulty or not. He might therefore think that there was no justification for a plea to the relevancy. He would consider that he would be entitled to have a debate in order to have the plea repelled so that a proof simpliciter[13] could take place. In that way, he would know that all he had to do at the proof was lead sufficient evidence and he would win. If he understood, or thought he understood, the point which was being made by Mr X in his pleadings regarding relevancy, i.e. material breach, then he might agree that a proof before answer would be appropriate. He might concede that the issues were of, "mixed fact and law"[14] and the legal issue could not be resolved until the court had decided the facts.

---

[13] In other words, a proof as opposed to a proof before answer.
[14] A phrase which is used often in this context.

Problems can arise, however, when a party takes a plea to the relevancy of an opponent's case and it is not entirely clear what the legal argument is. This problem has lessened somewhat because of the requirement in the OCR and RCS to give advance notice of such arguments for the purposes of a debate/procedure roll hearing. Nonetheless, there can be tactical advantages in making the other party explain the legal "trick" which he thinks might have a bearing on the outcome of the case rather than agree a PBA. At a PBA, he might only find out the "catch" when evidence has been led, and it is too late to retrieve the position.

It is often thought that most defenders will want a debate when they have taken a preliminary plea because they want to argue for dismissal of the action. There is a tactical advantage to a defender in doing so because, in a sense, the defender has nothing to lose. If he wins the argument, the action is dismissed. If he loses the argument, i.e. the court decides the pleadings are not irrelevant, the court would fix a proof or a PBA and the defender has another bite at the cherry after evidence is led. This approach means that a pursuer might often be very glad to agree a PBA to avoid running the risk of having the action dismissed at debate. He may not, by doing so, find out exactly what argument the defender is going to produce out of his hat once the "proof" part of the case is finished.

If a party has a preliminary plea against an opponent, the opponent might want to have the plea dealt with at debate or at least satisfy himself exactly what the point of the plea is if the opponent is willing to agree a PBA. It should be stressed that the appropriate procedure to follow does not depend simply upon what the parties think or agree. The court has to sanction that procedural approach and in many cases the court will have its own view, after hearing argument, as to what would be appropriate. The court will ultimately decide what procedure to follow.

Arguments about whether a case would be appropriate for proof, PBA, or debate occupy a considerable amount of court time and procedure. It can be said that there are few cases in which some legal issue does not have to be resolved after evidence is led, and yet some of the most complex cases are often decided on pure matters of fact.

Even more difficult is the tactical question of whether it would be in the interests of one or other party to have a PBA in any case or not. This issue is most frequently and conveniently discussed in the context of an action of damages for personal injury. It may be possible to amplify the explanation about the role of a PBA and the procedural niceties which surround the fixing of a PBA by reference to a well-known personal injury case. It should be noted that this was decided at a time when many actions for personal injury were dismissed at debate.[15] Nowadays, debates are positively discouraged in personal injury actions and require to be specifically justified in other procedures. Expressing

---

[15] Perhaps reflecting the attitudes of the day that not every accident should give rise to a claim. Things are very different now!

the arguments in the case very simply, the issue was whether the pleadings disclosed that the defender owed a duty of care to the pursuer. The persons to whom a defender might owe a duty to take reasonable care (the "neighbour" of *Donoghue v Stevenson*[16] fame) were persons whom the defenders could reasonably foresee as being likely to suffer injury as a consequence of some act or omission on their part.

In the case of *Miller v SSEB*[17] a child was injured whilst playing in a **18–05** council house from which the tenant had been decanted prior to the house being demolished. The council had asked the electricity board ("SSEB") to remove their services prior to the demolition taking place. The SSEB had done so to a certain extent but there was still some supply of electricity to fittings within the house. Some unknown person had entered the house after the SSEB had completed their work, and had vandalised the electric fittings in such a way as to cause a section of electric wire to be exposed. No one was supposed to be in the house, but the pursuer was playing there and he gripped the exposed wire as a result of which he suffered a shock.

This description is a summary of what was being alleged in the written pleadings by both parties. The pleadings of both parties do not contain precisely detailed averments of all the minute matters of fact which make up the whole background to the case. Clearly, the defenders were not in a position to know the truth or otherwise of some of the things which the pursuer was alleging, e.g. how the pursuer came to be there and what he was doing, and the pursuer was not in a position to know the truth or otherwise of some of the things which the defenders were alleging, e.g. what arrangements the defenders had made regarding the security of the electric wiring. There was no doubt, however, that there was sufficient in the written pleadings of both parties to enable them both to accept that they had full and proper notice of what the other party was saying[18] and, accordingly, of the general facts which they were likely to try and establish and which their opponent would be trying to prove.

The defenders took the case to debate and argued that the pursuer's claim should be dismissed because it was irrelevant. The argument was that, on the basis of the written averments for the pursuer, and accepting that those averments were true for the purposes of the debate, it could not be said that, as a matter of law, the defenders owed a duty of care to the injured boy. Moreover, it could be argued that there was nothing to demonstrate that the defenders had in fact been negligent, i.e. had failed to comply with any duty of reasonable care which might have been incumbent upon them. Furthermore, it could have been argued that any negligence on the part of the SSEB (not that this was conceded) could

---

[16] *Donoghue v Stevenson*, 1932 S.L.T. 317.
[17] *Miller v SSEB*, 1958 S.L.T. 229.
[18] If not, they would have taken pleas to lack of specification.

be said to have caused the accident. It could have been argued that the accident was caused by the fault of the third party and/or by the fault of the boy himself and the defenders did not do anything or admit to doing anything which could possibly be said to have caused the accident.

At debate, the judge in the Court of Session decided that there was no duty of care incumbent on the defenders. He looked at the pursuer's averments and indicated that he felt they were not sufficient to indicate that the defenders could possibly owe a duty to the pursuer. The Inner House agreed with him on appeal. On appeal to the House of Lords, the House of Lords expressed the view that it was simply not possible to say at the stage of debate that there was no duty on the defenders in the circumstances of that case and that a court could not decide that it was beyond argument that the defenders had not been negligent. In essence, the House of Lords said that there were many interesting questions to be asked and answered about the whole background. The averments gave sufficient notice of the types of things which were being alleged. Some of the things being alleged might not in fact be proved. Some of them might be proved in a qualified or amended way. Some of them might be proved and expanded upon or added to. Until the full circumstances of the whole case had been explored in the evidence—and remember that many of the allegations on both sides were unknown to each other and might well be disputed—it was not possible to make any pronouncement on the law applicable to that particular case. Accordingly, it was considered appropriate that the form of proof in the case should be a PBA. The court could first decide, after applying the rules of evidence, what facts had been established from the whole variety of facts alleged and then the court could decide, on the basis of the proven facts, what the applicable law was.

18–06   If the case proceeded to proof it was quite possible that the pursuer might have been unable to prove exactly how the accident happened. He might have been unable to prove by inference or otherwise that anyone else had interfered with the electricity supply. The defenders might establish that it was more likely that the pursuer himself had vandalised the electricity supply. There might have been very good justifiable reasons for not removing all of the electricity supply to the house so that the failure to do so may have been in accordance with normal and good practice. All of these matters of detail would be impossible to decide until such time as a proof had been heard. It can be seen that, if the facts came out in some of the ways suggested above, this would have an effect upon the law applicable to the case and upon the question of whether it could be established on the facts that there was some fault or breach of a duty of care on the part of the defenders which actually caused the accident.[19]

---

[19] An extremely interesting case in which there was a difference of opinion in the Inner House as to whether an action should be dismissed at debate or not, and one in which the underlying principles discussed in the text above were fully canvassed was *Mitchell v Glasgow City Council*, 2008 S.L.T. 368. The case was decided in February 2008 and it is understood that it has been appealed to the House of Lords.

In many personal injury accidents, the court might not be able to make any final decision as to whether a duty of care did arise or whether a defender had failed to comply with a duty of care which did arise until it heard evidence about the precise nature of the relationship between the parties and the precise circumstances of the accident.

On the one hand, this can mean that a defender who considers that the pursuer may have problems in establishing legal liability in the circumstances can keep his cards close to his chest, agree a PBA, and leave the pursuer's claim to fail because he has failed to establish sufficient facts to give rise to a duty of care. If the pursuer was unaware or had not fully appreciated that such a particular argument arose and that certain specific facts had to be proved in order to establish a duty of care, then he would lose the PBA simply as a result of failing to lead sufficient evidence.

On the other hand, it can be argued that if the defender has taken a plea to the relevancy of a pursuer's averment, then it is in the interests of the pursuer to insist that the case proceed to a debate so that he can at least find out what the defender's arguments are. This proposition is less valid now that we have procedures in OCR (r.22.1 note) and RCS (note of arguments)[20] for giving advance notice of legal arguments and indeed a r.22.1 note is intended to circumscribe any legal arguments which can be made at a PBA as well as at a debate.[21] If the defender's argument is that the pursuer may not have pled a relevant case against him because, to make out a relevant case, the pursuer would have to make certain factual averments, then this would give the pursuer the opportunity to amend his case and make the appropriate factual averments if they were supported by evidence. Sometimes it might seem to the pursuer that the defender's plea to the relevancy is not particularly valid and he might be content just to let the matter proceed to a PBA. Most pursuers seem to be happy to accept a PBA but the problem for them is that there might be a sting in the tail. If there is any question mark over the relevancy of the claim, then it would certainly be beneficial to a party against whom a preliminary plea has been taken to insist that that plea should be at least argued and hopefully disposed of before the matter proceeds to a proof.[22] If it is not disposed of at debate, then the pursuer should know the full nature and extent of the submissions which are likely to be made after the conclusion of the "proof" part of the PBA.

JURY TRIAL

Jury trials in Scotland can now only take place in the Court of Session **18–07** and only in particular types of action. Formerly, jury trials could be

---

[20] See Ch.16.
[21] See r.22.1(4).
[22] See also *Gibson v Strathclyde Regional Council*, 1993 S.L.T. 1243 and *Argyll and Clyde Health Board v Strathclyde Regional Council*, 1988 S.L.T. 381.

taken in the sheriff court as well as the Court of Session but the right to jury trial in the sheriff court was abolished in 1980. Parties have always been entitled to take a personal injury action to a jury trial in the Court of Session for the last 150 years or more. There was an upsurge in interest in jury trials in about the mid-1990s. This interest was prompted by the realisation that substantial awards of damages might well be made by juries which were significantly in excess of what judges would make and accordingly agents acting for pursuers were, and are, anxious to capitalise on this. A jury trial cannot take place if there is a genuine issue of law[23] to be resolved in the case or where there is some special reason advanced for it being unsuitable for a jury.[24] All cases of the type which can competently be decided by a jury are regarded as being suitable for a jury, and it is for a defender to demonstrate that there is a special reason for not sending it to a jury. It might be thought, therefore, that most personal injury actions in the Court of Session would have proceeded to jury trial but, as a matter of practice, it is only recently that the procedure has been looked at again.[25] In the light of the comments made by Lord Hope in the House of Lords appeal in the case of *Girvan v Inverness Farmers Dairy (No.2)*,[26] and Lord Rodger in *McLeod v British Railways Board*,[27] it might be that the right to a jury trial in Scotland will in due course be reserved for only one or two special types of claim.[28] It can be expensive and time consuming to take a case to jury trial and there is no doubt that there is a degree of unpredictability about jury decisions which is not particularly satisfactory to the purists.[29]

PRACTICE AND PROCEDURE RELATING TO PROOFS

18–08 In general terms, any proof is required to be conducted continuously.[30] Some proofs[31] may be completed in a couple of hours. Some proofs can last several days. In practice[32] it is often not possible to secure sufficient days before the same judge to enable a case to be heard on consecutive days. Different courts have different administrative arrangements

---

[23] Of the type which might justify a PBA.

[24] There are numerous recent reported cases relating to whether an action is "suitable" for jury trial—rather illustrating the significance of this form of hearing in personal injury claims.

[25] In England, a jury trial for a personal injury case is very much an exception.

[26] *Girvan v Inverness Farmers Dairy (No.2)*, 1998 S.L.T. 21.

[27] *McLeod v British Railways Board*, 2001 S.L.T. 238.

[28] Although there is no sign of any legislative change.

[29] Nor to defenders who have had to pay large (but not US-style) damages awarded by a jury, nor to pursuers who lost their case but were not sure why.

[30] i.e. the evidence is all to be heard at the one time albeit that the proof might stretch over two or three consecutive days.

[31] Especially where parts of the evidence are agreed in advance.

[32] In particular in the sheriff court.

regarding the fixing of proofs. Some courts will ask the parties to estimate the number of days which would be required for a proof and will be content to set aside the appropriate number of days. Estimates of the length of time a proof might take can be notoriously inaccurate, but it should normally be possible to secure a sufficient number of days to have the case heard continuously.[33] It is possible now[34] to have a partial proof or a split proof on one particular aspect of a case rather than on the whole case.[35] For example, in a reparation action, one can have a proof on liability and a proof on the quantification of the claim heard separately. Indeed, the rules now permit proofs on any particular aspects of a case to be taken separately.[36] It is quite likely, however, that for some time to come most proofs will not be split, and the following text ignores that possibility.

EVIDENCE

As previously indicated, the proof is all about evidence and the leading **18–09** of evidence in order to establish disputed facts. In broad terms, that evidence can be oral evidence of a witness, affidavit evidence of a witness, or documentary evidence. The parties have to consider what witnesses need to be cited and called and what productions need to be lodged in order to support their claim. There are rules about this. There are also rules designed to avoid the need to have witnesses attend in person. These rules are rarely invoked,[37] and the present practice is to have all evidence given by witnesses present at court who are subject to examination and cross examination. Whilst the courts are sympathetic to the principle that people should not be inconvenienced by being called as witnesses where this is unnecessary, there is no practice whereby a written statement of a witness will be regarded as taking the place of the evidence of the witness without any qualification.[38] It should also be noted that all but a minority of cases will be conducted in open court. Recent changes in the rules of the Court of Session and the sheriff court have allowed parties to ask the court to permit evidence to be given by a witness by way of a "live link". In addition, the rule allowed parties to

---

[33] In reality, however, this can be a major headache for all concerned.
[34] OCR r.29.6, r.40.12(3)(j) commercial action; RCS r.36.1, r.47.11(1)(b)(ix) commercial action.
[35] This does not seem to have proved particularly popular but it may do so in time.
[36] An interesting recent example is *Noble v De Boer (No.2)*, 2004 S.L.T. 1085, in which there was disagreement about the effect of findings made in one proof as ruling the facts in a subsequent proof in the same case.
[37] For reasons we shall see.
[38] It is necessary to mention this specifically because there may be a popular misconception (influenced by some practices in England) that witnesses do not need to attend court—in almost all cases witnesses must attend court.

make submissions by a live link. Whether this will be used in practice remains to be seen.[39]

Establishing facts without leading evidence

18–10   There are circumstances in which facts can be established in a case without the necessity of leading oral evidence from a witness:

(1) admissions on record—if, on a fair and proper reading of the record, averments by one party are admitted by the other or indeed where there is an implied admission[40] then that fact or those facts do not need to be proved.[41] There can sometimes be difficulty in identifying precisely what fact has been admitted, which can be overcome if the averments are clear and simple;

(2) parties can agree a joint minute of admissions[42] in connection with any matter of fact about which evidence might have been led. At the options hearing, the sheriff is empowered to make orders about the lodging of a joint minute of admissions or agreement in relation to matters of fact in connection with any proof which is allowed.[43] In practice, most sheriffs would not canvas the precise terms of any joint minute of admissions at that stage and might simply encourage the parties to agree what they could, e.g. the quantification of a simple claim. In any event, it is open to the parties prior to a proof to discuss and agree a joint minute of admissions and this is done quite often. The precise terms of the joint minute of admissions can be important[44];

(3) the parties can take advantage of a procedure known as a notice to admit.[45] These rules provide that, at any time after proof has been allowed, one party can intimate to the other a notice calling on him to admit certain specific facts. These have to be facts which relate to an issue averred in the pleadings and, inter alia, they could be the facts that a particular document which has been lodged in the case is an original document or is a true copy of an original document so as to avoid any formal evidence about the document itself. Once a party sends to another a notice to admit,[46] the other party has 21 days in

---

[39] Act of Sederunt (Rules of the Court of Session Amendment) (Miscellaneous) 2007 (SSI 2007/7) introduced a new RCS r.93.1 for the Court of Session and Act of Sederunt (Ordinary Cause, Summary Application, Summary Cause and Small Claim Rules) Amendment (Miscellaneous) 2007 (SSI 2007/6) introduced new rules for all sheriff court actions. Both commenced on January 29, 2007.

[40] See OCR r.9.7.

[41] In addition to this, in Court of Session procedure there is scope for a party to lodge a minute of admission of any matter regardless of whether it is formally admitted in the pleadings.

[42] This is a formal document lodged with the court and signed on behalf of both parties.

[43] See OCR r.9.12(3)(a), (b).

[44] See the case of *Lenaghan v Ayrshire and Arran Health Board*, 1994 S.L.T. 765.

[45] See OCR r.29.14; RCS rr.28A.1 and 28A.2.

[46] It could relate to one, or to a 100, individual facts.

which to intimate a notice of non-admission of any one of the facts. This would be done by simply advising the other party of the fact or facts which were not being admitted. If a notice of non-admission is made, then the fact remains disputed. If no notice of non-admission is made, then the party will be deemed to have admitted that fact which no longer requires proof. The court can allow a party to amend or withdraw an admission made in this way on such conditions as it sees fit. The party who serves the notice must lodge a copy of it in process[47];

(4) evidence on commission—where a witness who would normally be **18–11** required to attend court and give evidence is unable to do so for certain good reasons[48] then it is open to the party who wishes to lead that evidence to ask the court to have the evidence of the witness taken on commission.[49] Putting the matter very simply, the court would take the evidence of the witness separately and at a convenient time and place. The evidence can be taken by a judge but it can equally be taken by someone appointed by the court such as an advocate or a solicitor. The witness would be examined and cross examined as if it was a proof and his evidence would be noted by a shorthand writer. The transcript of that evidence would then be lodged with the process in the case so that when the proof was heard, the transcript of the evidence of that witness would effectively be read into the evidence given at the proof itself. There are particular rules about commissions to take evidence. A recent rule change has permitted parties to apply to the court to have the proceedings before the commissioner recorded by video recorder.[50]

(5) certain written statements can be received as evidence in a case in the Court of Session.[51] It is not clear exactly how this is intended to operate and it is rarely used;

(6) renouncing probation—both parties are entitled to advise the court that they do not wish to have any proof on matters of fact. This would normally be on the basis that all of the material facts were admitted. At any time after the closing of the record the parties can lodge in process a joint minute to the effect that they renounce probation and they can at the same time lodge a statement of admitted facts and

---

[47] It was felt that this whole procedure might avoid the unnecessary leading of a number of matters of evidence in proofs but, for some reason, the procedure has not proved very popular and it is infrequently used.

[48] Age, illness, infirmity, or other substantial reason—not inconvenience or personal preference.

[49] Not to be confused with a commission to recover documents.

[50] Act of Sederunt (Sheriff Court Rules) (Miscellaneous Amendments) 2008 (SSI 2008/223) for the sheriff court and Act of Sederunt (Rules of the Court of Session Amendment No. 4) (Personal Injuries Actions etc.) 2007 (SSI 2007/282) for the Court of Session.

[51] RCS r.36.8 provides the criteria which have to be met and the procedure for having such statements received as evidence. See *Glaser v Glaser*, 1997 S.L.T. 456.

productions. If the parties do this, then the sheriff can and will order a debate to take place on the agreed facts.[52]

These are the principal examples of situations where matters of fact will not require oral evidence of witnesses. Although efforts have been made to persuade parties to use other forms of evidence so as to minimise the calling of numerous witnesses or the leading of evidence which may not be controversial, these have not been particularly successful. The norm is still for parties to lead oral evidence to prove all but the most trivial or formal of facts.

Witnesses

(1) Witness precognitions

18–12   These are entirely private documents prepared by the solicitor for any party whose purpose is to give the solicitor for that party[53] some prior knowledge of what the witness is likely to say when giving evidence in court. There is a skill involved in taking reliable precognitions which are invaluable for the proper conduct of the case. They have no status as evidence in their own right.[54] The witness cannot come into court and simply refer to what his precognition says. Precognitions of witnesses are not used as evidence or as productions in civil cases in Scotland. This is in contrast to the position in England, where the "proofs"[55] of witnesses are lodged and are regarded as evidence.

(2) Lists of witnesses

There are rules in the different forms of procedure regarding the necessity to lodge with the court and intimate to the opponent a list of the witnesses a party is proposing to call.[56]

(3) Citation of witnesses

If a witness is required to attend court by a party to the action, then he must be sent a formal citation. The citation requires him to attend at court at a particular time and place. It advises him that he is entitled to claim his travel and other expenses and be paid these expenses before he actually attends as a witness if he requests payment before his attendance. There is a penalty on the witness if he fails to attend and steps can be taken to ensure his attendance.[57] It is not absolutely essential to cite

---

[52] This is relatively rare.
[53] Or counsel for that party.
[54] Although see *Highland Venison Marketing Ltd v Allwild GmbH*, 1992 S.L.T. 1127 and *Ellison v Inspirations East Ltd*, 2003 S.L.T. 291.
[55] Just to confuse matters, this is the English equivalent of precognition.
[56] These will be dealt with in detail later.
[57] This will be dealt with later.

a witness to give evidence in a proof.[58] If the witness turns up by informal arrangement, then the fact he has not been cited is neither here nor there. The practical benefit of providing a witness with a formal citation, however, is that if he fails to turn up, then the solicitor will be able to provide a certificate to the court to show that the witness has been properly cited. A case can be adjourned if a witness who has been properly cited fails to turn up. If a witness fails to attend but has not been properly cited it is unlikely that the court would adjourn. Special provisions may now be made for child witnesses or "vulnerable witnesses" as defined in the legislation.[59]

(4) Examination of witnesses

When witnesses are giving evidence, the witness will first be put on oath[60] by the judge. Then the witness will be examined by the party calling him, cross examined by the opponent or opponents, and then (if appropriate) re-examined by the examiner in chief. This is not the place to discuss the examination and cross examination of witnesses but it should be noted specifically that, in civil cases, hearsay evidence from any witness is perfectly admissible. It may carry little weight. It might be irrelevant and pointless. Nonetheless witnesses can, e.g. be asked about what other people might have said about an issue without any objection. This is in stark contrast to the rules regarding criminal cases.

(5) The care of a witness

A witness in a case is not allowed to be present in court whilst other witnesses are giving their evidence. After he has given evidence, then he may be required to wait in the court. In current practice, after giving evidence, most witnesses are excused from remaining in court. Witnesses are not to discuss their evidence with other witnesses in the case and steps are usually taken to ensure that this does not happen. If the witness is in the middle of giving his evidence and the case is adjourned, it is then sensible to ensure that he does not spend any time with others who have yet to give their evidence or indeed others who have given their evidence beforehand. The exclusion of witnesses from hearing other evidence in the case before they themselves have given evidence does not apply to the party to an action who might, of course, be a witness himself. Accordingly, the defender in a case who is going to give evidence himself can quite properly sit in court and listen to the pursuer and the pursuer's witnesses give their evidence.[61] Furthermore, an expert witness who is required to give evidence of his specialist opinion, is entitled to sit

---

[58] Although it is recommended in every case, including citation of one's own client.
[59] Vulnerable Witnesses (Scotland) Act 2004 (asp 3).
[60] Or asked to affirm.
[61] After all, it is his case.

in court and listen to the evidence of facts upon which his subsequent opinion is to be sought. The party who wishes to call him can ask for leave to allow him to sit in court and this is perfectly permissible. However, he is not supposed to sit in court whilst any opposing expert is providing his own expert opinion in relation to a similar matter.

(6) Recall of witness

It is open to the court and to the parties to ask for a witness to be recalled in certain circumstances.[62]

Productions

18–13   These are generally any documents which the parties want to put before the court as part of their proof of the disputed facts. They should be lodged some time before the proof. There are specific rules regarding productions, including how these should be lodged and when they should be lodged. The rules are slightly different in the different forms of procedure. One point worth mentioning is that a party may want to lodge a document simply for the purposes of enabling him to cross examine a witness, with a view to attacking the credibility or reliability of a witness. An example might be a witness questionnaire form completed by a witness in terms contradictory to the evidence he is giving in court.[63] The general view is that it is not necessary to lodge as a production a document which is going to be used to cross examine a witness.[64] However, it may be necessary to lodge as a production something which is going to be used solely to cross examine a *party* as opposed to a "witness" to the action.[65]

Rules regarding witnesses and productions

18–14   There are different rules regarding witnesses and productions in the different forms of procedure available in Scotland. This can be confusing and it might be helpful to summarise the main provisions applicable to each form of procedure.

Court of Session ordinary action

(1) Witnesses

18–15   There is no specific provision in the 1994 Rules regarding the intimation or exchange of a list of witnesses. This is, however, dealt with in

---

[62] See the Evidence (Scotland) Act 1852 s.4 and the Civil Evidence (Scotland) Act 1988 s.4.
[63] This is not like a precognition because it will be the actual words of the witness.
[64] Based upon *Paterson & Sons v Kit Coffee Co Ltd* (1908) 16 S.L.T. 180.
[65] For a more detailed discussion of this see *Robertson v Anderson* Unreported OH May 15, 2001, Lord Carloway.

Practice Note No.8 of 1994. This provides that, not later than 28 days prior to the proof, each party must give written intimation to every other party in the case of a list of their witnesses and must lodge a copy of that list in the court process. If a party wishes to call a witness not on the list, then, strictly speaking, he would need the leave of the court and a good explanation would be required.[66]

(2) Citation of witnesses

Witnesses are cited by virtue of a form of citation.[67] Citation is done by registered post, or by first class recorded delivery post, or by messenger at arms. A certificate of citation of a witness is provided in Form 36.2-B or C as appropriate.[68]

(3) Productions

Rule 27.1 provides that, if a party is founding on a document or has adopted as incorporated in his pleadings a document,[69] then he must lodge it at the same time as founding upon it. The other party is entitled to see these documents and they should be lodged in process. If they are not lodged, then the opponent can make a motion for recovery of them.

All productions which are intended to be used at a proof shall be lodged in process not later than 28 days before the diet of proof. Otherwise, the document cannot be used at the proof except with the consent of the parties or with the leave of the court.[70] A copy of every production shall be lodged for the use of the court at the proof not later than 48 hours before the proof.[71]

There are specific rules regarding attendance of witnesses and, inter alia, arrangements for looking after witnesses at court.[72]

Personal injuries actions and commercial actions

The specific rules regarding witnesses and productions in personal injuries actions are dealt with in Ch.6 and, in commercial actions, Ch.7.   **18–16**

Sheriff court ordinary actions

(1) Witnesses

The parties have to exchange a list of their respective witnesses within 28 days of the allowance of proof. The list should contain the name,   **18–17**

---

[66] In practice, parties often allow each other a degree of latitude in complying with this rule.
[67] See RCS Form 36.2-A.
[68] See RCS, r.36.2
[69] See Ch.3.
[70] See RCS r.36.3.
[71] See RCS r.36.4.
[72] See RCS r.36.9: there are no such provisions in the OCR for sheriff court cases.

address and occupation (where known) of the witness. The list requires to be lodged with the court at that time.[73] If a party wants to call as a witness a person who was not on the list, then he can only do so with the consent of the opponent or with the permission of the court.[74]

(2) Citation and attendance of witnesses

Citation of a witness in an ordinary action will be done by registered post, first class recorded delivery or by sheriff officer. It is done on a form[75] with a period of notice of seven days. In other words, for a citation of a witness in an ordinary action to be valid, it has to be done at least seven days before the proof diet itself.[76] If a witness fails to attend court having been properly cited, then he can be compelled to attend.[77]

(3) Productions

Any document founded upon in a party's pleadings, or any document which is adopted or incorporated into the party's pleadings must be lodged as soon as it is referred to by that party in the pleadings.[78] If this is not done and the other party who wishes to investigate the merits of the case or the defence to the case has to obtain a court order for that document to be produced to enable them to carry out enquiry, then the motion for recovery of that document will be done at the expense of the party who failed to lodge it as required.[79] This is rarely a problem.

Within 14 days of the allowance of proof, each party should intimate a list[80] of the documents which are or have been in his possession and control which are to be used at the proof together with details of where these documents are.[81] The opponent can inspect the documents in that list. If a party does not do this and the opponent objects to the document being used at the proof, then it is necessary to obtain permission from the sheriff to use the document. The intention behind this rule was to give early disclosure of the evidence in the case to an opponent. In practice, solicitors tend not to intimate such a list. This failure is rarely objected to in practice.

All productions to be used at the proof shall be lodged in the court process not later than 28 days prior to the proof itself. A party cannot use

---

[73] See OCR r.9.A.3
[74] See OCR r.9.A.3(2)
[75] Form G13.
[76] See r.29.7.
[77] See rr.29.9 and 29.10, compelling the attendance of the witness under pain of arrest and imprisonment.
[78] See r.21.1.
[79] See r.21.2.
[80] Only a list, not copies of the documents.
[81] See OCR r.9.13(1)–(3).

any production which has not been lodged at the appropriate time unless by consent of the opponent or with the permission of the sheriff.[82] A copy of every production should also be lodged for the use of the sheriff at the proof not later than 48 hours prior to the proof.[83]

Summary causes

(1) Exchange of list of witnesses

18–18

There is a requirement in the rules for the parties to exchange details of their respective witnesses, within 28 days of the date of fixing the proof.[84] Similar rules apply where there is a failure to do so, as apply in ordinary actions.

(2) Citation of witnesses

This is done by Form 26 and witnesses must be given not less than seven days notice of the proof.[85] The methods of service on a witness in a summary cause action are the same as for an ordinary action and similar penalties apply in respect of any failure to attend a summary cause proof as would apply to an ordinary action.

(3) Productions

There is no specific requirement to lodge documents founded upon in the pleadings at the time when the pleadings are made. It is reasonable to expect that if a document is to be relied upon as part of the proof of a claim,[86] then it will be lodged along with the summons for warranting.

There is no requirement to provide a list of documents upon which you are proposing to rely and which you might have in your possession to your opponent.

All of the productions in a summary cause proof have to be lodged along with an inventory not later than 14 days before the proof date itself. Notice of the lodging of the inventory should be sent to the other party at the same time.[87] Productions in a summary cause action lodged with the court in advance of the proof can be borrowed.

There are special rules regarding party litigants who may be entitled to borrow productions in some cases under special conditions. See r.17.3(4). There is some concern that party litigants may not return productions adverse to their interests.

---

[82] See r.29.11.
[83] See r.29.12.
[84] See r.8.6 of the SCR.
[85] See r.29 of the SCR.
[86] e.g. an invoice.
[87] Copies of the productions themselves should be sent to the opposing party. See r.17.1(3).

Small claims

(1) List of witnesses

18–19   No list of witnesses is required and there is no necessity to exchange details of witnesses. The sheriff may give directions to parties regarding the evidence which should be led, if evidence as such is necessary.[88]

(2) Citation of witnesses

Similar rules apply to the citation of witnesses for a small claim full hearing as apply to a summary cause proof. In essence, this means that witnesses have to be cited on seven days notice. Similar forms of citation as for summary cause proofs are used and similar penalties would apply in respect of a failure to attend.

(3) Productions

There is no specific rule about lodging productions founded upon in the statement of claim. However, in practice, if some document is being relied upon, then it might be expected to have that document attached to the statement of claim in the original summons. It is also open to a party to lodge a document simply by handing it over at the hearing.

Rule 16.1(1)—This provides that if a party is going to found upon any document or article in his possession which is reasonably capable of being lodged (e.g. a letter admitting a claim)[89] then he shall lodge that item or items with the sheriff clerk along with a list of the items lodged no later than seven days prior to the full hearing. He shall send a copy of that list to the other party.

Rule 16.1(3)—This provides that a party cannot use any other document at the full hearing other than those produced either with the summons or at the preliminary hearing or lodged seven days prior to the full hearing unless this is consented to by the opponent or unless the court grants leave to allow this to be done.

Shorthand writer

18–20   The evidence taken at an ordinary action in the sheriff court, an ordinary action, personal injury action and a commercial action in the Court of Session will normally be noted verbatim by a shorthand writer. There is no provision for the recording of evidence given at a proof in a summary cause action or in a small claim action other than recording by the sheriff taking notes himself.

The particular provisions regarding the recording of evidence in the sheriff court are contained within OCR r.29.18 and generally speaking

---

[88] Rule 9.2(4) of the small claim rules.
[89] But probably not a faulty washing machine.

provide that the evidence shall be recorded by a shorthand writer or by tape recording. There are quite specific rules about this, to which reference can be made.

In the Court of Session the provisions regarding recording of evidence are contained in RCS r.36.11. The rules are substantially the same. The recording of evidence in Court of Session proofs by way of tape recording is fairly common and by contrast it is fairly uncommon in sheriff court proofs. Formerly, all evidence was recorded by shorthand writers. The transcripts of the evidence given in the case will be prepared only if required by the parties or the court.[90]

CONDUCT OF PROOF

The conduct of a proof itself requires, inter alia, advocacy skills, knowl- **18–21** edge of the rules of evidence, and a clear grasp of the detailed facts of the case. The person conducting the proof must seek to provide an orderly presentation of the evidence and an orderly presentation of legal arguments. By the time an action has proceeded to a proof, both competing parties may often have accumulated a vast array of documents, court pleadings, and correspondence. It is beyond the scope of this book to discuss the detailed conduct of a proof, but a brief explanation of what is involved will help to put all of the foregoing rules into some practical context. From the perspective of a solicitor or advocate acting for a pursuer, the only documents which would be relevant and should be collated as preparation for a proof are likely to be the following:

(1) an up-to-date record showing the pleadings of the parties at the time of the proof;
(2) any notice to admit and relative notice of non-admission;
(3) a copy of any joint minute of admissions;
(4) a copy of the inventory[91] of productions for the pursuer together with numbered copies of all of the productions;
(5) a copy of the inventory(ies) of productions for the defender together with numbered copies of the productions themselves;
(6) a list of the witnesses for the pursuer;
(7) precognitions of all of the pursuer's witnesses including updated precognitions where necessary;
(8) a list of the witnesses for the defender;
(9) precognitions of the defender's witnesses or at least so many of the defender's witnesses as could be precognosced;
(10) preparatory notes for the examination and cross examination of the various witnesses;

---

[90] Practice varies between the Court of Session and the sheriff court.
[91] Or inventories.

(11)   preparatory notes together with any appropriate legal authorities to
       support any submissions on the facts or the law[92] or in relation to
       matters of admissibility of evidence or objections to evidence
       which can be anticipated.[93]

The proof should not be a haphazard and all embracing enquiry into the
circumstances of a claim but a carefully focused enquiry into specific
relevant facts and perhaps also the law applicable to them.[94] Detailed
preparation for a proof can be a time-consuming process, but some
would say that it really ought to start with the raising of the action and
continue until the proof itself. The pleadings and procedures we have
been discussing should, of course, be utilised with the goal of making
the proof easier to win.

18–22   What happens at the proof itself can vary infinitely, but it may be
helpful to have some general appreciation of the principal features one
can expect in the "normal" proof.[95] We will use as an example a sheriff
court proof in an ordinary action. Proofs in the Court of Session will normally be conducted by counsel,[96] and the practice is different in certain
respects although the principal features are very much the same.

Once it has been determined on the day of the proof that the proof
is in fact going to go ahead, the case will be called and the parties will
usually confirm that they are in a position to proceed. The court may be
advised of any preliminary matters. For example, if there is a joint
minute of admissions agreed between the parties, then this would be put
before the court at that stage. If the parties have reached agreement on
any other matters which might not be apparent from the pleadings then
the court would be advised. If there were any possible difficulties with
witnesses or with their availability throughout the proof then this might
be explained. There is no speech by either side explaining to the sheriff
what the case is about and what the respective parties are proposing to
prove. A reading of the record will disclose that.[97] Once any preliminary
matters have been dealt with, then the parties would commence the
proof by the pursuer leading his evidence.

In the usual case, the pursuer would lead at a proof, but there are special circumstances in which the defender would be required to lead.
Leaving that to one side, the pursuer's solicitor would normally lead the
pursuer as a witness first. There is no absolute requirement to do this.[98]

---

[92]   At the conclusion of the proof/PBA.
[93]   During the proof.
[94]   It is not necessary to deal with questions of law in a proof but only in a PBA.
[95]   A few years in practice will show that such a proof does not exist.
[96]   Or a solicitor advocate.
[97]   This is not done formally. Often, the sheriff will go off the bench, read the record and
       also look at the proposed productions to give him a basic idea of what the case is about.
[98]   However, if the pursuer gives evidence after he has been sitting in court listening to
       his witnesses—as he is entitled to do—then this might reduce the weight to be
       attached to his evidence.

After leading the pursuer first, it is entirely in the hands of the pursuer's solicitor to decide what other witnesses to lead and what order to lead them in. Even if he has given the court a list of the witnesses and given the opponent a list of the witnesses cited, there is no obligation on him to call any or all of those witnesses. It is a matter of judgment for the solicitor for the pursuer to decide how to deploy his witnesses and whether to use as evidence any productions which have been lodged. The simple lodging of a production in itself does not make the production evidence. There may be a joint minute of admissions agreeing that the production is evidence of something or other but, otherwise, productions are normally "spoken" to by witnesses which would involve the witness explaining what the production was, who had written it, and what general significance it might have in relation to the matters in dispute.

Any witness will be examined, cross examined and re-examined. It is also possible for a witness to be recalled in certain circumstances and this would probably be done at the end of the case. If a matter arises in the course of the proof about which a witness who has already given evidence was not asked, then it would be open to the court to recall, or to allow a party to recall, the witness. This is relatively unusual.

It is always possible that, during the course of a proof, a party will realise that he might need an additional witness or witnesses and has either not appreciated this or has overlooked the fact. It would be open to him to ask the court to be allowed to add additional witnesses. The court has a discretion to allow this and if, e.g. it seems that the additional witnesses are speaking to matters which the defender might want to contradict, then the court might allow an adjournment to give the defender an opportunity to consider whether he has additional witnesses. Again this would happen rarely. The proof should normally be taken continuously.[99]

18–23 While a witness is giving evidence, it is possible that a party could object to questions asked of the witness by the opponent. If an objection is taken on grounds of admissibility, relevancy or otherwise, then the grounds for the objection should be stated to the court. The sheriff should then enquire of the questioner what response he has to the objection to the question and if the questioner agrees with the objection, then the question will simply be struck out. If the questioner does not agree with the objection, then there can be an argument about the objection taken. In some circumstances it is appropriate to have the witness leave the court when the argument takes place because the arguments can often be about not just what the witness has been asked but about what he might be asked in the future. After hearing the submissions from the parties in relation to any objection, the sheriff will decide the objection. It is not uncommon for the sheriff's decision to be to allow a question to be asked, "subject to competency and relevancy", and this means that the sheriff will not decide there and then whether the question is objectionable but

---

[99] OCR r.29.17.

will allow the witness to answer the question and then consider the issue
at the submissions at the end of the case.

After the pursuer has led all of the witnesses he wishes to lead, he
should advise the court that he is proposing to close his case. It would
be recorded by the court that the pursuer had closed his case at that point
and then the court would hear the defender's proof. It is open to a
defender not to lead any evidence at all. He may consider that, after
hearing the pursuer's witnesses, the pursuer has not established his case.
He is perfectly entitled to take the view that there is no need for him to
lead any evidence but, if a defender decides not to lead any evidence,
then the court is entitled to draw the most favourable inference in favour
of the pursuer on any matter about which the defender could have led
evidence but did not do so.[100] The defender would lead evidence from
his witnesses in the same way as the pursuer leads evidence. The witnesses would be examined, cross examined and re-examined. Any productions lodged by the defender in order to support the defence would
have to be spoken to by the witnesses or agreed by a joint minute. After
the defender has led all of the evidence he wishes, then he would advise
the court that he is closing his case. That effectively ends the hearing of
all of the evidence in the case.

The next stage after the hearing of evidence as set out above is for
the parties to make submissions to the sheriff. There are many cases
in the sheriff court where the sheriff takes the view that he ought to have
the shorthand notes of evidence transcribed before he hears final submissions about the case. If this is not required, then the parties may
proceed straight into the submissions immediately after the evidence
has been heard.[101] The submissions might involve going through the evidence of the witnesses which were led, encouraging the sheriff to accept
your witnesses in support of the other witnesses, pointing out consisten-
cies or inconsistencies in the evidence and arguing about the credibility
and reliability of individual witnesses. The purpose of these submissions
will be to demonstrate to the court that any dispute on the facts should
be resolved in your favour.

Although the proof is supposed to be continuous, it is quite common in
practice for the proof to be adjourned after one day and not to be taken on
the next day or days. This is regrettable, especially in cases where the principal issues between the parties come down to matters of credibility of
witnesses. An adjournment may, however, allow time for shorthand notes
to be transcribed and available for the next proof date or it may be desirable for a variety of good reasons. The practice in the Court of Session is
to allow a number of days for the proof as a matter of course[102] so that a

[100] See *Johnstone v City of Glasgow District Council*, 1986 S.L.T. 50.
[101] Although sometimes a short adjournment would be sought to give the parties time to
prepare what they were proposing to say.
[102] All proofs for each week are scheduled to start on Tuesday.

case will normally be completed over the period of time allocated. It is rare for a transcript of the evidence to be obtained before hearing submissions in a Court of Session action.

CONDUCT OF JURY TRIAL

18–24

It is not intended to provide anything more than a rough introduction to what happens in a jury trial. Reference should be made to *Greens Annotated Rules of the Court of Session 2008/9*, Ch.37 and the notes relevant thereto for an excellent description of the details of the modern practice in jury trials.[103]

When a case is to be heard by a jury, the pursuer will have to give the jury at the outset certain specific questions to answer. These are called issues. Similarly, the defender can put questions to the jury and these are called counter issues. If there is disagreement about the issues or counter issues which are appropriate, these would have to be resolved or the jury trial could not take place. The questioning of witnesses in a jury trial is not, in principle, significantly different from that in a proof. However, the jury alone decide the facts. Since a jury trial can only be fixed if there is no question of law still to be decided, then it is the decision on the facts which is the only matter in dispute and the only matter the jury requires to consider. The function of the judge in a jury trial is simply to ensure that the parties adhere to the rules. The judge can give the jury some general direction but cannot tell them how to decide the facts and he cannot give them any indication as to what award they ought to be making. At the end of the hearing of the case, the jury is then asked whether they answer the issues in one way or another, and they will also be asked to award damages in respect of certain heads of damages as set out in the issues. The jury does not give any reasons or explanation for its decision on the issues.

---

[103] See also Hajducki, *Civil Jury Trials*, 2nd edn.

CHAPTER 19

DECREES

19–01 A decree is the order of the court containing the court's decision about the case or some part of it. Essentially, it is the "verdict" of the judge in the case. A decree would be granted by the court in response to what the pursuer asks for in his written pleadings[1] or what the defender asks for in his written pleadings.[2] Whilst the word "decree" describes the decision or order made by the court, reference to "the decree" normally denotes the official document issued by the court once the order has been made. This contains the authenticated details of the court decision or order. It should properly be called an "extract decree" as it is a copy of the court decree "extracted" from the records of the court. Extracting a decree has practical significance. The extract of the decree will be required if steps have to be taken to enforce the court's order for a defender to make payment.[3]

Of course, there can be many decrees where the court makes orders or decides something which does not involve any payment whatsoever. For example, a decree of declarator of rights of one kind or another or a decree ordering a party to do something.[4] The granting of a decree may be sufficient to enable the successful party to enforce his rights, but the extract of the decree may be required for other practical or administrative purposes. In the final analysis, the decree is just a piece of paper which does not automatically guarantee that a party will in fact obtain satisfaction of his debt or the achievement of his aims in the litigation. However, the decree will constitute the authority of the court to enable him to take the other steps which he might require to enable him to enforce his rights. In practice, the granting of a decree and the obtaining of an extract decree may be the first steps in the process of recovering money which is due to the client. That process is called doing diligence and we will deal with this briefly later in the chapter.

---

[1] In his crave and plea(s) in law.
[2] In his pleas in law.
[3] There are many cases in which the decision itself is sufficient to make the defender pay up, and many cases also where payment has to be wrestled from him.
[4] See Ch.13.

TYPES OF DECREE

Initially we shall identify and define the common types of decree which **19–02** can be granted by a court with a very brief introduction to what these decrees are. We shall then go on to look at the particular decrees in more detail and consider the rules of court which have a bearing upon the decrees. Many decrees will fit more than one of these definitions:

(1) decree in absence—this is a decree granted in favour of the pursuer when the defender does not respond formally in any way to the service of an action against him and does not take even the preliminary steps required to contest the litigation;

(2) summary decree—this will be granted in favour of a pursuer[5] in a defended action if and when the pursuer successfully moves the court to do so, on the basis that the defender's written pleadings are not considered by the court to disclose any real defence to the claim or part of it;

(3) interim decree—this will be granted in favour of a pursuer where the defences contain, or can be construed as, an admission of part of the pursuer's claim;

(4) decree by default—this is a descriptive name for any decree granted against either party because of some procedural lapse by that party. For example, one can have a decree for payment by default because of a failure to lodge defences on time. One can have a decree of dismissal by default because of a failure to attend court when obliged to do so;

(5) decree *de plano*—this describes any decree granted in favour of the pursuer when the court decides that the defence is irrelevant or where the case has not been defended properly.[6] In these circumstances, the court would be prepared without hearing any evidence about the pursuer's claim to grant decree in his favour;

(6) decree of dismissal—this is a decree in favour of a defender. It would be granted when the court decides that the pursuer's case is incompetent or irrelevant or has not been pursued in accordance with the rules. In other words it is a final disposal of the case without any hearing of evidence about the merits of the case;

(7) decree for payment, or decree as concluded for or decree as craved—these are all descriptions of a decree in favour of a pursuer for what he is seeking from the court. He can ask the court for a decree for less than the sum he was suing for.[7] He cannot ask for more than the sum for which he is suing in his writ.

---

[5] It can also be sought in a counterclaim by a defender.
[6] i.e. some failure to comply with procedural requirements.
[7] e.g. where the defender has made some payment to account of a debt after an action has been raised.

   (8) decree of absolvitor—this will be a decree granted in favour of the defender and will usually be granted after the court hears evidence in the case and decides that the pursuer has lost the case on the merits;

   (9) decree *in foro*—this is a description of any type of decree (either for the pursuer or for the defender) granted at any time in the action after the parties have, "engaged in the litigation". This description would apply to any of the decrees described above except for a decree in absence;

  (10) final decree—this is a statutory descriptive name for a decree granted in a sheriff court action only. It is a decree which, taken along with any other decrees in the case, disposes of the whole subject matter of the case including any liability for expenses. The term is significant primarily in connection with the procedure for appeals from the decision of a sheriff.[8]

19–03   It should be noted that these distinctions and definitions are not absolute. For example, there are provisions in the rules whereby, in very particular circumstances, some decrees in absence could be regarded as decrees in foro.[9] As a practical example of the interplay between these definitions consider a case where a pursuer's solicitor was absent from a calling of a case at the options hearing in a sheriff court ordinary action. The court might well decide that this merited the grant of a decree against the pursuer with expenses. This would not be a decree in absence. It would probably be a decree of dismissal by default. It would also be a decree *in foro*. In fact, it would also be a final decree.[10]

Particular Decrees

Decree in absence

19–04   This is not uncommon (about 70 per cent of sheriff court actions are undefended). It requires a more detailed explanation than the other types of decree. As we have seen in the earlier chapters, once the pursuer has served an action on the defender the defender will have time to respond to it. If the defender fails to respond, the pursuer can apply for a decree in absence. The "absence" is an absence from the litigation process entirely.[11]

    The courts have to balance a number of conflicting considerations when devising procedures to deal with such circumstances. The defender's failure to respond could arise for a number of reasons including error or

---

[8] See Ch.20.

[9] See r.7.5 of OCR 1993 and r.19.1(7) of RCS 1994; and also see *Rae v Calor Gas Ltd*, 1995 S.L.T. 244.

[10] But remember that "final" does not mean "unappealable".

[11] The following provisions apply *mutatis mutandis* to counterclaims. See the individual rules for details.

ignorance on his part. No court would be particularly comfortable grant-ing a decree against an absent defender whose lack of knowledge of the procedures prevented him defending himself. On the other hand, the pur-suer should not be prevented from taking a decree to which he may be entitled as early as possible. Generally, the court will be prepared to grant a decree in absence if it appears that the defender does not wish to defend the case. However, the defender should not be deprived of an opportunity to put forward a legitimate defence simply because he failed to comply with a technical requirement of procedure at the very outset of the case.

The courts have special rules dealing with decrees in absence. They also have special rules dealing with the recall of a decree in absence. The rules applicable in the different forms of procedures are different but the underlying principles are the same. Usually the only method of over-turning a decree of any sort is by an appeal to a superior court, but in the case of a decree in absence, appeal is not required to recall it. In some of the procedures we will look at, if a defender faced with a decree in absence applies to the court to overturn that decree, then the decree will be overturned automatically. In other circumstances, most notably in ordinary actions in the sheriff court, the defender must provide an expla-nation for his failure to appear and give advance notice of the nature of his defence before the court will recall the decree.

Particular rules regarding decrees in absence

Court of Session ordinary actions

Decree in absence. The rules can be found at r.19.1 of the RCS. After **19–05** the pursuer serves the summons in such an action the defender must appear and lodge defences within seven days of the calling of the case. If he fails to do either then the pursuer can enrol a motion for a decree in absence. He will normally also seek expenses. The court must be satisfied that it is competent to grant the decree[12] and the court has a dis-cretion whether to grant such a decree or not, but it will normally do so.

Recall of decrees in absence. The rules regarding recall are contained **19–06** in rr.19.2(1)–19.2(7) of the RCS. Generally speaking, a defender who is resident in the UK, and against whom a decree in absence has been granted has seven days from the date of the decree to ask for recall of that decree. He would do so by lodging a motion to that effect along with his defences and he would ask the court to receive the defences. There are certain administrative requirements also, but, if they are met, then the court will automatically grant recall of the decree. No question of the nature or the content of the defence to the case will arise at that point.

The rules are slightly different for a defender outwith the UK against whom a decree in absence has been granted. Where he has failed to

---

[12] e.g. that the court has jurisdiction to deal with the case.

intimate an appearance by marking the summons[13] then he is given somewhat more time to seek a recall of the decree. However, such a recall is not automatic. He must apply within a reasonable time of knowing that there was a decree against him, up to a maximum of one year. When he lodges defences along with his motion for recall of the decree his defences would have to disclose a prima facie case on the merits before the motion would be granted.[14]

Court of Session personal injuries actions and commercial actions

19–07   The same rules regarding service, obtaining of a decree in absence, and recall of a decree apply in these procedures as applies to the procedure in a Court of Session ordinary action.

Court of Session petition procedure

19–08   This whole procedure is fundamentally different from the procedure in ordinary actions. The rules about decree in absence are different, although the general principles are effectively the same. The procedure requires a respondent to lodge answers to the petition served on him within a set time. If there is a failure to lodge answers (which is the only procedural step which the respondent is required to take initially in a petition), this will probably lead to the petitioner enrolling a motion for the order sought. The granting of that motion and of that order will, in effect, amount to a decree in absence.

Recall of such a decree depends upon whether the respondent is resident within the UK or not. If resident within the UK then the same procedures as set out in rr.19.2(1)–19.2(7) of RCS apply. Where the petition has been granted in absence against a person outwith the UK then the rules are slightly different.[15] The court is still willing to recall the decree in absence but requires an explanation for the failure to lodge answers and will consider the strength or otherwise of the defence before reaching a decision on the recall of the decree.

Court of Session judicial review procedure

19–09   Similar provisions apply as with petitions. A failure to answer the application for judicial review will give rise to a decree being granted in absence. There are no specific rules for the recall of a decree in absence in judicial reviews and existing rules for recall in petition procedure will apply. In practice, it is perhaps a little unlikely—given the nature of

---

[13] However, not when he fails to lodge defences after marking the summons—the difference being that if he has marked the summons he obviously does know about the action against him.

[14] See *Bank of Scotland v Kunkel-Griffin*, 2005 G.W.D. 7-90, 1st Div; Unreported OH November 2, 2004.

[15] See r.14.9(3).

these proceedings—that a defender who actually does want to defend the application will fail to comply with the procedural requirements of lodging answers.

Sheriff court ordinary action

The rules for obtaining decree in absence in these actions are contained **19–10** in Ch.7 of the OCR rr.7.1–7.7. After the defender receives service of a sheriff court writ, he has to lodge Form O7 within 21 days. If he fails to do so, the pursuer can apply for a decree in absence. Administratively, he would do so by completing the details on the printed form which comprises the reverse side of the warrant for service which would have been issued by the sheriff clerk. The form contains a space for the sheriff clerk to certify that no Form O7 has been lodged. The solicitor will fill in the blanks in the printed forms asking the court for whatever decree is appropriate together with expenses.[16] The solicitor will sign this form and return the principal initial writ, the principal warrant, the completed form on the back of the warrant and the certificate of execution of service of the writ to the sheriff clerk. The papers would then be put before the sheriff in chambers and, if it is competent to do so,[17] then the sheriff will grant decree.

Recall of decree in absence. This is dealt with in Ch.8 rr.8.1(1)–8.1(5) **19–11** of the OCR. Recall of a decree in absence in a sheriff court ordinary action is done by means of a document known as a reponing note. It is necessary to consider this in a little more detail because reponing notes are important.[18] They can be quite contentious. A pursuer who has gained his decree against a defender who is trying to avoid paying a debt which is undeniably due (or so the pursuer thinks) will not take kindly to an effort by the defender to take this away from him. A defender who has allowed a decree to pass against him for a sum which (he thinks) should not be due will be desperate to have it recalled before diligence is done on the decree.

In practice, many pursuer's agents who have served proceedings in cases where they know it is very likely that they will be defended, simply do not consider it worthwhile to minute for a decree in absence. This is on the basis that the opponent would be bound to repone, and it is quite likely that the court would grant a reponing note if there was a genuine defence. If they take a decree in absence, this would simply cause expense and delay. Again, in practice, many reponing notes will not be opposed by a pursuer where it might be acknowledged by a pursuer that

---

[16] Also called a minute for decree.
[17] e.g. provided the court has jurisdiction or provided the order sought is a competent order.
[18] It should be noted that the rules are slightly different for defenders outwith the UK. See OCR r.8.1(4A).

there was an explanation for a failure to appear and there is a genuine defence of some kind. However, reponing notes are still argued quite frequently, especially in relation to actions of payment.

A reponing note will normally contain:

(1) a note of the details of the decree in absence which is to be reponed and any diligence which might already have been done on the decree;
(2) an explanation for the failure to lodge Form 07 in time;
(3) the defender's proposed defence; and
(4) a request to the court to recall the decree and to issue a Form G5.

19–12   The reponing note will be lodged with the sheriff clerk along with the appropriate fee. The sheriff will pronounce an order for service of the note and the order will give a date on which the court will hear parties on the question of granting the reponing note or otherwise. The defender will then serve a copy of the note along with a copy of the court order[19] for a hearing on the pursuer. At the hearing the sheriff will consider the terms of the note and hear arguments from each side. He has a discretion to grant the note or not.

In the case of *Forbes v Johnston*[20] the Inner House indicated what the proper approach of the court to reponing notes ought to be. The defender has to set out an explanation for his failure to appear and give details of his defence. The explanation does not have to be a "good excuse" (although that would help). The statement of the defence should normally be full and clear. The court will consider both of these factors before taking a discretionary decision whether to grant it or not. If it is apparent in the reponing note that there is a genuine defence on the merits or, at least, a genuine defence on the quantification of the claim, then the court is likely to grant a reponing note and recall the decree.[21]

There are different views as to whether, and to what extent, the court is confined at the hearing on the reponing note to the contents of the note itself. It is arguable that any matters which are going to be raised in the submissions at the hearing on the reponing note should at least be outlined in the reponing note itself.[22]

If the reponing note is granted, then the case just proceeds as if the date of grant was the date of expiry of the period of notice and the normal court timetable would operate from then. It is possible to appeal against the refusal of a reponing note but it is not possible to appeal against the grant of a reponing note. If a reponing note is unsuccessful then it is not possible to lodge another one at a later date.

---

[19] Or interlocutor.
[20] *Forbes v Johnston*, 1995 S.L.T. 158.
[21] See *Thompson v Jardine*, 2004 S.C.L.R. 806.
[22] See *Guardian Royal Exchange Group v Moffat*, 1986 S.L.T. 262; *Johnston v Dewart*, 1992 S.L.T. 286; and *Ratty v Hughes*, 1996 S.C.L.R. 160.

Sheriff court summary cause

The words "decree in absence" do not appear anywhere in the SCR **19–13** but, in summary causes, decrees similar to a decree in absence can be granted in two situations namely:

(1) where there is a failure to return the form of response by the defender; and
(2) where, although the appropriate form has been lodged, there is a failure by the defender to turn up or be represented at the first calling of the case.

Recall. This is done by virtue of r.24.1 of the SCR.[23] This allows the **19–14** defender 14 days from the execution of a charge or arrestment following upon a grant of decree in the above circumstances in which to apply for a recall of that decree. This is done by lodging a minute as in Form 30 with the sheriff clerk. This should contain a note of the proposed defence. The clerk fixes a hearing and the minute is then served on the pursuer. At the hearing, the court "shall recall the decree". In summary causes, therefore, the recall of the decree is automatic provided a party has complied with the procedural requirements.[24] A party is only allowed one opportunity to recall.

Sheriff court small claims

As with summary causes the words "decree in absence" do not appear **19–15** in the rules. If a defender fails to lodge a form of response, or fails to turn up or be represented at the hearing under r.9.1, then a decree can be granted provided it is competent for the court to do so.

Recall. This is done under r.22.1 of the Small Claim Rules 2002. The **19–16** procedures are similar to the procedures under summary causes as discussed above. Recall is automatic provided that the procedural requirements have been complied with.

Summary decrees

It is one consequence of our traditional system of pleadings that a **19–17** defender can lodge defences which consist of a simple denial of the facts of the dispute and a bald refusal to accept any liability for payment. This can delay the pursuer obtaining a decree against him for some time. The earliest the pursuer might be able to obtain a decree in these circumstances might be after a successful debate or procedure roll hearing at which the pursuer will argue that the pleadings in the defences are

[23] See *City of Edinburgh Council v Ure*, 2004 S.C.L.R. 306—a summary cause action for recovery of possession.
[24] In *Clydebank Housing Association v Mc Emerson*, 2004 S.L.T. (Sh. Ct) 25, the defender did not provide the necessary information in Form 30 and it was refused.

irrelevant. This would be unobjectionable, if a simple denial was a genuine and meritorious defence, but it is not acceptable if the defence is purely dilatory. A motion for summary decree is a very significant procedural mechanism which can be deployed when the defender appears to be attempting to take advantage of the formal system of pleadings and is simply frustrating a pursuer in his attempts to obtain a justified decree promptly. A pursuer is entitled to seek a summary decree in any case where, after defences have been lodged,[25] the court can be satisfied that there is no valid stateable defence.[26] Although applications for a "summary-type" decree are frequently used in other jurisdictions, they are more rare here and this is partly explained by the fairly strict conditions which have to be satisfied before such a decree can be granted.[27] The Scottish courts are generally reluctant to grant summary decree.

19–18 *Court of Session*

The rules regarding summary decree are now contained in Ch.21 of the 1994 Rules. A pursuer can apply for such a decree in most actions in the Court of Session. The application can be made at any time after defences have been lodged and the grounds for the application would be that, "there is no defence to the action, or a part of it, disclosed in the defences".

Rules 22.2(3)–22.2(5) provide that the procedure is to be by motion which has to be intimated not less than 14 days before it is enrolled. The court can grant the motion or not and, at the hearing on the motion, can order any party to produce any relevant document and/or lodge an affidavit in order to support his position. Even if a motion is refused a party can make a further motion if there has been a change in circumstances.

At the hearing of the motion the court is entitled to do more than interpret the pleadings strictly. It can go behind the pleadings to some extent in order to try and assess the true merits or otherwise of the defender's defence.[28] In determining an application for summary decree, the court should proceed with caution and there must be, "near certainty as to the absence of a defence".[29]

---

[25] Also despite the fact that they make no admission of liability to the pursuer.
[26] For a recent authoritative discussion about summary decree see *Urquhart v Sweeney*, 2004 G.W.D. 11-242.
[27] As authoritatively explained by the House of Lords in *Henderson 3052775 v Nova Scotia Ltd*, 2006 S.L.T. 489.
[28] For a range of decisions on this provision see *Rankin v Reid*, 1987 S.L.T. 352; *Ingram Coal Co v Nugent*, 1991 S.L.T. 603; *Daks Simpson Group Plc v Kuiper*, 1994 S.L.T. 689; and *Lord Advocate v Chung*, 1995 S.L.T. 65. Also very useful is G. Maher, "Summary Decree in the Court of Session" 1987 S.L.T. (News) 93, 101.
[29] See these examples: *Firth v Blinkbonnie Developments* Unreported OH February 7, 2007, Lady Paton; *Albyn Realisations (Festival Cars) Ltd v Levenfleet Ltd* Unreported OH June 20, 2007, Lord Brodie; *Advocate General for Scotland v Montgomery* Unreported OH July 10, 2007, Lady Paton; *Stewart v Pure Ltd* Unreported OH March 26, 2008, Lord Glennie; *Aedas Architects Ltd v Skanska Constructiuon Ltd* Unreported OH April 17, 2008, Lord McEwan.

Sheriff court ordinary actions

The sheriff court has power to grant summary decree under Ch.17 of **19–19** the OCR. The provisions are virtually identical to those in the RCS, although the period of notice is the same as for any other motion.[30] A good example of the approach to summary decree in the sheriff court is the case of *Whiteaway Laidlaw Bank Ltd v Green*.[31] In that case, the sheriff principal said:

> "Summary Decree will not pass against a Defender who appears to have the basis of a stateable defence but who has expressed it badly; on the other hand Summary Decree will not be refused merely because there is a drafting error or a lack of detail in the Pursuer's pleadings. There will be some cases in which a Defender is justified in stating a bald denial or putting the Pursuer to proof, but such cases do not include those in which the Pursuer's pleadings and productions indicate that there is a prima facie case calling for an answer especially where the facts founded upon by the Pursuer are within the Defender's knowledge".

The use of motions for summary decree is surprisingly rare, given the benefit of a successful motion[32] and the power which the court has to put some pressure on a dilatory defender during the hearing of such a motion.[33] The sheriff can order any opponent of such a motion to produce any relevant document and/or lodge an affidavit in order to support his position.[34]

There is no procedure for a motion for summary decree in any of the other forms of action which we have been considering in this book. However, in summary cause and small claims actions, the sheriff has power at the first calling of the case to make a decision on the merits which could be likened to the process of granting summary decree.

Summary decrees and reparation actions

Interesting issues can arise in relation to motions for summary decree **19–20** in reparation actions. These can be of particular practical significance. If

---

[30] i.e. seven days. NB: in commercial actions it is just 48 hours—OCR r.40.11.

[31] *Whiteaway Laidlaw Bank Ltd v Green*, 1994 S.L.T. (Sh. Ct) 18; the case was concerned with an earlier version of the rule but the principles remain the same.

[32] See *ITS Drilling Services v Qualitank Services Ltd* Unreported (Sh. Ct) June 22, 2004, Sheriff Principal Young.

[33] A recent example from the sheriff court is *J. Sykes & Sons (Fish Merchants) Ltd v Grieve*, 2002 S.L.T. (Sh. Ct) 15. A sheriff court case in which an award of summary decree was unsuccessfully appealed by the defender to the Inner House was *Clydesdale Bank Plc v McCaw* Unreported Ex Div. May 24, 2002, in which the defender, who represented herself plainly had no defence.

[34] This could be very effective if the opponent's pleadings are skeletal and obscure but the power is little invoked or used for reasons which are not entirely obvious.

we assume that, in a reparation action, the defender puts forward a defence which is a denial of liability but completely lacking in any detail, then the pursuer may have a number of procedural options including an option of making a motion for summary decree. In some reparation actions, a defender can quite legitimately and reasonably maintain a defence which is no more than a simple denial of the pursuer's allegations about the accident. There are particular types of accident in which that would be perfectly understandable and not open to challenge.[35] On the other hand, there may be many situations where a skeletal defence or a bare denial could be regarded as no defence at all.[36] In a motion for summary decree the court can go behind the bare denial and it is interesting to note how far, and in what circumstances, they are prepared to do this.[37]

Interim decrees

19–21   An interim decree for part of the sum claimed or in part satisfaction of the conclusions or craves in an action can be granted by the court at an early stage of procedure. This would be done where there was an unqualified admission or a concession by the defenders in their written pleadings which would enable the court to reach a decision that some part of the claim was indefensible.[38] This will usually apply where some part of the pursuer's claim can be considered on its merits independently of the claim as a whole.[39] The court can dispose of part of the case by granting a decree in favour of the pursuer, e.g. a decree for payment of part of the sum sued for, whilst allowing the action to proceed to a proof or some other form of procedure in relation to the other parts of the claim.[40] A motion for interim decree could be made orally with leave of the court at any time when the case calls in court, but it would be prudent for a party to make a written motion or otherwise give notice of the intention to move for interim decree.[41]

Decree by default

19–22   Generally speaking, this is a decree granted by the court in favour of either the pursuer or the defender because one or other of them has failed to comply with a procedural requirement. It can involve a failure to

---

[35] See *Keppie v Marshall Food Group*, 1997 S.L.T. 305; the report contains a list of all the relevant cases on the point at that time.
[36] See the case of *Campbell v Golding*, 1992 S.L.T. 889 and *Cooper v Northern Scaffolding Group Plc*, 1997 S.L.T. 157.
[37] A recent reported example is *Pope v James McHugh Contracts Ltd*, 2006 S.L.T. 386.
[38] See, e.g. *Southern Cross Commodities Property Ltd v Martin*, 1991 S.L.T. 83.
[39] See *Malcolm v Park Lane Motors Ltd*, 1998 S.L.T. 1252, in which there was discussion about the relationship between interim decree and summary decree.
[40] See, e.g. *Stanley Miller Ltd v Ladhope Developments Ltd*, 1988 S.L.T. 514.
[41] A rather unusual case on this is *William Miller Plumbing Contractors Ltd v James Lumsden Ltd*, 2000 S.L.T. 1425.

lodge documents,[42] a failure to comply with a specific order, a failure to turn up at a hearing, etc. There are specific rules dealing with default. It can give rise to complex procedural arguments primarily because of the unfortunate consequences which could flow from what may be no more than human error.

It is important to note that there are very subtle differences of definition and categorisation of decrees of default between the sheriff court and the Court of Session. These differences can have a significant practical effect and detailed reading of the rules is recommended as the distinction is not easy to understand.

Court of Session ordinary action

19–23 This is dealt with in RCS r.20.1. The court has a wide discretionary power to grant decrees by default for a failure to comply with procedural requirements, and the rule gives examples of particular situations which would entitle a court to grant such a decree and the type of decree which it can grant.

Sheriff court ordinary action

19–24 The rules are contained in Ch.16. This defines default more broadly. It provides that, where a party is in default, the sheriff may:

(1) grant decree as craved;
(2) grant decree of absolvitor with expenses;
(3) grant decree of dismissal with expenses; or
(4) make such other order as he thinks fit to secure the expeditious progress of the cause.

The frequency with which actions were being affected by some kind of default, meant that many cases had to be appealed to cure an administrative oversight which can occur in even the best run court action. The rules give the sheriff an opportunity to temper the draconian measure of granting some kind of decree if he thinks that the circumstances merit it. Often the sheriff will continue the case to a futher hearing to give a party an opportunity to explain or excuse a default.

The significance of the distinction between decree by default of dismissal and decree by default of absolvitor relates to the plea of res judicata. This is a plea to the effect that the merits of the case have already been decided by a competent court in an action between the same parties, and accordingly the unsuccessful party should not be allowed to pursue a subsequent action in similar terms. The practical significance is that, if a party suffers decree by default in one action, he may be unable to pursue the remedy by raising the same or a similar action again.

---

[42] However, a failure to lodge a minute of amendment after the court has allowed a party to amend is not a default. *Catterson v Davidson*, 2000 S.L.T. (Sh. Ct) 51. The point is that the amendment is "allowed", but not "ordered" by the court.

Putting the matter broadly, a decree of dismissal cannot justify a plea of
res judicata. In other words, if a pursuer's claim has been decided by the
court granting a decree of dismissal by default, he can usually raise it
again. He cannot do so if the decree was absolvitor.[43] In that case, the
party could have lost his right to obtain his remedy by virtue of a simple
oversight on a matter of procedure.

It is always open to a party to ask the court to excuse the default by
exercising the dispensing power.[44] Although this discretion will not be
exercised automatically, the courts can often be persuaded to do so
where the justice of the situation requires it and where the default is
relatively minor.[45] It is also open to the court to take the view that the
proper way to punish a default on the part of a solicitor for a party is to
make a finding of expenses against the solicitor.[46] If the court does
have an impression that a party, by his general conduct in the case, is not
seriously pursuing or defending the claim then the court would be
unsympathetic to any individual default.

A decree by default is appealable,[47] and if appeal is taken in these circumstances it is sensible to lodge what ought to have been lodged or to
cure any omission which gave rise to the default in the first place. It is
also helpful to demonstrate clearly that there is a genuine and stateable
case or defence on the merits.

Decree de plano

19–25   This is a decree granted in favour of a pursuer where the court
decides, without hearing any evidence, that the averments of the
defender are irrelevant.[48] The court takes the view that these averments
do not amount to a defence of the pursuer's claim at all so that the pursuer is entitled to decree as craved or as concluded for.[49] One of the most
common situations in which decree *de plano* may be granted is in a case
where the pursuer takes a plea to the effect that the defences are irrelevant because they are skeletal.[50] As an illustration see the case of

---

[43] This is a complex and potentially confusing area of procedure. For some guidance see
Waydale Ltd v DHL Holdings (UK) Ltd, 2001 S.L.T. 207.
[44] See Ch.1.
[45] See *Samson v Fielding*, 2003 S.L.T. (Sh. Ct) 48.
[46] Many of the cases on default relate to failures to attend at a peremptory diet where the
solicitor has belatedly decided to withdraw from acting or where there is doubt about
representation.
[47] In *Canmore Housing Association Ltd v Scott*, 2003 S.L.T. (Sh. Ct) 68, the pursuer failed
to appear at a peremptory diet and the sheriff granted decree of dismissal by default.
The sheriff principal took the view that the sheriff could not be said to have exercised
his discretion in the particular circumstances because he had not continued the case for
an explanation for the failure of the party to appear.
[48] See *Lutea Trustees Ltd v Orbis Trustees Guernsey Ltd*, 1998 S.L.T. 471.
[49] See the case of *Manheath Ltd v H.J. Banks & Co Ltd*, 1996 S.L.T. 1006.
[50] See, e.g. the case of *Grampian Hydraulics (Buckie) Ltd v Dauntless Marine
Engineering & Supply Co Ltd*, 1992 S.L.T. (Sh. Ct) 45.

Strathaird Farms Ltd v G.A. Chattaway & Co,[51] in which the sheriff considered the defender's averments to be irrelevant and granted decree *de plano* for £5,000. It is interesting to note that, on appeal, the sheriff principal overturned that decision, allowed the appeal against the decree *de plano* and then sustained the defender's plea in law to the effect that the court had no jurisdiction. He granted decree of dismissal in favour of the defender.

Decree of dismissal

Effectively this means that the pursuer's case is "thrown out" by the court. Usually the court has reached the view that the pursuer has not plead a relevant case or has not pursued the case in such a way as to entitle him to a proof of his averments.[52] Actions will often be dismissed after a debate where one of the defender's preliminary pleas has been upheld.[53] **19–26**

There are some differences of detail between the sheriff court and the Court of Session when it comes to providing rules about procedural lapses which might give rise to a decree of dismissal.

In the Court of Session there are particular provisions, e.g. in rr.22.1(2) and 22.3(1), providing for particular defaults which would give rise to a decree of dismissal. One example is a failure to lodge an open record.

In the sheriff court, r.16.2(2) provides that the sheriff may grant a decree of absolvitor or dismissal on a default as defined there.[54]

Decree for payment or decree as craved or concluded for

In cases where a pursuer is seeking a decree for interdict, or declarator, or for a party to do something in particular (a decree *ad factum paestandum*),[55] then it is important for the pursuer to state precisely in his writ the decree he is seeking. This is particularly relevant in relation to decrees of implement and interdict.[56] **19–27**

In the case of decrees for payment of money, the decree can, in appropriate circumstances, order payment in a foreign currency.[57]

---

[51] *Strathaird Farms Ltd v G.A. Chattaway & Co,* 1993 S.L.T. (Sh. Ct) 36.
[52] See *Steelmek Marine and General Engineers' Trustee v Shetland Sea Farms Ltd,* 1999 S.L.T. (Sh. Ct) 30.
[53] See, e.g. *Charisma Properties Ltd v Grayling (1994) Ltd,* 1996 S.L.T. 791; *Lennox v Scottish Branch of the British Show Jumping Association,* 1996 S.L.T. 353; *Duncan v Beattie,* 2003 S.L.T. 1243.
[54] For a good example of the distinction between the two see the case of *Group 4 Total Security Ltd v Jaymark Developments Ltd,* 1996 S.L.T. (Sh. Ct) 61.
[55] See Ch.13.
[56] For examples, see *Grosvenor Developments (Scotland) Plc v Argyll Stores,* 1987 S.L.T. 738 and *Retail Parks Investments v Royal Bank of Scotland Plc (No.2),* 1996 S.L.T. 52.
[57] See, e.g. *Commerzbank AG v Large,* 1977 S.L.T. 219; *Fulleman v McInnes' Executor,* 1993 S.L.T. 259.

A decree for payment will normally include an appropriate figure for interest. Generally, in actions for payment, interest will commence to run from the date of citation of the defender and will be awarded by the court up to the date of decree at the judicial rate. Eight per cent is the "judicial rate" applicable to all court decrees granted after April 1, 1993.[58] In actions of reparation, it is open to the court to grant decree from the date when the accident happened which will be considerably earlier than the date of citation. Decree would be granted for the combined amount of the principal sum plus interest up to the date of decree, and then interest would run on that combined amount from the date of decree until the defender made payment. It is, however, open to a pursuer to seek a variable rate of interest or a rate of interest higher than eight per cent provided this can be justified.[59] It should be noted that the Scottish Law Commission published a *Discussion Paper on Interest on Debt and Damages*,[60] and this includes a detailed summary of the current law on interest.[61]

Although it is simply a special kind of decree for payment, note should be taken of an "instalment" decree where, in certain circumstances, a debtor would be found liable to make payment to a pursuer by way of instalments rather than all at once.[62] This arises under the Debtors (Scotland) Act 1987 s.1 where a debtor makes an application to the court seeking a "time to pay direction" before the time that decree is granted, provides details of his income and outgoings and offers to pay by instalments. This is only competent in certain circumstances and reference should be made to the Act for details.

Decree of absolvitor

19–28   Effectively this means that the court absolves the defender from any obligation to the pursuer (usually an obligation to pay money) in connection with the subject matter of the dispute. The court assoilzies[63] the defender and this will be done after there has been a proof on the merits of the case. A decree of absolvitor will always be a decree *in foro*. A decree of absolvitor alone will not be a final decree and it would not become final until expenses were dealt with.[64]

---

[58] The interest rate can be amended from time to time.

[59] See the cases of *Bank of Scotland v Davis*, 1982 S.L.T. 20; *Royal Bank of Scotland v Geddes*, 1983 S.L.T. (Sh. Ct) 32; *Royal Bank of Scotland v Dunbar*, 1985 S.L.T. (Sh. Ct) 66.

[60] Scottish Law Commission, *Discussion Paper on Interest on Debt and Damages*. The Stationery Office, 2005. Scot. Law Com. Discussion Paper No.127.

[61] See also Lord Reed in *Wilson v Dunbar Plc*, 2008 S.L.T. 301.

[62] The latter being known as an "open decree".

[63] Pronounced "ah-soil-ease".

[64] See, e.g. *Gallagher v Strathclyde Regional Council*, 1996 S.L.T. 255 and *Waydale Ltd v MRM Engineering*, 1996 S.L.T. (Sh. Ct) 6.

Decree in foro

This is simply a descriptive name for any decree which is not a decree **19–29** in absence. It is a shortened version of the phrase, "decree *in foro contentioso*", or, "decree *in foro litis contestation*". In broad terms it can be described as being any decree which is pronounced in any case once it can be said that the parties have engaged in contesting the litigation. It can be used to describe any decree pronounced after the parties have joined issue in the action.[65] There is no immediate significance in the fact that a decree is a decree *in foro* or not, but its significance is in relation to the question of whether subsequent proceedings on the same topic can be attacked as being *res judicata*.[66]

Final decree

As has been explained, this is really a descriptive name for a decree **19–30** in the sheriff court which, either on its own or taken in conjunction with other orders of the court, disposes of the whole subject matter of the case including expenses. It is defined in s.3(h) of the Sheriff Courts (Scotland) Act 1907.[67] The relevance of whether something is a final decree or not relates primarily to the procedure and timetable for appeals in sheriff court actions.

ENFORCEMENT OF DECREES

The procedures for enforcing decrees comes under the law of diligence. **19–31** It is beyond the scope of this book to deal with the practicalities of enforcing decrees. Reference should be made to the textbooks noted below.[68]

There have been numerous changes in the methods and mechanisms for doing diligence lately. A useful source of up-to-date information and explanation is the website of the Accountant in Bankruptcy.[69]

---

[65] See the case of *Esso Petroleum Co Ltd v Law*, 1956 S.L.T. 105.

[66] There is an interesting discussion on decrees *in foro* in *McPhee v Heatherwick*, 1977 S.L.T. (Sh. Ct) 46, in which Sheriff McPhail discusses them.

[67] There is a full discussion of this in *Kerr v Strathclyde Regional Council*, 1988 S.L.T. (Sh. Ct) 42.

[68] Dawn McKenzie, *Debt Arrangement and Attachment* (Edinburgh: W. Green, 2003); Gerry Maher and Douglas J. Cusine, *The Law and Practice of Diligence* (Edinburgh: Butterworths, 1990); Cusine and Maher, "Diligence", *Stair Memorial Encyclopedia*, Vol.8.

[69] At *http://www.aib.gov.uk* [Accessed August 25, 2008]. See also *http://www.moneyscotland.gov.uk* [Accessed August 25, 2008].

CHAPTER 20

APPEALS

20–01 We have seen in the previous chapters how court actions are conducted at the different levels of the hierarchy of courts in Scotland. When any civil court in Scotland makes a final decision in relation to a civil litigation this will normally be subject to review by way of appeal to a superior judge or court. In some circumstances, decisions by the inferior judge or court which are not finally determinative of the case[1] can also be subject to review by way of appeal. Often this right of appeal will arise in relation to incidental decisions only if the judge at first instance grants leave to appeal to the superior court.

An appeal would proceed on the basis that the judge at first instance made the wrong decision and this can cover a number of possible criticisms. These include arguments that the decision was incompetent, that the judge exercised his discretion unreasonably, that the decision was wrong in law, or that the judge did not have sufficient evidence or other material before him to justify the decision which he made. Although there are extensive rights of appeal across the whole spectrum of civil litigation in Scotland, appeals are not encouraged and there have been relatively recent changes in the rules of procedure relating to appeals which have reduced the possibility of appeals being marked for no good reason. Formerly, a party could proceed with an appeal to a superior court simply by indicating that he wished to appeal the judgment at first instance and no more than that. In all forms of procedure now there has to be some prior indication of the grounds of appeal, so that the appellate court, and the opponent, will have prior notice of the points to be taken on appeal and some outline of the arguments to be advanced at appeal.

Most clients who are unsuccessful with their litigation or some part of it will instinctively want to appeal, but it should be noted that no appeals involve a rehearing of the evidence in the case.[2] Generally speaking, the decision of a judge at first instance in relation to matters of fact[3] is not

---

[1] But may have procedural or incidental significance for the conduct or progress of an action.
[2] Very rarely there might be a request for hearing additional evidence.
[3] Including what evidence was accepted, what witnesses were believed or not believed and the conclusions the judge reached about the facts of the litigation.

susceptible to review.[4] If the judge's decision depends in whole or in part upon his interpretation of the legal principles applicable to the dispute, then an appeal might well be directed to that aspect of his judgment. It is regarded as desirable that judgments of any court should not easily be subject to review, otherwise litigation would be open-ended. Repeated appeals on various incidental or procedural matters prior to a final decision in the case would delay a litigation significantly and they are discouraged. In the final analysis however, if a party loses a case before a judge at first instance, and after evidence has been heard about the case, he may have the opportunity to seek review of that decision all that way up to the House of Lords.

This chapter is concerned with the procedures and practice applicable to appeals in general.[5] Before considering the detailed procedures, however, it is important to understand exactly what rights of appeal exist in the different forms of procedure which we have been considering. We shall confine ourselves to the main forms of procedure and initially outline in broad terms the rights of appeal which are available.

COURT OF SESSION

Outer House—There is no right of appeal from a sheriff court judgment to the Outer House. There are some rights of appeal against incidental interlocutors of the Lord Ordinary to the Inner House provided leave is obtained from the Lord Ordinary. There are some rights of appeal to the Inner House against incidental interlocutors without any leave. There is a right of appeal to the Inner House against a final judgment of an Outer House judge. In the Court of Session, any application to review the judgment of a Lord Ordinary is called a "reclaiming motion" and the proper terminology is that a party will "reclaim" the interlocutor to the Inner House rather than "appeal" the interlocutor.

20–02

Inner House—The Inner House primarily has an appellate jurisdiction. Appeal can be taken there from the sheriff court in appropriate cases and from the Outer House. If an appeal is taken to the Inner House either from the sheriff court or from an interlocutor of the Lord Ordinary[6] and the Inner House reaches its own decision, a party can appeal this further to the House of Lords. The proper terminology is to call the appeal from the Inner House to the House of Lords an appeal.[7]

---

[4] For circumstances in which it can be reviewed see *Thomas v Thomas*, 1947 S.C. (HL) 45.

[5] It does not deal with appeals to the House of Lords.

[6] As a reclaiming motion.

[7] It should be noted that it is not possible to "miss out" the Inner House as a level of appeal and go straight to the House of Lords from the decision of a Lord Ordinary.

SHERIFF COURT

(1) Small claim

20–03   There is no right of appeal in small claim actions in relation to decisions by the sheriff on incidental procedures in a small claim. There is a right of appeal against a final decision of the sheriff, but that appeal can only be taken on a point of law.[8] The right of appeal only entitles a party to appeal to the sheriff principal. There is no provision for any further appeal upwards from him in a small claim action.

(2) Summary cause

20–04   There is no right of appeal against a decision by a sheriff on incidental procedures in a summary cause. There is a right of appeal against a final decision in a summary cause, but again this is only on a point of law. The right of appeal only entitles the party to appeal to the sheriff principal but, in contrast to small claims, there is a further right of appeal available from the decision of the sheriff principal to the Court of Session.[9] This further appeal can be taken if, and only if, the sheriff principal certifies the case as being suitable for such an appeal.[10]

(3) Ordinary action

20–05   Some rights of appeal are available in ordinary actions against decisions of the sheriff on incidental matters provided that the leave of the sheriff is obtained.[11] There are some rights of appeal against decisions of the sheriff on incidental matters without any leave. There is a right of appeal against the final decision[12] of the sheriff to the sheriff principal or alternatively directly to the Court of Session.[13] If an appeal is taken against the sheriff's judgment to a sheriff principal, then the sheriff principal's judgment following the appeal can itself be appealed to the Court of Session. An appeal against a final decision of the sheriff can be taken on matters of fact, or on matters of law, or both.

It is worth re-emphasising that the highest level one can go on appeal from a decision in a small claim action is the sheriff principal on a point of law only. The highest level for a summary cause action is usually the sheriff principal with a very limited onward appeal. The highest level for any final judgment of a judge at first instance in either the sheriff court

---

[8] The sheriff's decision on the facts is final and not subject to review.

[9] This would be to the appellate court of the Court of Session, namely the Inner House.

[10] This might arise when the case raises an important point of law which might be of significance for other litigations. See, e.g. *SSEB v Elder*, 1980 S.L.T. 83, a claim for electricity charges of £6 (pre-small claims), which raised a question of principle and was certified as suitable for the Inner House.

[11] The obtaining of leave is dealt with at para.20–19, below.

[12] See para.20–20, below.

[13] It should be noted that the sheriff principal can be "missed out" as a level of appeal from the judgment of a sheriff.

or the Court of Session is the House of Lords, but an appeal can only be taken to the House of Lords after the appeal has first been heard by the Inner House. It is possible in the extreme case[14] for a decision of a sheriff to be appealed to the sheriff principal, and then for the decision of the sheriff principal to be appealed to the Inner House, and then for the decision of the Inner House to be appealed to the House of Lords. It will be appreciated that this would be an expensive and lengthy process and it is only likely to happen in exceptional cases.[15]

COMMON LAW POWERS ON APPEAL

Before we go on to consider the statutory powers given to appellate courts, it should be noted that there exists what has been described as a "supereminent" or overriding power of any appeal court to recall any interlocutor by a judge at first instance which is incompetent. The circumstances in which that power may be exercised in the different procedural regimes we are considering may be unclear, and it is rarely invoked.[16] **20–06**

STATUTORY PROVISIONS REGARDING APPEALS

Court of Session

Outer House—The provisions regarding appeal are contained in ss.18 and 28 of the Court of Session Act 1988. Section 18 provides that every interlocutor of the Lord Ordinary shall be final in the Outer House but subject to review of the Inner House. Section 28 provides that any party to a case initiated in the Outer House who is dissatisfied with an interlocutor pronounced by the Lord Ordinary may, "except as otherwise prescribed" reclaim against the interlocutor within such a time and in such a way as may be prescribed in the rules. Accordingly, in contrast to the sheriff court position, the interlocutors which are susceptible to appeal are detailed in the rules rather than in the primary legislation. **20–07**

Inner House—Section 29 of the Court of Session Act provides that any party who is dissatisfied with the verdict of a jury in a civil jury trial[17]

Although very unusual.
[15] See *Donoghue v Stevenson*, 1932 S.C. (H.L.) 31; *RHM Bakeries (Scotland) Ltd v Strathclyde Regional Council*, 1985 S.L.T. 214; *Laing v Scottish Grain Distillers Ltd*, 1992 S.L.T. 435.
[16] See *Lord Advocate v Johnston*, 1983 S.L.T. 290; *VAG Finance Ltd v Smith*, 1988 S.L.T. (Sh. Ct) 59; *City of Glasgow District Council v McAleer*, 1992 S.L.T. (Sh. Ct) 41; *City of Edinburgh District Council v Robbin*, 1994 S.L.T. (Sh. Ct) 51.
[17] See Ch.18.

can apply to the Inner House for a new trial on various specified grounds. In particular circumstances, the Inner House can substitute its own verdict.[18]

There are statutory provisions in s.32 of the Court of Session Act 1988 regarding appeals from the judgment of the sheriff or sheriff principal which have been mentioned above. The principal provision to note is that, where an appeal is taken to the Inner House from the judgment of the sheriff principal or the sheriff proceeding on a proof, the Inner House shall specify in its decision the facts material to the case which it finds to be established by the proof and express how far their judgment proceeds on matters of fact or on matters of law. It shall also specify the several points of law which it means to decide. The reason for this is that the judgment of the Inner House on any such appeal, i.e. after a proof, shall be appealable to the House of Lords only on matters of law.[19]

The statutory provisions regarding appeals to the House of Lords from the Inner House are contained in s.40 of the Court of Session Act 1988. It is competent to appeal from the Inner House to the House of Lords without leave against a judgment on the whole merits of the case, or against an interlocutory[20] judgment where there is a difference of opinion among the judges, or where the interlocutory judgment sustains a dilatory defence and dismisses the action. Furthermore, appeal is competent with leave of the Inner House against any interlocutory judgment other than those mentioned above. It is specifically provided that it is not competent to appeal to the House of Lords against the interlocutor of a Lord Ordinary unless that interlocutor has first been reviewed by the Inner House.

Sheriff court

(1) *Small claims and summary causes*

20–08   The basic statutory provision relating to appeals is contained in s.38 of the Sheriff Courts (Scotland) Act 1971.

(2) *Sheriff court ordinary actions*

The provisions regarding appeals in an ordinary action are contained within ss.27 and 28 of the Sheriff Courts (Scotland) Act 1907. Section 27 deals with appeals to the sheriff principal. It provides that these shall be competent against all final judgments[21] of the sheriff and also against interlocutors:

(a) which grant or refuse interdict;
(b) which grant interim decree for payment of money or make an order *ad factum praestandum*;

---

[18] See *Cleisham v British Railways Board*, 1964 S.L.T. 41.
[19] See *Martinez v Grampian Health Board*, 1996 S.L.T. 69.
[20] Be that incidental or procedural.
[21] As defined in para.20–20, below.

(c) which sist an action;

(d) which allow or refuse or limit the mode of proof;

(e) which refuse a reponing note; or

(f) against which the sheriff grants leave to appeal.[22]

Section 28 of the Act deals with appeals to the Court of Session. It covers appeals to the Court of Session from the sheriff[23] and the sheriff principal. These appeals are competent against a final judgment or against any interlocutors:

(a) which grant interim decree for payment of money;

(b) which sist an action;

(c) which refuse a reponing note;

(d) against which the sheriff or sheriff principal has granted leave to appeal.

RULES REGARDING APPEALS

There are significantly different rules of procedure for appeals under the **20–09** various forms of procedure dealt with in this chapter. The reader's attention is directed to the specific rules mentioned and a summary of the contents of the rules is provided.

Court of Session

There are a number of rules regarding appeals in the Court of Session **20–10** because the Court of Session deals with a large number of different types of appeal. There are rules relating to reclaiming.[24] There are rules relating to the handling of appeals from inferior courts, i.e. from the sheriff or sheriff principal. There are also rules regarding various appeals under statute in which the jurisdiction of the Court of Session is somewhat similar to the jurisdiction of the sheriff court in summary applications. We shall concentrate on the first two. It should be noted that the rules contain a number of administrative and procedural details which will not be discussed and reference should be made to the precise terms of the rules for full details.

Reclaiming

This is dealt with in Ch.38 rr.38.1–38.21 of the RCS. The principal **20–11** rules are as follows:

---

[22] Which means in theory against any interlocutor of any kind if the sheriff is disposed to grant leave.

[23] In which the appeal to the sheriff principal has been missed out.

[24] i.e. appealing from the decision of a Lord Ordinary.

316 *Civil Procedure and Practice*

Rule 38.2—This provides that any party to a cause who is dissatisfied with an interlocutor pronounced by the Lord Ordinary and who seeks to submit that interlocutor to review by the Inner House shall do so by reclaiming. However, some specific interlocutors are not open to being reclaimed.[25]

Rule 38.3—This provides the time limit within which reclaiming must be done. An interlocutor disposing of the whole subject matter of the cause or the whole merits of the cause may be reclaimed against without leave within 21 days after the date on which the interlocutor was pronounced. An interlocutor:

(a) disposing of part of the merits of a cause;
(b) allowing or refusing proof, proof before answer or jury trial;
(c) limiting the mode of proof;
(d) adjusting issues for jury trial;
(e) granting, refusing, recalling or refusing to recall interim interdict or interim liberation;
(f) in relation to an exclusion order under s.4 of the Matrimonial Homes (Family Protection) (Scotland) Act 1981;
(g) granting, refusing, or recalling a sist of execution or procedure;
(h) loosing, restricting or recalling an arrestment or recalling in whole or in part an inhibition on the dependence of an action or refusing to do so;
(i) granting authority to move an arrested vessel or cargo;
(j) deciding that a reference to the European Court should be made,

may be reclaimed against, without leave within 14 days after the date on which the interlocutor was pronounced. Any interlocutor other than those mentioned in the rule may be reclaimed against, with leave, within 14 days after the date on which the interlocutor was pronounced.

Rule 38.4—This contains seven types of interlocutor or decision in which specific provisions are made regarding reclaiming with leave. Reference should be made to the rule.

Rule 38.5—This deals with applications for leave to reclaim and provides a procedure whereby this shall be done. Broadly speaking, it is done by motion brought before the Lord Ordinary whose judgment is to be reclaimed. Since the reclaiming motion has to be enrolled within 14 days of the interlocutor complained of, the application for leave to reclaim has to be enrolled as soon as possible so as to allow time to mark the reclaiming motion within the time limit.

---

[25] It is necessary to check the specific rules for details.

Rules 38.6 and 38.7—There is a simple form of motion for review pro- **20–12** vided in the rules, and when a motion is enrolled for review the reclaimer has to lodge a reclaiming print. The reclaiming print is in the form of a record and must contain the whole pleadings and interlocutors in the case and (where available) the opinion of the Lord Ordinary. In a case of mistake or inadvertence, the Inner House may allow a motion for review to be received outwith the reclaiming dates and any motion for extension of time has to be made along with the motion for review.

Rule 38.7A—In certain cases, a party who wishes to reclaim specified interlocutors must seek early disposal of the reclaiming motion.

Rule 38.8—A reclaiming motion[26] will have the effect of submitting all of the previous interlocutors in the case to review, even at the instance of the other party.

Rule 38.11—This provides that where appeal is taken against a decree by default which has been granted against a party in respect of his failure to lodge a step of process or other document, then a motion for review of the interlocutor granting that decree will be refused unless the document is lodged on or before the date on which the motion is enrolled.

Rules 38.13 and 38.14—These provide that if a party wants early disposal of a reclaiming motion he shall include in his motion for reclaiming a request for early disposal.[27] If the appellant does not seek early disposal then the respondent can do so by completing an appropriate form. The Inner House hears the motion for review along with any additional motions or issues, including a motion for early disposal and then will make an appropriate order. Reclaiming motions against incidental or procedural interlocutors must request early disposal. It is open to an opponent to object to the competency of a reclaiming motion, and there is a procedure whereby that objection can be dealt with. Where there is no objection to competency, then the Inner House shall, without hearing parties, order grounds of appeal to be lodged.

Rule 38.16—This provides that an order for grounds of appeal shall **20–13** require the reclaimer and any respondent who wishes to bring under review the decision of the Lord Ordinary to lodge grounds of appeal in process within 28 days after the date of the interlocutor making the order. The grounds of appeal have to consist of brief specific numbered propositions stating the grounds on which it is proposed to submit that the reclaiming motion should be allowed. On lodging the grounds of

---

[26] With one exception.
[27] NB: by r.38.7A he must request early disposal in certain cases.

appeal the party has to lodge three copies in process and send a copy to every other party. A party who has lodged grounds of appeal can at any time apply for leave to amend the grounds of appeal. A failure to lodge grounds of appeal can lead the Inner House to refuse the reclaiming motion without any hearing, either at its own instance or on the motion of a respondent.

Rule 38.17—This provides that once grounds of appeal are lodged the reclaimer shall apply by motion for an order for hearing. The order for a hearing can be to the summar roll for hearing[28] or for the cause to be heard in the single bills.[29] If there is an issue regarding competency which has not been decided as provided above then the motion requesting an order for a hearing shall also require the attendance of counsel so that the competency issue can be argued at that time.

Rule 38.19—This contains a number of provisions regarding various procedural matters in an appeal. Reference should be made to the precise rule but, broadly, it provides that where, in a reclaiming motion the opinion of the Lord Ordinary has not been included in the reclaiming print[30] or where it is sought to submit notes of evidence or documents for consideration by the court in the reclaiming motion, then the reclaimer has to lodge an appendix incorporating such documents within three months after the case has been appointed to the summar roll. If it is not considered necessary to lodge an appendix then the reclaimer has to advise the deputy principal clerk and the opponent of this. If the respondent wants to submit notes of evidence when the reclaimer does not, then the respondent will incorporate the notes of evidence or documents in an appendix which is to be lodged within the time limit provided. If the reclaimer fails to lodge an appendix as required then the respondent can apply by motion to have the reclaiming motion refused.

Rule 38.21—If a party wants to amend his pleadings after a reclaiming motion has been marked then he shall apply for a direction as to further procedure in relation to that amendment. If it is considered by the Inner House that the proposed amendment makes a material changes to the pleadings it may simply recall the interlocutor of the Lord Ordinary reclaimed against and remit the case back to the Lord Ordinary for a further hearing.

Appeals to the Inner House from an inferior court

20–14   For present purposes we shall simply consider the question of appeals to the Inner House from the sheriff court and the rules regarding such

---

[28] The summar roll is a list of cases which have been appealed to the Inner House.
[29] The single bills is the motion roll of the Inner House.
[30] Because there is no written opinion at the time when the reclaiming motion is lodged.

appeals are dealt with in Ch.40 of the RCS. Again the rules relate largely to administrative matters. They are intricate and are somewhat difficult to follow without detailed knowledge of the administrative processes in the Court of Session. Reference should be made to the detailed terms of the rules and the intention here is simply to give a broad appreciation of what is contained within the rules in Ch.40. The rules are from 40.1–40.21, and there are similarities between the provisions applying to such appeals and the provisions applying to reclaiming an interlocutor of the Lord Ordinary.

The important rules to note are:

Rule 40.2—This provides that where leave to appeal is required, an application for leave shall be made in the first instance to the inferior court although there may be circumstances in which leave to appeal can be sought from the Inner House. There are provisions for how that may be done.

Rule 40.4—This provides that an appeal from an inferior court shall be made within an appropriate period and if there is no specific period prescribed by the enactment by virtue of which the appeal is made then the period within which the appeal has to be marked is 21 days after the date on which the decision appealed against was given or the date on which written reasons were issued or the date on which leave was granted, whichever is the later. There are provisions regarding the way in which an appeal should be marked.

Rule 40.5—An application to allow an appeal to be received outwith the time prescribed for marking an appeal has to be included in the note of appeal. Difficult questions arise as to time limits and applications for leave to appeal out of time. There may be an issue as to whether an application for leave to appeal which ought to have been made to the sheriff before an appeal was marked should go to the Inner House or to the court of first instance.

Rules 40.6 and 40.7—Once an appeal has been marked then the relevant sheriff court process should be forwarded to the Court of Session within four days. Within 14 days after receipt of those papers each party seeking to appear in the appeal has to give his details to the deputy principal clerk of the Court of Session and then within 28 days of the receipt of the process in the appeal the appellant has to lodge a process and an appeal print. Appeals against interlocutors which are not final judgments have to be marked for early disposal.

It is also possible to sist an appeal for a period of time thereby preventing the time limits provided in the rules being exceeded.

Rule 40.9—A failure to comply with the formal requirements of the **20–15** appeal can mean that the appellant can be deemed to have abandoned the appeal. The respondent can within seven days insist upon it by complying with the appropriate requirements. An appellant can, within seven days after the date on which the appeal has been deemed to be abandoned, apply by motion to be reponed and that motion may be granted on such conditions as to expenses as the court thinks fit. Seven days after the date on which the appeal is deemed to be abandoned the deputy principal clerk will simply return the papers to the inferior court.

Rule 40.11—This provides for a party seeking early disposal of the appeal and it is open to the Inner House to appoint the case for early disposal.

Rule 40.12—Objections can be taken to the competency of appeals and there is specific provision that if the deputy principal clerk considers an appeal may be incompetent he may refer it to a single judge before it is brought before the Inner House at all. The judge has various powers including the power to have a hearing on competency and the power to refuse the appeal without a hearing on the ground it is incompetent.[31] Any such decision is final and not subject to review.

Rules 40.13 and 40.14—If there is no objection to the competency of the appeal then the Inner House will order grounds of appeal to be lodged. The grounds of appeal have to be lodged within 28 days of the date of the interlocutor ordering them and the provisions regarding the form and content of grounds of appeal have already been noted in the earlier rule.

Rule 40.15—This provides that within seven days after the period prescribed for lodging grounds of appeal the appellant will apply by motion for an order for hearing, and the court can appoint the case to the summar roll for a hearing or direct that it be heard in the single bills. If questions of competency of the appeal have been reserved, then they can be dealt with at the motion for an order for hearing. The appellant has to lodge an appeal print in the form of a record. There are provisions also regarding the lodging of appendices which are very similar to the provisions noted above and will not be repeated.

Rule 40.21—This was introduced with effect from March 1, 2004,[32] and allows an appellant to apply to address the court in Gaelic[33] if the original proceedings were so authorised.

---

[31] See *Sheltered Housing Management Ltd v Aitken*, 1998 S.L.T. 515 and *McArthur v McArthur*, 1997 S.L.T. 926.

[32] By the Advice and Assistance (Scotland) Amendment (No.2) Regulations 2004 Amendment Regulations 2004 (SSI 2004/305).

[33] As opposed to Greek in which some appellants are fluent!

Appeals under statute

It is not intended to deal with these appeals in any detail. The Court **20–16** of Session has jurisdiction to deal with various statutory appeals and these are usually dealt with in the Inner House although there can be circumstances in which a statute might provide an appeal to be heard by a Lord Ordinary. The specific provisions are contained in Ch.41 of the RCS and reference should be made to the rules themselves. The types of application and the ways in which they have to be set out are provided in detail. Amongst other things the appeals relate to Exchequer appeals, appeals under the Pension Appeals Tribunal Act 1943, appeals under the Representation of the People Act 1983, and appeals under Social Security Acts.

Sheriff court

Small claim

Rules 23.1–23.5 deal with the procedure for an appeal to the sheriff **20–17** principal. The appeal is taken by lodging a note of appeal in a prescribed form in which the party requests the sheriff to provide a stated case.[34] The note of appeal will also specify the point of law upon which the party proposes to proceed with the appeal. The note of appeal has to be lodged not later than 14 days after the date of final decree. The rules provide that the party lodging the note of appeal (the appellant) will intimate the lodging of the note of appeal to his opponent (the respondent). The sheriff then has to issue a draft stated case with findings in fact and law or a narrative of the proceedings which took place before him. The draft stated case should also include appropriate questions of law and should contain a note stating the reasons for his decisions in law. This will be sent to both parties in the appeal and they have 14 days within which to lodge suggested adjustments. The respondent, who will not have had an opportunity to make any representations about points of law by that stage, can then state any point of law which he wishes to raise in the appeal. The sheriff does not have to accept any suggested adjustments by the parties to the stated case, but if he proposes to reject any adjustments then he must fix a hearing on the proposed adjustments before finalising his stated case. Within 14 days of the expiry of the period for adjustments, or alternatively within 14 days of any hearing on the adjustments, the sheriff will then produce a final version of the stated case which is signed by him and which forms the basis of the appeal hearing along with any productions or documents used in the case itself. The point of law arising at the appeal and argued before the sheriff principal will be confined to the point of law or points of law specified in the

---

[34] This is a document in which the sheriff—who is unlikely to have issued a written judgment in the small claim action—will set out the circumstances of the case, the procedure in the case, any evidence heard in the case, and the reasons for his decision.

322   *Civil Procedure and Practice*

stated case unless a very good reason is given for extending the scope of
the appeal.

There are special provisions regarding appeals in connection with a
time to pay direction.[35] An application for leave to appeal has to be made
on a prescribed form within seven days of the decision and must specify
the question of law upon which the appeal is to proceed. If leave to
appeal is granted the appeal has to be lodged and intimated on a prescribed form within 14 days, and the sheriff must state in writing the
reasons for his original decision.

Summary cause

20–18   The rules regarding appeals in summary causes are contained in
Ch.25 of the SCR rr.25.1–25.7. Again, reference should be made to the
precise terms of the rules themselves, but the procedure for appeals is
virtually identical to that applying in an appeal in a small claim and will
not be repeated here.

It has already been noted that it is possible to appeal from the sheriff
principal to the Court of Session in a summary cause and the provisions
regarding this are contained in r.25.7. A party can apply on a prescribed
form for a certificate of suitability for appeal[36] to the Court of Session
from the sheriff principal and must do so within 14 days of the date
of the final decree. The sheriff principal will hear the parties or their
solicitors on this, and decides whether to grant or refuse the certificate.

Ordinary actions

20–19   The interlocutors which can be appealed are specified in the statutory
provisions which we have already considered, so the rules regarding
appeals in an ordinary action deal simply with administrative and procedural issues. They are contained within Ch.31 rr.31.1–31.11 of the OCR.
The principal features of the rules are as follows:

Rule 31.1—Any appeal must usually be taken within 14 days after the
date of the interlocutor which is to be reviewed.

Rule 31.2—If leave to appeal is required before an appeal can be taken
then an application for leave to appeal must be made within seven days
after the date of the interlocutor appealed. If leave to appeal is granted
then the appeal must be marked within seven days after the date when
leave was granted.

---

[35] Where a defender proposes to make payment of a sum due by him by instalments.
[36] The form does not need to include any specific reason or justification for the proposition that the case is suitable for appeal to the Court of Session. The hearing of the appeal
before the sheriff principal might or might not have raised matters which would
apparently merit further consideration.

Rule 31.3—This provides for the form of appeal to the Court of Session and the details can be noted in the rule.[37]

Rule 31.4—This provides for a form of appeal to the sheriff principal. The appellant has to lodge a note of appeal in the prescribed form. Amongst other things, the note of appeal must contain grounds of appeal, which shall consist of brief specific numbered propositions stating the grounds on which it is proposed to submit that the appeal should be allowed. This was something of an innovation in the 1993 Rules because formerly a party could appeal simply by intimating that he wished to appeal. He wrote on the process that he wished to appeal and he did not have to state any specific grounds of appeal at all until the appeal hearing itself. It is clearly far more desirable for a party to state grounds of appeal in advance, although the rules also provide that a party can amend the grounds of appeal at any time up to 14 days before the date assigned for the hearing for the appeal. A copy of the note of appeal and any amendment has to be sent to the opponent and once the note of appeal has been lodged a date should be fixed for the hearing of the appeal.[38] If the sheriff against whom the appeal has been taken has not provided a note regarding the decision appealed against, then the party who lodges the appeal should at the time of lodging the appeal ask the sheriff to write a note setting out the reasons for his decision so that this is available when the appeal is heard.

The rules contain a number of administrative provisions which we do not need to consider, but it is provided that the sheriff principal shall hear parties at an oral hearing of the appeal or on the motion of the parties and, if he thinks fit, dispose of the appeal without ordering an oral hearing.[39]

Once a party has appealed, then an opponent can cross appeal, and in that case he would lodge a note of the grounds of his cross appeal not less than seven days before the date assigned for the hearing of the appeal and send a copy of this to every other party in the case. The rules provide that after an appeal has been marked the appellant is not entitled to abandon it unless with the consent of the other parties or with the leave of the sheriff principal.[40]

---

[37] The form for marking an appeal is extremely simple. More details of the appeal will be required later, once the papers have been transferred to the Court of Session for the purposes of administering the appeal.

[38] Although there may be good reasons for delaying the fixing of the date, e.g. a party requiring to apply for legal aid for the appeal.

[39] This is relatively unusual. A practice is now developing of preparing written submissions for an appeal which might supplement or perhaps, eventually, replace an oral hearing of an appeal. That is a development of practice. There are no rules requiring this, although it is generally found to be helpful and can reduce the time taken in appeals.

[40] Primarily, this is intended to cover a situation whereby a party, by abandoning his appeal, could prevent his opponent proceeding with a cross appeal.

PARTICULAR ASPECTS OF APPEALS

(1) Final judgment

20–20 It will have been noted that in many situations there has been reference to appeals being competent after "final judgment" in the sheriff court. Broadly, a "final judgment" is a judgment which either alone or in conjunction with other interlocutors in the case disposes of the subject matter of the case and deals with the question of liability for expenses. Whether a judgment is a final judgment or not can often be a matter of controversy.[41] The rules in the Court of Session do not base time limits for reclaiming upon the date of a final judgment. Their equivalent time limits are based upon the interlocutor which disposes of the whole merits of the cause. It is interesting to see that what this meant in practice was not entirely understood by practitioners and the Court of Session went to the length of issuing a notice[42] confirming what the court considered to be the proper interpretation of the rule.[43] In Court of Session cases, whether the interlocutor deals with expenses or not is immaterial in deciding whether it is a final judgment.

(2) Leave to appeal

20–21 It will be observed that some appeals are only competent if leave is granted. It is regarded as desirable to discourage incidental appeals so that appeals in relation to incidental or procedural matters need the permission of the sheriff or the judge before they can be taken. When considering an application for leave, the judge who made the decision has to exercise his discretion as to whether to allow leave or not. Amongst other factors he will have to consider the delay and cost which an appeal might cause and the benefit or consequence of a successful appeal.[44]

(3) Effect of an appeal

20–22 Putting the matter broadly, the marking of an appeal in any case will suspend the operation of the decree and suspend all execution upon the decree until the appeal has been heard. The marking of an appeal can open up all of the previous interlocutors in the case including interlocutors which were not themselves appealable at the time.[45]

---

[41] For a detailed explanation of this see Macphail, *Sheriff Court Practice*, 3rd edn, paras 18.33–18.36. See also *DTL Gas Supplies Ltd v Protan Srl*, 1999 S.L.T. 397 and *Japan Leasing (Europe) Plc v Weir's Trustee*, 1998 S.L.T. 224.

[42] Like a practice note, although its origins are not entirely clear.

[43] The time limit is 21 days and will run from the date of the interlocutor against which appeal is being taken, notwithstanding that expenses have not been decided. Rule 38.3(2) and notice dated February 6, 1997.

[44] This is discussed in more detail in Macphail, *Sheriff Court Practice*, 3rd edn, paras 18.50–18.54.

[45] See Macphail, *Sheriff Court Practice*, 3rd edn, paras 18.68–18.71 and r.38.8 of the RCS.

(4) Additional proof

As a general proposition, the hearing of an appeal will not involve **20–23** the hearing of any additional evidence in the case or a rehearing of the evidence in the case. However, there is a provision in s.27 of the 1907 Act permitting a sheriff principal to allow additional proof.[46]

(5) Conduct of an appeal

Although it is not within the scope of this book to discuss the detailed **20–24** presentation of an appeal it may be helpful to give an indication of the general submissions which would normally be made[47]. This is intended only as a very broad guide indeed, and it is extremely difficult to reduce the complexity of submissions in an appeal to a standard formula of any kind. Appeals against interlocutory judgments will involve parties making submissions to the court regarding the procedure in the case and making submissions regarding the legal principles and practice which ought to have been applied. They will normally involve a detailed explanation of the relevant facts and a discussion about the appropriate legal principles. The appellant will explain to the appeal court what is being appealed against and what order he wants the appeal court to make. If the appeal is against a decision in which the judge has a discretion, it is necessary to satisfy the appeal court that he exercised that discretion unreasonably.[48]

In cases where there has been a final judgment following a debate, the appeal will concern itself entirely with matters of law based upon the pleadings. The record which was the basis for the hearing of the debate or procedure roll hearing which gave rise to dismissal will be available to the appellate court. If there is any amendment proposed then this will have been dealt with in accordance with the rules as previously discussed. In the absence of amendment prior to the appeal, the hearing will usually be, in essence, a further debate on the same point.

An appeal against a final judgment following upon proof at which detailed evidence has been led would probably be presented along these lines:

(1) a broad explanation of the nature of the case;
(2) the relevant procedural history of the case up to the appeal;
(3) confirmation of the decision being appealed against;
(4) what matters are or are not in dispute for the purposes of the appeal;
(5) what particular findings in fact made by the judge at first instance are to be varied/recalled/supplemented;

---

[46] This is extremely rare and would probably involve remitting the case back to the sheriff for such proof. See Macphail, *Sheriff Court Practice*, 3rd edn, para.18.81 for further details.
[47] This is covered in detail in Hennessy, *Practical Advocacy in the Sheriff Court*, Ch.12.
[48] See *Royal Bank of Scotland Plc v Malcolm*, 1998 S.L.T. 331.

(6) the interlocutor which is ultimately to be sought from the appellate court;
(7) a detailed exposition of the case by (a) reading of the record, the contents of the judge's interlocutor and note, and (b) the reading of the notes of evidence at least insofar as these are relevant to the point at issue in the appeal;
(8) presentation of detailed arguments in accordance with an outline and highlighting individual points;
(9) submissions on the expenses of the appeal.[49]

DECISION OF THE APPELLATE COURT

20–25   The appellate court in dealing with an appeal can do any of the following:

(1) adhere to the original decision;
(2) recall the original decision;
(3) adhere to the original decision in part or recall it in part;
(4) vary the original decision;
(5) remit the case back to the sheriff or judge of first instance for particular reasons;
(6) dismiss the appeal; or
(7) grant the appeal and substitute a completely different decision.

PARTICULAR APPEALS

Appeal against the exercise of discretion

20–26   An appeal against the exercise of a discretion by a judge of first instance is discouraged. The appellate court will not interfere with such a decision unless it is satisfied either that the judge exercised his discretion upon a wrong principle or that, his decision being so plainly wrong, he must have exercised his discretion wrongly. If an appellate court is considering the judge's exercise of discretion it is not sufficient for them to say that they disagree with him, and if the matter had called before them they would have decided the matter differently. They have to reach the view that he was plainly wrong. They might have reached a different decision themselves but that would not be sufficient for a successful appeal if they accept that the decision the judge at first instance reached was a decision which he was at least entitled to make.[50]

---

[49] Which will usually follow success in the appeal. See Ch.20.
[50] See the cases of *A v A* [1985] 1 W.L.R. 647 and *Brown v Brown*, 1985 S.L.T. 376.

Appeal against an apportionment of liability

In reparation actions, the judge at first instance will sometimes be **20–27**
asked to decide whether a pursuer contributed to the accident and a
reduction ought to be made for contributory negligence or whether two
or more defenders contributed to the accident in different degrees.
A judge's decision on contributory negligence or on the apportionment
of liability between various defenders will rarely be appealed successfully. This type of appeal is discouraged and would only succeed if the
judge has, "manifestly and to a substantial degree gone wrong".[51]

Appeals against awards of damages

Again these are discouraged. In relation to claims for financial loss as
part of damages an appeal would only be allowed where there has been
the use of wrong facts, the application of wrong principles, or where the
judge's decision is manifestly unfair.[52] In cases where the court has
made an award of solatium for the personal injury suffered by a pursuer
and the defender wishes to appeal against this as being too high (or
indeed in a case where the pursuer wishes to appeal against it as being
too low) the appeal court will be slow to interfere with the judge's decision. An appeal would only be successful where the sum awarded is out
of all proportion to what the appellate court thinks should have been
awarded.[53] Particular considerations apply in relation to awards of damages by a jury. Such awards can only be reviewed on appeal if they are
excessive to the extent that the award amounts to a gross injustice.[54]

Appeal against award of expenses

An appeal to a higher court against an award of expenses made by an **20–28**
inferior court is very severely discouraged. Appeals on expenses generally are not welcomed and they will only be considered where there has
been an obvious miscarriage of justice.[55]

---

[51] See the case of *McCusker v Saveheat*, 1987 S.L.T. 24, for an illustration.
[52] See the case of *Blair v FJC Lilley Marine*, 1981 S.L.T. 90.
[53] See the case of *Bowers v Strathclyde Regional Council*, 1981 S.L.T. 122, where the award was considered to be "wholly unreasonable".
[54] See the very detailed discussion of this in *Girvan v Inverness Farmers Dairy (No.2)*, 1998 S.L.T. 21.
[55] See the case of *Mason v Foster Wheeler*, 1984 S.L.T. (Sh. Ct) 5.

CHAPTER 21

EXPENSES

21–01 It may not have been apparent to the reader but litigation actually costs money. This simple fact is one of the most significant practical features present in most litigation. Media reports of high profile cases may well convince clients that not only does a court case cost money, it costs vast sums of money and the costs are virtually uncontrollable. That is not true, but the expense of litigation can in many cases be high in proportion to the sum claimed. There is no doubt that a realistic assessment by a solicitor, at the outset of litigation, of the cost of pursuing it, or defending it, can be a powerful disincentive to a client to proceed. All the more so, if the likely costs are going to be out of proportion to the sum at stake. On the other hand, there are clients who simply insist on litigating, or feel that they have to litigate as a matter of principle (or for some other reason) and are not particularly concerned about cost.

It is important to make clear what is meant by the "expenses" or "costs"[1] of a court action. A client who instructs a solicitor to pursue or defend a litigation will normally be liable to pay his solicitor's fee for doing any work on his instructions in the litigation. That is a contractual arrangement between them. So the immediate expense of the litigation to the client is going to be his solicitor's bill.[2] Putting the matter very broadly, during the litigation itself, various steps taken by the parties on their own initiative, and other steps required by the court during the procedural stages of the action, will attract a fee. If the client succeeds with the action, then he should be able to recover that fee from his opponent. If he loses, then he is likely to have to pay that fee to the opponent. The fees which one or other side can recover from the unsuccessful litigant are termed the "judicial expenses".[3] At the same time as the judicial expenses are being incurred, that same work will attract a fee which the solicitor can charge to his client. Generally speaking, the fees which a solicitor contracts to charge his client are likely to exceed the amount he can recover from an unsuccessful opponent,[4] so there is usually a shortfall between what the litigation costs the client (his agent/client bill) and what he can recover from the opponent (the party/party bill).

---

[1] Which is really the English term for expenses.
[2] This can be termed the "agent/client" expenses.
[3] Also called "party/party" expenses.
[4] For reasons which shall be explained.

Sometimes a solicitor will contract with his client to the effect that he will accept the judicial expenses he can recover from the opponent in full settlement of the fee he will charge the client. Another option might be for him to do the case on a speculative basis. Basically this means that the solicitor agrees that he will pursue the claim but will only be entitled to a fee from the client[5] if the client is successful in the claim. The quid pro quo for that agreement would be that the client agrees that if the claim is successful, then the solicitor shall be entitled to charge a fee up to 100 per cent more than he would normally be entitled to charge. This kind of arrangement can be found in some personal injury claims, although there is no reason in principle why it should not apply to other types of action.[6] The rules contain a definition of what "success" in the cause is. This covers a settlement whereby the client receives money, or a settlement in kind, or where the case has been concluded by a decree which, on the merits, is to any extent in his favour.

It is extremely difficult to understand the real practical significance of judicial expenses in a litigation without repeated first-hand experience. Disputes about judicial expenses are frequent and sometimes it may seem that arguments about judicial expenses assume more importance than the merits of the case itself. Recovery of the maximum amount of judicial expenses from the opponent can make a very substantial differ-ence to the cost of the litigation to the client.[7] A good understanding of court practices, procedures and rules, and a good appreciation of the principles applicable to the recovery of judicial expenses in the court where the litigation is taking place, will enable a litigator to conduct the case in such a way as to minimise the cost of the litigation to his own client.[8] That is his professional obligation.

The choice of litigating in one court rather than another, the choice of **21–02** specific procedures during an action, and many other significant choices made by one or other party during the course of an action, are as likely to be influenced by costs, as by any nice points of law or practice. One of the first questions a client will ask before embarking on any litigation, or defending any litigation, is likely to be whether the opponent can be forced to pay the client's legal bill. The answer to that question depends first, and crucially, on whether the client wins the case or not. If he wins, then the court will almost certainly make an award of expenses in his favour.[9] The next question which arises, however, is whether this award

---

[5] i.e. the "agent/client" fee.

[6] The provisions regarding fees in speculative cases are contained within r.42.17 of the 1994 Rules of the Court of Session. The statutory basis entitling a solicitor and client to reach agreement on a speculative fee is s.61A(3) of the Solicitors (Scotland) Act 1980, inserted by s.36(3) of the Law Reform (Miscellaneous Provisions) (Scotland) Act 1990.

[7] And to the opponent.

[8] Regardless of the outcome of the litigation.

[9] In principle, therefore, he is likely to be able to recover at least some of the money he is contractually bound to pay his lawyer from the other side.

of expenses will cover all of the expenditure which the client will have to pay his lawyer for handling the case from start to finish? The answer to that question is that "it depends".[10]

The client might not be entitled to recover the whole of his own lawyer's bill from the opponent even when he "wins" because:

(1) the court reaches a decision at the end of the case, that he is not entitled to recover some or all of the judicial expenses; or
(2) some of the expenditure in the account of judicial expenses is not the kind of expense which could ever, in principle, be recovered from an opponent; or
(3) the charges he has to pay his solicitor for individual items of work legitimately done on his behalf (as per the contractual fees which the solicitor is entitled to charge the client), are higher than the amount he can properly recover from his opponent for that same work (as per the prescribed scale of fees which a party to a particular litigation is entitled to charge the opponent).

Indeed, the difference between the judicial expenses, which he can in principle recover from the opponent, and the amount which he has to pay to his own solicitor for the work he does in the litigation, can arise from a combination of any of the three factors mentioned above. In order to explore this topic further we are going to look at the following:

(1) What precisely is meant by judicial expenses?
(2) What are the basic principles on which awards of judicial expenses are made?
(3) What is the appropriate rate of charges (otherwise known as the scale of fees or table of fees) applicable to any particular litigation?
(4) Are there any exceptions or specialities relating to that principle?
(5) Once the court has made an award in principle and has set the appropriate rate of charges in principle, how are the detailed figures calculated and decided?

If it is necessary to ask the court to adjudicate on the precise amount of the judicial expenses payable in any ordinary action this is done by the court auditor and the process is called "taxing" an account.[11] If a hearing is required for that purpose, the hearing is called a "taxation". It is important to remember, however, that whatever the court might decide about judicial expenses which can be recovered from an opponent, the client will always have his contractual obligation to pay his own solicitor's bill at whatever rate or on whatever scale has been agreed between them.

---

[10] As all good lawyers might say.
[11] NB: it has nothing to do with the Inland Revenue!

1. What Do We Mean by Judicial Expenses of Litigation?

The judicial expenses of litigation comprise solicitors' fees, counsels' fees **21–03** (where applicable), VAT, and outlays incurred by the solicitors on behalf of their client in preparing and presenting any case for litigation. These are the costs which, provided they are reasonably incurred in the litigation, can be recovered from the opponent subject to the detailed rules which will be discussed. The actual figures quoted as an illustration are the figures applicable, as at November 2004, to an ordinary action in the sheriff court or Court of Session.[12] The figures applicable on April 1, 2008 are higher.[13]

Solicitors' fees

They are charged at a rate applicable to that particular type of litiga- **21–04** tion and can be charged either on a "detailed" time basis, i.e. so much per hour or quarter hour, or on a "block" fee basis, i.e. so much for a particular piece of work regardless of the time actually spent on it. For example, the fee for adjustment of pleadings in a sheriff court ordinary case could be a time charge, (say) four hours at £x per hour, or the block fee of £255. The Court of Session block fee[14] would be £458.70. The table of fees applicable to judicial expenses for solicitors in actions in the Court of Session is contained in r.42.16 of the RCS, and the actual charges within that table can change from time to time. The table of fees for solicitors in actions in the sheriff court is contained in an Act of Sederunt[15] and the actual charges within the table can change from time to time by way of Act of Sederunt.

Counsels' fees

These are recoverable from the opponent in Court of Session actions **21–05** as a normal element of judicial expenses, although in odd cases it is open to a party to argue that the case should never have been raised in the Court of Session and therefore counsel's fees should not be recoverable from the other side. It is possible to include in the judicial expenses of a sheriff court action fees due to counsel for conducting the proceedings or part of the proceedings, but this can only be done if the court sanctions the employment of counsel.[16] This might be requested because the

---

[12] Keeping up to date with the latest tables of fees is, needless to say, rather important. They can change quite frequently.

[13] For sheriff court actions they can be found in the Act of Sederunt (Fees of Solicitors in the Sheriff Court) (Amendment) 2008 (SSI 2008/40) and for the Court of Session they can be found in the Act of Sederunt (Rules of the Court of Session Amendment) (Fees of Solicitors) 2008 (SSI 2008/39).

[14] Which encompasses a little more work than the sheriff court "block".

[15] Act of Sederunt (Fees of Solicitors in the Sheriff Court) (Amendment and Further Provisions) 1993 (SI 1993/3080).

[16] i.e. grants a motion by either party requesting the court to approve the employment of counsel for the case.

case was considered by the solicitor to be too difficult, complex or important for him to do himself. A party is always entitled to use counsel if he wishes, but the expense of counsel can only be recovered from the other side if the court ultimately sanctions his employment.[17]

VAT

21–06   In simple terms, this can be charged against the unsuccessful party as part of the judicial expenses where the successful party, who has been awarded expenses, is not VAT registered. If he is VAT registered, then he would be able to reclaim the VAT on his own solicitor's bill in his own VAT returns, so the opponent is not required to pay the VAT on the judicial expenses.

Outlays

21–07   These can form quite a substantial part of the judicial expenses of litigation. The more expensive outlays, which can increase costs quite considerably, would include, e.g. the cost of an expert report for use in the litigation (easily costing £750 or more), the cost of specialist medical reports required for a personal injury case (£300 or more), and the expenses of witnesses attending court to give evidence. Witness expenses can be substantial if the witnesses are coming from far away and incurring loss of earnings, etc.[18] or charging a fee in the case of expert witnesses. A further expense will be court dues. The court dues have increased considerably over the last few years as it is the intention of the Scottish Court Service to reduce the level of public subsidy to the courts and cover a large part of the costs of running the court service by payments from those who actually use it.

2. Principles Regarding Awards of Judicial Expenses

21–08   Since most cases are settled, the courts frequently do not have to adjudicate on expenses. A party settling an action will normally be compelled to agree to pay the opponent's judicial expenses as a condition of the settlement, but the parties can agree to deal with the opponent's expenses in any way they think fit.[19] It is often an important part of any

---

[17]   That is by no means automatically done. An example from the sheriff court is *Mason v Foster Wheeler Power Products Ltd*, 1984 S.L.T. (Sh. Ct) 5.

[18]   There are rules about witness expenses. See, e.g. the Act of Sederunt (Rules of the Court of Session Amendment) (Fees of Solicitors, Shorthand Writers and Witnesses) 2002 (SSI 2002/301) and Act of Sederunt (Fees of Witnesses and Shorthand Writers in the Sheriff Court) 1992 (SI 1992/1878), as amended by Act of Sederunt (Fees of Witnesses in the Sheriff Court) (Amendment) 1999 (SI 1999/188).

[19]   Including agreement to pay the other side's expenses on an agent/client basis, i.e. the opponent would effectively pay the successful party's lawyer's bill so that there would be no shortfall.

negotiation for settlement of a claim that the expenses are to be paid at a set figure or at an agreed rate and this might not necessarily be the rate in the court scale fees. The expenses (actual and anticipated) of a court action can often be a very significant factor in negotiations for settlement, especially where the total expenses are as much as, or more than, the value of the claim.

Assuming the expenses fall to be decided by the court, the decision which the court is required to make is primarily the decision as to which party should be liable for expenses as a matter of principle, not a decision as to what the actual figure for expenses should be. The award dealing with liability for expenses, in principle, is entirely within the discretion of the court. It can make awards dealing with the expenses of any particular stage of a case, in relation to any particular matters of procedure, and in relation to the action as a whole. Frequently, the court will not be asked to make any finding of expenses until the conclusion of the case, but there is nothing to stop a motion for expenses occasioned by procedure in some part of the case being made at an appropriate stage. Indeed, the court can make such an award of expenses on its own volition.

The general principle upon which the court makes an award of expenses can be taken from Lord President Cooper in *Howitt v W. Alexander & Sons Ltd*[20]:

"An award of expenses according to our law is a matter for the exercise in each case of a judicial discretion, designed to achieve substantial justice, and very rarely disturbed on appeal. I gravely doubt whether all of the conditions upon which that discretion should be exercised have ever been, or ever will be, successfully imprisoned within the framework of rigid and unalterable rules, and I do not think that it would be desirable that they should be . . . If any party is put to expense in vindicating his rights, he is entitled to recover it from the person by whom it was created, unless there is something in his own conduct that gives him the character of an improper litigant in insisting on things which his title does not warrant."

In that same case, Lord Russell said: **21–09**

"It appears to me that in dealing with expenses at the close of a contested suit, the court may in some cases proceed inter alia on the view that the rights of the parties are to be taken to have been all along what the ultimate decree shews . . . In our courts, the exercise of the judicial discretion in awarding expenses has always been regulated by the wide principle of doing justice to the parties in each particular case, regarding . . . its particular circumstances,

---

[20] *Howitt v W. Alexander & Sons Ltd*, 1948 S.L.T. 334.

including the averments of parties, the evidence adduced, the conduct of the parties, and the ultimate result."

Whilst the broad principles are clear, and, generally speaking, the award of expenses follows success, the application of that principle to different circumstances has produced a whole range of results which defy easy and simple analysis. Factors which would have a bearing upon the award of expenses include (1) the particular circumstances of the case; (2) the contribution of each of the parties to the fact that litigation occurred at all; (3) the length and expense of the litigation or some part of it; and (4) the conduct of the parties before and during the litigation.[21]

3. WHAT IS THE APPROPRIATE SCALE OF FEES?

21–10 Apart from making the all-important finding of which party is liable for expenses of all or part of the procedure, the court will adjudicate on one other crucial issue, namely the scale of judicial expenses which should be payable. Normally the losing party would have to pay the expenses on the scale appropriate to that form of procedure, but there may be circumstances in which it can be argued that the scale should be reduced. The court has discretion to award expenses on a different scale to the norm if other circumstances merit this. The court can even award judicial expenses on an agent/client basis, i.e. on the basis that the fee chargeable by the solicitor to the client can in fact be charged to the unsuccessful opponent.[22]

As an illustration of the practical effect this might have on the amount of judicial expenses[23], consider a Court of Session ordinary action in which the final award of expenses has been made on different scales. On the Court of Session scale, the block fee for instruction[24] would be £651.30 plus (automatically) a fee to counsel for drafting the summons of about £300. On the sheriff court ordinary action scale (without counsel) the block fee would be £693.90.[25] On the summary cause scale it would be £166.35.

---

[21] A sample of cases on expenses follows: *Stevenson v Western Scottish Omnibuses Ltd*, 1990 S.L.T. (Sh. Ct) 55; *Woods v British Steel Corp*, 1974 S.L.T. (Notes) 24; *Alvis v Harrison*, 1989 S.L.T. 746; *William Nimmo and Co Ltd v Russell Construction Co Ltd (No.2)*, 1997 S.L.T. 122.

[22] Examples of cases where awards of expenses were made on different scales are: *McIntyre v Munro*, 1990 S.L.T. (Notes) 177; *Rooney v F.W. Woolworth Plc*, 1990 S.L.T. 257. See particularly what was said in *McIntosh v British Railways Board*, 1990 S.L.T. 637 at 641A–D.

[23] Applicable at April 1, 2008.

[24] Leaving aside work done pre-litigation which will be mentioned later.

[25] This would include the solicitor's fee for drafting the writ.

4. SPECIALITIES

There are some specialities regarding judicial expenses which should be borne in mind.

(1) Events prior to litigation itself

The court can decide that even though a party was "successful" with **21–11** his claim, he should not be entitled to the judicial expenses because he did not give the opponent any opportunity to pay him before the action was raised. On the same theme, but from a different perspective, if the actions of the other party have in some way encouraged a party to raise an action which was ultimately held to be plainly ill founded, and the party could not reasonably have known this prior to raising the litigation, the court could decide that the "successful" defender should not be awarded expenses. This is perhaps just a particular illustration of the discretionary power which the court has in expenses. The court in these cases focused their criticism on the party who could reasonably be said to have "caused" the litigation.[26]

(2) Caution for expenses

Court expenses can be very high. A client may hope that he will get **21–12** his costs back from his opponent on a successful conclusion of the case. He may fear that he is going to spend money advancing his claim (or defence) and the opponent is then going to abandon the case or lose comprehensively but have no money to pay the judicial expenses. It may be prudent and highly desirable, if these are legitimate concerns, to try and obtain some guarantee or security for the payment of judicial expenses, and there are circumstances in which the court can make such an order. Procedurally, this is done by making a motion for the opponent to find caution for expenses. The court has discretion whether to grant this or not.[27] Special provisions apply to limited companies where there is always the possibility of an individual using the protection of a company's corporate identity to litigate without the any risk of real liability for expenses.[28]

---

[26] See *Cleghorn v Fairgreaves*, 1982 S.L.T. (Sh. Ct) 17, *Cellular Clothing Co Ltd v Schulberg*, 1952 S.L.T. (Notes) 73, *Crombie v British Transport Commission*, 1961 S.L.T. 115.

[27] The best, recent, and authoritative view of the whole issue is the well-known case of *McTear's Executrix v Imperial Tobacco Ltd*, 1997 S.L.T. 530. The report contains details of many of the other cases on caution for expenses. See also *Thomson v Ross*, 2001 S.L.T. 807 and *William Dow (Potatoes) Ltd v William Dow*, 2001 S.L.T. (Sh. Ct) 37.

[28] See s.726(2) of the Companies Act 1985. See also *Medicopharma (UK) BV v Cairns*, 1993 S.L.T. 386 and *Merrick Homes Ltd v Duff*, 1996 S.L.T. 932.

(3) The significance of legal aid

21–13   This has very important practical implications for much litigation. If a pursuer has legal aid to pursue an action, that fact has no particular significance for awards of judicial expenses if he is successful with his claim. However, if a legally-aided pursuer (or defender) loses his case and is found liable in principle to pay his opponent's judicial expenses, he can make a motion to the court to have that liability to the opponent reduced.[29] This entitlement arises from the terms of s.18(2) of the Legal Aid (Scotland) Act 1986. The court does, however, have discretion as to whether to make a modification or not and there are certain factors which can and should be taken into account in exercising that discretion.[30] In practical terms, if the pursuer is unemployed and has a legal aid certificate which shows that he has no contribution to make to the Scottish Legal Aid Board towards his own solicitor's costs, his solicitors will normally make a motion to the court for the pursuer's liability for expenses of the defender to be modified to nil. There is often little realistic alternative for the court but to grant such a motion. This leaves the successful defender winning the case and having to pay his own solicitor's bill which he cannot recover from the pursuer. It means that a legally-aided pursuer (or defender) can litigate in the knowledge that it is unlikely to cost him anything by way of expenses even if he loses. There are certain restricted situations where the successful litigant, opposing a legally-aided party, can recover expenses from the Scottish Legal Aid Board itself,[31] but these are few and far between.

(4) Awards of expenses prior to the conclusion of the action

21–14   Notwithstanding that there is often one single and general award of expenses at the end of an action in favour of the successful party, there can also be individual and specific awards of expenses in relation to particular parts of procedure during the conduct of the case. A motion can be, and often is, made by a party in these circumstances seeking specific awards of expenses. It is open to a judge to consider arguments about expenses during a hearing at any of the earlier incidental procedures in the case. If a party makes a motion for the expenses of some particular part of the proceedings, the judge can:

(a)   make an award one way or the other;
(b)   reserve the question of expenses, i.e. not make any award at the time although he might come back and reconsider this later;

---

[29]   By being modified to a particular amount or (quite often) reduced to nil.
[30]   See *Otterwell v Gilchrist*, 1998 S.L.T. (Sh. Ct) 63 and *Cullen v Cullen*, 2000 S.L.T. 540. A recent case in which the principles were fully argued is *McNeish v Advocate General for Scotland* Unreported OH July 30, 2004.
[31]   Most notably when a legally-aided person is unsuccessful in an appeal to the House of Lords.

(c) find no expenses due to or by either party, i.e. decide that neither party can claim the judicial expenses from the other in respect of that particular matter; or

(d) make the expenses for that part of procedure "expenses in the cause" which means that the expenses of that part of procedure will simply follow the final and general award of expenses to be made in the case as a whole.

(5) Payment of expenses as a penalty for delays, failures or defaults in procedure

There are many situations where one party takes some procedural step **21–15** which is plainly going to cost all parties additional expense in a litigation. An obvious example is by lodging a late minute of amendment which has the effect of changing the issues in a case shortly before a proof and might mean additional procedure which would not have been necessary if the pleadings had been properly drafted. Another example might be a late motion to discharge a proof where it is clear that at least one side will have done preparations for it. Whilst the court can refuse to allow such motions, or can regard failures to comply with the rules of procedure as fatal, it is not unusual for a judge to allow such "irregular" procedures, but to penalise the party responsible by holding them liable for the expense incurred and the additional expense which this might cause. In extreme cases, the court can find a party responsible for the whole expenses of the case to date, or the expenses of whole stages of the case, if it is apparent that there have been serious failures in the proper conduct of the case. In this way, a party who might ultimately be successful, and entitled to an award of expenses in principle because of this, might have very substantial awards of expenses of parts of the procedure made against him.

(6) Payment of expenses as a condition precedent of further procedure

Sometimes the court will use the award of expenses in a court action as **21–16** a means of ensuring that the parties are seriously intending to proceed. In extreme cases, where the conduct of a party is such as to suggest that he is not seriously or properly pursuing or defending the litigation, the court can make an award of expenses against that party and make it a condition that those expenses should be taxed and paid before any further procedure will be allowed in the action. If the party does not pay the expenses, then that would constitute a default in complying with a court order, and it would entitle an opponent to ask for a decree of dismissal of the action by default.

(7) Award against solicitor

Sometimes the court will decide that in the interests of justice it is **21–17** appropriate to make an award of expenses against the solicitor rather than against the client. This can be in a situation where unnecessary or inappropriate procedure has been caused by the actions of the solicitor, and there is no good reason why the client should suffer further by having to pay for it. This does not happen too frequently.[32]

(8) Certification of witnesses and skilled witnesses

21–18   As pointed out above, witness expenses can be quite a significant cost of court proceedings and it is important to ensure that they are fully and properly recovered as judicial expenses from an opponent. In the first place, the client is responsible for the expenses incurred to a witness in having him attend court and give evidence on his behalf. Sometimes a witness can be present at court but not called or, at least, not called that day. It might be problematic whether he was actually in attendance for the case on one day or another, and in practice this uncertainty can cause difficulties. Furthermore, skilled or expert witnesses are (unlike lay witnesses) entitled to charge fees for attending and are also entitled to charge for certain preparations, etc. which they have to make prior to giving their evidence. It is necessary to take some procedural steps to ensure that such witnesses are recorded as being present and are noted by the court to be skilled or expert witnesses, so as to avoid any doubt about the entitlement to recover their costs as part of the judicial expenses. This involves making a motion to the court as appropriate asking the court, e.g. to certify a witness as being present at court, although not called or, e.g. to certify him as being a skilled witness.[33]

(9) Additional fee

21–19   It is open to the parties to ask the court to award them an additional fee at the conclusion of the litigation. This is a fee additional to what they are entitled to recover from the opponent under the appropriate table of fees. This can be justified on a number of different specified grounds including the complexity and difficulty of the case. If the court awards an additional fee then the opponent has to pay this as judicial expenses, which is obviously of benefit to the client.[34] The procedures for obtaining an additional fee and the assessment of that additional fee are different in the Court of Session and the sheriff court.[35]

---

[32] An interesting example is the case of *Reid v Edinburgh Acoustics Ltd (No.2)*, 1995 S.L.T. 982. In this case you will see reference to most of the other previous cases on this point. See also *Bremner v Bremner*, 1998 S.L.T. 844.

[33] See the case of *Mains v Uniroyal Englebert Tyres Ltd (No.2)*, 1995 S.L.T. 1127. Also *Merrick Homes Ltd v Duff (No.2)*, 1997 S.L.T. 53; *Earl v Kvaerner Energy Ltd*, 2002 S.L.T. 1167 and *Jones v George Leslie Ltd*, 2005 S.L.T. (Sh. Ct) 113.

[34] It does not do the solicitor any harm either!

[35] There are no recent reported examples of sheriff court decisions on the point but for Court of Session cases see *Gray v Babcock Power Ltd*, 1990 S.L.T. 693 and *Young v Blue Star Line Ltd*, 1998 S.L.T. 109.

Court of Session—rule 42.14 of RCS

In the Court of Session, after a party obtains an award of judicial **21–20** expenses in his favour, he can make a motion to the court for an additional fee. This is usually made at the same time as the motion for expenses but it can be made later. The court will then decide whether an additional fee is due or not. The additional fee will be sought on the basis that one or more of the factors mentioned in r.42.14(3) which include complexity, importance, etc. justify it. If the court approves the granting of an additional fee, it will normally say no more than that it considers an additional fee to be appropriate because the case fits the requirements of one or more of the specified factors. It is then left to the auditor when taxing the account to decide what that additional fee should be. The more factors the court considers to be present in a particular case, the more the additional fee is likely to be, but it is for the auditor to decide the amount.[36]

Sheriff court—Act Of Sederunt (Fees of Solicitors in the Sheriff Court) (Amendment and Further Provisions) 1993, Schedule 1, General Regulation 5

In the sheriff court the factors which go towards justifying an addi- **21–21** tional fee are identical to those applying in the Court of Session. The procedure is usually by a written motion, asking the court to allow a percentage increase in the fees in order to cover the responsibility undertaken by the solicitor in the conduct of the case. There is no limit to the percentage increase which can be allowed, but, in contrast to the position in the Court of Session, the court, and not the auditor, will decide what the amount of that percentage increase should be. The court will hear arguments from the parties and will then make a decision which will govern that point for the purposes of the auditor's taxation of the account. Once the auditor decides the total of the account at taxation, he simply increases the fees element of the account by the prescribed percentage.

(10) Appeals

Since the award of expenses by any judge is a discretionary award, it **21–22** is difficult to appeal against such an award. Indeed, appeals against decisions of judges on questions of expenses only are very much discouraged. They can succeed only if there has been, "an obvious miscarriage of justice in the award".[37] As can be seen in some of the cases quoted above, that is not to say that there are never any appeals against awards of expenses.

---

[36] A recent illustration is *Petrie v North Milk Cooperative Ltd* Unreported OH March 26, 2005.
[37] See *Caldwell v Dykes* (1906) 14 S.L.T. 67.

5. Taxation of accounts

21–23   Once the court has decided:

(1) as a matter of principle, who is going to be liable for expenses;
(2) what aspects of the case they are going to be liable for the expenses of;
(3) what scale of expenses is to apply; and
(4) any of the other specialities mentioned above,

the court's interest in the expenses is virtually at an end. The successful party will usually make up an account of judicial expenses and send this to his opponent. If a contra-award of expenses[38] has been made in relation to part of the proceedings, then the opponent will prepare and submit a contra account. Parties will usually try to reach agreement on what the proper judicial expenses are. There is no obligation to do so. If they cannot reach agreement, then the account, known as the, "Judicial Account of Expenses for the Pursuer/Defender", will have to be lodged with the auditor for taxation.

The auditor of the Court of Session is an official of the court and he has responsibility for taxing, amongst other things, all accounts relating to Court of Session actions. In sheriff courts, each separate court has an auditor who is often the principal sheriff clerk for the court and carries out the functions of auditor on a part-time basis. In Glasgow, for historical reasons and because of the volume of business, the auditor is a court official and is engaged full time in taxing accounts. It is the function of the auditor to "tax" or assess the judicial account of expenses to ensure that the charges are in conformity with the tables of fees and otherwise to see that they are proper and reasonable. He does so by reference to the award of expenses made by the judge in the case, and by reference to any individual awards of expenses which might have been made during the case. He also takes into account any court interlocutor with regard to additional fees, etc. With that as his base, he will then consider the detailed charges in the account. He has a wide discretion. He can consider the account himself and form opinions about the propriety or level of any of the charges, hear any specific challenges to the account which the paying party might raise, and he can allow specific charges, disallow them, or reduce them as he sees fit. Where accounts include outlays, he has to satisfy himself that they are properly vouched and that they are reasonable. The auditor charges a fee for the taxation which is added to the account and which will usually be payable in full by the party against whom the original award of expenses was made.

21–24   It is not possible to give anything more than a broad indication of the basic principles upon which taxation proceeds. Two general matters should be noted:

---

[38] i.e. an award of expenses for some part of the proceedings which has been made against the party who obtained a general award of expenses.

(1) It may or may not be possible to recover as judicial expenses, any, or some, of the expenses incurred prior to the actual raising of the court action. In r.42.10 RCS, only such expenses are allowed as are reasonable "for conducting the cause" in a proper manner. In the sheriff court, reg.6 of the general regulations in Sch.1 of the Act of Sederunt only allows a party to claim the "proper expenses of process". These provisions formerly prevented recovery as judicial expenses of many charges for work done before the court action commenced. The position has changed somewhat recently by the introduction of a block fee in both Court of Session and sheriff court tables which allows a charge as judicial expenses for all work which the auditor is satisfied has reasonably been undertaken in contemplation of, or preparatory to, the commencement of proceedings—the fee being up to a maximum of £417.35 in the Court of Session and £383.80 in the sheriff court.[39]

(2) Just because work relating to the case during the course of the litigation has been done by the solicitor for one party does not mean that this will automatically be recoverable from the opponent. The auditor can refuse to allow some charges which, on the face of it, were incurred in connection with the litigation. Rule 42.10(1) RCS, provides that, "only such expenses as are reasonable for conducting the cause in a proper manner shall be allowed".[40] Similarly, general regulation 8 of the sheriff court table states:

> "In order that the expense of litigation may be kept within proper and reasonable limits, only such expenses shall be allowed . . . as are reasonable for conducting it in a proper manner."

General regulation 9 also allows the auditor (provided the issue has not been specifically dealt with by the court) to disallow certain expenses. He can do so if it appears to him that that the successful party has proved unsuccessful on any part of the cause, or has, through his own fault, caused some expense. That specific provision is understood to reflect what the auditor in the Court of Session would adopt as his normal approach to such issues.

PROCEDURE AT TAXATION

Court of Session

The provisions regarding taxation of accounts in the Court of Session **21–25** are contained within the RCS, and, in particular, Ch.42 of the rules,

---

[39] It is important to realise, however, that if one does extensive, and quite proper, work for a client before raising an action on his behalf, one will not be able to insist on recovering from the opponent the fees for that work beyond the limit mentioned.

[40] See *Ahmed's Trustee v Ahmed*, 1993 S.L.T. 390.

paras 42.1–42.16. In order to have a judicial account of expenses in the Court of Session taxed, it is necessary to lodge an account of expenses with the court not later than four months after the final interlocutor on which a finding for expenses is made. Written intimation of the lodging of the account and a copy of the account must be given to the opponent who is liable to pay the expenses. Once the account is lodged with the process in court, the process is given to the auditor. The auditor then fixes a date for the taxation to take place and he intimates the date to the parties interested in the account.

The parties then attend at the diet of taxation.[41] Practice Note No.3 of the Court of Session 1993 provides, inter alia, that, at least three working days before the taxation, the auditor must receive a note of all outstanding points of objection to items in the account and a copy of those objections must also be sent to the other party. This gives them advance notice of the points which are going to be argued and, if there are any authorities bearing upon the objections which are being taken, then these should be referred to. Full arguments should be made before the auditor.[42]

The auditor then adjudicates on the individual items in the account. Anything which is not allowed or is reduced in the account is "taxed off". At the conclusion of the diet of taxation, the auditor will then total up all of the sums which have been taxed off. He will add on any sums which have been added to the account (he has power to add appropriate charges which might have been omitted) and he will then reach a final figure which represents the taxed account.

The auditor then prepares a report of the taxation and sends the process back to the appropriate court department at which time he lets the parties know that he has done this and confirms the date when this has been done. Any party to a case who has appeared or been represented at the taxation can state an objection to the report of the auditor, and he does this by lodging in the court process a note of objections within 14 days after the date of the report. He also has to intimate a copy of the note of objections to his opponent. He then applies by motion for an order to allow the note to be received and to have the auditor state, within 14 days, the reason for his decision in relation to any items to which the objection has been taken. The auditor can state his response by minute which is lodged in the process and then, once that has been done, the party who lodges the note of objections will arrange with the court administration for a hearing to be fixed before the appropriate court. At the hearing on objections, the court can do a variety of things and can order the auditor to amend his report to give effect to the decision of the court in relation to any matter to which successful objection has been taken.[43]

---

[41] Although there is nothing to prevent them agreeing the account at any figure in advance of the taxation.

[42] See *Griffiths v Kerr*, 1992 S.L.T. 1024; *Magee v Glasgow City Council*, 2003 S.L.T. 777.

[43] *Magee v Glasgow City Council*, 2003 S.L.T. 777; *McNair's Executrix v Wrights Insulation Co Ltd*, 2003 S.L.T. 1311; *Tods Murray WS v McNamara*, 2007 S.L.T. 687 and *Coyle v Auditor of the Court of Session*, 2006 S.L.T. 1045.

Sheriff court

The rules for taxation of expenses in the sheriff court are contained **21–26** within Ch.32 of the OCR and, in particular, rr.32.1–32.4.

Assuming the parties cannot reach agreement, the account will be lodged for taxation. This is done by preparing a principal of the account and lodging this with the process for taxation. Once that has been done, the account and the process will be given by the sheriff clerk to the auditor of court.

Once the process and the account have been given to the auditor, the auditor will assign a date for taxation not earlier than seven days from the date he receives the account from the sheriff clerk and he will intimate that diet to the party who lodged the account. The party who lodged the account then will send a copy of the account and intimate the date, time and place of the taxation to every other party.

At the diet of taxation itself, the same procedure will follow as applies in the Court of Session. There is no provision in the sheriff court rules for prior intimation in writing of any specific objections being taken to the account. If an objection is taken which requires consideration, or detailed argument, or further vouching, then the auditor might adjourn the diet of taxation, for such a purpose.

In any event, after the auditor has decided the various points, he will adjudicate upon the total of what has to be taxed off and he will then certify what the total of the taxed expenses ought to be. Once he does that, he will transmit the process with the account and his report back to the sheriff clerk. After this is given back to the sheriff clerk, the matter is put before the sheriff to grant decree for the actual amount of expenses as taxed.

Before the case is put back to the sheriff for decree for expenses as taxed, it is open to an opposing party to lodge a note of objections to an account.[44] He can only do so where he actually attended the diet of taxation. He must lodge a note of objections within seven days of the diet of taxation or if the auditor has reserved any points for consideration, within seven days of the date in which the auditor intimated his final decision on the point. The sheriff can dispose of the objection in a summary manner as he sees fit. It may not be unusual for the sheriff to fix a hearing on a note of objections so that the party can make submissions to him in support of their opposing contentions regarding the account.

Summary cause expenses

The court procedures for assessing expenses in a summary cause **21–27** action in the sheriff court are quite different[45] although the general principles of liability for expenses are the same as set out above. Rule 23.3

---

[44] See *Erskine v Russell*, 2003 S.L.T. (Sh. Ct) 2 and *Cowan v Ramsay*, 2005 S.L.T. (Sh. Ct) 65.
[45] See Ch.11.

of the SCR provides that the sheriff clerk must, with the approval of the sheriff, assess the amount of expenses in accordance with the appropriate table of fees for summary causes.[46] The sheriff clerk hears the parties in relation to any claim for expenses after the merits of the case have been dealt with. The successful party has to lodge an account with the sheriff clerk and both parties can be heard on it. Once the sheriff clerk assesses the appropriate award, he reports to the sheriff and the case calls in court for the sheriff formally to approve his assessment. Any objection can be taken before the sheriff at that time.

A recent change in the rules[47] provides, alternatively, that the sheriff may on his own initiative, or if asked by any party, or the sheriff clerk himself may, on cause shown, have a summary cause account remitted to the auditor. This option applies to all summary causes raised after January 1, 2003 and might be used where larger and more complex accounts are under consideration.

There is a separate scale of fees for summary cause personal injury claims, which have their own procedures.[48] This was introduced in anticipation of a change in the jurisdiction limits for summary causes which was expected to lead to an increase in the number of personal injury actions proceeding by way of summary cause.

Small claims expenses

21–28   These general principles do not apply in small claims, where, in the normal case, there is no detailed argument about liability for expenses or the amount of the expenses. In a small claim, the sheriff may award expenses not exceeding £150 to the successful party in a case for a value up to £1,500, and he may award expenses of 10 per cent of the sum sued for in cases where the value of the claim is between £1,500 and £3,000. That is all he can do, unless there are special circumstances. The circumstances include a case where the defence has not acted in good faith, and a case where there has been unreasonable conduct on the part of either the pursuer or defender.[49] If a sheriff decides that these circumstances do exist then he can award expenses on the summary cause scale.

A party litigant may be awarded certain outlays and expenses by virtue of the Litigants in Person (Costs and Expenses) Act 1975.[50]

---

[46] The charges in that table are substantially less than the comparable charges for an ordinary action.

[47] Act of Sederunt (Summary Cause Rules) (Amendment) 2002 (SSI 2002/516) para.2(4).

[48] See Ch.11.

[49] Sheriff Courts (Scotland) Act 1971 s.36B.

[50] See r.21.6(4).

CHAPTER 22

HUMAN RIGHTS LEGISLATION AND RULES OF CIVIL PROCEDURE

THE LEGISLATION

It is beyond the scope of this book to discuss the details of the relevant **22–01** legislation but a very basic overview will suffice for the purposes of this chapter.[1] Section 57(2) of the Scotland Act 1998 makes it unlawful for the Scottish Parliament, the Scottish Executive, or the Lord Advocate to act in a way which is incompatible with Convention rights. The Human Rights Act 1998 which came into force on October 2, 2000 was enacted in order to incorporate into UK law the European Convention on Human Rights and Fundamental Freedoms 1950.[2] It is necessary to read both Acts in order to understand the legal status of Convention rights in Scots law. For our purposes, the principal article in the Convention which impacts upon the practice and procedure of the civil courts is art.6(1) which gives all persons a right to a fair trial.

This chapter gives a brief selection of some recent reported and unreported cases in which issues regarding Convention rights and civil court procedures or practices have been considered in Scotland. It is not intended as a comprehensive review of all such cases. The reader may find it interesting to refer to the Scottish Executive's Legal Studies Research programme research findings entitled, *The Use of Human Rights Legislation in the Scottish Courts*.[3] This provides a good introduction to the whole subject and a snapshot of the effect of human rights legislation on civil and criminal law along with its impact on the courts, public policy and administration, and the legal profession. The paper researched the use made of human rights legislation in the Scottish courts between May 1999 and August 2003. Most of the cases considered were in the field of criminal law. Difficulties in conducting accurate research in civil cases hampered any full analysis in the field of civil law.

---

[1] For further reading see Francis G. Jacobs and Robin C.A. White, *The European Convention on Human Rights*, edited by Clare Ovey and Robin C.A. White, 3rd edn (Oxford: Oxford University Press, 2002); Lord Reed and Jim Murdoch, *A Guide to Human Rights Law in Scotland* (Edinburgh: Butterworths, 2001); and Lord Reed (ed.), *A Practical Guide to Human Rights Law in Scotland* (Edinburgh: W. Green, 2001).

[2] Referred to throughout this Chapter as the "Convention".

[3] Paul Greenhill et al, *The Use of Human Rights Legislation in the Scottish Courts*. Scottish Executive, Social Research, 2004. Legal studies research findings No.54/2004.

However, the indications were that a significant number of human rights issues in civil cases related to civil procedure and practice. The findings concluded that human rights law had an important, but only a "moderately significant" impact on Scots law and practice generally.

It is interesting to consider the arguments which have been deployed in the cases to which we will refer and even more interesting to note that, by and large, our civil procedures and practices stand up to the test of compatibility with Convention rights. It is axiomatic that all rules of procedure should promote and follow the principles of natural justice, regardless of human rights legislation.[4] That being so, the "right to a fair trial" contained in art.6(1) of the Convention can be seen as no more than an expression of long-established principles in Scotland. In recent judgements, there has been debate about the inherent power which both the sheriff court and the Court of Session have to regulate their own procedures, a power which operates within the existing procedural rules but can also operate as a supplement to those rules. It should really come as no surprise that most arguments that procedures and practices in the Scottish courts are contrary to the Convention have not proved successful.

There have been certain specific procedural devices which have been subject to criticism as not being compatible with other Convention rights. This has given rise to certain minor changes in procedure and practice. It is to be hoped that most areas of possible incompatibility have already been identified and amendment made. It is assumed that any future rules or any future changes to the existing rules will take full account of the requirement of compatibility.

Consideration of the following cases will perhaps reinforce the reader's understanding of certain areas of civil procedure and indicate certain areas in which change might be possible. Some of the cases have already been referred to in the appropriate chapters but it is felt that there is no harm in re-emphasising the points which have been decided.

THE INHERENT POWER OF THE COURTS

22–02 The courts will require parties to conduct the litigation before them in accordance with the appropriate procedural rules. The Court of Session has power to regulate its own procedure by Acts of Sederunt.[5] Procedure in the sheriff court is regulated by the Court of Session following recommendations by the Sheriff Court Rules Council and again this is done by Act of Sederunt. In this way, the courts provide a procedural framework within which a fair trial can be conducted. Both courts have, within their rules, a general dispensing power which entitles the court in certain circumstances to excuse failures to comply with the rules. This dispensing power can be

---

[4] See Lord Johnston's opinion in the criminal case of *McGibbon v HM Advocate*, 2004 S.L.T. 588.

[5] See s.5 of the Court of Session Act 1988.

seen as a reasonable restriction on draconian remedies of granting decrees or dismissing actions as a result of a simple failure to observe a "technical" requirement in the rules. The absence of such a power might make the court more vulnerable to a challenge on fairness. For example, if the procedural rules meant that a substantial action was dismissed and could never be raised again because a document was lodged five minutes later than it should have been, and there was no mechanism whatsoever available in the court procedures to excuse such a minor default, then the procedure might not be regarded as compatible with art.6(1).

In addition to the power to regulate procedure by Act of Sederunt, the Court of Session also has an inherent power to regulate its own procedure, allow certain matters to be rectified, and dispense with the requirements of a rule.[6] In the sheriff court, the sheriff also has power to regulate procedure in an action before him without reference to specific rules provided that the sheriff exercises the power in a way which is not inconsistent with statute or the statutory rules of court.[7]

PROCEDURAL CHANGES AS A RESULT OF THE CONVENTION

There have been three specific areas in which there have been obvious changes in procedure where existing procedures were found to be plainly incompatible with other Convention rights.   **22–03**

1. Inhibition on the dependence—This is a procedure whereby a pursuer can prevent a defender from disposing of any heritable property during a litigation until such time as the litigation has been concluded. Formerly, when an action was first raised, and before a defender even knew of its existence, a pursuer could automatically obtain an order from the court allowing him to inhibit the defender. In the case of *Karl Construction Ltd v Palisade Properties Plc*[8] this was challenged as being incompatible with art.1 of the First Protocol to the Convention which provided that every person was entitled to the peaceful enjoyment of his possessions. The challenge was successful. The decision was followed in the case of *Advocate General for Scotland v Taylor*[9] in which the Inner House stated that the relevant rules of court in relation to this matter were not compatible with the Convention but the court could regulate its own procedure and alter the terms of the rules. For the time being, therefore, a practice was suggested which would cure the incompatibility and it was envisaged that a formal change in the rules would be required. A formal change in the rules was   **22–04**

---

[6] This power was discussed and authoritatively affirmed in *Tonner v Reiach and Hall*, 2007 S.L.T. 1183.

[7] See the case of *Newman Shopfitters Ltd v MJ Gleeson Group Plc*, 2003 S.L.T. (Sh. Ct) 83 and also *Wilson, t/a TW Contractors v Drake & Scull Scotland Ltd*, 2005 S.L.T. (Sh. Ct) 36.

[8] *Karl Construction Ltd v Palisade Properties Plc*, 2002 S.L.T. 312.

[9] *Advocate General for Scotland v Taylor*, 2003 S.L.T. 1340.

subsequently introduced.[10] Thereafter the Bankruptcy and Diligence etc. (Scotland) Act 2007 led on to rules for what is now termed "interim diligence" in both the Court of Session and the sheriff court. The rules for granting interim diligence are now much stricter.[11]

22–05 **2. Arrestment on the dependence**—An arrestment on the dependence operates in a similar way to an inhibition on the dependence and the same criticisms were applied to that procedure.[12] A change was subsequently made in the rules to cure the incompatibility with art.1 of the First Protocol to the Convention.[13] The power to arrest and inhibit on the dependence remained with the courts, but a pursuer had to make out a clear case before a judge justifying arrestment or inhibition on the dependence before authorisation is granted. The rule changes referred to in para.22–04 also applied to arrestments on the dependence.

22–06 **3. Applications under the Administration of Justice (Scotland) Act 1972**—These applications relate to the recovery and preservation of property in the possession of others in respect of which issues might arise in court proceedings which might be likely to be brought in the future. The best known example of this type of application is the "dawn raid" in which a party, unknown to the opponent, obtains an order from a judge entitling him to enter the defender's premises and to secure and retain property in the defender's possession before the defender has any chance to protect his interest or indeed has any idea that proceedings have been raised or are in contemplation. It was recognised at an early stage that this procedure was again incompatible with art.1 of the First Protocol to the Convention and, without any significant delay, changes in the rules in both the sheriff courts and the Court of Session were introduced. Again, the power to grant such an application remains but there are detailed provisions to ensure that it will only be granted when a judge is satisfied that it is necessary and justifiable by virtue of compelling material presented to him at the time of the application.[14]

---

[10] Act of Sederunt (Rules of the Court of Session Amendment No.6) (Diligence on the Dependence) 2003 (SSI 2003/537).

[11] Act of Sederunt (Rules of the Court of Session Amendment No.3) (Bankruptcy and Diligence etc. (Scotland) Act 2007) 2008 (SSI 2008/122) and Act of Sederunt (Sheriff Court Rules Amendment) (Diligence) 2008 (SSI 2008/121), both of which came into force on April 1, 2008.

[12] See *Fabtek Engineering Ltd v Carillion Construction Ltd*, 2002 S.L.T. (Sh. Ct) 113; *Irvings Curator Bonis v Skillin*, 2002 S.L.T. (Sh. Ct) 119 and 2003 S.L.T. (Sh. Ct) 27; *Maguire v Itoh*, 2004 S.L.T. (Sh. Ct) 120.

[13] As in fn.10, above. In the sheriff court, the matter was dealt with by the Act of Sederunt (Ordinary Cause, Summary Application, Summary Cause, and Small Claim Rules) Amendment (Miscellaneous) 2004 (SSI 2004/197).

[14] See Act of Sederunt (Rules of the Court of Session Amendment No.4) (Applications under Section 1 of the Administration of Justice (Scotland) Act 1972) 2000 (SSI 2000/319) effective from September 7, 2000; see also Act of Sederunt (Summary Applications, Statutory Applications and Appeals etc.) Rules Amendment (No.2) (Administration of Justice (Scotland) Act 1972) 2000 (SSI 2000/387) effective from November 3, 2000.

CHALLENGES TO EXISTING PROCEDURES AND PRACTICES

In the following cases the parties have attempted to challenge procedural **22–07** steps taken in civil actions as not being compatible with the Convention. In many of the cases, arguments about a breach of the human rights provisions are presented as supplementary to other arguments. A very brief outline is given of each case but reference should be made to the cases for details.

1. The requirement for a party to find caution for judicial expenses has been challenged on the basis that this imposes an unfair restriction on an individual because it does not give him an unqualified right of access to the courts. Accordingly his right to a fair trial has been prejudiced. The challenges have so far been unsuccessful.[15] The research paper mentioned in this chapter refers to a successful appeal where it is understood that the amount of caution fixed by the court was successfully challenged as being disproportionate. Unfortunately, the details of the case are not known.

2. A challenge was made to the power of a sheriff who granted a decree by default because the pursuer failed to proceed with his action within a reasonable period of time. This challenge was unsuccessful because the sheriff principal decided on appeal that the court had an inherent power to regulate its own procedure and was perfectly entitled to grant a decree by default in the circumstances. Indeed, a failure to do so could be seen as prejudicing the defender's right to a fair trial by allowing a hearing in an extremely old case which had been dormant for many years.[16]

3. A challenge was made to the requirement that an artificial person (in other words, a company or a partnership) had to engage a lawyer if it was to be represented in proceedings before the court. The pursuer was a partnership between husband and wife and the husband wanted to represent the partnership. There has long been a general rule that a partnership requires legal representation and cannot be represented by an individual partner. The challenge was unsuccessful on the basis that the sheriff principal considered that it was appropriate and proportionate for any court to impose requirements of that kind because this helped to ensure the proper administration of justice.[17]

4. A challenge was made to a decision made by a sheriff in which it was argued that he had failed to give one side an opportunity to be

---

[15] See *William Dow (Potatoes) Ltd v Dow*, 2001 S.L.T. (Sh. Ct) 37 and *Cairns v Chief Constable of Strathclyde Police*, Unreported IH October 22, 2004.

[16] See *Newman Shopfitters Ltd v MJ Gleeson Group Plc*, 2003 S.L.T. (Sh. Ct) 83; see also *Wilson, t/a TW Contractors v Drake and Scull (Scotland) Ltd*, 2005 S.L.T. (Sh. Ct) 36, which followed the decision in *Newman*.

[17] See *Clark Advertising Ltd v Scottish Enterprise Dumbartonshire*, 2004 S.L.T. (Sh. Ct) 85.

heard on a certain aspect of the case. The challenge was successful but its success owed as much to the common law and the principles of natural justice as it did to the Human Rights Act and the Convention. The sheriff principal took the opportunity to set out his understanding of the basic principles which would be required to ensure that a fair trial is available under our current procedures. It is worth repeating what he said:

"Under the Human Rights Act 1998 it is unlawful for the Court, as a public authority, to act in a way which is incompatible with a Convention right. In this case, the relevant Convention right is the right under Article 6(1) to a fair trial or, in the language of Article 6, a fair hearing in the determination of her civil rights and obligations ... The concept of a fair trial has been developed in the jurisprudence of Article 6. It includes the right to equality before the law, or equality of arms, which demands that all parties before the Court should be given the same procedural facilities for advancing their case ... both parties must be afforded an equal and reasonable opportunity to present their own case and to learn their opponent's case and respond to it under conditions which do not substantially advantage or disadvantage either side ... Accordingly, each party must have an opportunity to have knowledge of and to comment on all evidence adduced or observations filed with a view to influencing the court's decision and must be able to participate properly in the proceedings before the Court. The opportunity to have knowledge and comment must be a genuine one ... The party should have a reasonable opportunity to present his or her case under conditions that did not place him or her at a substantial disadvantage viz a viz his or her opponent ... A formal opportunity will not suffice, because justice must be seen to be done. The case law of the European Court of Human Rights attaches great importance to appearances and emphasises the increased sensitivity of the public to the fair administration of justice."[18]

5. A challenge was made to the right to a jury trial for the assessment of damages in a personal injury case on the basis that the provisions for the conduct of a jury trial were such that there was a substantial risk of the defenders not having a fair trial and the jury not reaching a fair decision. In essence, it was suggested that any jury trial in a personal injury case was not a "fair trial". Concerted arguments to this effect were advanced in the undernoted cases but all of them were unsuccessful.[19]

---

[18] See *Richardson v Rivers* Unreported (Sh. Ct) August 23, 2004, Sheriff Principal Macphail.

[19] *Gunn v Newman*, 2001 S.L.T. 776; *McLeod v British Railways Board*, 2001 S.L.T. 238; *Sandison v Graham Begg Ltd*, 2001 S.L.T. 1352 and *Heasman v J.M. Taylor & Partners*, 2002 S.L.T. 451.

6. A challenge was made against the granting of a motion for decree in absence in a Court of Session action on the basis that the rules regarding decree in absence against someone resident outwith the UK were harsher than the related provisions in the Convention and in the EC Regulations upon which the rule was based. The judge took the view that the automatic right available to such a defender to recall a decree in absence perhaps afforded greater protection than the appeal provisions in the Convention and the Regulations and accordingly the rules were not incompatible with the right to a fair trial.[20]

7. An argument that the use of surveillance by private investigators in a personal injury claim was contrary to art.8(1) of the Convention was unsuccessful in the particular circumstances of the case. The judge considered that the enquiries and surveillance were reasonable and proportionate steps for the defender to take in the course of investigating the case brought against him and did not infringe the pursuer's rights under art.8 of the Convention.[21]

8. A challenge was made under art.6(1) that it was incompatible with the Convention that the same sheriff who refused the pursuer's motion should consider (and refuse) his further motion for leave to appeal against the original judgment. The court took the view that the original decision on the merits and the subsequent decision on leave to appeal were so intimately linked that there could be no breach of art.6 if the same judge decided both questions. Indeed, the judge who heard the substantive issue was best placed to decide whether to grant leave to appeal.[22]

9. A challenge was made to the leading of hearsay evidence at a proof on the basis that it was incompatible with the right to a fair trial because the other party was unable to examine the person who allegedly made the original statement. This challenge was unsuccessful and the court took the view that there was no fundamental objection to the use of hearsay evidence in the Convention jurisprudence nor was there any absolute rule that all parties had to have equal access to those whose statements might figure in hearsay evidence. In any event, as a matter of fairness, the other party had the opportunity to present its case and lead evidence in such a way that did not place it at a substantial disadvantage in the litigation.[23]

10. A successful challenge was made to the decision of a sheriff who granted decree against a defender in an action for recovery of possession of heritable property on the basis of a breach of art.6(1). The sheriff had recused herself from an earlier calling of the case

---

[20] *Bank of Scotland v Kunkel-Griffin* Unreported OH November 2, 2004.
[21] *Martin v McGuiness*, 2003 S.L.T. 1136.
[22] *Umair v Umair*, 2002 S.L.T. 172.
[23] *Irvine v Arco Atholl Ltd*, 2002 S.L.T. 931.

because of prior knowledge of the defender's behaviour. She did not do so at a later hearing at which she granted decree. The sheriff principal concluded that, "a fair minded and informed observer" would consider there was a real possibility of bias.[24]

It is quite likely that, over the next few years, further challenges will be made to our civil procedures on the basis that there is an incompatibility with one or other Convention right. Party litigants have proven themselves to be very enthusiastic in pursuing arguments based on general breaches of their human rights. It will be apparent from this chapter that the courts have had little difficulty in concluding that the vast majority of our procedures and practices are Convention compliant and, as this issue is now very familiar to those involved in the making of rules of procedure, it is perhaps unlikely that future rule changes will impinge upon Convention rights. Whether it becomes necessary in future years to expand upon this brief illustration of the impact of human rights legislation on the rules of procedure in the civil courts remains to be seen.

---

[24] *Aberdeen City Council v Robb*, 2004 S.L.T. (Sh. Ct) 21.

INDEX